W9-DHI-705

NADIA
Captive
of Hope

Autobiographies and Memoirs of Women from Asia, Africa, the Middle East, and Latin America
Geraldine Forbes, Series Editor

SHUDHA MAZUMDAR
MEMOIRS OF AN INDIAN WOMAN
Edited with an Introduction by Geraldine Forbes

CHEN XUEZHAO
SURVIVING THE STORM
A Memoir
Edited with an Introduction by Jeffrey C. Kinkley
Translated by Ti Hua and Caroline Greene

KANEKO FUMIKO
THE PRISON MEMOIRS OF A JAPANESE WOMAN
Translated by Jean Inglis
Introduction by Mikiso Hane

MANMOHINI ZUTSHI SAHGAL
AN INDIAN FREEDOM FIGHTER RECALLS HER LIFE
Edited by Geraldine Forbes
Foreword by B.K. Nehru

THE WOMAN WITH THE ARTISTIC BRUSH
A Life History of Yoruba Batik Artist Nike Davies
Kim Marie Vaz

THE WOMAN WITH THE ARTISTIC BRUSH
A Life History of Yoruba Batik Artist Nike Davies
Kim Marie Vaz

NADIA, CAPTIVE OF HOPE
Memoir of an Arab Women
Fay Afaf Kanafani

NADIA
Captive
of Hope

MEMOIR OF AN ARAB WOMAN

Fay Afaf Kanafani

Introduction by
Lisa Suhair Majaj

AN EAST GATE BOOK

M.E. Sharpe
Armonk, New York
London, England

An East Gate Book

Library of Congress Cataloging-in-Publication Data

Kanafani, Fay Afaf.
Nadia, captive of hope : memoir of an Arab woman / Fay Afaf Kanafani.
p.   cm—(Foremother legacies)
"An East Gate Book"
Includes index.
ISBN 0-7656-0311-X (cloth : alk. paper).
ISBN 0-7656-0312-8 (pbk : alk. paper).
1. Kanafani, Fay Afaf. 2. Arab American women—Biography.
3. Arab Americans—Biography. 4. Women—Civil rights—Arab countries.
5. Women and war—Arab countries. 6. Beirut (Lebanon)—Biography.
7. California—Biography. I. Title. II.Series.
E184.A65K36   1998
956.92'504'082—dc21   98-39925
CIP

Printed in the United States of America

The paper used in this publication meets the minimum requirements of
American National Standard for Information Sciences—
Permanence of Paper for Printed Library Materials,
ANSI Z 39.48-1984.

BM (c)   10   9   8   7   6   5   4   3   2   1
BM (p)   10   9   8   7   6   5   4   3   2   1

I dedicate this work
to those who are the source of my love,
my sons and my late husband, Fuad

Contents

Preface

I have no problem looking into my memory and recovering the look, sound, smell, and even my emotional reaction to events from very early childhood. But for me to imagine sitting down to write a book was unthinkable. The science of language has never been my strong point, something proven time and again in school. In grammar school, my classmate Iso and I used to cheat by exchanging homework: she would do my French and humanities and I would do her math and science.

I acquired my statistical training late in life and entered a career in that field partly because I was stronger in science and mathematics than I was in languages and literature. That is why, after I came to settle in the United States in 1985, I decided I would have to take classes in English grammar and literature to be able to attend the classes in art I loved most. But Dorothy, my beautiful and serene English instructor, discovered a different side of me, one I was not aware of. She saw in my written assignments a gift for writing fiction. "Are these your stories or did you copy them from a magazine?" she asked. "No," I told her, "I am translating them from my diary. These stories are about my own life."

From then on Dorothy began to pay special attention to my writing, and she finally said, "You have the material here for a valuable book." But she also said, "Your English has a long way to go before you could be published in the United States. Why don't you publish these stories in Arabic and the work could be later translated into English."

I did not have the courage to tell my wonderful teacher that reading my diary opened deep wounds that I have carried throughout life. It is all so personal that seeing the events I endured and the names of those cruel people in Arabic script makes me sick. The familiar letters seem to jump off the sheets and glare back at me with a vengeance. I could not tell Dorothy that it was easier for me to express my feelings in a foreign language even if I did have to struggle to find the right words. Nor did I think she would understand that a foreign language has a neutral quality and that writing in it could help me deal with the cruelty of the wars that have so dominated my life. I knew that living in the United States and writing in English let me pretend that the wars in the Middle East were someone else's wars and that it was not me, but rather someone else, who endured their horror and suffered great loss.

In writing this true story I replaced actual names with fictional names. In this way I can protect the privacy of the people involved.

Mine is an old story that is as young as the new wars that explode every now and then in this world. It was only yesterday that I heard my own footsteps echoing up and down the staircase of my home in Beirut, where I grew up surrounded by abusive kin, and on the staircase of my home in Haifa, where I was married, bore children, and became a widow with three children in the midst of a vicious war.

These events are now in the past. My apartment in California is the present. It is my bridge to the future, the new world I am building. With me is my beloved late husband Fuad, whose soul never deserted me. Because of the eternal bond between us, this work is dedicated to him and my sons.

I have decided to donate the proceeds of this book to a fund to support women who write about women's rights in the Middle East. Their writings will contribute to our understanding of women in the Middle East and enlarge the hopes and dreams of women all over the world.

I am at peace now.

Fay Afaf Kanafani
May 1998

Acknowledgments

I owe a debt of gratitude to those who made this memoir come to life. In addition to family members, relatives, and warm-hearted house companions who loved me from my birth, I would like to thank a number of people.

First, thanks go to the editor of this memoir, Apostolos Athanassakis, Professor of Classics at the University of California Santa Barbara. He has edited my recollections with insight and sensitivity. Lisa Suhair Majaj, Visiting Scholar in Women's Studies at Northeastern University, who writes on Arab, Arab-American, and third-world women's literature, very kindly pored over the manuscript to write the introduction. Geraldine Forbes, Distinguished Teaching Professor of History and Director of Women's Studies at State University of New York at Oswego, and the general editor of this series, has guided me at every step. I thank them for believing in Nadia's story.

I want to thank all the friends who supported and encouraged me as the memoir developed: Dorothy from Berkeley, Larry from Berkeley, Nagat from Washington, D.C., Susan from Saint Louis, Nuha from Venis, Artine from Berkeley, Nadeem from Mission Viejo, David from Berkeley, Catalina from Oakland, Muna from El Cerrito, Wafaa'' from San Leandro, and many other friends who accompanied me through the long journey of writing this memoir, never doubting it would be done. For those whose names are not on this list, you are in my heart.

Introduction

The poet Muriel Rukeyser once wrote, "What would happen if one woman told the truth about her life? The world would split open."[1] Fay Afaf Kanafani's autobiography, *Nadia, Captive of Hope*, provides one such act of truth-telling. An Arab woman's penetrating account of her life, set against the backdrop of some of the most tumultuous periods of Middle Eastern history, *Nadia* recounts Afaf's experiences in Lebanon and Palestine from the close of World War I in 1918 to the Israeli invasion of Lebanon in 1982. Informed by critical analysis, political insight, and feminist critique, the narrative portrays life under the colonial mandate system, the dispersion of Palestinians during the creation of the state of Israel, and the destruction of civilian life during Lebanon's civil war. It also provides insight into the role of the family in Arab society, the social constraints placed on both women and men, and the possibilities of resistance. Situating the events of her life within a context delineated by colonialism, war, political conflict, and social change, Afaf makes clear that Arab women's issues cannot be viewed in isolation from the problems confronting their societies at large. As such, she gives voice to a feminist awareness grounded not in Western discourse, but in her own experiences and identity as a Muslim Arab woman.

Afaf, called Nadia in this narrative, was born in Beirut, Lebanon, on February 21, 1918. She was the sixth child in a family of ten children, two of whom died in infancy. Her mother, Ban, born to a family of jurists and scholars of distinguished religious status, had defied social convention and familial pressures in order to marry Kareem Rajy, the son of a merchant family possessing education and wealth, but of lower social status. Ban's defiance of tradition was particularly daring within the social context of the time, in which personal identity, social status, and economic welfare were largely determined by clan affiliation and familial relationships. However, her independent spirit was soon muted within a marriage troubled by her husband's reckless and domineering personality, by his sexual fecklessness, by financial difficulties, and by disputes with the extended family. Her acquiescence to a lawsuit initiated against her mother by her husband, who wanted to gain possession of Ban's share of the ancestral mansion, wrought further schisms within the family, creating an atmosphere of tension and discord.

Afaf's childhood was spent within this troubled familial context. As a young girl she was subjected to her father's abuse (including sexual abuse), to her older brother's aggressive dominance, and to her mother's hostility. She early developed a feminist awareness of the social devaluation of women and girls, and of the ways in which women may be co-opted into supporting the system that oppresses them. She also developed a strong sense of selfhood. Even as a child, she insisted on the value and integrity of her female identity, expressing outrage at the suggestion that she must regret having been born a girl. Although isolated from the extended family by her father's feud, she was nonetheless able to create her own sustaining emotional context through close relationships with a maternal aunt and a beloved family servant, and through her sense of connection to her grandfather, whose portrait hung in the family hall.

Afaf's birth coincided with major political events: the end of World War I, the collapse of the Ottoman Empire, and the establishment of European colonial mandates in the Middle East. Lebanon, where Afaf grew up, came under the French mandate, while Palestine, where she moved to as a teenage bride and lived until she was made a refugee by the creation of the state of Israel, came under the British mandate. This political context permeates the text, situating the events of Afaf's personal life and, at times, occupying a central role in the narrative. Her autobiography begins as the Ottoman regime leaves Lebanon and the French and English enter—a change in power with direct impact on Afaf's father, who was employed by the local Ottoman pasha. The Ottoman Empire, with its capital in Istanbul (the city where Afaf's father, like so many other young Lebanese and Palestinians during this period, received his education) had controlled the Arab region for four centuries. But the Ottoman entrance into World War I on the side of Germany and Austria, and the 1916 Sykes-Picot agreement dividing the Arab region into zones of European influence, marked the wane of Ottoman dominance. The Allied victory left Britain and France in control of the region of Greater Syria, which included present-day

Syria, Lebanon, and Palestine. Although the Treaty of Versailles provided for the nominal independence of the Arab countries formerly under Ottoman rule, it required that European states assume mandates over these countries. By the close of World War I, Ottoman rule in the Middle East had been replaced by colonial Western rule, with Britain assuming the mandate over Palestine and Iraq, and France taking control of Lebanon and Syria.

Afaf's autobiography narrates a life lived within this colonial framework—first in French-controlled Lebanon, then in British-controlled Palestine, and finally, after the loss of Palestine, in a newly independent Lebanon already showing signs of the internal conflicts that were later to erupt in war. The colonial legacy was of particularly fateful significance in Palestine, where the British government supported Zionist aspirations despite the threat these posed to the local inhabitants of Palestine, whose rights the British authorities had also pledged to uphold. The Balfour Declaration of 1917 had stated, "His Majesty's Government view with favor the establishment in Palestine of a national home for the Jewish people . . . it being clearly understood that nothing shall be done which may prejudice the civil and religious rights of existing non-Jewish communities in Palestine."[2] This declaration, which facilitated greatly increased Jewish immigration, "revolutionized Zionist prospects overnight."[3] Meanwhile, organized Jewish land purchases, an explicit policy of excluding Arab labor from Jewish economic enterprises and Jewish-owned land, and discussions about "transferring" non-Jewish populations[4] out of Palestine quickly made clear the inefficacy of the proviso protecting non-Jews. The contradictions enshrined in the Declaration thus set the stage for the decimation of Palestinian life that Afaf's narrative so powerfully recounts.

The colonial legacies shaping the region during Afaf's childhood and young adulthood delineated not only political and geographical parameters, but every aspect of life. While the British colonial policy tended to concentrate on administrative and economic dominance, the French colonial policy was based on an assimilationist policy carried out though the establishment of French schools and the imposition of the French educational system on local schools. As the Lebanese writer Etel Adnan notes, "The French . . . created in Lebanon, and imposed on it, a system of education totally conforming to their schools in France, an education which had nothing to do with the history and geography of the children involved."[5] The religious missions of other Western countries also established schools aimed both at gaining religious converts and at consolidating a presence in the region, and "French missions multiplied in pace with the arrival of rival Anglo-Saxon missions."[6] It was to these foreign schools that middle- and upper-class Lebanese and Palestinian families, seeking to augment their social status and display their wealth, often sent their children. While state schools were slower to provide educational resources for girls than for boys, foreign missionary schools educated both boys and girls from around the mid-nineteenth century.[7] But because educational opportunities were class-based, girls from lower-class families had significantly less access to education. (As a family servant in the narrative tells Afaf and her sister, "Girls don't go to school in my village. . . . Girls have to work until they are married" [p. 37].) Educational opportunities were also slanted toward Christians. Indeed, "of 650 primary schools reported in Mount Lebanon at the end of the nineteenth century, only 13 were Muslim or Druze."[8]

In Afaf's own family, education, at least primary education, appears to have been taken for granted for both girls and boys, if for no other reason than to boost the family's social prestige. Indeed, Afaf and her siblings were sent to foreign instead of local schools, the boys to a secular French lycée that accepted Sunni Muslims (considered more amenable to French dominance than Shi'ite Muslims), and the girls to an American mission school that did not require Christian catechism. Although Kareem's financial recklessness later made it impossible for his children to attend private schools, even the public school that Afaf was forced to switch to was run on the French system. The most immediate impact of this foreign-dominated education was multilingualism: Afaf, like many Lebanese, gained fluency in Arabic, English, and French. The same was true in Palestine: Afaf writes of her pleasure, as a married woman in Haifa, that the Catholic Carmelite school she sent her son to offered instruction in both French and English. However, she also hints at more troubling implications of this educational system; in particular, the failure of parochial and other foreign-dominated schools to ground Arab children in their own cultural and religious heritage.

The matter-of-factness with which primary education for girls is treated in the autobiography suggests the impact of the social and economic changes taking place in the Arab world during this period. Forces of nationalism and modernization, shifting demographic patterns, new modes of transportation, new forms of media, an increase in the publication of newspapers and books, greater access to education, a growing secularization of society, and the rise of an Arab feminist movement (particularly in Egypt, but with a presence in Lebanon and Palestine as well) were bringing about significant changes in the social codes governing everyday life for both women and men. These changes increased the opportunities available to women, opened new possibilities for social relations, and shifted the balance of power within traditional social and political structures. While in some countries women's feminist awareness preceded nationalist consciousness,[9] nationalism often gave impetus to the movement for women's emancipation, as did the work of some writers connected with the Islamic reform movement.[10]

Although Afaf does not address these developments explicitly, the implications of these sweeping social changes are evident throughout her memoir, often through seemingly minor narrative details. For instance, she recounts a childhood memory of going out with her parents for a drive and noticing her mother looking "carefree and pretty without her veil and topcoat"— her father had insisted that his wife remove her veil and topcoat as soon as they leave the carriage (p. 27). The incident suggests the extent to which veiling, instead of being an imperative for Muslim women, was often context-specific and class-related; it suggests, too, the social pressures middle- and upper-class Lebanese must have felt to appear "modern." Other incidents in the narrative make clear that the range of acceptable social practices during the time was quite broad. For instance, in a later episode, the teenage Afaf is chastised by her brother Anwar for wearing a short skirt to go downtown in Beirut. Her fiancé Marwan protests, pointing out that modern fashions are, after all, a common sight in Beirut, and furthermore arguing that if they, as men, have the right to dress as they please, then so does she. Although Marwan's egalitarianism later proves inconsistent, the difference between these male views on a young woman's right to personal choice is striking.

While changing social and political conditions created new opportunities for women, however, they also highlighted the resilience of old social structures. The most significant and enduring of these structures was the family. By tradition, patriarchal and extended, and based on a hierarchy of sex and age, the Arab family has historically served as the basic unit of social organization and of socioeconomic production. As such, it has provided the primary source of support for individuals. At the same time, however, its hierarchical structure has often made it a locus for the oppression of those, such as women and minors, who occupy a lower status within its stratified system.

The tremendous role, both positive and negative, played by the family is evident throughout Afaf's autobiography. Situating her personal struggle for autonomy within the context of a broader familial and social context of rebellion and restraint, Afaf makes clear her awareness that while traditions can be resisted, their power structures cannot easily be overthrown. Her narrative gives voice to an experiential feminism grounded not in theory, but in an intrinsic awareness of the social power vested in males and the corresponding limitations placed on females. An outspoken child, the young Afaf insisted on her right to speak her mind, to go to school, to interact in the world. However, her ability to resist traditional structures of power was limited by her position within a society stratified by hierarchies of both gender and age. As her older sister Nora points out, "You know what happens in our society to girls who defy the rules" (p. 64). Although Afaf's own struggle for personal autonomy was constrained by the gendered roles she occupied—first as daughter, then as daughter-in-law, wife, widow, and mother—her self-assertion was predicated on the attempt not to *escape* familial roles so much as to redefine these roles on her own terms.

This attempt to redefine traditional roles is particularly evident in Afaf's account of her arranged engagement at the age of thirteen and marriage at the age of seventeen. When her father accepted an offer of marriage on his daughter's behalf from the Rajy family, wealthy relatives from Palestine[11] whom he hoped to exploit financially, Afaf, furious at being made an economic bargaining chip in her father's schemes, reacted with rage and denial. But she had little leverage against the combined forces of her father, her equally avaricious brother, and her mother, who felt threatened by Afaf's open critique of her father's and brother's predatory sexual behavior toward the household's female servants, and who wanted her daughter out of the house. Married off as a minor, Afaf was not even allowed to sign the official marriage records on her own behalf, nor to attend her own wedding ceremony (p.88–89).

Despite her limited agency, however, Afaf nonetheless managed to retain an element of self-determination. When her family tried to prevent her from completing her school certificate, arguing that education was of little value to a girl about to be married, she managed to sneak out of the house to take her final exams. She eventually chose to acquiesce to the marriage, recognizing that it offered an avenue of escape from her abusive family situation into a household that promised, instead, affection, financial security, and support for her educational goals. (Indeed, on leaving her parents' home for that of her parents-in-law she experienced what she describes as a sense of rebirth.) Despite the admonitions she had received about a woman's lot in marriage and the need to submit to her husband, the teenage bride had the courage to insist on her right to personal autonomy, including sexual autonomy, within the bounds of the marital relationship. As she told her sister-in-law, "I have the right to prevent my husband from violating my body" (p. 141). In refusing the sexual component of the role of wife, while nonetheless claiming the familial role of daughter-in-law, Afaf sought to redefine, rather than reject altogether, the gendered roles thrust upon her. Although her efforts to resist sexual relations with her husband ultimately failed, her striking defiance of societal and familial expectations and of her husband's physical power suggest an intrinsic feminist awareness of the role of resistance in individual empowerment. As she writes, recounting an argument with her husband in which she refused to accept his authority, "To this day I remember how much better I felt, how all it takes sometimes is a slamming door" (p. 133).

However, Afaf's resistance was necessarily located within a broader social context that circumscribed individual agency. In Palestinian and Lebanese society of the time, the extended family functioned as both a support system and a locus of control for women and men alike. For those who accepted the system, the extended family offered protection, support, and financial assistance, but also authoritarian constraint. For those who rejected it, there were few options. While men clearly had more rights and opportunities within the system than women, they too were trapped by intertwined structures of support and constraint that wove a web of dependency difficult to resist. As Afaf's husband told her after their marriage, "Our whole lives were planned the moment we were born. . . . The apartments where we have to live; the schools, languages, and futures we have and the wives we have to marry, all these decisions are not for us to make. . . . Do you know that when your Uncle Ahmad first spoke of you it was as a future daughter-in-law, not as a wife for me? I was not consulted" (p. 149). By accepting the protection and support of her in-laws, Afaf realized, she had assented not only to her husband's authority, but also to that of the family system more generally. Indeed, she acknowledged, "It was the love and compassion that my in-laws bestowed on me that crippled me . . . it was the family structure and its efficient shock absorption system that did me in. My in-law's love turned out to be a prison that was all too secure for me to leave" (p. 203).

The extent to which familial protection compromised individual agency is particularly evident in Afaf's description of issues of medical care. Both Afaf's father and father-in-law were reluctant to allow the women in their families to be treated by male doctors in public settings—not because they wanted to deny them adequate medical treatment, but because they wanted to spare them the presumed "humiliation" of such an experience, and hence to safeguard their own honor. When Afaf had tonsillitis, for instance, her father-in-law refused to let her be operated on in the hospital; instead, the operation was carried out at home. When Afaf, still a minor, was pregnant with her first child, the issue of whether she would give birth at home or in hospital was determined by the elders of the family; neither her opinion nor that of Marwan was deemed relevant. As Afaf writes, "The where and how of our baby's delivery had been exhaustively discussed by the *grown-ups* of the family . . . nobody cared to get my opinion on a matter that usually concerned the *grown-ups* only" (p. 179; italics mine). Even Marwan was not able to persuade his father to allow Afaf to give birth at the hospital, where she would be cared for by an obstetrician.

However, despite the encompassing power of the family and tradition, Afaf was nonetheless able to assert her will in certain areas. For instance, although she had no say about either the circumstances of her delivery or the circumcision of her baby, she was nonetheless able to convince Marwan to depart from the traditional dictate that the first male child be named after his paternal grandfather. Indeed, in a creative gesture, she had the baby "choose" his own name by writing several choices on slips of paper, wadding up the slips, and allowing the baby to bat at them until only one was left. The scene makes clear Afaf's commitment to the concept of self-determination, not only on her own behalf, but on that of her children as well.

Afaf's struggles for personal autonomy within her marriage were played out within an increasingly troubled political situation. She arrived in Haifa, Palestine, in 1935—the year before the General Strike paralyzed the country. Her narrative provides a rarely voiced woman's perspective on Palestinian life during the crucial years leading up to the creation of the state of Israel. The increase in immigration after the Balfour Declaration of 1917 had resulted in the creation, under British protection, of a largely European settler population committed to the goal of creating a Jewish state. Palestinian landowners, many of them absentee owners, were often tempted by the high prices offered by the Jewish Land Agency for their land. But such sales had devastating consequences. As Thomas Reid, a dissenting member of the Palestine Partition Commission, wrote in 1938, "Land so purchased becomes Jewish for all time, . . . [it] cannot be leased to any non-Jewish tenants, and . . . a clause in the leases forbids the employment of non-Jewish labour on such land. . . . Probably nothing has produced more communal ill-will in Palestine than this Jewish system of economic penetration."[12] The sale of large estates on which Palestinian peasants had lived for generations created a growing class of displaced peasants who flooded into Palestinian cities as refugees. By 1936, according to one observer, there were around 11,000 people living in shantytowns on the outskirts of Haifa.[13] The economic crisis was accentuated by the Jewish Trade Union Organization's campaign in the 1930s to discourage Jewish employers from employing Arabs, and by economic preferences and concessions given by the British Authority to Zionist groups.[14] Arab-Jewish tensions were also accentuated by the British use of Zionist task forces in their police force. Hostilities grew, culminating in the General Strike of 1936 and the rebellion of 1937–1938 that followed the announcement of the Royal Commission's plan for the partition of Palestine.

Palestinian women, as well as men, mobilized in response to the political situation. In 1929, the first congress of Palestinian women submitted a declaration to the British High Commissioner, protesting against 1) the Balfour Declaration, which they described as "the sole cause of all the troubles that took place in the country, and which may arise in future"; 2) Zionist immigration "in view of the political and economic situation of the country"; 3) the enforcement of the Collective Punishment Ordinance; and 4) police maltreatment of Arab prisoners.[15] While Afaf did not play a personal role in the nationalist movement, from her arrival in Palestine she realized the importance of educating herself politically, and quickly determined to "listen and watch carefully, combining new information with common sense and my instinctive reactions to events" (p. 133). Her political insight soon gained her the respect of her husband, despite his disagreement with her political views, as well as that of his colleagues and friends.

In charting the impact of the political situation on middle- and upper-class Palestinians, Afaf's autobiography provides insight into the variety of political views among Palestinians of the time. Palestinians of an older generation and wealthier background, such as her in-laws, tended to cling to the hope that the authorities would retain control of the situation and that things would "clear up"—the phrase Afaf describes as "the Arab motto of the time, the crippling footnote to every statement" (p. 241). Although patriotic (for instance, Afaf's father-in-law staunchly rejected his son's advice that he safeguard his assets by investing outside Palestine), these Palestinians seemed unable to encompass the enormity of the changes overtaking the country. Others, like Marwan's boss, who as director of a Palestinian bank wanted to support a national agricultural industry and to assist the rural Palestinian population, found their patriotic ideas pitted against pragmatic imperatives. A few, like Marwan, tried to remain uninvolved. But none remained untouched by the situation. Afaf herself quickly developed sympathy for the Palestinian rebels, and for the rural poor, whose plight during the strike went largely unnoticed.

Afaf came of age amid this politicized context. Over the course of her twelve–year residence in Palestine she gave birth to three sons (one amid the Italo-German bombing of Haifa in 1940), weathered epidemics of typhoid and meningitis, established a manageable, if difficult, relationship with her husband, and fell in love, against all traditional dictates, with a Christian family friend, Nadim. Her narrative recounts intense political discussions, making clear the wide range of opinions on Zionism among both Jews and Arabs. It also makes clear the growing impress of the political situation on everyday life. Although Afaf's position within the well-off Rajy family sheltered her from some aspects of the political situation, on one of her trips between Beirut and Haifa, she too was caught in the growing conflict when a violent border incident erupted between British and Zionist forces and Arab rebels.

In 1947, a Palestine partition plan was accepted by the UN General Assembly, and the British announced their impending withdrawal from Palestine. The increasing violence on both sides spurred the Rajy family to move to Acre, where they had family ties. Marwan, however, refused to leave Haifa and his job, and Afaf and the children stayed with him. When Zionist fighters took over their neighborhood, the family rented an apartment near the children's school. But tragedy struck in January, 1948, when Marwan, determined to go to work despite the political situation, set out on an unsafe road and was killed. A few months before the final demise of Palestine, Afaf was thus left a twenty-nine-year-old widowed mother of three, caught between the dictates of tradition and a disintegrating political context.

Afaf's narrative after her husband's death recounts her struggles to take responsibility for her children within this context of complete political and personal crisis. Although she wanted to take the children home to Haifa, her father-in-law refused, fearing for their safety. Haifa fell to the Zionist forces in April 1948. When Acre too fell under occupation, the once-wealthy Rajys, who had now lost everything, fled, along with hundreds of thousands of Palestinians, to Lebanon.

The declaration of the state of Israel on May 15, 1948 marked the end of Palestine as Afaf had known it. Some Palestinians, like the Rajys, had already left their homes to escape the escalating hostilities, planning to return when things "cleared up." Others fled in panic in the wake of terrorist incidents, such as the massacre of villagers at Deir Yassin,[16] or else were forced out by "the deliberate policy of the Israeli army."[17] Almost two-thirds of the Arab population of Palestine became refugees. The impact was devastating. In Afaf's words, "The future looked like a bowl of fire that whirled around us and ravaged everything it its way—people, land, cultures, everything" (p. 248).

In Lebanon the Rajys sought shelter with relatives, while Afaf went to her parents, who had lost their own inherited mansion to creditors and were living in a rented apartment. But her still-brutal father made life miserable for them. In addition, he pressured her to send the children, as tradition dictated, to their paternal kin. To protect the children, she was finally forced to comply. The narrative describes Afaf's growing awareness of the limited options for women once their place within the social structure is jeopardized. Although as a wife she had enjoyed the protection and support of her family-in-law, as a widow she had few options: either she could remarry, further weakening her control over her children's destiny, or she could remain at her parents' house as a dependent of her father and brothers. While her parents-in-law might have helped her, their sudden destitution made such assistance impossible. All they could offer her was the role of second wife to their younger son, whose first wife was barren: Afaf indignantly refused the proposition. Nadim, the man she had fallen in love with in

Palestine, followed her to Beirut and urged her to marry him, and Afaf was pressured by her brother, eager to rid himself of his responsibility for her, to accept the offer. However, recognizing that such a marriage would mean the definitive loss of her children, since their paternal relatives would never let them be adopted by a Christian, Afaf refused to consider it until the children had grown up. Meanwhile, she struggled to keep her eldest son out of an orphanage, as her brother tried to turn both her parents and her parents-in-law against her.

Despite the enormity of the catastrophe and the numbing traditional constraints circumscribing her possibilities, Afaf was nonetheless able to formulate a plan of action to take charge of her life and reclaim her children. As she remarked shortly after Marwan's death, "In reality, a young empty-handed widow who belonged to a closed society such as mine could have one of only two providers: her in-laws or her parents. . . . But since both of my legal custodians were broke—the Rajys financially, and my parents ethically—why shouldn't I be my own provider? Practice began the very next day" (p. 237). Against familial opposition, she took secretarial courses and began looking for a job. Finding a position as an embassy secretary, she moved temporarily to Baghdad, an experience that widened her horizons, gave her increasing self-confidence, and sharpened her feminist analysis. Nadim followed her to Baghdad, insisting once again that she marry him. But Afaf, convinced that marriage would make it impossible for her to fulfill her responsibilities to her children, rejected his ultimatum. Instead, she returned to Lebanon, found a job, and went back to school, once again defying familial dictates.

By this time, Lebanon was in the throes of political and social change. Afaf describes the shifts taking place in 1952, when Camille Cham'oun's presidency held out the promises of internal political and social reform and of ending French control over the country. However, despite the changes promised by the reformist coalition that brought Cham'oun to the presidency—changes extending from land redistribution to women's suffrage[18]—Lebanon was experiencing deepening sectarian divisions, as frustrations grew on the part of the Muslim majority over dictatorial Maronite rule. From the first creation of "Greater Lebanon" by the French, who annexed parts of Syria to Mount Lebanon to construct a "national home" for Maronite Catholics, the state was constituted as "a grouping of sectarian communities . . . each [with] its own power structure, its own laws governing . . . personal status, its own courts and judicial procedures, its own deputies in parliament, its own political parties, frequently, its own schools and distinct educational orienta- tions often hostile to that of other communities, its own hospitals, health, and social agencies."[19] The organization of the state was heav- ily weighted in favor of the Maronites—even though their privileges, such as Maronite monopoly over the presidency, were at odds with the demographic reality. This sectarian organization and imbalance of power set the stage for the civil war that was to devastate the country.

Amid this volatile political context, Afaf's personal situation was also in flux. After obtaining a job as a clerk in the newly established Ministry of Education and Fine Arts, Afaf won UN and American scholarships to programs in Lebanon and then the United States. It is at this point, Afaf writes, "that I began to feel free from the fear of insecurity that complicated my past. At home, I was still the daughter of my own overprotective family and a member of the Rajys' unwieldy clan. I was content to have a steady job. But the doors to a brighter future and a challenging career were flung wide open for me and I began to sense a new woman emerging within me" (pp. 307–308). After a year in the United States, Afaf returned to Beirut, where she developed a friendship with the colleague who headed the cabinet of her ministry, Fuad Salem—a man she describes as her soul mate, someone who restored her faith in male-female relationships. The friendship shifted to romance, and in 1965, when the last of Afaf's children had left home and Afaf finally felt free to put her own life first, the couple married. In 1971 they built a home in the mountains of Lebanon and looked forward to a life of tranquility together.

But once again Afaf's life was devastated by political violence. During the 1970s, increasing economic disparities, the role of the Western powers, especially the Unites States, in arming and training rightist Maronite militias and Israel's numerous cross-border raids and military incursions into Lebanon brought about a coalescence of leftist and progressive groups in Lebanon. This progressive movement came together with the Palestinian resistance to oppose Israeli aggression, and, to some extent, to work for social and economic justice for the disadvantaged.[20] While rightist Maronite leaders—who had long seen in Zionism a reflection of their own aspirations for a national "home" for Christians—called for a strengthening of ties with the west, the Progressive Front called for Lebanon to dismantle sectarian privileges and turn toward the Arab world.[21] The conflicting aspirations for Lebanon held by Maronite exclusionists, "Greater Syria" nationalists, and pan-Arab nationalists were defined along both sectarian and class lines. Out of this context of deepening national, political and social tensions civil war erupted in 1975, catching Afaf and her husband in its crossfire.

Following a fisherman union's strike in Sidon and its violent suppression, and the massacre of a busload of Palestinian and Lebanese families by Kataeb (Maronite) gunmen on April 13, 1975, a fierce wave of violence swept Lebanon. The fighting pitted Maronite militias against Palestinians and their Lebanese allies, Christians against Muslims, and the rich against the poor and dispossessed.[22] Exchanges of rockets, mortars and incendiary bombs devastated the country, while sniper fire and other forms of violence and brutality claimed large numbers of lives. Civilians were explicitly targeted: huge numbers of people were kidnapped or killed at roadblocks on the basis of the religion listed on their identity cards. As Tabitha Petran writes, what were "essentially social and class conflicts quickly assumed a sectarian character, as Christians and Muslims in mixed villages fought each other" and "cleansing" operations were carried out by the Maronite right.[23]

Meanwhile, foreign parties played an increasing role in the Lebanese conflict. Israel assisted rightist forces, launching raids on refugee camps and villages in both the north and the south, supplying armaments (heavy weapons, rockets and tanks as well as lighter arms), and providing military training and strategic advice, while also expanding its control in the border region.[24] In the spring of 1976 Syria intervened militarily on a large scale. This Syrian intervention initiated the "Arabization" of the war, as other Arab countries sent forces to Lebanon. At the same time, an "unacknowledged, American-inspired working alliance of Syria, the Maronite right, and Israel" emerged.[25]

By the end of the 1975–1976 phase of the war, between 25,000 and 40,000 Lebanese and Palestinians had been killed, and 60,000 people had been wounded. Most victims were under 20 years old. Six hundred thousand people, mostly Muslims, had been evicted from their homes and districts and made into refugees. The war also took a huge toll on the country's infrastructure: its hospitals, schools, offices, and sewage, phone, electricity, water and transport systems. The end of the 1975–1976 war provided little respite; in 1978 Israel invaded and occupied the south of Lebanon and Syria bombarded East Beirut. In 1979 Israel again invaded Lebanon and initiated a war of attrition against the south. Another 5,000 to 7,000 people were killed in the 1977–1980 violence.[26]

On June 5, 1982, Israel launched, with what Israeli Foreign Minister Yitzhak Shamir termed the "total accord of the United States,"[27] a massive invasion of Lebanon, aimed at destroying Palestinian nationalism and the Palestinian infrastructure in Lebanon. In the south alone, over 20,000 Lebanese and Palestinians were killed, over 40,000 were wounded, 15,000 were herded into concentration camps, and 600,000 people were left without shelter. In West Beirut, which came under Israeli siege, civilians were targeted by phosphorus rockets, cluster bombs and concussion bombs; at least 80 percent of the casualties in West Beirut were civilians.[28]

Like countless others, Afaf and her husband were caught in the middle of this violence. During the 1975–1976 war Fuad was seriously injured when their home was shelled by a militia group; he remained in a coma for fourteen months and woke to a state of paralysis. The couple moved to Beirut to be closer to medical care, and Afaf spent the next six years shuttling between her job and hospital rooms as she cared for her husband. Then in 1981 Afaf suffered a heart attack. Another heart attack struck her in 1982, in the midst of the Israeli invasion. Separated from Fuad by the violence, Afaf was sent to the United States for medical treatment. Meanwhile, Fuad was taken out of Beirut by his family to escape the Israeli bombing, which destroyed the family home. Amid the devastation, the couple lost touch with each other. After finally obtaining information on Fuad's whereabouts, Afaf returned from the United States to be reunited with him. But a few days after her return, he died. The autobiography ends with Afaf's poignant description of this final reunion and final loss.

As the narrative of one woman's life, Afaf's autobiography takes its place within a tradition of Arab women's autobiographical and feminist writing. The late ninteenth century had seen the rise of what Margot Badran and Miriam Cooke, in the introduction to *Opening the Gates: A Century of Arab Women's Feminism*, term "invisible feminism"—feminist ideas, expressed in journals, literary salons and other forums, that were not necessarily identified as such. (Badran and Cooke define "feminism" as "an awareness by women that as women they are systematically placed in a disadvantaged position; some form

of rejection of enforced behaviors and thought; and attempts to inter-
pret their own experiences and then to improve their position or lives
as women."[29]) During the time period covered by Afaf's autobiography, Arab feminist discourse had begun to assume a more public role.
By the 1920s, public, organized women's movements had begun to
emerge in Egypt, and by the 1930s and 1940s, there were women's
organizations in Lebanon, Syria, Iraq, and Palestine. These movements
were grounded in the struggle for dual (national and feminist) liberation, as women organized to respond to the political crises confronting
their societies. Thus, for instance, the Egyptian Feminist Union was
established following the revolution against British colonial rule in
Egypt, in which feminists had participated. Similarly, in Palestine,
women came together to oppose the British mandate and the Zionist
colonization of Palestine. In 1938 and 1944, Palestinian women joined
with other Arab feminists in pan-Arab conferences, and in 1944 the
Arab Feminist Union was formed.[30]

    Afaf's autobiography also fits within a more general tradition of Arabic
autobiography. Although it is sometimes supposed that autobiography is a
literary genre peculiar to Western culture,[31] historian Leila Ahmed notes
that it is "an anciently known form in Islamic-Arabic letters."[32] There
were no autobiographies by women in classical Arabic literature,[33] but
many Arab women's autobiographies have been published throughout
this century, many of them explicitly feminist. These include the posthu-
mously published *Harem Years* by Huda Sha'arawi, often termed the first
Arab feminist memoir; Fadwa Tuqan's *A Mountainous Journey: A Poet's
Autobiography*, Raymonda Hawa Tawil's *My Home, My Prison*, Fatima
Mernissi's *Dreams of Trespass: Tales of a Harem Girlhood*, Nawal El
Saadawi's *Memoirs from the Women's Prison*, Jean Said Makdisi's *Beirut Fragments: A War Memoir*, and others.[34]

    As an Arab woman autobiographer writing in English, Afaf con-
fronts several tasks. While all autobiographers grapple with the tension
between lived life and the literary narration of this life, women autobiographers must, in addition, negotiate gendered constraints on their
articulation. Writing within social contexts that have historically deval-
ued women's lives and experiences, women autobiographers seek to
narrate "the journey of a female self striving to become the subject of
her own discourse, the narrator of her own story."[35] Women of non-
Western backgrounds writing in English for Western readers confront
a further task, that of educating their readers about unfamiliar cultures

and histories. Finally, Arab women writers must struggle with a particular set of received stereotypes that not only depict Arab women as
mute victims of a patriarchal and misogynist Islamic culture, but that
also portray Arabs in general as "enemies" of Christianity, democracy,
civilization, and the West. These stereotypes, based on a long tradition
of Orientalist discourse,[36] have been accentuated by contemporary
hostilities toward Islam as the new "enemy" of the West since the
waning of the Cold War, and by the skewed stance of the United States
in the Arab-Israeli conflict. Ironically, these stereotypes have also been
perpetuated by a thread of Western feminist discourse that views third
world women as in particular need of "rescue" from the presumed
inherent oppressiveness of their cultures, that implicitly holds up Western culture as the model for women's liberation, and that tends to view
third-world women as discovering their voices only upon exposure to
Western feminist discourse.

Afaf's feminism, in contrast, is the product of her own environment,
her own culture, and her own experiences. Offering penetrating obser-
vations about women's roles, social constraints, and the destructive-
ness of male history, Afaf makes clear that the feminist projects of
transforming social relations and furthering women's autonomy are
shaped by local contexts. Within her feminist critique, elements often
assumed to be responsible for Arab women's oppression, such as
Islam, play a minor role. Practices such as veiling and polygamy, often
considered to be standard practice in Islamic societies and to be imposed on Muslim women against their will, emerge in the narrative as
both class-related and context-specific. Indeed, although Afaf does not
hesitate to criticize the overriding role of family and tradition in Arab
society, she nowhere suggests that Islam is responsible for the difficulties she faces. Rather, what references she does make to Islam are
largely positive; she mentions, for instance, the spiritual comfort she
derives from her sense of connection to her grandfather, a religious
leader who wrote essays seeking to minimize the differences between
different religious groups in Lebanon.

The publication of Afaf's autobiography comes at a time when,
despite the increasing numbers of self-representations of Arab women
available to English-speaking readers, the stereotypes delineating Western views of Arab women remain markedly in place. Afaf's memoir
presents one woman's account of her life, her society, and her times.
Her narrative offers a personal portrait of constraint and defiance, op-

pression and resilience, resistance and transformation. Throughout, it underscores the inadequacy of stereotypes to render the reality of an individual life. Analytical, self-critical, passionate, and sometimes poetic, Afaf provides insight into the truth of that most famous of feminist dictums, that the personal is political. At the same time, tracing a struggle for autonomy played out within contexts of overwhelming political devastation and personal loss, she accentuates the often-forgotten inverse of this dictum: that the political is also personal.

Afaf's journey has not been easy. Childhood experiences of abuse and domination, constraints on personal autonomy, the loss of home, husband, belongings, and country not once, but twice—these might have crushed a woman of lesser spirit. But against the most difficult odds, Afaf prevailed. Her narrative is imbued with the strength, resilience, humanity, commitment, and vision that have sustained her through eighty years. *Nadia, Captive of Hope* stands as testimony to the world-shaking act of telling a woman's life.

Notes

1. Muriel Rukeyser, "Kathe Kollwitz," *A Muriel Rukeyser Reader,* ed. by Jan Heller Levi (New York and London: W.W. Norton, 1994), 217.
2. Quoted in Charles D. Smith, *Palestine and the Arab-Israeli Conflict* (New York: St. Martin's Press, 1988), 55. For a discussion of the debates surrounding the drafting of this Declaration, see Smith, 50–55.
3. Walid Khalidi, Introduction, *From Haven to Conquest: Readings in Zionism and the Palestine Problem Until 1948* (Washington, DC: Institute for Palestine Studies, 1987), xxvii.
4. For a study of the concept of "transfer" in Zionist ideology, see Nur Masalha, *Expulsion of the Palestinians: The Concept of "Transfer" in Zionist Political Thought, 1882–1948* (Washington, D.C.: Institute for Palestine Studies, 1992). See also Benny Morris, *The Birth of the Palestinian Refugee Problem, 1947–1949* (Cambridge and New York: Cambridge University Press, 1987), 23–28.
5. Etel Adnan, "Growing Up to Be a Woman Writer in Lebanon," in *Opening the Gates: A Century of Arab Feminist Writing,* edited by Margot Badran and Miriam Cooke (Bloomington and Indianapolis: Indiana University Press, 1990), 7.
6. Tabitha Petran, *The Struggle Over Lebanon* (New York: Monthly Review Press, 1987), 30.
7. Badran and Cooke, *Opening the Gates,* xxviii.
8. Petran, *Struggle Over Lebanon,* 31.
9. Badran and Cooke, *Opening the Gates,* xxiv.
10. Albert Hourani, *A History of the Arab Peoples* (Cambridge, MA: Belknap Press of Harvard University Press), 344.
11. It was not unusual for families in this region to have branches in both

Lebanon and Palestine. As Tabitha Petran explains, "Until the World War I peace settlement, no international frontier separated Palestine from southern Lebanon . . . centuries-old social and economic bonds made of southern Lebanon a relatively prosperous economic unit; Haifa, then the most important port of the east Mediterranean coast, was the economic capital. During the period of the mandates the economic unity of the region persisted, while social relations between Arabs of southern Lebanon and those of northern Palestine continued to be intimate" (*Struggle Over Lebanon*, 65–66).

12. Thomas Reid, "Reservations on the Plans for the Partition of Palestine 1938," in *From Haven to Conquest*, 418.

13. See Sarah Graham-Brown, *Palestinians and Their Society, 1990–1946* (London: Quartet Books, 1980),128.

14. For instance, the British favored Jewish enterprises with tariff concessions and gave Zionists concessions to build a power station on the Yarmouk River and to exploit Dead Sea potash. See Graham-Brown, 164.

15. See Graham-Brown, *Palestinians and Their Society, 1990–1946*, 168.

16. For an account of this massacre, see "A Jewish Eye-Witness: An Interview with Meir Pa'il," in *Remembering Deir Yassin: The Future of Israel and Palestine*, edited by Daniel A. McGowan and Marc H. Ellis (New York: Interlink Publishing Group, 1998), 35–46.

17. Hourani, *A History of the Arab Peoples*, 360. See also Benny Morris, *The Birth of the Palestinian Refugee Problem, 1947–1949* (Cambridge and New York: Cambridge University Press, 1987).

18. See Petran, *The Struggle Over Lebanon*, 48–49.

19. Ibid., 16.

20. Ibid., 17.

21. Ibid., 95–96.

22. Ibid., 165–166, 168.

23. Ibid., 175–176, 183.

24. Ibid., 182, 206.

25. Ibid., 203, 206.

26. Ibid., 227–228

27. Quoted in Ibid., 275.

28. Ibid., 275–276.

29. Badran and Cooke, *Opening the Gates*, xv-xvi.

30. Ibid., xxiv.

31. See, for instance, George Gusdorf, "Conditions and Limits of Autobiography," trans. James Olney, in *Autobiography: Essays Theoretical and Critical*, ed. James Olney (Princeton: Princeton University Press, 1980), 29.

32. Leila Ahmed, "Between Two Worlds: The Formation of a Turn-of-the-Century Egyptian Feminist," in *Life/Lines: Theorizing Women's Autobiography*, edited by Bella Brodzki and Celeste Schenck (Ithaca and London: Cornell University Press, 1988), 154.

33. Ibid., 155

34. Huda Sha'arawi, *Harem Years: The Memoirs of an Egyptian Feminist, 1879–1924* (London: Virago Presss, 1986); Raymonda Hawa Tawil, *My Home, My Prison* (London: Zed Press, 1983); Nawal El Saadawi, *Memoirs from the Women's Prison* (Berkeley and Los Angeles: University of California Press,

1986); Fadwa Tuqan, *A Mountainous Journey: A Poet's Autobiography* (Saint Paul, MN: Graywolf Press, 1990); Jean Said Makdisi, *Beirut Fragments: A War Memoir* (New York: Persea Books, 1990), Fatima Mernissi, *Dreams of Trespass: Tales of a Harem Girlhood* (Reading, MA, and New York: Addison-Wesley Publishing Company, 1994).

35. Francoise Lionnet, *Autobiographical Voices: Race, Gender, Self-Portraiture* (Ithaca and London: Cornell University Press, 1989), 91.

36. See Edward Said, *Orientalism* (New York: Vintage Books, 1979).

Lisa Suhair Majaj
Visiting Scholar in Women's Studies
Northeastern University

NADIA
Captive
of Hope

1

February 21, 1918

I owe the reader an explanation for the choice I made to begin this memoir on the day I was born. On that day, the body of a newborn would barely manage to split away from the womb safely, let alone remember.

Memories are known to be piled up and installed in the brain. The power that commands those memories is something else, I have discovered. It is the spiritual power of our existence, our soul. I have thought about this many times through the years, and my thoughts reach deep into the mysterious pool of that existence to listen to those memories. They are inside me, irrecoverable and yet ever present from my youngest years. They brighten the light by which my tiny footsteps roam this earth.

* * *

The room was quiet. On a large bed, surrounded by sheets, bowls, jars, and towels, lay a young woman, motionless. The yellow kerosene light fell on her closed eyes and on the taut muscles of her small face. The only sound was that of the heavy February rain that might not stop for days.

Suddenly, her hands clutched the cover of her bed as a contraction seized her back and spread around her bowels. She opened her eyes with a moan. "Sara! Sara!"

The door of the room flew open and a large woman rushed to her side. "Come on, dear Ban. Push hard now! Don't let that contraction go in vain." She dipped a towel into a ceramic bowl half filled with warm water and dabbed at Ban's face and neck.

"It smells like Damascus," Ban said in a weak voice.

"What?"

3

"The perfume on the towel. Kareem ordered it when we were in Damascus after the wedding." Giving in to fatigue, Ban shut her eyes, carried away by her sweet memories:

The silver-gray horse kicked excitedly under his bearded rider, and the groom calmed him as they waited to start their weekly ride to the country. Ban, waves of golden hair streaming behind her, rushed out and with the groom's help jumped up and sat behind her father, apologizing for the delay, when she suddenly saw him.

He stood next to the old eucalyptus tree, only a few steps away from the garden gate of her house, watching . . . a young man, carrying his tall, lean frame straight in a fitted blue coat and an immaculate white cotton shirt. He seemed unaware of how handsome he was, with his round, freshly shaved face and large brown eyes that met hers in a quick glance before the restive colt trotted away.

Ban did not know who he was or where he came from. Nor did she understand why the fleeting glance she had exchanged with the stranger had sent the blood racing through her veins. She knew, though, that seeing him waiting by that old eucalyptus every morning filled her with joy. She would dress quickly on her way to school and gulp down her cream cheese sandwich and oranges so she could go downstairs before her sister Salma to peek around the garden gate, looking for him. He was always standing there next to that tree, unaware of her watchful eyes.

But one morning, when Ban unlocked the gate and slipped her head out, she gasped! His face was less than two yards away from hers. She felt trapped in her own game.

"Please don't go, Miss Mehdi!" the young stranger whispered breathlessly. "I know who you are, and I don't mean to scare you. I live one block away, and have often watched you ride with your father or ride out in the carriage. I would be honored if you would let me introduce myself properly." He saw panic in her eyes and stepped behind the tree as Salma approached.

The groom came around to help the two sisters into the carriage. Ban could not take her eyes away from the man's intent gaze, oblivious to her sister Salma, who watched with open mouth, then tugged at her sister's sleeve. "Ban! Stop it!" Ban's face turned crimson and she looked away. An awkward silence fell between the two sisters.

That evening, as they put their nightgowns on, Salma asked, "Who is that young man? What does he want from you? You know we are not supposed to show our emotions to strangers!"

They settled onto a large Persian cushion. Ban told her sister the

Nadia's Grandpa Mehdi, 1873, Beirut, Lebanon

whole story, finding all the reasons a seventeen-year-old could think of to justify her romantic feelings. "If you hadn't dropped in on us without any warning, I would have known all the answers to those questions," Ban retorted.

The youngest daughter of the eminent Sheikh Mehdi, patriarch of a family prominent among the upper class of professionals that included lawyers and judges, Ban little knew then that the handsome Kareem Rajy was destined to become the one and only man in her whole, long life, even though her family—as tradition dictated—did not mix with his. They were money-making merchants, but belonged to the *other* class.

A strong spasm shook Ban's body. Old Sara was dozing, sitting with her back toward the corner. The rain seemed to have stopped.

Within her belly, the tiny body struggled. Ban moaned, and Sara was next to her. "That's it, dear Ban. Don't give up. Concentrate on breathing and pushing." The midwife touched Ban's brow soothingly. "I think it's time to go get Salma." Just moments later, as two heads bent over her, Ban's body stiffened with sharp pain. A piercing scream was heard before she fell back onto the wet sheets. A purplish six-pound infant slipped out to life . . . a life that would experience abundance, love, deprivation, terror, sacrifice, and determination in a struggle for personal integrity against uncivilized tradition.

"Darling, look at her!" My father's cheerful voice brought Ban back. "She looks very much like you. See?" He lowered my bundled body close to her.

"Oh, Kareem! Let me look at her; she is so tiny. I hope you don't mind having another girl." My mother's arms were weak as she took me and brought me close to her bosom.

"I do not mind girls as long as they look like you." He bent down and kissed her tenderly on both cheeks. "Do you think there is some correlation between girls and wars?" he teased. "When Nora was born, the war came right after, remember? And now the next girl seems to have come just in time to celebrate its end!"

Soon after Kareem left, Salma came in smiling and set a tray of fresh juice, chicken broth, and sauteed fruits with a pinch of cinnamon next to Ban. "I am so happy you presented us with such a healthy, beautiful girl, Ban, my love. Now give me that little one and have some food. I have a hunch she is going to be mine for some time. I felt such a wave of compassion the moment I held her tiny body. I hope you don't mind if I call her Miss Mehdi until you decide on a name for her!" She held me tenderly and then she left the room, her face shining with pride.

Salma lay awake on the nursery couch all night, unable to recover from the shock of Kareem's behavior toward her earlier. Nor could she decide whether she should leave the Rajys' home immediately or wait until her ailing sister improved. She felt sorry for Ban, who loved her husband too much to believe that he could attack another woman and force himself on her physically. That was the dark side of Kareem's nature, which Salma had never expected from a man who worshiped his wife and had dragged the Mehdis and the Rajys into a long-standing feud to marry her. Although Kareem had often teased Salma for her austere style of dress and plain appearance, this was the first time he had made harsh comments about her being single for so long and tried to physically violate her. It would break her heart to let his frivolous attempt separate her from a sister she loved more than anything in the world, should he react to her refusal by creating some kind of scandal against her.

When she finally made her decision, it was to confront him rather than risk losing a sister who needed her support at that point more than ever before. Kareem had filed a lawsuit against the Mehdis concerning his wife's share of her father's estate, and Salma was the only member of that house who maintained a relationship with the couple.

Kareem was stretched out on the large sofa in the living room, fully dressed under the crocheted afghan covering his legs. His eyes were closed when Salma crossed the carpeted room quietly and sat by the window. The rain had started again and the early morning February wind sent wet leaves tossing and falling.

Kareem massaged his forehead and opened his eyes. "Salma! How long have you been sitting there?"

"I could not sleep." Her back turned toward Kareem, Salma sobbed miserably. "I still can't believe you would behave so frivolously and betray the trust of our kinship. You could at least respect Ban's condition!"

"You just don't want to understand! My intention is your happiness. But you have never given yourself the chance to discover your own sensuality!"

"Obviously I cannot win with you treating this issue so arrogantly. All I want now is that you stay away from me until Ban recovers her health." She rushed from the room, seeking refuge in the nursery. Bending over my tiny body, she buried her hot face in the soft folds of the baby blanket, filling her lungs with the sweet scent of the newborn.

Handsome in his elegant gray suit and flowery red tie that brought out the warmth of his tan skin and brown eyes, Kareem, on his way to work, stepped in to see the recovering new mother. Two days had passed since the delivery and Ban looked rested. "Good morning, angel, did you sleep well? I'm afraid I'll be gone all day. A special occasion is being planned to celebrate the end of the war at the pasha's residence, and it's important that I stick by his side now. You can't imagine how rich this Turkish businessman is, Ban. Once the war is over, we will prosper again. You just wait and see. I promised on our wedding night that you would never regret leaving your family's fancy life for a modest marriage with an empty-handed, loving husband." He kissed her and hurried down the staircase to the street.

The bedroom door swung open again as five-year-old Anwar and Nora, who was younger by a year, waddled in, followed by Salma, dragging along baby Sami, the Rajys' two-year-old son. "Well, hello, Anwar," Ban exclaimed as Nora stood apart watching. "Jump up here and have a look at your little sister." She took a deep breath as she looked at her children's faces. "You know, Salma, I still feel a pain in my heart when I think of my two poor little ones. Did you notice how much this baby looks like Aida? How can I look at her hazel eyes and not remember the poor little babies I lost during the war?" Sorrow filled Ban's voice, as she remembered her two dead babies lost during the early years after World War I. "Five years since my little son Nadi was gone. Six since Aida died. But my heart still cries for them." She turned her head to hide her tears.

Salma held her sister in her strong arms. "You must not dredge up that grief now. Save your strength for the surviving ones. Hand me my precious baby now and give those three some attention." She carried me out of the room, whispering, "Yes, my little one. You are as beautiful as that poor girl was. I promise to look after you and pray that you live."

When Kareem returned home that night, the house was dark except for the blue flame of a kerosene lamp in Ban's bedroom. Ban was standing next to the window, wearing a long blue nightgown with an embroidered blue silk robe. Her golden hair was pulled into a chignon crowned with two white lilies. The two beds, pushed next to each other again, had been freshly made with soft blue linen. A white wool blanket was folded at the foot of each one. The couple would be back together.

"Sorry I'm so late, angel." Kareem's tender voice sent her pulse jumping with joy. He crossed the room in two strides and took her into his arms. "Oh, sweetheart, you look more breathtaking than ever. I have missed you so much! Ban, please don't let us be separated like this anymore."

She knew he was referring to the issue of having babies, which was more devastating to her than to him. "But you always forget that I am not in this alone; it is your fault as well," she said.

"Come on, Ban, I have repeatedly told you that the only way to get rid of that problem is abortion. But you refuse my advice."

She heard the reproachful hint in her husband's tone and preferred not to press that painful issue at that moment. "Come, sit down and tell me about your day."

"Let us celebrate your safe delivery, first thing." He took off his black wool coat and necktie, handed them to Ban, and bent down to unbutton his boots.

Ban poured water into a ceramic bowl for him to wash his hands and offered him a towel. "Now sit down and relax. I'll see what Salma made for supper." She went to the side table and lifted a linen kerchief from a tray, then carried the tray with both hands to the low divan. Stretched out on the cushions, Kareem watched her delicate feet step silently on the thick red and black carpet, feeling relieved that she had gained back her vivacity.

He kept his eyes on her as he ate. "I really look forward to the times we spend together in this little room when the whole world is asleep. But soon I'm going to find a larger apartment in an area that has better schools for the kids."

"Can we afford that now? The war is barely over, and you're already working long hours. What is wrong with the local school Anwar attends?"

"Oh God, Ban! You call that shabby, decadent place a school? All those people do is recite old Arabic lyrics and chant monotonous prayers over and over. None of those tutors is qualified to be called a teacher."

"I don't see what choice we have, Kareem, apart from the parochial schools of our friends the Christians. Do you want our children reading the Bible and reciting catechism instead?"

"Beirut is changing. For as long as I can remember, we have had only Muslim or Jesuit schools to choose from. But now there is the French lycée for boys, which is totally secular, and some missionary schools where non-Christian students are not forced to attend classes on religion."

"We can't afford that! Salma told me about the astronomical fees some of my cousins pay for their sons who attend the lycée."

Kareem's face reddened. "No cousin of yours is superior to me! Nothing is going to stop me from becoming just as prominent as any Mehdi! Please trust me, Ban. These are not things for you to worry about." He took a deep breath. "So it is decided, then. We will have Anwar's enrollment papers by summer. A colleague at work who has two sons at the lycée has recommended our son. I'm sure he will be accepted."

"What do you mean, recommended? I thought the lycée would accept anyone who could pay."

"Well, they seem to favor the Christians more than the rest of us in this country. Otherwise, they want to make sure the Muslims they choose are broad-minded and tolerant. Since I am of the Sunni faith, I don't have to worry; the Sunni families have seldom caused any problems for the French. They want to keep it that way." He went on. "We can register Nora in the American school for girls downtown. Most of the distinguished Muslim families are sending their daughters there, and no catechism is imposed."

"It's a long way to those schools. Do you want Anwar and Nora taking the tramway?"

"The tramway is perfectly safe, and I want our kids to be independent. Anyway, we are going to have our own carriage soon!"

Ban's eyes widened. "Kareem, don't exaggerate. Where would you park a carriage on this narrow street? And the groom? And the horses?"

"So now you know why I want to find another place to live." He grabbed her shoulders lovingly. "I sometimes wonder whether this is the same ambitious Ban I fell in love with so many years ago! I thought you resented the long years we spent in that tiny room always depending on my parents. And what do you think was the reason for that miserable time?" He looked into her eyes, surprised at the hesitation he saw. "Money, angel, is the solution to all our problems. Let me do what I see fit and things will be fine for all of us."

On a hillside street several miles above the stone buildings of old Beirut, the sound of galloping horses slowed down and came to a halt at the steps of the Rajy home. It was the pasha's carriage that Kareem was allowed to use on that special day. A military parade was taking place at the harbor, and the children had been promised they could attend. Anwar and Nora were dressed for the occasion and sent down to the entrance of the building to wait for their father and for the carriage to arrive. Anwar, who had been running around the narrow street, stopped and looked with wide eyes, and Nora stood behind him, clutching her old rag doll tightly. The street went silent as neighbors, debating over the pushcart loaded with freshly unearthed potatoes, onions, spinach, and parsley, stopped their discussion abruptly, and young boys left their game of marbles to circle the fancy carriage. They ran their fingers over the large metal wheels and the shiny body that had the look one saw only in foreign magazines.

Climbing onto the gray velvet front seat next to his father, Anwar peeked out at the boys, his eyes dancing proudly. Nora squeezed between Aunt Salma and Maria, the children's nanny, who held two-year-old Sami on her lap, as Kareem looked up at the house where Ban waved at him from behind their bedroom window.

"I guess we're ready now, Saleem," Kareem called to the groom. Then he looked at Salma. "Are you sure you wouldn't prefer to move to the front seat next to me and let Anwar sit with Maria and Nora? That will give you more room."

"Oh, no. I am quite all right here," Salma said quickly, evading his eyes.

"All right, then," Kareem said, turning to the groom. "Tell the coachman to proceed. Have him take the long route round the peninsula." Digging into his vest pocket with two fingers, Kareem pulled out a round gold watch, checked it, and continued. "We have lots of time. The parade won't start before ten."

The carriage rolled smoothly down the alley, then turned onto a large gravel road heading west where the homes were set far apart. The hills were green with date, olive, pine, and eucalyptus trees rising over trellised jasmine vines.

"Beirut looks so different now from when we were kids," Salma reminisced, breathing the sweet air deeply and gazing over the steep hills dotted with a wide variety of colorful buildings. Beyond them the mountains separated the peninsula from the inland area to the east. "I still remember the small old house in the downtown area where my parents used to live. When father decided to buy a piece of land overlooking the town, his friends were adamant that it was not safe to live outside the city walls."

"Papa," Anwar complained, "when are we going to see the parade? I'm tired."

"Calm down, son. We'll be there soon. See that big stone building down on the other side of the city? That is the French school you will start attending next year. Few families can afford to send their children to that school." He glanced at Salma, who responded with a pale smile to his outburst of vanity.

"What about Nora? I hope she won't be there, too."

"Don't be silly, Anwar. You know girls don't go to boys' schools. But she will attend one as good as yours when the time comes. Nora's American school is not far from where we are now. In fact, I suggest we stop there for our picnic. The grounds overlook the Place des Canons, where all the action is, and we can watch the parade from there."

The carriage rolled noisily onto the steep slate road that passed the American hospital and university and led downward to the old part of the city. The horse's springing gait echoed sharp and rhythmic off the high stone walls siding the road.

"Children, look down there! See the big ships?" Salma held Nora up and pointed with her gloved forefinger to the azure sparkling waters. The usual fishing fleet of shallow-water boats was nowhere to be seen that morning. Instead large gray warships cruised around the shores flying colorful foreign flags.

"Papa, are those big ships our friends?" Anwar asked, his eyes full of wonder.

Kareem paused before he answered. "They are British and French ships here to show that the Allies are now in power, not Turkey. They seem to be friends now. By the time you are all grown-up, perhaps we will know whether they are truly our friends." There was a bitter tone to his voice.

"Is the pasha supposed to be down there with the officials?" Salma asked, trying to change the cold mood that had fallen over them.

"No. For now, it wouldn't be appropriate for a Turkish dignitary like the pasha to attend. Politically speaking, the Allies are the conquerors."

"Will his business be jeopardized now that the Turks are no longer in power?" Salma began to suspect the reason for Kareem's bitterness.

"Oh, no. The pasha is a well-established businessman. In fact, he could be better off now. Our new regime is as much in need of him as he is of them." He looked at Salma sharply. "You're not thinking that my work for him would raise suspicions."

The blood rushed to Salma's face. She lowered her voice. "You cannot deny me that concern since I am part of your load. Ban told me about your plans. A larger house, expensive schools for Anwar and Nora, a carriage, and the new baby. I know you work hard and deserve all of it, but other people are going to be jealous, and that might bring you bad luck."

"Luck has nothing to do with what I am doing." Kareem sounded amused. "I want you to trust my judgment and support me, especially when talking with Ban." His face became serious again. "Working for the pasha is not my only venture. I work part-time for some commercial businesses also."

Coming into a small square with an ivy-covered church dominating one side, the Rajy carriage slowed and joined a line of other carriages rolling toward the Place des Canons. "Papa, look there! Do you see those funny soldiers? Why are they carrying those long guns? Why are their skins so dark?" Everyone in the carriage followed Anwar's bewildered eyes to where an infantry of the French army auxiliary lined both sides of the road. The heavy-set African men were dressed in ill-fitting fatigues, their long legs planted several feet apart. "Those are the Senegalese troops who fought with the French army. They come from Africa, where everyone is as dark as they are."

"Don't worry, Anwar," Salma added, as he still looked puzzled. "You will see people from all around the world today and learn about them when you attend your new school."

"There it is." Kareem nodded toward a stone compound on a small hill at the side of the road. He knocked on the groom's window with the silver top of his ebony cane and waved for him to stop in the yard of the American church and school. "Maria, see that the kids play where you can keep an eye on them," Kareem said. "Miss Salma and I will stay in the carriage and watch the parade from here."

Gathering her skirts, Maria stepped down with Sami in one arm and the picnic basket in the other. Anwar galloped ahead of her, chasing white butterflies over the daisies and red poppies that bordered the yard. Nora followed, hanging from the maid's sleeve. They were on a large, elevated lawn shaded by old oak and cypress trees. A low stone wall surrounded the grass and the two-story school, Gothic church, library, and music hall.

"Do you know, Salma, this is the first time so many foreign troops have paraded on our soil." Kareem's eyes were distant. "During my two-year stay at the Institute of Engineering in Istanbul, I saw many parades and ceremonies that included representatives of countries from all around the world. Istanbul is a great city, one that attracted the attention of powerful nations. But it makes me uneasy to see our port jammed with these huge warships and our little plaza surrounded by so many foreign faces and troops."

"What are you afraid is going to happen?" Salma looked puzzled. "I thought once the war was over, there would be nothing to fear."

"In a way you're right. But these winners have to share the booty. France and England are allies now, and yet they have been long-time enemies. I'm afraid we might be caught in the middle of their bargaining. Didn't you ever hear your father talk about these political matters? I'm sure he was aware of how France and England keep an eye on this part of the world."

Salma answered, "I would hear him discuss social and political matters with my brother on occasion. It was well-known that France had worked for many years to establish her position among certain segments of this country. But I did not expect a serious conflict among the Allies over us. Did you?"

"There are always stories about secret foreign plans to take over this country. Well, we are quite vulnerable. Under Napoleon, France tried to invade this front of the Mediterranean and failed. Now, having defeated the Turks, the Allies have set as their top priority to divide the empire into small states so they can control it. One thing is certain, though. France will be given control over us because of the support she has from the Catholic community in the Lebanese mountains. For many years France has taken upon herself the task of protecting those minorities from invaders." A knock on the carriage window stopped him.

"Thank you, Saleem," Salma said, taking a wooden tray of fruit and stuffed flat bread from the groom.

Salma looked at the food, pleased and smiling. "Are you hungry?" She turned to Kareem.

Before he could answer, a deafening explosion shook the air, and the carriage jerked as the horse whinnied and pulled at the bit. Blood rushed to Kareem's face. "So this is the music of celebration!" His voice was filled with contempt. "That was a military salute. See that big warship across the harbor? You can see the smoke hovering above it."

At one-minute intervals, eleven more blasts echoed in the surrounding mountains and reverberated over the sunny town where suddenly all activity came to an end.

Anwar's hard elbow dug into my shoulder. "Nadia is cute, Nadia is smart. She can talk and sing and dance and tell wonderful stories," he mimicked. "As if that were so unusual for a four-year-old!"

"Anwar!" my mother cried. "Stop your silly arguments! You're too hard on your little sisters." She closed her eyes for a moment.

"You never find fault with Nadia, and neither does my father," Anwar burst out defiantly. "He always punishes me but never touches her!"

"Your father never punishes you unless you have done something wrong. Now let's finish this work before your father and the packers come."

The Rajys were preparing to move to the new home that Kareem had long fought for. It was a luxurious floor in the Mehdi home which Ban inherited as part of her father's estate. But Kareem had to file a lawsuit against his mother-in-law and get a court order to gain control of that property. The hostile interactions dragged on for years, creating a barrier between the two families that tore at Ban's heart. It lasted as long as they all lived. By paying off Salma for her share, Kareem put his hands on the spacious upper floor and the large backyard and gardens surrounding the Mehdis' valuable mansion.

Nora helped me collect the dolls Anwar had thrown across the hall, saying they were useless rags that should not be taken with us to the new house. That's when I ran to our room and threw myself face down on the stiff mattress. "Oh, Aunt Salma," I groaned quietly. "Why did you have to leave me in this house? Why didn't you take me with you?" Sobs shook my body while her soft voice echoed in my ears.

"Sorry, honey, I can't stay with you any longer, but I shall come to see you often. I will never love anybody more than you."

Nora came in with some lemonade, set it on the low table, and knelt next to me. "Every time there's an argument, you cry until you've worn yourself out. Here, let me clean that face of yours."

The cool, wet cloth felt good against my skin. I closed my eyes. The soft fragrance of the soap reminded me of Aunt Salma. How I missed snuggling into the smooth folds of her flannel nightgown!

"Why do you have to tell on your brother every time he teases you?" Nora's eyes were fixed on mine. "He is the first son in our family," she warned. "Standing up to him will only make your life miserable. Take my advice, Nadia. In the long run, our parents and everyone else will support him, not us."

"No, I'm not going to follow your advice, first son or not! We all have the right to love something as long as we harm no one. You love to read stories; I love to make dolls and look after them; he loves to chase girls. . . ."

"All right, all right! Do it your way, Nadia. Here, drink your lemonade and let me show you the books I dug out of the trash that your mother wanted to leave behind."

"Good morning, Miss Nadia." I liked the sound of Maria's husky voice. She was as dear to me as my dolls and the only one who looked after them when I was away. She was opening and closing drawers, chatting about the things she had to do while we went to visit the new house. Unfolding an old pink knit dress, she said, "Most of your clothes are packed. I hope this still fits you."

"Oh no, not that one. It was torn when Anwar chased me. Please find another dress, otherwise my mother will ask me how it happened. I don't want her to get mad at me, because she is very sick. Every morning she looks sick."

"Don't worry, sweetie. Your dear mama tires easily because of her present condition, but she is not sick. She has a very tiny baby in her stomach." Maria pulled a white cotton dress over my shoulders as we talked. The rough skin of her palms tickled my bare arms. "Now I want you to be a good girl, and try to be nice to her. The next few months will be hard on her with all the changes that will be happening in her life from now on."

"If my mother is busy with the new baby, why doesn't Aunt Salma come back here and help?" Maria shot a strange look at me and left the room. Oh, how I wanted Aunt Salma to come back!

"Did you finish packing, Nadia?" My mother's musical voice brought me out of my dreams.

"My dolls are all packed." Encouraged by her smiling eyes, I continued. "I am going to make some new little dolls for the baby you hid in your stomach."

She stepped inside the room and closed the door. "What are you talking about? Who told you I hid a baby in my stomach?" She sounded amused.

"I was worried that you were sick, but Maria said you put a tiny baby inside your stomach. Mama, what happens if the baby wants to eat or play?"

Her soft hand tapped my head and pulled me close. "Babies feed off their mothers. As for play, well, they have a lot of space to move around. But I want you to keep this between you and me as our secret, agreed?"

"You know what, mama? I am going to make a tiny baby and swallow it. Then both of us will have the same secret!" I felt thrilled with the new game, but she grabbed my arm tightly.

"This is not a game for little girls to play. Nadia, I warn you, you will be forbidden to play even with one single doll if you ever think of swallowing one. Do you understand?" My arm was becoming numb under her grip. "Eating dolls!"

Nora's light movement woke me up early, but I did not move. Lying on my stomach, I kept my eyes closed and tried to guess what was going on in the house by listening to all the noises. Sami complained that Anwar had locked him out of their room. Papa's footsteps shuffled on the terrace tiles as he watered his delicate gardenias. Maria banged her copper pots and pans on the coal stove as she cooked our Sunday breakfast, seasoned fava beans with lots of garlic.

"I knew you were pretending. I wanted to see how long you would play your game." Nora's serene face towered over me after she rocked my body face-up.

"Why are you all dressed up?" I was envious of her fine hair neatly braided and tied with yellow ribbons that matched the embroidered daisies on the front of her white dress.

"Well, you know we're going to see the new house today, and you'd better get dressed in a hurry."

My parents, cool and elegant in their linen clothes, sat on the front seat of our carriage with Akram, my two-year-old brother, between them. I stood in front of my father, holding onto the side of the seat.

"Stand still now, Nadia," my mother said calmly. "We'll be at your grandma's in fifteen minutes. Watch out for the bundles at your feet. Those are the crystal chandeliers from the dining room." I had the feeling she was avoiding looking at my father.

"Ban, you have been acting as if I have committed a crime. How long is it going to take you to start accepting things?"

Her answer was barely audible. "So much is happening, and I am not feeling very well lately, you know." She looked as though she was about to cry, and I almost bit my tongue as I tried to stop myself from telling papa about the baby inside my mother that was making her sick.

"Please, don't try to fool me. I can read you like an open book. You've been delaying our move for weeks. I have begged you to go see the work that has been done on the house these last few months, but for some reason you always pretend you cannot do it." He seemed not to care that she was crying, and he went on. "You are entitled to inherit a share of your father's house. Is it right for a family as large as ours to squeeze into a small apartment while your mother pretends she doesn't have enough money and keeps us from living in that house all these years?"

My mother's body shook inside her blue linen cape, and her lace veil was wet with tears. The feeling of guilt over the lawsuit she had signed against her family, together with her old conviction that her father had never forgiven her for hiding her relationship with Kareem from him, was closing in on her soul. Those were issues she could never discuss with Kareem.

"When I heard the verdict in court and I knew we had won our case, I wanted to fly to you and see your happy face. But no, you turned against me. Please, Ban, give me the chance to prove how serious was the promise I made to you on our wedding day. How can you deny me that? Aren't you happy that the court verdict, after seven years of expense and struggle, gave you what your beloved father wanted you to have?"

"Please, Kareem, don't make it harder than it is already. People don't understand how you could go against my mother as you did. Everyone blamed me for taking your side so blindly."

"I don't care about anyone else. I want you to understand. When we get there, I want you not to listen to anyone who tries to come between us." They turned away from each other and sat in silence.

"Mama, what happened to Nora and the boys?" I felt lonely and confused.

"They'll be along shortly. The walk from our apartment to the new house might take half an hour. I have a surprise for you. How would you like to spend some time with Aunt Salma while you are waiting for Nora and the boys? Then you can all play in the back yard for the rest of the day."

"I didn't know Aunt Salma would be at the house we are going to. Are you sure she will be there?"

"Of course; that's where she lives. Your Grandma Mehdi, your Aunt Fatima, and her four kids live there too. But Aunt Salma is engaged to be married and she will soon leave home, too." Her sad eyes were as clear as the blue sky.

"Mama, which is Grandma's house?" I tugged at her sleeve. My father grabbed my face with his large hand and forced me to meet his gaze.

"That is not all Grandma's house anymore. We own the top floor, and soon we will be living above her. From now on you are to call it our home."

Our carriage rolled onto a large clean street where two-story sandstone houses set far apart were surrounded by walnut, almond, persimmon, and citrus trees. Except for a couple of carriages parked in front of the high gates, the street was empty.

Saleem knocked. Long moments passed before the gate creaked and a pair of dark, questioning eyes stared at us. "Yes?" The voice sounded uncertain. "What do you want?"

"This is Miss Nadia. Master Rajy has brought the young miss to pay a visit to her respected aunt."

"Come, miss." The woman held my arm with her strong hand. She pulled me in and slammed the gate. She wore a long brown cotton dress, and her head was wrapped tightly with white muslin. A white rope girded her thin waist, and from it two large keys dangled noisily.

"Take off those shoes, miss, and tell me which aunt you wish to visit." She bent down, unbuttoned my white leather shoes, and handed me a pair of worn-out slippers. "You can put them on, miss. They are clean."

The large slippers flapped clumsily as we crossed the marble entryway to wooden doors with glass arcades arching above them. I heard the sharp voices of children arguing. Then the door opened and two boys raced past us, their bare feet flying.

"Is that you, Nadia?" The warm, familiar voice filled the dark lounge. "Oh, honey, how I've missed those beautiful eyes!" Aunt Salma stooped down and pulled me as close as she could. I can still smell the fragrance of her hair.

"Who brought you here?" She asked.

"Mama and Papa. They went to park the carriage in the backyard before coming upstairs. Aunt Salma, will you come and live with us now that we will be upstairs? Mama said you want to marry someone and move away. Our house will be much bigger now. Why don't you move in with us?"

"You know how much I would love to do that, Nadia." She held my hands and looked into my eyes. "But I will be marrying someone who works in another city. I think you know what a lady does when she marries someone who lives far from her home. I have to live in his house." She smiled at me. "But I will be living in a lovely summer resort town in the north, and I can invite you for long visits to my own home. How would you like that?"

"Oh, Aunt Salma, I would rather live with you than with my parents. My brothers scare me and make me sick sometimes."

"Don't worry. You are growing fast. Soon you'll be big and strong and nobody will bother you." Her voice calmed me.

"Who are those boys who ran out of here a minute ago? They aren't yours, are they?" My heart felt light as I joked with her.

"You naughty little thing!" Her tickling fingers made my chest bubble with laughter. "Come with me. It is time you met everybody here. Aisha?" she called to the woman who had let me in earlier. Aunt Salma bent down, smoothed my hair, and straightened my blouse. Her eyes were a few inches away from mine. "Don't worry, love. Grandma and Aunt Fatima have nothing against you. It will be all right." How did she know how frightened I was to meet those two ladies for the first time?

We followed Aisha down a long hallway. Above us, the ceiling shook and I heard loud hammer blows. I held back. "What is all this pounding?"

Salma smiled faintly. "It is the sound we have been living with ever since your father started remodeling the upstairs so that you can move in. Don't ask such questions when you are with your grandma. She has been taking this matter rather hard."

"Doesn't she love us? Is that why she never came to visit us?"

"How could she not love her own kin? No, it's just that she would rather have you visit her in her house. That is why I am very happy you came."

At the far end of the hallway we entered a tall door into the *dar,* the spacious main hall with other doors leading off into bedrooms and lounges. We went into the first room on our left.

A huge framed picture faced us from the opposite wall as we entered the *liwan,* the large rectangular room off the dar that was used as a family room. The larger-than-life face that looked back at me seemed familiar. The calm, slanted eyes appeared to be smiling. The white turban was pushed slightly back, showing a furrowed, tranquil brow that reminded me of my mother. It was a man draped in a dark wool *jubba.* Only the sinewy back of his skinny hands folded on his lap showed the whiteness of his skin.

I knew he must be my Grandpa Mehdi.

Glass cabinets filled with books lined the high walls, and from an open window, warm rays of sun touched my bare legs. The room smelled crisp and clean, like a freshly ironed sheet. "Mother, this is Nadia, your beautiful granddaughter." Aunt Salma's hands pushed me lightly toward the picture. Then I saw two bright blue eyes looking at me intently. Beneath the picture, on low carpeted cushions, sat a real person!

"Do you want to come closer, young girl?" A steady voice moved smoothly through the spacious room. "Didn't your parents teach you how to greet a grandma? Maybe they were too busy plotting the end of that grandma!" The eyes sparkled.

"I assure you this child has fine manners, Mother. She is my favorite niece!" Aunt Salma carried me across the thick red and blue carpet to an aged lady in a white dress and scarf who held herself as straight as the old man above her.

She stretched out her hand, and I took it into both my hands and brushed the back of it with a soundless kiss. She looked at me for a long, very long moment, and then kissed me on both cheeks. The silky touch of her skin reminded me of my mother. So did her fragrance. I knew I was going to love her.

"My goodness, Salma. What is this child doing here?" A sharp voice pierced my ears. "Mother, don't you see she has stepped on your dress?" A young lady, thin as a whip, stood in the middle of the room. Her almond-shaped, pale eyes were as sharp as her voice. Her head was tightly wrapped with an immaculate white kerchief.

"Fatima, this is your niece, Nadia," Grandma said cheerfully. She helped me out of her lap. "Say hello to Aunt Fatima."

This new aunt did not look happy to meet me. "So this is your famous Nadia." Her eyes looked accusingly at Aunt Salma. "Each one of my four children is ten times better than this skinny child of that crazy man." She turned around and left the room.

When the reception room, the *salia,* as we called it in the new house, was fully furnished, it was a wonderful surprise for me to see a life-sized framed portrait of Grandpa Mehdi on the wall. It was a gift from Aunt Salma to her younger sister Ban as a token of reconciliation in the feud that had existed between the Mehdis and the Rajys from the time Kareem had married Ban against her mother's wishes.

My mother's beautiful eyes looked at me with confusion as I prayed she would understand how much I loved to go into that quiet lounge and look at the paintings on the walls and the warriors on horseback pictured in the carpets; they seemed to talk to me. But mostly I loved that room because my grandfather was there, and sometimes he smiled at me when I talked to him. His serene old visage offered me a ray of hope and love I could never feel from my living relatives when they talked to me face to face. It would be many years before I became aware that he had been my guide to the divine light that directed me through the worst of times.

"Please, Mama, don't be mad at me. I promise to take off my shoes next time."

"There won't be any next time, Nadia. And don't give me any of those answers about talking to the pictures and paintings; that's stupid. Now you wait here; I want your father to know what has been going on. Oh, what did I do to deserve such a crazy child!" Taking a few steps backward, she turned away and fled.

I was alone in the large sun porch that stretched along the west side of the dar. Off the porch, a long balcony looked down a straight road all the way to the Mediterranean waterfront. Clear glass doors and windows topped with arches of stained glass brought light and warmth into the porch and the hundreds of plants that thrived year round. Blue shadows fell on the white walls of the porch where pale green sprouts climbed toward the high ceiling along strings pinned with tiny blue nails. A pang of hunger gripped my stomach and I wondered when someone was going to call me for dinner. Suddenly the doorbell rang. I shivered as I listened. My father would scare us all when he returned from work. Not until he could wash and change for dinner would we be able to talk to him. But that evening my fear of him was doubled because I had made my mother angry. I could barely hear her soft words. "Quick, Maria, run down and get his bags."

His loud, commanding voice filled the hallway. "What are you waiting for, Anwar boy? Hurry up." Anwar was supposed to have rushed down to unbutton father's boots.

A short time later the electric lights that topped the artificial candlesticks adorning the center hall were switched on and I saw my parents sit on the purple damask easy chairs in the corner next to the porch. My mother seemed to have forgotten me as they discussed a possible trip to Egypt. Then, after a moment of silence, I heard her say, "Kareem, I want to talk to you about Nadia."

"Is something the matter with her tonsils again?"

"No, nothing like that. It's just that she is turning into a strange, willful girl. It's beyond me to understand what pleases or upsets her."

"She's only five, angel. She has always been different, but I thought her extra energy pleased you."

"The girl is mixed up. She says strange things and seems to have a hard time accepting the fact that she is not like the boys." I felt my face heating up. Why was she saying that? I did not want to be a boy. In fact, I would hate to be one, if it meant that I became as rude as Anwar and Sami. They looked stupid chasing girls, sneaking around when we changed or washed, so they could see us naked.

"Oh, Kareem, this is serious." My mother went on. "I really think we have to do something before it is too late. Remember I told you that whenever I'm not home she goes and hides in the salia? She says she's been talking to the paintings, and that her grandfather's portrait smiles at her!"

"I think we should send her to school with Nora this fall. Her wild mind needs some discipline." He made it sound as if going to school was a punishment, but the idea sounded wonderful to me.

"When Nora started, they did not accept girls until they were six."

"Don't worry, I'll go talk to Miss Horn. When she finds out how capable Nadia is, she'll let her in."

"Madame, do you and Master Rajy plan to have dinner with the children?" Maria's voice rang out in the hall.

"Yes, we will be coming. Make sure they are all in their seats."

As soon as their footsteps died away, I tiptoed through the hall to my room at the far corner, jumped into bed, and pulled the covers over me.

My father's left eyebrow arched while his forefinger glided down the season's shopping list my mother had prepared. "Hats, gloves . . . Ban, do you know what size the girls wear?"

She seemed unsure. "I know Nora is a B60, the largest in the girls' line. As for Nadia, shall we take her with us?"

"Good idea." He shoved the list deep into his pocket. "I must take care of some things at the stables. I'll be back for you in half an hour." His voice echoed as he went down the long flight of stairs to the stables.

I jumped up with excitement. "Mama, what should I wear?" The unfinished jasmine blossom necklace I had been threading dangled from my arm as I followed my mother to the kitchen.

The carriage rolled down our quiet street as passing boys played on the sides of the road near their homes. I remembered Anwar bragging that only rich families could send their children to foreign schools, which closed on Saturdays and Sundays. Those who went to the free public schools were home only on Fridays.

I sat straight between my parents, listening to them plan our day. After shopping we were to have lunch at the wharf in Sidon.

We turned onto a crowded street leading to the harbor where the fancy shops—Orozdi's and Abira's—were located. The noise and

movement dazzled me. Next to us the electric tramway clanged with a
terrible noise as the driver kicked the metal brake, and people jumped
in and out of the open rows of iron benches or hung with one arm to
the iron handles. Mules brayed, beggars wailed, men carrying goat-
skins of water, juice, or milk shouted to the crowds, and iron cart-
wheels rumbled over the pavement. Through the chaos came the
rhythmic sound of the coffee carrier who clicked his tiny pile of empty
demitasse cups. When a customer appeared, the carrier lifted the
gleaming brass pot above his head with a great flair and poured a long,
dark stream into the tiny cup.

Under his brown leather apron the licorice carrier wore only a long
cotton shirt. A red felt tarboosh pushed to the back of his head showed
his sun-browned forehead, and across his chest was a huge goatskin
bag filled with the cool licorice drink. With one hand he played a
beautiful, resonant tune using two brass bowls, and with the other he
held the nozzle of his goatskin bag and squirted the dark liquid into the
bowls for thirsty passersby.

Once the carriage had been loaded, we left the harbor plaza and
turned southward on the dusty seaside road. Gradually, the city noises
gave way to the sound of waves and seagull shrieks. I relaxed my head
on the padded seat, looking into the distant, clear horizon where nothing moved.

"Don't sleep now, Nadia. I know you are tired, but I want you to
enjoy the ride." My mother's veil was pulled back, and she took off my
hat, reached into her huge handbag, and pulled out a face towel and an
enamel flask she carried when traveling. "There, baby, this will
freshen you and keep you awake." I closed my eyes as she wiped my
face with a cloth soaked in rosewater.

"Mama, when will we be able to eat?" I kept my voice low so my
father would not hear me.

"Kareem, are we going to pass by that famous bakery?" she asked.

"We'll be there in about fifteen minutes. Do you need to stop?" My
father sounded as if he had something else on his mind.

I could not believe that the small, three-sided shack, half the size of our
kitchen, could serve so many people, or be so well known. At a
wooden table against the back wall I could see a short man, his stooped

back turned toward us, his arms moving quickly as he patted the white cookie dough. In the corner there was a round, earthen oven, and the fire blazing in its square opening gave the only light inside. Another man used a long wooden paddle to thrust tray after tray of dough into the oven. The cookies went in pale and limp, and came out looking as brown and crisp as wasps' wings. The aroma tingled in my throat, and I could hardly wait as a third man counted twelve puffy cookies, placed them on several layers of newspaper, and handed them to my father, slipping the metallic piasters Papa gave him into the pocket of his grease-smeared apron.

As we left the crossing, the paved road unfolded into the higher elevations like a serpent, gliding through fields of golden wheat and green groves of orange, lemon, and almond trees. To our left, patches of okra laced the blond and brown soil that rested on the lap of the purple mountains. To the right, all the way down to the stretch of foaming tides, the vivid green of the banana plantations shared the uneven land with the gray sugar cane shoots that tilted inland under the restless sea winds.

I felt content and relaxed against the cool seat, watching the black swallows sweep through the sky, their wings almost never flapping.

"Nowadays, a car is no longer just for leisure." My father's animated voice cut into my reverie. "With all the roads being built between the capital and the towns in the mountains, it is imperative to have one."

"But how can we afford one? A car requires a driver, a garage, fuel. Are you sure you are earning enough for all that extra expense?" A pinch of nervousness shook my mother's voice. "In fact, I wonder sometimes how you have managed lately with the remodeling of the house, the new expensive furniture, and the stables. I know very little about the way you earn your money, and I worry sometimes. Your mother has her worries as well."

"What do you mean by that? And what does my mother have to do with this?"

"Oh, you know how she likes to stick her nose into everything. She feels our lifestyle is too extravagant, and she blames it on me. She thinks you could be heading for disaster just to satisfy me."

"She is crazy!" my father snapped bitterly. "She repeats what my brother Ahmed tells her, and you know how jealous he is."

She cut him short. "Your father too worries, Kareem. He seems to blame you for the fire that broke out in the workshop where you worked last year, remember?" A thick silence fell between them. "You never told me you were fired from there."

"Why are you bringing up this story now? God, Ban, I hate to see you turning against me whenever some relative chooses to attack me. There was no evidence behind that accusation. And I was glad they fired me; I was tired of working for others." His face was taut with anger, and his hands reached up to press both sides of his head.

"But what now, Kareem? It scares me to see you without a serious job for almost a year now. You spend most of your day around the stables and the weekends at the races. How can you manage?"

"You should know by now that those horses are the source of our income. You cannot imagine the money in that trade! Look at me, Ban. The horse trade is an extremely challenging business. You go to those secluded farms in the wilderness where, if you have the right instinct, you can pick up the finest fillies and colts, care for them for a few months, and sell them for enormous profit! Doesn't that sound reasonable?"

"How should I know? I cannot tell you what is good and what is bad. All I know is that I am scared for you and for all of us." She sounded tired.

"That is why I want you to trust me, angel. Did I ever disappoint you?"

As we approached the sea, a low set of wooden shacks emerged from the haze. "There, Ban. This man fries the freshest fish." We were met by a fisherman who seemed to be the only person around. "Welcome to the Fisherman Cafe, master." His large bare feet did not seem to mind the hot sand. Tall and heavily built, he strode into the pergola, grabbed two wooden chairs with one hand and a square bamboo table with the other, and set them on the sand under a green palm-leaf trellis.

Suddenly, I noticed that my mother looked carefree and pretty without her veil and topcoat, which my father had insisted she take off the moment we left the carriage. The fresh warm air gave her color, and her hair blew around her face. At that moment, she exuded a special glow that often radiates from a woman during pregnancy, as I later became aware. Her eyes were free of that look of fear I often saw in them but never understood.

2

June 1923

I opened my eyes. Nora stood at the foot of my bed, hanging onto the iron bedpost. Her eyebrows looked funny, like arches drawn above her eyes. My parents, their heads a few inches away, were talking quietly. The pale electric light encircled their heads with two net-infested halos. But the light blurred my vision and shot hot arrows deep behind my eyes.

"Mama, look, she's awake!" Nora sounded surprised.

"Nadia," my mother called, "why were you screaming? Are you in pain?"

My arm moved up to my brow. "My head, it is burning." I had to make a huge effort to answer, my teeth were so tightly clenched.

"Kareem, she has a very high fever. Don't you think we should call the doctor?" Mama's cool hand felt wonderful on my forehead, and I wanted her to keep it there.

"It's three o'clock in the morning," my father said. "Nora, go wake up Maria. Tell her to bring some vinegar and cold water. She'll know how to keep the fever down until dawn."

"How about having her drink from the horror cup? That might stop her nightmares," my mother said.

"Oh, Ban, how can you think of such a thing? A silver cup engraved with some words from a holy book will not help her now." Anger flashed between them.

"Sometimes people need to turn to God, Kareem."

"What is wrong with Miss Nadia?" Maria burst into the room with a glass bowl in one hand and a cotton face towel in the other. The vinegar fumes prickled my nose as the bowl came close.

"This will make you feel better," my mother whispered, putting the cool towel on my forehead. She sent Maria for more towels and a large bowl of crushed ice. She wet the towels and placed them over my palms. I closed my eyes, soothed by the coolness that spread through my pounding head, down my back, and all the way to my toes.

When Dr. A. Nasser came in later, I was propped up on my father's bed where every sick child was placed in preparation for the doctor's visit. The rest of the time during an illness we were put on a small sofa between our parents' beds. Dr. Nasser had a lean face and sharp, piercing eyes under thick black eyelashes. His straight nose settled into a bush of a black and white mustache that covered most of his mouth and made me wonder whether he had another mouth somewhere else.

With a nod to my mother, he asked, "How are you Mrs. Rajy?" Then, without looking at her, he put his black box down on the foot of the bed, and snapped it open. "Well, well, miss, you look fine. What was wrong with you last night?"

My mother helped me lie down and pulled my fresh white nightshirt up. For a moment I thought I was going to cry. His hand looked like a large spider, and the touch of his bony fingers on my stomach sent a chill over my body. I looked into my mother's eyes, "Am I going to die, Mama?"

"Relax, Miss Rajy, please," the doctor wheezed through his mustache. "Sit up straight. Turn this way, please." His cold stethoscope glided around my back, making short stops like a train. At each stop he called, "A deep breath, miss."

"I'm sick, Mama." My hand shot up to press my lips. She grabbed a basin and held it under my chin. When my stomach finally stopped heaving, she whispered, "Well, Doctor?"

"I'm afraid it looks like typhoid. But I wouldn't worry too much. As I recall, your family has been inoculated." The doctor sounded cheerful, but my parents looked as guilty as two small children.

"Nadia was sick at the time the others had their shots," my father said. "And my wife did not have her yearly vaccine either. She was a couple of months pregnant at that time."

"In that case, you must sterilize all the bedding and dishes the child uses." He finished scribbling on a blue pad. "I'll come back in a few days to see how she's doing. As far as you are concerned, Mrs. Rajy, I want you to stay away from this room and be sure to watch your diet. Typhoid is not known to affect an unborn child, but we would rather take the necessary precautions. You need rest at all times."

"What are we going to do, Kareem? The boys will be through with school soon, and we can't keep them in the city with this heat just because of her." "Don't worry, angel. When the schools close, my sister Huda will look after her with Maria. You can take the kids up to the summer house, and I'm sure we can find a maid to help you up there."

"How about you? Now that we have a car, can you drive up to see us each day instead of only on weekends as you used to?"

"Of course. That's one of the reasons I wanted the car so badly. Now let me go over and tell Mother we want Huda to stay with Nadia. Dr. Nasser's clinic is on my way and I'll stop and pick up the medicine, too."

∼C

"Here's some thick broth for you, honey." Maria helped me sit on the edge of the bed. "You need to move your feet so they won't become stiff."

"Maria, may I have a piece of bread or a biscuit? Please?" My head spun every time I sat up, and my teeth ached. For a whole week I had had nothing but water, broth, and juice.

"No bread, Nadia. The doctor said no solid food until your fever is gone."

I hated that doctor. "Why, Maria? I'm so hungry I could chew your finger when you wipe my mouth."

Maria left and I looked around the room. Even with its shining brass beds, velvet and lace drapes, and huge beveled mirror, it was a prison to me. My brothers and sisters were not allowed to enter, and my mother didn't come to bed until very late. I thought of sneaking out to find some food when I heard Maria's voice in the hall. "I'm sorry, Doctor, Master Rajy is not here. He took the family to the beach just fifteen minutes ago." I pulled the cotton quilt over my head.

"And how is our young lady today?" A pleasant voice entered the room.

I peeked over the cover and saw a man standing near me all in white like an angel. He was taller than any of the men I knew, and his oval, freshly shaved face was very tan, as if he had been at the beach too long.

"This is Dr. Nasser Jr.," Maria said with a big smile.

"My father left a note asking me to pay you this visit. He was called out of the city early this morning." His honey-colored mustache did not dip into his mouth like his father's.

"I want to eat some food, Doctor. Maria has been filling me up with water and broth until I feel like a drum."

"Let's see what we can do about that." He pulled a chair close to my bed, sat down, and set his small leather bag between his long legs. "Where is her fever chart?" he asked Maria.

She handed him the notebook she kept on the marble-topped chest. "I take the thermometer to Madame, and she reads it and keeps a record of it."

His lean arm shook the glass instrument that looked like a flattened pencil, and then put it into my mouth. "I know, Miss Rajy, how unfair it is to keep you from having your regular food, but I'm sure you would rather eat less and live longer, am I right?" Our eyes met, and his open smile cheered me a tiny bit. "The medical books tell us very little about how to treat this fever. Since the disease affects the digestive system, we advise you not to burden your stomach with heavy food for perhaps two to five weeks. Don't look so frantic now, I don't think your case is that bad. You seem to be doing very well." He reached for the thermometer, his face brightening as he looked down at the thin line. "If you keep being such a good girl, I think this coming week will see the end to your misery." A funny way to cure sick people, I thought, but I liked the way he talked to me as if I were an adult.

"How about some yogurt, Miss Nadia, while I pour water for Dr. Nasser to wash his hands?"

"Nadia? Is that your name, Miss? I've always liked that name." A wave of peace seemed to have filled the room. I sat on the side of the bed, swinging my feet with contentment, eating the smooth, sweet yogurt.

"Since your father has left the city, will you visit us instead?" I could not tell him his father scared me.

"I work at the French hospital during the week and only return home on weekends," he said, wiping his hands. "I have told your friend here how to help you keep on improving. For every glass of water you drink, she can treat you with a delicious meal. How about puddings, jello, rice, potatoes?" He bent down and patted my head. "See you next Saturday." He took a few strides and then he was out of the room.

"Well, now, Miss Nadia, we have a few hours before they all come back from the beach. You can rest, and I will finish packing. Your father wants to move the family to the summer house tomorrow, since it is Sunday."

"I know. And then Aunt Huda's eyes will watch over me all the time while everybody else is enjoying the summer." I felt so sad, tears filled my eyes.

Maria came to my side. "I'll be here with you, remember? You will have all my time, and we can catch up on our storytelling."

Suddenly the quiet was broken by banging doors and Papa's thunderous voice. "Maria, where are you?"

"Something is wrong!" She ran out of the room.

My mother's fever shot up to the end of the thermometer. Maria and Nora fussed over the ice and vinegar pads, then put the cold towels on her feet as well as on her palms and forehead, waiting for old Dr. Nasser to return. My father, of course, would never have allowed a young doctor to examine his wife.

"This is an acute case of typhoid, Mr. Rajy. The same treatment we recommended for the young miss will also be followed for Madame."

"Nadia's fever is better. Do you think she should remain here or can she join the other children?" asked my father.

"I prefer you keep her here, preferably in another room. This house is well aired and cool, and the medical help available in those mountain villages is not as good as in the city." His piercing eyes turned to me. "My son told me you are doing fine, Miss Rajy. Good for you."

"When did he see her?" asked my father, suddenly very alert.

"When I was called to the emergency today, I asked him to see her this morning in my place. Don't worry. Waled has grown up to be a very serious young doctor. He graduated last year from the French Medical School in Beirut, and won a scholarship to study tropical diseases in Paris. He will be leaving in October."

I had the feeling that my father's concern was that a young man had examined his daughter rather than how medically qualified he was to treat her.

I waited for Maria to come to bed, watching as the lights flicked off in my parents' room, then in the dar. She had been sleeping in Nora's bed for the last two weeks since my sister went to the summer house with Aunt Huda and the boys.

Finally, Maria tiptoed into the room. Pretending to be asleep, I closed my eyes and pulled the light cotton cover over my ears. The narrow bed squeaked, then I heard her heavy breathing.

I could not stop thinking about the small village in the nearby mountains. That afternoon the doctor had said Mama could join the family by the end of the week. So our ordeal was almost over. My mouth watered as I thought of the sweet figs in the trees that surrounded the house we rented from Um-Imad each summer.

In the middle of the night a strange noise awakened me. It was pitch black. I heard a moan and then some scuffling right next to my bed. Then Maria's low voice, pleading, "Leave me alone, master, please. I can't stand this anymore."

"Move out of here," a thick, husky voice ordered. My father!

More scuffling, and then quiet sounds of movement were swallowed by the thick darkness of the hall. I waited for a long time, but Maria did not come back.

2C

"Are you deaf, Nadia?" My father stood at the foot of my bed. "Do you know what time it is?" He shot a glance at his wristwatch. "Almost eleven. Your mother wants to see you."

I went looking for Maria. She was not in her room, in the attic; her dresser drawers were pulled out and her clothes were scattered all over the floor.

I went to the west terrace at the front of the house hoping to find her there. Perhaps she was tidying the couch where my father slept on hot nights. The terrace looked neat, the bedding put away, and the mosquito net drawn back and hooked to the lamppost as usual.

A lump came up in my throat, and a strange fear shot through me. I went to the cement baluster and peered through the narrow slits to the main street, which stretched all the way to the harbor. Down the road, I saw the familiar figure, walking slowly toward the house, hands deep inside the pockets of her black Sunday coat. But it was not Sunday. Why did she have to go to church?

I ran inside to wash and change before I got into trouble. As I was combing my hair, I heard Maria's loud voice coming from my mother's bedroom. My hand froze in mid-air. I had never heard my mother and Maria argue like that. A moment later, Maria rushed down the hall as if chased by a ghost.

"Good morning, Mama." I managed a little smile as I entered her room. "Did you want to see me?"

"Yes, Nadia. Come sit here." Her small hand tapped the side of her bed. I looked at her freshly ironed nightgown, the dry, taut skin of her thinned-out face, and her carefully combed hair. So Maria did see to my mother's morning toilette, I thought. Sitting so close to her cheered me up. She smelled like a rosebud.

"This has been an unfortunate beginning to our vacation, Nadia. I know how much you love being in the mountains each summer and how disappointed you've been to have to stay in the city these past weeks. The time we spend in that fresh mountain air is special for all of us."

"Mama, if you are happier in the mountains, why don't we live there all the time?"

"Oh, Nadia, you never cease to amaze me with your funny ideas and dreams. How do you think we could survive in the mountains? Do you think you could just run from orchard to orchard picking fruit off the trees? The people who live there work hard to plow the fields, feed the cattle, pick the figs and grapes, boil the milk. It is not like our life in the city."

"But you don't have to wear your veil," I said, "and I can play games with the boys and climb the trees. . . . My friend Omar told me last summer that I could climb any tree I wanted around their house, because they own the whole lot. Is that true, Mama?"

"Yes, some people are able to own their mountain homes and maintain them year-round. Omar's family lives in Jordan where his father holds a high position in the King's Chambers. But stop all this now and let me tell you why I called you. Maria is leaving us. She wants to go back to her family."

I looked into her eyes hoping to see she was joking. "What do you mean, back to her family? For good?"

"Yes, for good."

"Why, Mama? Is it because . . ."

"She is retiring. Her family needs her."

"Excuse me, Mama. I want to go see her." I jumped down from the bed, but her fast grip caught me.

"No, Nadia. I want you to hear what I am going to say. Your father and I believe that you have depended on Maria too much, it's time for you to use your strong will to be more self-reliant."

"Mama, please let me go. I promise from now on I will do everything myself, please."

⁓℃

Maria was in the kitchen setting out the plates for lunch. I stood for a moment, watching as her hands went on with the work she had been doing since I first knew her.

"You have not eaten anything today. I'm sorry, dear child, it's all my fault." She seemed not to know that I had spoken to my mother.

"I know everything, Maria!" Doubt clouded her eyes and her hands hung in the air.

"What do you mean you know everything?" Our eyes met for a few seconds and then I fell into her large, loving arms.

⁓℃

"They're here, Aunt Huda. The car is here!" I could hear Sami yelling at the top of his lungs as our car sputtered into the driveway. He was jumping on the porch of the stone house, looking tan and rumpled.

Abdo, our driver, climbed out of his seat and rushed to open the door to the back seat where Mama waited, smiling. Sick from the long drive, I took a deep breath of mountain air.

As I stepped onto the uneven ground, my heart throbbed. The one-story house stood among a grove of fig and almond trees. Its gray limestone walls seemed to have been carved on a day as old as the surrounding ridge.

Nora waited until I had kissed and hugged everyone, then we clung to each other for a long time. "Oh, Nora, I missed you so much. It was so sad without you down at the house."

"We'll talk later, Nadia," Nora yelled as she rushed toward the house in response to my mother's summons.

I stretched out on the porch bench and closed my eyes. The crisp mountain breeze began to ease the throbbing in my temples.

"This is for you, miss. Your Aunt Huda said fresh lemonade is good for car sickness." A lean young girl bent down to offer me a cold glass of it on a brass tray. Two thick braids of black hair fell from beneath the loose white chiffon that covered her head.

"Do you live around here?" I asked.

"I am Alia, your new maid." Her soft words carried a distinct mountain accent.

"I like your name and your long, long hair." I sipped at the refreshing lemonade and smiled at her.

I waited anxiously for Nora after Alia had tucked me into bed that evening, thinking of all the things I would tell her.

"Are you still awake, Nadia? I had to stay with Akram until he fell asleep, or the boys would have kept him up." Nora spoke softly as she undressed. "You have really gotten thin. Haven't you been eating enough? When you arrived this morning your face was green." Her warm hand touched my brow and glided over my head.

"Oh, Nora, you would not believe how sad the last few days have been." I choked on a mounting sob.

"Don't cry, little sister. Is it because Maria decided to retire? My mother told me that her daughter was getting married and the family wanted Maria to come back and be with them. That's her right to go back to her family anytime, isn't it?"

"But that's not true. Maria didn't leave us because of her daughter or her family. She left because of what your father did to her." In the dim light I could see Nora's head jerk up as she looked at me strangely.

"What are you talking about?"

"She was sleeping in your bed. In the middle of the night he hit her and dragged her out of the bed, calling her bad names. And while your mother was sick he chased her around the house."

"You're crazy, Nadia. How dare you accuse your parents of such a disgrace."

"I am telling the truth, Nora. I waited for her to come back that night, but she never did. The next day I heard her argue with your mother, and every day after that she was crying and going to church. She told me it was the only place she could find peace and comfort. The last few days before she left, your mother did not even speak to her, and she told me to stay away from Maria, too."

We gazed at each other for a while in the darkening room. I wanted her to say something, but she finally lay down and pulled the thick cover around her. I could not tell whether she believed what I said, or whether she thought I had had another one of my countless dreams.

"Alia, where are you?" Alia was helping me comb the hair of all my dolls and arrange them in a row along my bed. Aunt Huda's head showed in the doorway. "What are you doing in the children's room? It's almost dinnertime and we need your help." I never saw Alia smile as she did the morning chores, followed by my aunt's scrutinizing eyes, but later in the day she sometimes sat with me, and told me how much she loved her family and her small village. She talked to me as if I were not a child.

One afternoon I had confided in her too. "Do you know, Alia, that I will be going to school this year?"

Her black eyes sparkled with amusement. "What will you do there?"

"Don't you know what's done at school?"

"Girls don't go to school in my village. We have a school for boys that's run by the clergy. My brother says if you can read the holy book you can read anything."

"Well, if you come live with us in the city, you could go to school there. Beirut has all kinds of girls' schools."

"Oh, Miss Nadia, you are very sweet. But if I come live with your family in the city, it will be to work, not go to school. My father needs the money very badly. Girls have to work until they are married."

"Mama, can I go with Alia on Sunday when she visits her family? Please, Mama, this Sunday only."

"Do you know that Alia's home is more than two miles away and you must walk there on a small footpath? Do you think you can walk there and back?"

"If Alia can do it, I can." I wanted so much to see the people Alia had been telling me about. I wanted to know why she loved them so much if they made her work since she was a child and took all her earnings while her brothers went to school.

"If Nora will go, too, I suppose you may."

We walked past the lush, spreading mulberry tree to the clearing where Alia's house stood on one end of a crushed limestone base. Branching out from the side of the small white-washed structure was the front wall of a large, unfinished room, its three arcades looking like suspended wings. On the other side, the house opened onto a porch where vines hung from a wooden trellis. An uneven yard spread down the hill, and except for the flock of hens and their chicks pecking around at a pile of discarded vegetables, everything was still.

"Where is everybody? It is too quiet around here," Alia said as we approached the house. Suddenly her twin brothers appeared from behind a tree.

"The hadj had to leave early today," Hadi volunteered. "He is going to a wake to say prayers before he goes to his other house for the week."

"Who is the hadj?" Nora asked.

"That's my father. Everybody calls him "hadj" ever since he visited the holy land in Mecca."

"But why would your father have another house?"

"That is where his second wife and four children live," Alia answered with a touch of bitterness.

"How can he manage two families? What does he do for a living?" I had never seen Nora so curious.

"Manal and Miriam, my younger sisters, work at the calico mill down in the valley. The three of us provide my father with all the money he needs." Alia sounded matter-of-fact, but Nora looked shocked.

"What about the boys?" I asked.

"We go to school," Hadi said proudly.

"*Ahlan wa'sahlan!* What a fortunate day it is to have you honor our land." Very much like Alia, but taller, the woman who stepped out of the house seemed too young to be the mother of a nineteen-year-old. Alia ran to her, grasped her hand, and while she touched it lightly with her lips, Um-Hadi bent and kissed the top of her daughter's head. "How are you, Alia?"

"I am fine, mother. Miss Nora and Miss Nadia wanted to come and meet you."

"I am grateful to both of you and to your kind mother for letting you take this long walk." She came closer and took each of us by the hand. "I hope you will look after my Alia once she is with you back in the city. I worry about her very much. It will be the first time she goes so far."

We stepped up to the house where thick log benches lined the wall. From the end of the porch I could see down into the spectacular valley. Natural mountain terraces unfolded down the hill, the varying shades of green as colorful as a handmade quilt. Way down, the land came upon the dark, winding river, then piled up anew, reaching to the distant sky.

⁓ℭ

Um-Hadi's soft voice called us in from the patio. "You will forgive our modest meal, young ladies. The honor is all ours that you will share our bread and salt."

The invocation "In the Name of God and His Grace" hummed around the low wooden table where Um-Hadi and her five children bowed their heads. I bowed my head, too. Surrounded by the mountains and the placid faces of these women and children, I felt a deep peacefulness that touched my heart the same way Grandpa Mehdi's eyes did.

⁓ℭ

I did not know what awakened me. The room was dark, and though my eyes were wide open, I could barely see anything. Only Nora's heavy breathing next to me could be heard. The whole house was quiet.

I started thinking about going to school. Suddenly it seemed a much more complicated matter than when we talked about it in the daytime. Nothing I had heard from my family made it sound simple or pleasant. My father saw school as our duty, a way in which we were taught to be grateful to him. My mother wanted only to have a few hours of peace. She had become helplessly melancholic as her pregnancy came closer to term.

My uniform was one Aunt Hind, my father's sister, had made for Nora three years ago and altered for me. When I learned I was to have an old uniform, I worried that maybe they weren't serious about keeping me in school. But my mother said that I would get new ones if I passed the three-month probational period the American school required of new pre-school students.

"Come on, you lazy girl." Nora's hand was shaking me.

I jumped up, feeling guilty for sleeping late on such an important day. When we were finally ready to go, Alia put my white linen hat on my head, tightened the ribbon of my black leather shoes, and handed me the enamel lunch box. "Is it too heavy?" She had a broad smile on her face. I shook my head, unable to open my mouth, barely holding back my tears.

Nora and I stepped down the stone stairs and the iron gate banged shut behind us. We were off to a great adventure!

We walked an endless time on endless paths. Finally we reached the end of the uphill grade, left the public road, and stepped onto a clean street lined on both sides with petunias. We walked down to a round, paved court surrounded by several stone buildings, huge trees, and green lawns. Could it be true, I wondered? Was this where I was to spend many years of my life? The place reminded me of pictures on cards that came with papa's plants from Europe. I felt light and happy.

"Come with me, Nadia. You look like a mess." Nora dug into her book bag and pulled out a clean handkerchief. She took off my hat, wiped my face, and smoothed my hair. "There," she said, straightening my uniform, "relax now, everything will be all right. At school you have to keep very quiet and talk only when you are spoken to, you hear?" I nodded assent while my eyes were fixed on the court where girls of all ages were gathered. Their excited voices and rather shrill giggling made a cheerful noise.

My mother was in bed recovering from the delivery of my baby sister Mae when I began my music lessons with Miss Annette. This tough middle-aged lady who spoke with an accented mixture of French, Romanian, and Arabic had been giving piano lessons to members of my family ever since the large German instrument arrived at our new house. She taught Mama, then Anwar, and Nora, the same tunes and songs we heard on the gramophone. Sami refused to sit next to a woman and take instruction from her, but ironically he was the only one of us who took music seriously. As a teenager he took piano and voice lessons at the conservatory in Beirut, where he developed his baritone voice for opera singing. I often sat with Nora when she practiced and learned to play songs, sweet songs I know to this day. When Miss Annette insisted on teaching me the same pieces my family had learned, I told her, "I want to play the other songs, not the ones we already know." I had watched her left hand move smoothly on the lower keys while she waited for our lessons to begin. The melodies she played that way made my head whirl. But for the Arabic songs she taught us she used the left hand only to play a hard, drumming beat.

"That is not what Madame told me to teach you." Her voice was hard, not like her music. "I teach your family the Oriental songs. To learn the classical European music you must learn a note system out of special books."

Days later my mother told me the story of Annette's sad life after her parents were persecuted in Romania. "She is working very hard to pay for her expenses. I want you to be good to her." I felt she did not care very much what kind of music I learned as long as Annette kept her job.

"Aunt Salma! When did you get here?" I could not believe my eyes, as I returned from school one day to see Aunt Salma sitting next to my mother in the *manzoul,* or guest room. Their heads were bent, looking at some papers they held in their hands.

"Nadia, baby, I didn't hear you come in! My child, you look gorgeous! How long has it been since I last saw you? You're going to school already?" She had her arms open, and welcomed me with her usual warmth.

"You are coming to stay with us, Aunt Salma, aren't you? I have so much to tell you about school."

"Yes, baby, I will surely stay long enough to bore everyone to death!" The fragrance of her body was so sweet. Her voice had such a lovely ring to it. As I tightened my arms around her neck, I realized that I loved her beyond words.

"Nadia, I want you to go wash and change," my mother interrupted. "I need to spend some time with Salma before dinner." The two sisters sat next to each other. They looked so different. Mama was small and

Nadia (front, far right) and Her Siblings

frail, while Aunt Salma was large and animated, and her pale eyes shone with love for everyone she saw. The big trunk in the corner of the room assured me she would be with us for quite a while, so I left the room.

Anwar was irritated because he was left with the younger children who were having dinner in the kitchen so my parents and Aunt Salma could eat alone. "You think I don't know what they're talking about? Well, you're wrong!" Anwar's face was red with anger as he looked at Nora's shocked face. "Yes, I know about the fight between your father and grandma. It's not a secret. All the aunts and uncles ask me funny questions—your father has dragged Aunt Salma into it, too. I'm tired of it!"

Nora stood up hastily, "I have homework to do, Alia. If you need my help, I'll be in my room." She looked frightened; I didn't know why.

As I lay in bed that night, I hoped Aunt Salma would come kiss me goodnight. I hadn't seen her all evening. After dinner, she and my parents had gone to the salia and closed the door. I had sneaked up to the door when no one was watching, and heard my father's strong voice vibrating through the thick wood.

"I don't care about the odor. It's my garden, and I am free to use it any way I please. If Salma hates horses and can't stand their smell, that's her problem."

"Kareem, the problem is not just with a couple of carriage horses. You have more than half a dozen horses down there, and as many grooms, stablemen, and valets." Aunt Salma's voice was calm.

"So what? This is a business!"

No sound came for a while; then my aunt's barely audible voice: "What business are you talking about?"

"Come on, Salma, do you think the money we need to maintain our lifestyle comes from the odd jobs I do for the pasha?"

While she no doubt suspected the truth, it must have seemed almost inconceivable to Aunt Salma that, in a society where the dominant religion forbids gambling, the son-in-law of an eminent patriarch like Sheikh Mehdi would be engaged in horse trading.

I woke up early to the sound of heavy rain hitting the window panes. It was Sunday, and the house was quiet. I longed to go to Aunt Salma's room. I had so much to tell her about school but it had been almost three days since she had arrived and I hadn't had a chance to be alone with her at all.

The door to the manzoul was ajar. When I touched the smooth wood, the brass hinges squeaked. Aunt Salma was sleeping on a mattress that had been placed on the floor next to the divan. I pulled up the side of the fluffy quilt and snuggled next to her.

"Well, Nadia, what a lovely surprise." She sat up, but instantly pressed her hand to her lips, her eyes closed tightly.

"Aunt Salma, is something the matter? You look very pale. What is wrong?" She was unable to talk. "You look the way my mother did when she had a baby hidden in her stomach."

Her eyes opened suddenly and an amused expression warmed her face. "What do you know about that, honey?" A little color appeared on her high cheekbones. "Sweetie, I can't wait for this miracle to come true. But remember my promise to you a long time ago? You will always be my first baby."

"Aunt Salma, how do you swallow a baby to have it in your stomach? When I ask my mother, she says I am nothing but trouble. Am I bad because I want to know?"

"As we grow up, Nadia, old questions get answered and new ones come up. Don't rush, honey! As for your question, we do not swallow the babies. God takes care of all such things. Now tell me about your school. How do you like it?"

"Oh, Aunt Salma, I wish you could go with me one day and meet my teachers and friends. And the big books on Miss Anderson's shelves have the most beautiful color pictures with letters written around them. When we line up to go into the classroom, Miss Horn plays the piano, but Nora says we don't have to sing with the other girls if we don't want to. She says these songs are hymns. But they sound the same as the music Miss Annette plays before our piano lessons. They are the songs she won't teach me! Anwar says I'm crazy to want to play church music on a Muslim piano!"

She put her hand on my head. Then, with a serious expression on her face, she said, "Your brother is just teasing you, honey. People sometimes tend to use God as an inspiration for their art and music, but that does not prevent any human being from enjoying such an achievement. After all, our religion teaches us that God is one for all of us on this planet. Oh, how I wish your Grandpa Mehdi were still alive so he could tell you all the beautiful things he knew about the Almighty God!"

"Good morning, Aunt Salma." Nora came in and closed the door. "I hope Nadia didn't disturb you too early."

"Not at all, dear Nora. I enjoyed her surprise visit very much. Come closer and let me look at you. You look lovely in that blue dress. Are those earrings new?"

Nora fingered the smooth golden pendants shaped like crescent moons. "My mother gave them to me a few months ago. They are the first pendants she bought for me."

"She won them in recognition of her excellent conduct at school. Her name is on the board in the assembly hall." I was proud of my sister, who was a good girl and all, but I didn't like to be as docile.

"Now, Nora, you tell me about your school."

"The teachers come from different countries; some are American, others come from France. And we have some British teachers, and some Lebanese. It's not difficult. We don't have nearly as much homework as Anwar does at the French school." She looked very sweet with her soft hair gathered at the nape of her neck and tied with a blue ribbon. I thought she would make a good teacher when she grew up. Her strong voice and serious eyes reminded me of some of the teachers I had seen at school. "Have you ever been to our school, Aunt Salma?"

I was surprised by Nora's question. A distant look clouded Aunt Salma's eyes. I snuggled closer to her.

"On a spring day, when your mother and I were in our teens, our father came home earlier than usual. Ban ran to take his jubba, as she always did, and he handed her the mail. 'Look at that, Salma,' Ban exclaimed, and she held up an invitation to Reverend and Madame Mehdi and family. It was from the American School for Girls, inviting us to their commencement in Beirut. In those days, all the families who were natives of Beirut were invited to the ceremony as special guests, though few Muslim families attended since they did not want to be seen celebrating Christian rituals.

"When we arrived we saw two young guards at the entrance to the school grounds. Ahmed dismounted from the high bench where he sat next to the coachman to announce us. In all the years he had worked at our house, I had seldom seen him wear his official outfit. Over his gray suit he wore a red valet coat with gold trim and buttons, and he had white gloves and a red tarboosh.

"The guard nodded, and our carriage rolled down the short drive toward the courtyard. Aisha made sure that our scarves were in the right position, away from our faces and loose enough to let our hair run down our backs. 'You look like a pair of white peace doves. God bless you,' she said.

"Our names were on the back of the chairs reserved for dignitaries. The principal, a tall, lean lady in her fifties, welcomed all guests in broken Arabic, and then she accompanied them to their seats. It was all very impressive. Something few Arab women had the chance to attend in those days."

"Hold still, Nadia." Aunt Hind's soft beautiful face and gleaming eyes brightened up the whole room. Yet on that day her voice sounded tired, as if it came from a deep hole. That sweet aunt, who was widowed very early in her life and left with three children to raise alone, had always baby-sat for her brother Kareem's family when he and his wife went away on one of their pleasure trips. Now she was working on our school dresses, and I didn't like the made-over garment she wrapped me with.

"Why can't you make our dresses like the ones in the fashion magazines, just like Mama's?"

I heard Nora's giggle from the other end of the room where she stood ironing.

"What's so funny, Nora? I don't like these sloppy clothes. The boys wear nothing but imported, ready-made suits. They can refuse to put on any of the shirts Aunt Hind alters for them if they choose. But you and I can't."

"What do you suggest we do? Become boys?" Nora said with scorn. "You would not be satisfied no matter what."

"Don't you dare say this to me!" I shrieked. "Just because I like my clothes to be as nice as Mama's and my brothers' does not mean I have to change myself. I know you want the same thing, but you don't dare to speak out. What are you afraid of? Everybody calls you 'old Nora' at school. You look older than Mama sometimes with your tight scarf and long skirts!"

"Stop it, Nadia! Let our aunt finish her job. Imagine a six-year-old girl wanting clothes as fashionable as her mother's." Nora sounded very quarrelsome. "I want you to stop saying 'us,' too. I am not interested in your fantasies. The problem with you is that you regret being born a girl and you are taking it out on all of us in this house."

That was such an insult that I threw myself forward, oblivious to the stool, Aunt Hind, and the pins. Stumbling on the unfinished hem, I charged toward the ironing board, then lost my balance. Confused, Nora thrust the hot iron toward me, hitting my right arm.

I heard my own frantic scream, and Nora's shrill cry; then, nothing, only darkness.

I couldn't move, so sharp was the pain in my arm, but the voices I heard sounded familiar. I wondered whether I was dreaming.

"Mama?" The moan came from my throat with the stab of unfamiliar pain. "Mama!" Sobs bubbled up, and I opened my tearful eyes.

Anwar stood in the middle of the room facing a tall man. They talked in low voices. The straight back of the man and his soft honey-colored hair seemed familiar.

"Hello, Miss Rajy. How do you feel now?" His warm fingers closed on my wrist. "Don't worry, everything is going to be all right." The pain persisted, but young Dr. Nasser's cheerful voice made me relax.

"Why am I here? Is Mama back?" It was confusing to lie on my father's bed while my parents were so far away.

"You have got quite a serious burn, and it will take some time to heal. You have to be patient, Miss Nadia. If you help us take care of you, the scar will be small."

Dr. Nasser looked at the frightened faces of my family who stood around the room. He reached deep into his black bag and brought out several small jars and bottles with white tags. He wrote on the tags and lined the jars on the dresser, then addressed Anwar. "The first three days are the most critical. I'll send somebody to dress the burn daily if I can't make it myself." He folded the stethoscope and pushed it back into his bag, then turned to me with a shy smile. "The medicine I gave you should work soon, Miss Rajy. Have a restful night." He snapped his bag shut and left.

For three days I lay in that room. Burning pain and horrible nightmares blurred my mind. Christmas was only a few days away, and I tried to think of the play I was to have been in at school. Six of us, chosen because we were small, were to have been the sheep around the manger. I closed my eyes and tried to remember that beautiful porcelain doll, the size of a real baby, that our teacher placed on the dry grass in the wooden manger.

I moved slowly from under the warm sheets. The house was very quiet. What day was it? I had lost count. The December chill froze my bare feet, and I sat on the side of the bed reconsidering my urge to get up.

The door opened and Nora peered in. My heart leaped; I had not seen her for three days.

"Good morning, Nadia. I didn't want to come in earlier because I thought you might be sleeping." Her large, sad eyes blinked a few times before they met mine. "Are you feeling better?"

"Yes, I guess the fever is gone." I felt awkward, still unable to move my right arm. Nora came closer.

"Nadia," she began, her voice barely audible. "It all went so fast, I don't know how I hit you. My God, I could have killed you, do you know that?" I had thought she was mad at me, but instead she was afraid.

"I don't know what is going to happen when our parents come back. Especially your father! When they find out they'll be furious—you, too, will have to lie. Yes, suffer the pain, live with the scar, and lie!" She turned to the window through which the pale morning sunlight came in.

"He doesn't need to know what happened. By the time they come back, I will be well." Her back was very still, but the sun gleamed on a line of tears that rolled down her cheeks. "I swear by God and the Prophet that I shall never tell, Nora." Guilt mounted in my heart for the sorrow I caused her. I slipped off the bed and went over to her. "Nora, please, forget about that skirt and don't be mad at me. I love you." My hand reached up to her shoulder, and she turned and grabbed my head, pressing it to her heart.

The staircase landing looked dark and eerie in the blue twilight haze when Aisha let me out of my grandma's back door. I ran up the first flight of stairs blindly, the soft soles of my sneakers barely touching the cold marble steps. I knew my father had forbidden us children to go down to Grandma Mehdi's ever since that heated fight between him and Aunt Salma over the abominable odor of his horses pervading the yard and over the annoying insects that swarmed the area because of his trade. But Aunt Salma, whom I had not seen since last fall, was there and I could not resist the temptation to visit with her and see her beautiful little baby who had come to meet his Grandma Mehdi for the first time since he was born in June. The top landing was bathed in yellow beams of light from the hall lamp. I prayed that the door would be open and I could sneak in without being seen. "Stop right there, Nadia!" My mother's voice lashed out at me from the shadowed terrace on my right. I saw her small frame moving toward me. "Where have you been until this hour?" She stepped forward and grabbed my arm.

My mouth felt dry. "I was downstairs at Grandma's. She's sick," I lied. In fact, Grandma's cook had made me wait until the *mughli* cooled down so she could give me a few spoons. This was a delightful rice and cinnamon pudding, garnished with all kinds of nuts, and prepared to celebrate the arrival of a new baby. It was my Grandpa Mehdi's habit that his family would offer that sweet to the parents of a newly born in their neighborhood whether they were rich or poor.

My mother's fingers loosened. "This is not the first time you have gone down there, is it?" I shook my head and opened my mouth to apologize, hoping she would forgive me, but she did not let me finish.

"Go to your room. I will talk to you later."

As I heard the gate bang, I reached out and touched her cold hand. "You won't tell Papa, will you?"

"Go now, and wash those hands before you go to your room." I galloped ahead, feeling, for some reason, that she, too, was afraid of him.

Alone in my room, I flung myself on the cushions next to my dolls. My arms reached out to the smallest one and held it close to my ear. I closed my eyes until I heard my parents settle in their favorite corner in the dar, where they liked to have a cup of tea and talk for a while before dinner. I moved closer to the door of my room, listening to see whether my mother would tell on me. But they seemed to be talking about some legal problem regarding the house, and my father's continuing animosity toward Grandma Mehdi, which now appeared to include both aunts, Fatima and Salma.

At the dinner table that evening, my parents looked tired and avoided looking at each other. The lump in my stomach was growing, with the fear that my father would make my mother sick as was always the case when her family was the source of their disagreement. My mother had promised to finish my costume for the commencement play which was to take place soon. I was to be a butterfly, and the stiff tulle wings were spread around the manzoul, waiting to be pasted with tiny, colorful circles. The full skirt my mother had sewed made me feel as light as a real butterfly.

"Are we going to finish my costume tomorrow as you promised, Mama?" I ventured as we were leaving the dining room for the lounge, where we would spend the rest of the evening.

"Yes, Nadia, we will finish it."

"I love you, Mama. You are as sweet as Miss Mary."

"Who is Miss Mary?"

"That's her teacher, Mama," Nora volunteered from her seat across the lounge. "All the kids like her very much."

"Miss Mary is the one who helped us make the commencement play and let me be the butterfly," I said. "You will meet her, Mama, when you see our play."

"I'm sorry, Nadia, I won't be able to attend your party this year. Your father and I have other plans." Her pale face had no expression at all.

"What do you mean, Mama?" Nora sounded alarmed. "You signed the invitations I brought from school!"

"I know, Nora, but I have other things on my mind besides your party." Her voice was decisive, but Nora did not yield.

"Are we going to go there alone? It will be late when the party ends. Who will bring us back?"

"Don't worry, Sharifa will be there, and Saleem too. They will keep an eye on you." As I looked at her grim face, I knew nothing would change her mind.

Nora sat on the side of her bed, her face tense with anger. "You don't understand, Nadia. How could you? This is your first year at school. You don't know what it means to have a maid and a coachman as stand-ins for your parents. They will have to use those fancy invitation cards and sit among the other parents in the seats with Mama's and Papa's names on them."

She seemed very hurt.

"Don't worry about the people around us, Nora. You can just watch me dance."

"Do you want my friends to think that those are my parents?" Nora turned off the light and stretched out on her stomach, her face flat on the sheet. It was too hot to use a cover. I heard the chirping of the crickets on the pine tree and thought of the cool nights in the mountains, of Alia's family and the breathtaking view across their slopes. I would have loved to live in that village if it weren't for my school, teachers, and classmates down in the city.

"Stop tossing and turning, Nadia. Go to sleep," Nora ordered.

I woke up to the feeling that my body was being carried from my bed. The crickets were quiet. I heard only my father's rapid breath. I snuggled in the soft silk of his shirt as he carried me down the hall.

"Papa, am I sick?" Half dreaming, I thought I was being carried away to my parents' room where young Dr. Nasser was going to examine me and Maria would come and take care of me.

"Hush," he whispered. He bent over his bed and slipped me under his covers.

I have no memory of that night—patches of some nightmare are still floating where our house used to stand, like leaves by the wind. The night, though, that night moved out of the house and, for years, locked itself in a corner of my soul, a dark and unvisited one.

3

May 1933

From behind the cement rail of the terrace balustrade I watched other families join mine in the street as they went on the last shopping spree of that very special day. It was Adha's Eve, the holiest celebration of the year. "Nadia will stay here," my father had said, "as punishment for her behavior." Long ago I had learned not to show the boiling frustration I felt when he turned on me with his twisted anger. The man was sick, and seemed unaware that I was no longer the six-year-old kid he had once abused with his loathsome caresses. I had shut my mind, like a thick wall built stone upon stone, against the accusations and punishments of my parents.

I turned around and ran inside the quiet house. "No, I shall never give up. Not ever!" My high-pitched voice hit the hallway walls.

"Please, Nadia, don't make things more difficult than they already are! Just try it on." The blue wool knit dress Nora had outgrown hung on her outstretched arm.

"If your father thinks he can control me by refusing to buy me new clothes or school material and books, he is wrong."

"Nadia, you shouldn't fight your father this way. You will end up having the whole family against you."

"Of course I am aware that everyone in this house goes along with him, especially my mother," I said bitterly. Nora's defensive tone had unleashed my anger.

"That's not fair, Nadia. What can your mother do? It's not as if he asks her permission before he does things! She is as concerned about you as I am, but she doesn't know how to reach you."

"Don't be naive! And don't fool yourself that I am the only one who is abused in this house. Do you think Anwar was taken out of school and sent to work behind her back? And what about you, Nora? On whose advice did you consent to leave school and get a job?" She

gasped as if I had revealed one of her personal secrets. "Do you remember how shocked you were when Alia told us that in her village
girls never go to school because they have to work as maids to provide
for their brothers and fathers?"

She flashed back a tearful wink. "But we had no other choice,
Nadia. We were broke, and your father's debts couldn't be paid off any
other way. Apparently he had resisted admitting his losses from the
horses for too long."

"To tell you the truth, Nora, I often feel that I have survived better
than all of you. Although changing from a private English school to a
public one run on the French system was quite an ordeal, at least I have
a school to go to, so far. . . . "

Adha with its four-day celebrations was an occasion when regular
rules and daily routines were replaced with splendid festivities and
feasts. Long after the lights went off in the bedrooms and the reception
area that night, the action continued in the service area, where the
chattering of voices and banging of pots and pans could be heard all
through the night. The turkey, which earlier that morning had lain
headless in a copper bowl waiting to be plucked, washed, and hung to
dry, was stuffed with rice and meat and mounted over a low fire to
simmer until morning. Now, supervised by my father, the long process
of making *maamoul,* the delicate Adha pastry, was being completed.
Ahead of time, my mother had shelled walnuts, almonds, and pista-
chios and seasoned them with sweetened blossom water and spices. I
loved to watch the family work in concert to prepare hundreds of those
rich crusts as my father rolled the limp, buttery dough, cut it into little
balls, and handed them to my mother, who would dig her forefinger
into each one, then smooth the hole quickly, and fill it with the crushed
sweetened nuts, and hand it back to him. He smoothed the dough again
to make sure the filling was well hidden, then pressed it with a wooden
stamp. I waited in suspense as he turned the stamp over and banged it
on the end of the marble counter to release the tiny pie. With the
utmost care, the perfect pastry was laid on a forty-inch-wide copper
tray made specifically for that particular recipe, one tray for each kind
of filling as indicated by the different stamp.

"Can I try?" I couldn't resist asking.

"You'd better finish your other chores, Nadia," my mother reminded me.

I picked up the shoe-polish box from under the hallway dresser and took it to the manzoul where the boys had lined up all the well-cleaned shoes that needed polishing.

"Still ironing?" I called to Nora as I entered the steamy room. The smell of new fabric and old cologne hung in the air.

"It might take another hour yet. Please, Nadia, open one of those windows before you use that stinky shoe polish in here."

The fresh breeze swept into the room as I flung the high panels wide open. "Nora! Come look!"

A glowing veil covered the houses on our street and the rest of the ancient city and made them appear as if they had walked out of a magic book. A ten-day-old moon, an uneven chunk missing from one side, headed down the violet horizon. Its pale light cast golden shadows on the slanting roofs. Adults and children carried their pastry trays through the streets to the bakery. Some strolled along, calling Adha greetings to each other, and others just stood on the sidewalk enjoying the scene.

Suddenly, in a blaze of light, hundreds of lightbulbs strung along the walls of the mosque flashed on. Above them rose the slender minaret, and from its tower came a solemn chant, the story of Ibrahim, the great patriarch for so many of us in the world. The muezzin's voice floated over the rooftops, commemorating the occasion of Ibrahim's offering his son to God, speaking to the heart of the pilgrims who at that moment were on their way up to Arafat Hill. The voice swelled as a chorus joined in. I could feel the shiver of emotion run wild under my skin.

I lay on my bed and dozed off for a while until the mournful sound of a bleating lamb cut through the quiet night. "Come on, young man, make it quick. I have quite a few more offerings to do tonight." The husky voice with a lisp sounded familiar. I went to the window. In the yard below Anwar was dragging our lamb to where Hadj Maarouf, the butcher, waited with a long knife in his hand and a thick apron hanging down to his feet. My father stood next to him watching. It was our tradition to buy a baby lamb six months before the feast and to fatten it. Children were warned not to go close enough to excite him, as the extra action could harden his muscles. I shut my eyes and put my hands over my ears, but still the hadj's words drifted up to me. "In the name of Almighty God by whose order you were made the Rajys' sacrificial offering on this holy Adha . . . " The prayer rang harsh as a death sentence. "Amen!" The three men's praise reverberated through the chilly night air.

The distant sound of the morning Adha prayer drifted into my room to awaken in me old memories. Oh God, how I missed being with Grandpa Mehdi on that holy night. His beloved picture, that refuge of my childhood, had been disposed of by my father after his big fight with the Mehdis over his race horse stables.

"I've been looking everywhere for you, Nadia. Mama said you could help me dress and fix my hair." My baby sister Mae, who had grown into a ten-year-old beauty with a glowing face and soft auburn hair, held three ribbons in one hand, a comb in the other, while her unbuttoned dress hung awkwardly on one side. I smiled into her sparkling brown eyes, my fingers working already on the dozen small buttons.

"I wish you had gone shopping with us yesterday, Nadia. Then maybe my father and Nora wouldn't have argued. Nora refused to let him buy anything new for her, saying she didn't need anything. When my mother argued with her, she said it was you who needed new clothes and shoes." Her large eyes gazed into mine as if waiting for me to say something, but my throat tightened.

Soon the doorbell was chiming and the house was echoing with chatter and footsteps as Adha callers began to arrive. From my room I could hear my parents' voices, mixed with several strange accents that I did not recognize. These visitors were talking all at once in high, excited tones that gave me a funny feeling.

"Come quick, Nadia." Nora ran in and grabbed my hand, pulling me toward the dining room.

"Who are those people out there?"

"Relatives from Palestine. They have come to pay their first visit to us, calling father, 'Cousin Kareem.' His name is Ahmad Rajy. Look at the packages they brought!"

The dining room table was covered with packages and pastry boxes. I recognized the baklava wrappers from Samadi's, a fancy confectioner in Beirut, and the long, elegantly wrapped boxes with shiny blue ribbon from Orosdi's. But the bags I peered into held golden apples, pears, and blood-oranges larger than I had ever seen before.

"What do these people look like?"

"You can see for yourself. Come, you have to help me serve the lemonade."

I saw his animated face the moment I stepped into the noisy dar. He was talking with my mother, who sat across from him next to my father. He wore an elegant suit, a white starched shirt, and a large red tie; the delicate French chair on which he sat seemed to barely contain his large frame.

Our eyes met and I felt the warmth of his admiring gaze. His ruddy face and gray hair reminded me of a physician I knew at the American School. He bent toward the lady sitting next to him and said, "Look at this one, Najla!" still looking at me with his cheerful eyes.

The heavy tray swayed in my arms. He sprang up and took it. "Allow me, child. This is too heavy for your delicate arms. Suad, serve these glasses, please."

A young lady who had been chatting with Anwar stepped forward. "Hello, Nadia. Your sister Nora told me about you." The delicate aroma of gardenias filled the air all about me as she bent and kissed my cheeks. She had the same large, heavily mascaraed dark eyes as the older woman. "I am your cousin Suad, and these are my parents."

"We have other children, too, but they could not come with us today." The man's fleshy hand reached for an empty chair and pulled it between him and his wife. Tapping on the velvet seat, he continued, "Please sit down, Nadia. I would like to know more about you."

The lady he called Najla took my hand and held it between hers. A long dark coat covered her to the ankles, and on her head she wore a pelerine like the ones Mama had worn many years ago. Feeling encouraged by her warmth, I asked, "Why do you have a different accent? You don't come from the mountains, do you?"

"You have never met anyone who lives in Palestine before?" Her soft voice sounded like a whisper.

"I don't know. But I do know where it is on the map, how big it is,

Nadia's Future In-Laws, c. 1928. Her Husband-to-Be Is Top Row, Far Right

and where the largest cities are located." They exchanged a quick smile over my head. "If you are part of our family, why do you live there?"

"When Palestine and Lebanon were still one country, the Rajys traded between all the big cities and ports around the Mediterranean. They had a prosperous business in grains and spices for several centuries, and had spread all over the Near East," said Ahmad Rajy.

"This is too precious a time to talk about business," Lady Najla interrupted. Her long arms pulled me off my seat, encircled my waist, and held me close. "Tell me, Nadia, is it true that you play the piano better than anyone else in the family?"

"We all play, but who said I was the best?" I turned and looked for help, feeling uneasy with the compliment.

"I did," Nora and Suad said at the same time. Hand in hand, the two looked as if they had known each other all their lives.

"Cousin Ahmad, who has seven sons and two daughters, asked us to accept his oldest son as a son-in-law." Mother's grave tone at the dinner table that evening alerted me to the seriousness of the afternoon visit. A hush fell over the assembled family, and all eyes turned to Nora. Only my father, apparently in a bad mood, went on eating as if he were alone in the room.

"Why didn't their son come with them so he could meet Nora and ask her if she would like to marry him!"

Mama ignored my question and went on. "He is twenty-four and is the cashier of the national bank in Haifa." She sounded impressed.

"His name is Marwan. He graduated from the French Jesuit boarding school in Beirut." Anwar spoke eagerly. "They seem to be very rich people. The father is quite influential in the bank where Marwan works."

"Does my sister Nora have to go live with them?" Sami looked at my mother, his eyes filled with intense curiosity.

"It isn't Nora whom they want as a bride to their favored son."

Nora looked away as I turned to her, and I felt my father fix a vengeful stare on me. Anwar was looking at my mother as if stunned.

My mother paused, and the room was silent. "Nadia is the one chosen by the father of the groom."

I gazed uncomprehendingly at the blank faces across the table, and something stopped inside me as if my heart had suddenly died. The meal was finished in silence.

As I went about my daily task of dusting the furniture in the dar, the two sad, dark eyes followed me around from a new picture on the piano. Trapped within a fancy leather frame, Marwan's face had no expression at all and showed no resemblance to his father or mother. What a funny way to travel in search of a wife, I thought. A giggle rose in my throat as I raised my arm and touched the grayish face with the soft tips of the white ostrich feathers.

"I bet you can't wait to touch that young man." Anwar's taunting words startled me.

"What do you mean, touch him?"

"Don't play games with me, little sister. I watched your tricks yesterday. Our poor uncle fell for your charming act the minute you squeezed yourself between him and his wife."

"You're crazy, Anwar, and blind, too! If you were really watching, you would have noticed that I was the one who was charmed by those two wonderful people. They showed me a respect and admiration that doesn't exist under this roof." I turned to leave but Anwar's strong fingers gripped my arm. "Let me go!"

"Oh no, miss big mouth!" He dragged me to the far end of the dar and into the salia where he pushed me into a chair and closed the door.

"Our parents have made a big mistake by indulging your wild stubbornness all these years. My father let you do whatever you wanted because he thinks you resemble your mother. But now he is no longer the boss. I am, dear sister. I'm the one who has given up my dreams to feed you and the rest of this family. Nora has done her share, too, and deserves to be relieved and rewarded, but not you." He stood over me looking pathetic with his matted hair and his far too small shirt.

"What did you expect me to do, leave school when I was ten and find a job? I bet you would like me to go to work as a maid at some house where a son like you could assault me the way you assaulted Alia." The words slipped out before I realized what I had said. He looked shocked and, having caught him off balance, I ran for the door.

Standing in the middle of the dar, my mother and Nora turned wide eyes at me as I charged in with Anwar close behind. Nora opened her arms and I buried my head in her bosom.

"What on earth are you doing, Anwar?" Mama stepped in front of him.

"Teaching this young girl a long overdue lesson! Didn't you see how she threw herself at Uncle Ahmad and his wife yesterday, using all of her tricks to allure them, to steal them from Nora, right from under her nose?"

"You are wrong, Anwar," Nora said. "Nadia had nothing to do with what happened yesterday. You should have talked to your mother first."

"What is this," Anwar yelled. "A secret plan between you two?" He looked as confused as I did.

"Nora is already spoken for, son," my mother said. "A promise was made a long time ago between your Grandma Rajy and her late sister Safia that Nora would be the future bride of one of the grandsons."

"But that old aunt left no eligible grandsons, unless you mean that homely protégé you call Radwan. He's in his forties, mother!" Anwar looked bemused. "Poor Nora!"

"Radwan is a gentle man with a big heart. He has been a great financial help to us these last few years. I don't know what would have happened to us if he had not . . . "

"We never asked him for any favors," Anwar interrupted. "Every time he lent us money, he locked your box of jewelry in his safe first!"

"Anyone would've done that," my mother said in defense of Radwan.

"Anyway, if Nora's hand was part of the deal, who knows what else he'll ask for. You'd better get them married now before his greed spreads any further."

I held my breath at this thought. Why had Nora never told me what was going on? Suddenly her actions began to make sense: her weekly trips to Radwan's family home; the special gifts she often brought back with her; the way she kept her face veiled, even when my mother did not. It had never occurred to me that these trips were part of an engagement ritual. Radwan came from a very conservative family.

"Last week, as you know," my mother continued, "we received a message from Judge M. T. Rajy that his brother Ahmad who lives in Palestine was on a trip to Beirut and would like to pay us a visit during the Adha celebrations. What you did not know, Anwar, was that he also indicated that Ahmad wanted to renew his relationship with us because he was in search of a bride for his oldest son and he wanted to know if we would welcome an offer from him."

"You mean those people didn't know anything about my sisters before they arrived yesterday?"

"Nothing except that we have three daughters and four sons." My mother paused then and, in a lower voice, she said, "And even if we chose to break our promise with Radwan's family, I don't think I could survive having Nora live so far away. She is the daughter I can depend on."

My head was spinning.

Back in the calm of our room, Nora and I stared at each other. "Is all this really true, Nora? My God, not even in my wild imagination could I have woven such an unbelievable story!"

"Please, Nadia, don't judge me yet. It is a complicated situation, parts of which I still am not free to tell you."

"So your mother didn't explain everything?" I felt more confused than ever. "Can you tell me, at least, how I fit into all this?"

"All I can say is that Uncle Ahmad has asked our father to give you in marriage to his son. Our father has accepted."

My knees gave way and I collapsed on the side of my bed. Nora rushed to my side and held me close. "What's wrong, Nadia? I had the impression you liked those relatives as much as they liked you. Why are you shivering? Are you afraid of being loved and wanted?"

"You make me feel you don't know me at all, Nora. I am not interested in getting married just because the parents of that shadow on the piano like me or I like them. But what's the use? No one in this house cares about what I want. Even you, Nora! You all share a secret plan against me. A plan to ship me away to an unknown husband who lives in a place none of you have ever been to." I pulled away from her and walked across the room to the window.

"What do you expect me to do? Rebel against my mother and father? I'm in the same situation as you, Nadia."

I stared aimlessly through the window.

The bitter deception by Nora and my parents had left me devastated. But as the four days of Adha ended and school started again, I was able to push the matter to the back of my mind, pretending that it was nothing more than a social amenity similar to the "arrangement" made for Nora and old Radwan.

Miraculously, none of my family brought the subject up again. As the days went by, I felt an easing of the tension between my parents and myself; my father seemed resigned, but my mother was determined not to give up.

Then, one day, I discovered among my clothes a new dress my mother had sewn. Shortly after that, a knitted sweater appeared. Twice she accompanied Nora and me to a ladies' shop and let us each select a pair of shoes, a belt, several kinds of lotion, cologne, and assorted soaps. We began to exchange an occasional joke, and I no longer sulked and fretted in the evenings. Still, I couldn't throw myself into my mother's arms and unburden my heart to her. Nor could we talk about the sad face on top of the piano.

At the beginning of June, a few weeks before we moved to our summer house, my father got his long-awaited job. He became superintendent of road construction, a tedious, low-paying job where he inhaled more dust than air, but he didn't seem to mind. Since he was working for nothing less than the Municipal Bureau of Public Works, he was convinced his job would be secure.

The evening my father received his first paycheck, he came home with bags of out-of-season fruit and freshly baked croissants. He noticed that my relationship with my mother had improved. So he started to make conciliatory gestures toward me—caressing my cheek after asking for a simple favor, or giving me a long hug when I served his morning coffee. I began to realize that it was not fear that caused my repugnance when he came close to me. It was a cold, sickening feeling, as if I were being pushed against a corpse.

Our summer house that year was in Broumana, a sophisticated town in Matn county, north of Beirut. The well-to-do residents lived in ornate villas and drove shiny cars to their offices in the capital where they held fine jobs. Because most of Broumana's inhabitants were Christians, European laymen and missionaries settled there and established very advanced schools. The British Boys' School was particularly well known among the wealthy Muslim families, who were delighted to have this foreign institution, with its imposing buildings and tennis courts atop a lush, forested ridge, so near.

Our modern three-bedroom apartment on the second floor of a four-story building had two large verandahs and three spacious balconies with a breathtaking view of the capital and the sea. Broumana's tennis club courts were on the other side of the narrow alley at the rear of our apartment. One morning, from the window of my room, I was watching Anwar play on the courts below. As soon as he saw me he yelled: "Nadia! See if Sami wants to play a few sets before the sun gets too high." When I told him Sami had left early for a long walk and wouldn't be back until after lunch, he paused, then yelled back, "All right, then. Why don't you bring his racket and come on down here?"

I ran to my room, put on a white skirt over my white knit nightshirt, stuffed my bare feet into my younger brother Akram's tennis shoes, grabbed Sami's racket, and took off. I couldn't imagine what was on my unpredictable brother's mind, but I was delighted to play with him.

"Nora, why did you refuse Anwar's invitation to go get an ice cream with him and his friends this evening? Don't you enjoy the company?" I had just washed my hair and was drying it in the bright afternoon sun; Nora was mending socks.

"It's not that I don't like his friends," she said. "I'm afraid they may not be interested in me."

"Why shouldn't they?"

"I'm not like you, Nadia. You like to go to parties, meet boys and foreigners, and be out in the world."

"Is it such a big deal to meet new people? I wish you could understand how important it is to me to know the world and be part of it."

I opened the closet and sorted through the dresses. I selected one my mother had made for me from one of the pieces of silk Uncle Ahmad had brought with him on his visit for the Adha feast. Looking in the mirror, I felt lit up inside. My soft, clean hair swayed around my tan face, barely touching the padded shoulders of the canary yellow dress.

"Oh, Nadia, you look beautiful in that dress. I haven't seen it on you before. Turn around and let me see how it fits." Nora reached to the hem and pulled at the sides to straighten it. "That is marvelous! You will be a dazzling debutante tonight." She was all smiles.

"Actually, I've been reluctant to wear it because the fabric came to me as a gift from you know who. But now that Uncle Ahmad's ideas are forgotten, there's no harm in putting it on. Poor Uncle Ahmad, I wish I had known him under different circumstances. "

"You sound so sure you will never see him again, Nadia. How do you know he won't return one of these days to press his claim?"

"Well, we haven't heard from them since they left four months ago. I'm sure my situation with him is just like yours with old Radwan." Nora did not share my laugh.

"You know what happens in our society to girls who defy the rules," she said in a low voice. "Our parents are not fanatics like some. Still, things could get difficult for you. You're barely fourteen."

"Well, for the time being, I want to enjoy life, and you should do the same. Anwar has one friend I could talk with for hours. His name is Jim and his father teaches at Broumana School. I think you met him once when he came to borrow Anwar's racket, remember?"

The familiar roar of the Beirut shuttle bus that stopped across from our building came through the open door. Footsteps and agitated voices echoed up the stairway, my father's above the rest. "They are early today. I wonder why," Nora said and went to find out. I turned to the task of cleaning up again.

"Well, aren't we looking dressed up," Anwar called from behind me a few minutes later. His eyes swept over my body with admiration.

"I wanted you to be proud of me tonight. Do you like my dress?"

"Very elegant, indeed. I'm glad you dressed up, because there's a big surprise waiting for you in the lounge." He grasped my hand and pulled me through the hall.

"This is my sister Nadia," he announced as we entered the living room and stopped before a gentleman who sat on the large armchair facing my parents. "And this is Marwan Rajy, our cousin from Haifa."

"I am honored to meet you, Miss Nadia." The visitor, shorter than both of us, stretched out a stiff hand waiting to be met by mine.

It took me a while to grasp the fact that the man in the picture on top of the piano was here in the flesh. His thin chest seemed yet thinner in his gray linen suit. The sad, dark eyes quivered under his raised eyebrows, as if that cousin who suddenly materialized had expected a different reception.

"I am sorry you look so surprised to see me. Uncle Kareem has known for some time that I would visit at the end of August." His arm fell to his side as he shot a glance toward my father, whose eyes remained fixed on his teacup.

My mother's gentle voice softened the tense atmosphere, though her face was taut and pale. "Sit down, Nadia. Your cousin is going to spend his vacation with us. The rest of his family will be joining him tomorrow."

Nora started another round of tea, just as the sound of soft voices came from the hallway. My body tensed as I recognized Jim's voice.

"Please excuse me, cousin. I had a previous engagement to go out with some friends for an hour or two," Anwar said, touching Marwan's shoulder. "See you at dinner." He left the room without so much as a glance at me.

Unable to sit still, I jumped up and took the tea tray from Nora. I felt the sting of watchful eyes as I forced myself to serve each person calmly. Tears were already blurring my vision when I stepped into my room, feeling sick and praying to God to do something to save me. The unexpected appearance of that newfound cousin had forced me to face the reality of a fate I had been refusing to consider ever since the day my parents gave me away to someone whose picture was the only proof of his existence.

Nora came in and sat next to me on my bed. "It won't do you any good to keep running away from this situation. I know what you're going through, believe me. But there is little we can do if our parents support this engagement."

"How can you say such a thing after seeing that poor creature? I can't believe my parents would throw their own daughter into the hands of that sickly little man just because his parents happen to be wealthy relatives."

"Why don't you think more positively. This is the first time this gentleman has met you, too. He himself might reject his father's plan."

The wind was warm and dry that evening, promising a rare fogless sunset. On the top of a mountain less than two miles from the sea, Broumana was enveloped daily in humidity and fog. It was a funny kind of fog that surged uphill in the late hours of the afternoon, like a tidal wave, thick and foamy. People would joke that the best time to go fishing in Broumana was between five and seven in the evening when the sea came to their doorstep.

"Do you care for a drink, Marwan?" Anwar asked the guest as the two of them stepped onto the veranda, where I had set up the dinner table.

"What do you have?" They pulled a couple of chairs to the far end of the terrace where a clematis bush filled the corner with its distinct fragrance. "Not what you and I would like to have," Anwar said with a wink. "We have only soft drinks in this house."

"I am used to that at home." Their heads leaned close as they chatted informally, already using nicknames; somehow I couldn't trust Anwar's show of admiration for that self-conscious guest who seemed so much out of place.

Nora appeared with a white porcelain bowl heaped with tabbouli, piles of colorful herbs smothering crushed wheat. My mother handed me a silver plate of *sambousics,* and the appetizing smell of miniature meat pies made me feel dizzy with hunger.

"Bring those delicacies over here!" Anwar called from where he sat talking politics with the guest. "How could you have such a hard heart as to forget your beloved brother and his guest," he teased. He shoved one pie into my mouth as I leaned on him, then filled his hands and turned back to his companion, who declined his offer of a meat pie. "I have heard from the son of a man in the oil business that Palestine is benefiting from Iraq's oil glut."

"Yes, their refinery in Haifa has given our economy a great boost. We are flooded with money, and our pound is one of the strongest within the commonwealth. But still I feel uneasy. This prosperity benefits the foreigners more than the Arab people, and it makes our economy dependent on the actions of outsiders."

"You talk very differently from the few Palestinians I know in the city."

"I'm not the only one who's worried. My feelings are shared by most of the young men I know who have been educated in European institutions and have talked with foreign advisors and financial analysts. But our parents and their friends are not convinced by what we tell them. They refuse the idea that the purchasing of Arab land by Jewish corporations is part of the plan for establishment of a Jewish state in Palestine. They consider our fears and political theories to be based on rumors."

"It is hard to think trouble is coming when the country seems so prosperous. It sounds intriguing, though. I would love to get involved in some kind of business in Palestine and may need your advice one of these days." I did wonder how long that poor cousin from Haifa would take to fall into my conniving brother's hands. "I don't intend to spend my life working for others, especially not as a teacher, which is what my father expects."

"What a fantastic view you have from here. I love to see Beirut at night from such a height. It looks like a piece of jewelry nestled in the green velvet lap of the mountain." Hands inside the pockets of his tailored jacket, the visiting Rajy stood by the table contemplating the open horizon as I arranged the dishes. His long face looked very white in contrast to his dark hair, and his square, flat mustache. "Haifa is much smaller than Beirut, but it's growing fast. Since it's between a mountain range and a bay, it can only expand uphill toward Mount Carmel." His earnest voice faltered for a moment before he continued. "I am sure you will love it."

He must have seen me pull back slightly, so he continued. "Please, Miss Nadia, be patient and hear me out. Tomorrow my family will arrive in Broumana so our families can spend some time together. I don't know why you are so formal with me, calling me Mr. Rajy and avoiding me. Believe me, I do not intend to push myself on you. I would like very much to see a smile in those eyes of yours instead of fear and distress. What is it you are afraid of? I would never harm anyone, especially a nice sweet cousin like you."

"Dinner is ready!" Sami's voice saved me. He rushed onto the veranda carrying a heavy tray of sizzling lamb fillets and cubes of chicken breast high above his head and set it in the middle of the dinner table.

"Not for me, please, Miss Nora." Marwan reached out to Nora's arm as she started to serve him a big spoonful of green salad. "I cannot eat raw vegetables. Two skewers of meat will do."

"I have made some inquiries, Marwan, to find out how close the link between our families is," my father began as we sat around the table. "I have been unable to determine when our families first came across each other. Does your group in Palestine have any records of these matters?"

"I really don't know, Uncle Kareem. Such things have never been of importance to me. I'm sure my father can give you all the information you need when you talk with him. This subject is so close to his heart." Although he had a cheerful smile on his face, I detected a touch of sarcasm.

Marwan was standing next to my chair, his fingers fumbling unsuccessfully with the tiny silver latch of an exquisite, slender jewelry box which he held a few inches from my face. The latch snapped, and his shaky fingers nervously searched the shiny white lining folds of the box until they came out with a delicate golden wristwatch. "Please, miss, let me have the pleasure of putting this humble gift on your wrist. I hope you will accept this as a token of gratitude and appreciation of your grace."

"Thank you very much, Mr. Rajy, but you owe me nothing for doing my duty toward a guest. Please give this to someone who can wear it. It would look very expensive on a student as casually dressed as I am." That very expensive gift, however, remained in my father's temporary custody like all the other valuable jewelry the Rajys bestowed upon me before I went to live with them.

"Good morning, Nadia. Look at what came for you last night after you were asleep." On the last day of the Rajy family's vacation in Broumana, Mae laid on my bed a long package wrapped in the red paper and golden ribbon of Abira's exclusive shop. Her eyes were dancing with curiosity.

"Who brought it?"

"Anwar did when he returned from his trip to the city. He said cousin Suad chose it as a goodbye gift for you. Well, come on, open it."

I had a good idea what Suad had chosen for her parting gift to me. That family was trapping me in a web of affection, attention, and lavish generosity. For the last three days she had gone into town, accompanied by Anwar, to do her "last-minute shopping," bringing home for me three cashmere sweaters, half a dozen silk scarves, and two pairs of Italian leather gloves.

"Oh, Nadia, look!" Mae lifted an azure dress from the thin wrapping tissue and held the sheer fabric against her small body. "Are you going to wear it to dinner at the hotel tonight? Mama said I can't go because this is a formal party the Rajys have planned especially for you and Cousin Marwan."

"I'd better. I haven't yet worn anything Suad has given me. I don't usually wear such fancy clothes, but I want to show my appreciation at least this once." I went to the mirror and brought the thin crepe garment to my cheek, feeling its coolness. The warm blue color brought a magic shine to my eyes. I took a deep breath and decided I liked it.

"Did you get Suad's package, Nadia?" Anwar was sitting across the table from me. We were having lunch. He leaned against the back of his chair, and waited for an answer. I nodded silently, returning his keen gaze with unwavering eyes.

"Suad is amazing; she knows her way around Beirut better than we do. I've learned so much about all those fancy stores in the last three days. One would think they have no stores in their hometown the way she was buying clothes, draperies, towels, and kitchen goods. Those people have much to be envied for." Anwar's eyes met mine again with a cold, significant glance, and a strange chill crept down my spine.

Ceder's Hotel in Broumana, the five-story stone building where the Rajys were staying, stood high on the edge of a cliff directly over the Mediterranean. Its half dozen pointed arcades seemed to keep an eye on that ancient, restless sea.

"I wonder what one does to be rich enough to own such a huge building as this. Look at it!" Anwar sounded bitter. He and I were walking down the grassy alley between our apartment and the hotel.

"You scare me sometimes, Anwar. How can you be surrounded by all this natural beauty and think only of money? Behind that handsome, smart face I feel a cold force inside you."

"I hope you don't let such childish ideas influence your feelings about your cousin. I must be blunt with you, Nadia. Neither our parents nor I are going to let you spoil this heaven-sent gift that has fallen into our lap. I assure you that I'll do anything to keep these cousins in my hands. Such luck will never happen twice."

"As I see it, you don't need me to accomplish that. Suad has a crush on you. Isn't that enough?" A great romance seemed to have blossomed between Anwar and Suad. But it was a one-sided affair that Suad had fallen into, unaware that Anwar was using her to get her father's trust for financial purposes only.

Marwan met us at the wide steps of the hotel and led us through the spacious lobby and up the red-carpeted circular staircase to their third-floor suite. I slid my hand along the cool brass railing and gazed at the large oil paintings of birds and landscapes in their large gold frames.

The lounge of Uncle Ahmad's six-bedroom wing was bathed in sunlight coming from the French doors open to the terrace. White marble tables held large displays of hydrangeas. At the far end of the terrace chairs were scattered around a Ping-Pong table.

"*Ya halla!* Dear Nadia." Suad burst into the lounge with open arms and a radiant smile. Her milk-white cheeks smelled of the soft gardenia scent that had become familiar to me. She wore a pleated skirt, long and purple, and a fitted tan blouse of fine Valenciennes lace that covered her arms and shoulders up to the tip of her chin. Taking my hand she led me to an adjacent living room with several arrangements of chairs and couches. Anwar and Marwan were already seated on a leather sofa, their heads bent over a page of a local daily that came in the French language.

"Thank you, Nadia, for accepting my gift. The dress looks beautiful on you." Suad settled back against some pillows and pulled me next to her.

"I don't know how to thank you and your parents for all you have given me."

"We owe you more than you could possibly imagine, Nadia. Your frank, beautiful eyes and your warmth have brought our families close. For us, that is far more valuable than clothes or scarves. I have the feeling that we will be together for a long time."

Anwar's voice rose heatedly from where he and Marwan were engaged in serious talk. "That is outrageous! What can they accomplish by killing an old man? Besides, he's not the only Arab selling land to Jews, as you have said." We moved closer to hear what they were discussing.

"True, Jews have been buying land in Palestine for years," Marwan said. "Under the Ottoman Empire permits were issued, and religious groups from the Jewish European community acquired many acres of land they consider to be holy around Jerusalem and the Dead Sea. Since the purchases took place over a long period of time and seemed to be for religious purposes, no one paid any attention. But now the real motives of many of the Jews are becoming apparent. After World War I, the Zionists, who had worked underground for centuries toward the creation of a Jewish state anywhere in the world as long as their scattered people could reunite and be free to practice their religion, had finally agreed to take the offer made by the church and share with the Palestinians their small holy land."

"That sounds like some of the stories we read about in history books," I joked.

Marwan looked at me, but did not seem to hear my comment. "Quite a few Jews have already moved from the Arab countries, where they were told that soon a Jewish state would replace Palestine and the whole land would be called Israel," he continued.

"How can a foreign state be created out of nowhere and planted among such a hostile Arab world?," Anwar asked. "Are you sure you're not being given misleading information?"

"Anwar, if you had the chance to read, as I have, about the conditions under which Jews live in Europe and in other Christian countries, you would understand their feelings of alienation. Although they worked hard to please the Christians and acquired political and economic power in some parts of Europe, they have been unable to gain the acceptance and trust they wanted."

"So you're saying that all those European Jews are going to move to Palestine? The country is not large enough for its own population, let alone millions of newcomers!" I heard the disbelief in Anwar's voice, but Marwan continued evenly.

"That's not the only thing people are concerned about. Some are worried that Jewish interests extend beyond Palestine. Once they establish themselves there, what's to keep them from spreading their influence?"

"I wouldn't know, Marwan. You seem to know things that neither I nor my friends have heard about. I hope you're not involved with those nationalists!"

"Come on, Anwar, how could I be? The days are hardly long enough for the piles of work in my office. I have no time either for politics. In fact, most of my friends are not even Arabs. But that doesn't mean that I am blind to what's going on under our noses. Who knows how the winds will blow in one or two decades?"

"So you align yourself neither with your father's group, who are sure nothing fundamental is going to change in Palestine, nor with the radicals who advocate violence. Then where do you stand?"

"You might find this difficult to believe, but I want out. Out of Haifa, out of Palestine, and out of my family obligations if necessary."

Suad's audible gasp startled me. I looked at Anwar who was stunned by his cousin's strange pronouncement.

Before anyone could say another word, a bell rang in the hallway, followed by Uncle Ahmad's voice welcoming my family. A moment later Aunt Najla led my mother to a brown leather armchair and helped her take off her long maternity coat. "Sit down, Ban. You look tired."

A few minutes later the tall stained-glass doors that separated the lounge from an adjacent dining room rolled back smoothly. "Dinner is ready, ladies and gentlemen." A tall waiter in a white dinner coat stood at the side of the open door, a white towel hanging from his arm. He nodded for us to move to the table.

I had never been to such a formal dinner. The table sparkled with crystal, shiny silver, and heavy china. I rested my hands on the white linen tablecloth, touching the cool lace pattern with awe. A huge silver plate in the center of the table, filled with gardenia buds and tuberoses, left little space for the smaller silver bowls of green herbs, sliced lemon, and sesame butter dip.

Anwar was speaking to Uncle Ahmad. "I wonder, Uncle Ahmad, if you could tell us more about our family ties? We asked Marwan last week, but he seemed to know very little." I saw his hand reaching for Suad's under the table.

"It is my pleasure to tell you that since we met I have discovered information proving that our connection goes back almost a hundred years. At that time a Rajy daughter who was an only child to one of our clan was married to one of your great-great-grandparents. She left a new line of Rajys in your beautiful country. Two of her offspring are married to my brothers who live in Beirut."

He turned to my parents, who were listening attentively. "I hope you enjoy what Abou Tony has chosen for this special dinner. He has promised to serve a meal fit for this great occasion. Let us pray that the Almighty God blesses this beloved young lady who has brought nothing but joy into our lives. To Nadia."

The talk and laughter swelled around me hazily, while I felt weak with panic and fear. My parents would not let me catch their eyes for more than a second. They continued the chatter with carefree, lilting voices that seemed to expand, and bounce off the glittering crystal and silver.

"Did you read in the paper this morning, Ahmad, about someone who was shot and killed on the outskirts of Jerusalem?" My father's question seemed to make Marwan even tenser.

"Yes, that was a few days ago, in fact. I didn't know the man myself, but I had heard of him. There is nothing to the accusations against him, Kareem. He came from a well-known religious family and was a leader among the conservative groups that were quite active during the last few decades when the Turks were in power. He was too rich to involve himself in selling land to the alleged enemy, as some seem to believe he did."

"Then what do you think was the motive behind the assassination? The papers talk about nationalist radicals who want to dispose of anyone who cooperates with the Jews."

"To tell you the truth, I know very little about what those radicals are up to. Their leader is the son of a late hero who had fought against the British when Great Britain was granted the mandate over Palestine a decade ago. Supported by less than a dozen of his townsmen, the father fought from the hills of his village, vowing to die rather than let the British take over. And that he did. His son was born a few weeks after the battle and was called Shaheed to commemorate his father's martyrdom. Most of those radicals are kids like him, born and raised during the mandate in detention camps where their fathers were held because of their politics or their nationalism."

Anwar seemed intrigued. "How large is that group of radicals? What kind of public support do they have? Marwan and I were talking about this earlier, and from what he said, it sounds as if they are spread all over the country."

Uncle Ahmad shot an accusing glance at his son before answering. "Marwan and I differ immensely on this matter. He believes our country is heading for a disaster, though we seem to be enjoying great prosperity. He even wanted me to scale down my business in Palestine and invest here in Beirut. I would consider myself the worst of traitors if I did that. In spite of the fact that the origin of our tribe is somewhere between North Africa and Spain, and our great-grandparents were among the Muslims who moved eastward after their empire collapsed, one has to believe in a place where one's family has lived for genera-

tions. Palestine is the land where our parents and grandparents are
buried, and where I want my children to bury me, too. Don't you feel
the same way toward your country, Anwar?"

"Well, let's say I am loyal to the government that protects me and
my business. As long as my ships are unloading, I don't care who the
boss is." The familiar smile shone on my brother's face.

"I am pleased you have such a practical attitude. You will make a
good businessman. But we had better stop this discussion before our
guests feel sorry for us because we live in Palestine. Believe me, ladies
and gentlemen, we are on top of the world, and we miss nothing except
having all of you there with us."

Abou Tony had just finished taking away whole plates of chicken
pie when Uncle Ahmad pulled his chair from the table and asked to be
excused. "I need to have a few moments with cousin Kareem. What
have you prepared for dessert, Abou Tony?"

"That is my secret, Mr. Rajy. Would you like me to serve now?"

"No, we'll be back in a minute." Followed by my father, Uncle
Ahmad went out to the terrace and leaned against the rail. I could see
their shadowy figures through the corner of my eye. It took only a
minute, as Uncle Ahmad had promised. His hand reached into his
pocket, came out with a large envelope, and passed it to my father.
Quickly, my father slipped it into his pocket. The hands joined in a
final shake, and the shadows moved back to the light. I lifted my chin,
trying to ease the choking pain in my throat. Could that be the end?
Marwan was as silent as a statue.

Back in the lounge after dinner, I turned to tell my mother I felt tired
and wanted to go home when Uncle Ahmad put his arm around my
shoulders and swept me out to the terrace. "Come with me, dear Nadia.
I see that you are not as happy as we are about what is going on. Let
me explain."

The late evening chill had brought a stillness to the air, and the sky
was black and filled with stars. I followed Uncle Ahmad to the far end
of the terrace overlooking the old side of Broumana and the distant
eastern mountains. Most of the houses below were dark and quiet. The
pale street lights trembled in the chill of the mountain breeze.

"I am going to miss this beautiful place very much. You and your
family have made it impossible for me to ever forget it."

"Thank you, Uncle Ahmad, for everything you have done for me.

Your kind attention has made me know an affection I have never felt before."

"There is nothing as valuable as to see you happy and to help all your dreams come true." His smile was relaxed, but his tone was serious. I turned my head, sensing that he wanted to tell me something I wouldn't want to hear.

"Forgive me, daughter, for bringing up this subject. I feel I have no alternative since I see how strained the relationship between you and Marwan is. I feel terribly disappointed that he has failed to find the right way to approach you. You may not believe it, but that son of mine has never been close to a woman in his life. I don't think he knows what that means."

I held my breath, wondering whether Uncle Ahmad was going to change his mind about this whole matter. I waited.

"I am taking the liberty to talk to you directly for two reasons. First, I have come to realize that, despite your very young age, you are a person who appreciates straightforwardness. Second, the more I know your father, the surer I become that candor is not his style and that he would not talk to you openly about what this engagement means. If I am right, I want you to tell me why you are dreading our proposal. Do you really dislike Marwan that much?"

"I don't know if I dislike your son, Uncle Ahmad. But I do know that I don't want to marry anyone. Ever. All I want is to continue going to school and after that go to college."

"That is a great wish for a wonderful young lady like you. I am fully confident that you have the ability to reach your goal. But how do you plan to accomplish it? Would your father support you for all those years of education?"

I couldn't find the words to tell that serious man what my father felt toward me. I shook my head, trying to evade his inquisitive eyes.

"Well, then, why don't you let me take care of this? Once you are among us, you can do anything you want. We live in an area not far from the Technicom College—a well-known institution where courses in the arts, history, and literature are available—it's two blocks from our house."

"Oh, Uncle Ahmad, I would love to be part of your family. Not just because I could go to school, but because I love you and your family very much. But do I have to marry your son to go live with you? You have said that I am a new daughter to you, right?"

"I'm sure you know the answer to that, Nadia. You are a smart girl."
His brown eyes sparkled. "But don't worry, I promise to make your
life with us as comfortable as I can. You will not be marrying my son
Marwan alone. You will be our favored daughter and a preferred sister
to all my children." His warm hand caressed my hair as he whispered
several times, "Trust me."

The day after that dinner party, I fell ill with a bad case of jaundice that
dragged on for ten painful days. Yet in spite of the tight knot in my
stomach and the awful discoloring all over my body, the illness was a
blessing. It gave me time to think about the situation in which I was
entangled. I would have pretended that the whole episode was just
another one of my nightmares that I had grown to endure, were it not
for the envelope, bringing back the memory of that scene on the edge
of the terrace.

The envelope was there, bulging within the folds of my father's
clothes every time he came into my room to see how I was doing, to
see how his investment was.

I had survived. But the trusting, cheerful, fifteen-year-old girl was
gone. I looked into the mirror one morning at an ashen, yellow face
with angry eyes, eyes vindictive and bitter.

I wrapped my arms around my listless body. I closed my eyes to
everything around me. I vowed never to let any sinister wheeler-dealer
get close enough to hear my heart beat.

"What is wrong, Nadia? Are you in pain?" My mother stood behind
me, her arms pressed against her sides to support the bulge in her
stomach.

I began pulling the wrinkled sheets off my bed. "I'm all right. Do
you need me for something?"

"I think you know that in a few days when we are back in the city
some changes will take place now that you are engaged to your cousin.
Why don't you sit down so we can talk. . . ."

"What changes do you mean? Haven't we had enough drastic
changes?" I continued shuttling between the dresser and the bed, dis-
missing her invitation.

Tension colored her low voice. "One important change must be in
that attitude of yours. Most girls would be grateful to have half the

advantages that have fallen into your lap, yet here you are throwing yourself into fits and creating imaginary worries." She crossed the room and sat on the side of Nora's bed.

"How do you know my worries are imaginary? Were you ever pushed into the arms of a man you had never seen? Did your parents put you on a platter and sell you to the highest bidder? Don't you think you should be the last person to be the judge of such a matter? Aren't you the heroine of a legendary love story who defied her whole society to marry for nothing but a throb in her heart?" I stood shaking in the middle of the room, searching for any hint of compassion in her angry blue eyes.

A huge wall of silence fell between us. When she finally spoke, her voice was thin and remote. "Are you holding me responsible for what your father and his cousin have chosen to do? I wouldn't be surprised if you are. You have always blamed me for everything that happened between you and your father, most of which was of your own doing."

"Oh, what's the use of talking about this? You have never given a damn whether I live or die. If Aunt Salma hadn't been here when I was born, I probably wouldn't be here now to remind you of your failures. Why couldn't I have been born to parents like Aunt Salma or Uncle Ahmad, both of whom have kids because they love them, not because they want to use them."

"You are not in a state of mind to be reasoned with, Nadia. Sooner or later you will come to realize how wrong you are. But in the meantime life will take its course with or without your approval."

"Leave school in the middle of the year to learn how to be a wife and mother! So that's it. My God, Nora! I can't believe what I'm hearing. This school year is the most important one of my life. At the end of the year I'll have the diploma that will open many doors to me if I want to pursue a career."

"Calm down, Nadia! Why do you set your heart on something that might never come true?" Nora's voice was pained. "I'm sorry the news had to come from me. I thought you would enjoy having all this time to be with our new baby brother, to play music, to sew, to paint, or whatever."

"School may be a punishment for you, but for me it is my whole life. Don't you see? They know how much I love school, and here they are kicking the ladder out from under my feet. They hate me!"

"Nobody hates you. Parents, like children, have problems and make mistakes, but all in good faith."

"Don't talk to me about good faith. Remember the story about Radwan that my mother had to invent in order to keep Marwan's hands away from you? And then using me as bait so your father can dig deeper into Uncle Ahmad's pockets!"

"That story was not invented." Nora's voice was shaking.

"It was, too, and we both know it. I wasn't sure until at Radwan's wedding party I saw our mother's diamond necklace on the bride's neck." Nora started to interrupt me, but I went on. "That necklace was not a gift from our parents. Radwan was no dummy. He knew that your father hadn't been borrowing all that money from him with the intention of repaying it. Confiscating your mother's jewelry was mighty clever of him."

Nora was quiet for a while. "You never mentioned anything about that. It isn't like you to keep such a discovery to yourself."

"You led me to believe you didn't want to discuss this matter, and I respected your wish. I felt happy for you that Radwan needn't be on your mind any longer so the whole charade could end. My case is more complicated than yours, however, even though I've made it clear to everyone in our family that I'm not going to marry Marwan Rajy. The difference here is that your parents just wanted to use Radwan's infatuation with you, not to give you up. And contrary to your conception of your mother's helplessness, she can be quite willful when she wants. She's the one who wants me out of the house and as far away as possible."

"Are you saying that your father has no part in this at all?"
"I really don't know how his weird mind functions; all I can say is that no one can imagine how loathsome he is to me. Sometimes I feel I'm going to die when I see him looking at me that way. . . . Do you understand what I'm saying?"

She nodded calmly. Only her eyes showed the agitation. Only her tears spoke.

"But our mother could have stopped him if she had had the courage to stand by her child. She knew all along he was a cruel tyrant by nature, especially with those who resist him, but she closed her eyes to the cruel measures of intimidation he enforced on me for resisting him. My God, Nora, I was barely seven years old then! I knew nothing, but she knew. Think of it, Nora, think of drowsy children, of girls that can no longer trust the touch of their father's hands, that see in his eyes the unutterable."

4

May 1934

During the last two weeks of May, Madame Saint-Jean, our school principal, kept us after school for an extra hour of study in preparation for the exams we would be taking at the end of June. I was having difficulty concentrating on my work that day as her tall figure roamed between our desks. Her clear blue eyes seemed to see right through me. She had spent the best years of her teaching career in Lebanon and had a reputation for being a demanding teacher who would not let an unprepared student take the public exams. I was proud that she knew I would pass my exams with ease, but what if she could also see the turmoil inside me caused by problems at home? What if she knew I was counting the days until the exams, praying they would be over before things got completely out of hand?

After the birth of baby Fadi, my mother's health failed drastically. She had moved out of the master bedroom with my father and settled into the liwan by herself. She was fifty-two years old and weary of nursing the poor little boy who was the tenth child of her twenty-five-year matrimonial career. I took Fadi into my room and Sharifa looked after him when I was gone. A few years before she came to work for us, Sharifa had given up custody of her four children because she refused to live in the same house with her husband's second wife. My baby brother was a gift of mercy to both of us, and we cared for him devotedly.

Anwar had quit his job as soon as we came back from the mountains and had been running around with Kamal, Aunt Hind's son, who had been on his own since his father disappeared during World War I. "What more do you want from me?" Anwar had yelled to his father's face. "Your cousin Ahmad is not going to let you down, not since he and that sucker son of his got hooked in your filthy fingers!" My mother's scream split the air as the two muscular bodies charged at each other.

The lines in my history book blurred with the memory of that terrible scene. "Is everything all right, Nadia?" Her cool hand touched my brow. I knew Madame Saint-Jean could sense my agony.

I nodded. My throat felt dry.

"We have to hurry, Nadia. I smell rain in the air." Mabel, my classmate who lived around the corner from our house, stepped into the darkened schoolyard before me. Shadows were lengthening down the crowded street.

"Give me those books," Mabel said. "I'll put them in my satchel to keep them dry until you get home."

Voluptuous, feminine, and extremely attractive, Mabel was my opposite. As we ran hand-in-hand, I remembered the day we met, five years earlier, on my first day at the crowded public school. Our teacher had lined us up by height, telling us to stretch one arm to the shoulder of the girl ahead of us. As my fingers touched the smooth black uniform of the girl in front of me, a head of silken hair turned and a pair of green eyes looked into mine.

"You're new here, aren't you?"

Before I could answer, the ruler tapped at my back. "You two take desk number three. Mabel, lead the way."

Mabel and I were halfway home when big drops of rain began to splash down on us, and we were soon thoroughly drenched as we stumbled blindly down the rain-lashed road. A large limousine was blocking the foot of the stairs when we finally reached my house. The gate was wide open and light poured out of the front windows. Mabel turned and ran back to the road, forgetting to give me my books.

Loud shouting reached my ears as I climbed the last flight of stairs. I did not need to worry about being scolded for getting wet, because no one saw me. I was changing to dry clothes when Nora dashed into the room. She looked very pale and her hands were shaking.

"What's wrong, Nora? Who were those people shouting at Papa?"

"Awful thing! Disgrace! I'm glad you weren't here earlier when Uncle Ahmad and Marwan were still here. This place has been like a madhouse! I should have known this would happen sooner or later.

How could that father of yours be so abusive to those wonderful and generous people, thinking he could outsmart them? He thought he could fool the Rajys by squeezing as much money out of them as possible and then pulling the carpet from under their feet by canceling the engagement. He was never serious about your engagement to Marwan, Nadia." She sat down on the side of her bed and pulled me next to her.

"That's unbelievable! You mean all those stories about needing money to order jewelry or fabric for my trousseau were not true? He kept making excuses for why it was taking so long! How could he do that to Uncle Ahmad? And Marwan! He kept encouraging Marwan to come visit all last year. Was that part of the plot?"

"Well, even worse—listen to this! It seems Marwan had been giving your father extra money in exchange for a promise that the wedding plans would be speeded up. Uncle Ahmad knew nothing about that.

"Speeded up! The wedding date hasn't even been discussed yet! Almost nothing has been done to complete the embroidery for the bedding or lingerie, or to do all the shopping and sewing that Mama and Aunt Najla agreed upon." I felt confused and numb. The only thing I was sure of was my sympathy for Uncle Ahmad.

Nora reached for my hand. "I swear to you, Nadia, before this day I knew very little about what was going on. When the Rajys arrived this afternoon, I received them with joy and surprise. Hussein Rajy, Uncle Ahmad's older brother, came with him. You know how grim that man can be. But seeing the same grimness on Uncle Ahmad's face upset me greatly. Your father didn't look surprised at all when I rushed to tell him of their unexpected call. It wasn't long before their argument was echoing throughout the house. When I heard the accusations, the hard truth struck me like a thunderbolt."

"Are they going to make him pay back everything they gave him?"

"Well, the biggest surprise of all came when Uncle Ahmad left the dar, stopping for a minute in the doorway to say, 'I want nothing from you, Kareem. I regret not having taken seriously Hussein's warning about your unreliability. I thought it was because he wanted Marwan to be *his* son-in-law. But now I just want you to bundle up my little daughter-in-law as soon as possible so that I can come get her. I don't care about any trousseau or jewelry. I want to spread flowers and money on her path, just to see her happy. And, by God, I will.' He left Hussein behind to make arrangements for the wedding, since he lives in Beirut. He's still down there talking with Anwar." Nora stood up and opened the door to the dar. "I'll go find out what is being planned."

I sat in the dark, quiet room feeling my whole world crumble. Through the open door I could hear the men's voices as they walked into the hallway.

"One week will be enough to prepare for the *kitâb* ceremony." I recognized Uncle Hussein's austere voice, referring to the ceremony of signing the marriage contract. "It doesn't have to be a large one since the wedding party will be in Haifa, not Beirut."

My father answered weakly. "Next Friday will be fine for getting the marriage certificate. But I am not sure she can be ready in five months for the wedding. You know, Hussein, we have less than two months before summer, when very little will be done with school."

"Nadia will be busy studying for her exams, Papa. Can't this ceremony wait until after the finals? She is exhausted already." I was amazed to hear my sister's courage rise.

My father regained his commanding tone as he addressed Nora. "To hell with those finals! Who cares about that now? I don't want to hear you talking about that nonsense anymore."

"What difference does it make whether she has a diploma or not if she is going to be married?" Anwar said, concluding the reading of the verdict.

I pulled the quilt more tightly around my shoulders as I sat propped up against my pillows, sipping the fragrant herbal tea Nora had made for me. Although the early morning sun promised a warm cloudless day after the sudden rainstorm of the day before, I felt cold. A nagging headache and sneezing fits had kept me tossing all night.

Sharifa stepped into my room, carrying a pile of books which she set on the table next to my bed. "Your mother asked me to bring these to you. Miss Mabel was here asking about you. And your fiancé is here. He wants to know if you would like to see him. Master Anwar is with him. They are waiting for you in the salia."

My apprehension mounted as I hurried to the kitchen in my night-gown, washed my face and hands, and came back to my room. I put on a light cashmere sweater and a pleated linen skirt, dressing slowly, dreading this early morning visit. Yet something in me respected Marwan for returning immediately after last night's stormy encounter to claim his rights and for refusing to be intimidated by my father's shameful plot. I felt somehow accountable to him, knowing the contempt with which my father had treated him.

Sunshine poured in from the windows behind Marwan, illuminating his figure and making him appear taller than he was. "Good morning, Miss Nadia. I must apologize for disturbing you on your day off from school. But I realized we have very little time to prepare for the kitâb. Do you mind accompanying Anwar and me so we can select the rings today?"

Suddenly the reality of what last night's confrontation meant swept over me. My throat tightened with the familiar feeling of being trapped. I turned to Anwar, looking for comfort, but his steely glare offered no hope.

"When do you plan to go?"

"Right now," Anwar said, eyeing my short skirt critically. "You'd better go quickly and change into some decent clothes."

"What's wrong with what she has on? This outfit looks beautiful on her." Marwan's sudden compliment surprised me. "I wouldn't expect you to pay attention to such trifles, Anwar."

"It's not for myself that I'm concerned. Today is Friday and those people who fill the streets around the Gold Market to gather for their weekly prayers in the neighboring mosque are not used to seeing a fashionable young lady walking down the street half naked. They might get ideas."

"If they choose to come to the city, they must learn to accept our different ways of doing things," Marwan responded. "I'm sure you are aware that your sister is not the only one who follows modern fashions."

"That's not the point. Nadia is a Rajy and she should behave like the other female members of this household. Would your sister Suad dress like that? Believe me, Marwan, this girl has always been difficult. You will soon discover what you have on your hands if you start indulging her every whim."

"I think you're making a big issue out of nothing. If you and I have the right to dress as we please, why shouldn't your sister have the same right?"

With a sudden surge of protectiveness, I said, "Thank you both for your interest in my safety. Anwar is just joking, Cousin Marwan. Don't mind what he says. Let's get going." Yet a relentless voice in me argued, obsessively, that I had a brother who would have sold me for money or for favors—one who would do this in style, and with a smile that never deceived me.

It was almost noon by the time we arrived at the Jewelers' Market in the heart of the downtown area. We walked down a dark, winding alley and through a wooden gate into a large square paved with shiny blue slate, in the center of which stood a stone fountain with a weak stream of water where a crowd of men took turns washing their faces, hands, and feet in accordance with the Islamic rules of ablution before the prayer. Around the fountain were several round tables and wrought-iron chairs where shop owners and customers sat with their coffee and cigarettes. The entire market was roofed by an old saucer-like dome decorated with blue and red mosaics of birds and flowers, with brown patches in between where the ancient mosaic had crumbled. Electric light bulbs in white metal discs hung from this antiquated ceiling and shed their dim light all the way to the adjacent mosque.

It took us some time to reach Mr. Caspar's shop, circling around the maze-like alleys and crossing small squares crowded with people from all parts of the country. The rich city women, wearing dark linen suits with straight ankle-length skirts and tailored jackets, some with their faces veiled, others with hats or scarves, brushed shoulders with people from many other Arab countries. Villagers from the nearby mountains wore bright-colored cotton dresses, beads, and sequin-edged white cotton veils that draped their heads and shoulders but not their faces. Rows of shiny bracelets or the serpentine loops of a golden snake with red stone eyes and diamond teeth adorned their arms.

Mr. Caspar the jeweler, an old friend of my father's whom we called Uncle Cass, rose from his chair when we entered. "Anwar Rajy! What a surprise. What has brought you here?" The tall man reached out to grasp Anwar by the shoulder. Still holding Anwar, he turned to Marwan and then to me. "Is this the little Nadia I used to know? My God, how have you grown to be so beautiful?" He released Anwar and thrust a thin, bejeweled hand to me.

"My father sends his regards." Anwar was all smiles, happy with the warm reception. "This is Cousin Marwan Rajy, Uncle Cass. We have come to select a couple of wedding rings for these two."

The bushy gray eyebrows arched upward for a second, then his steady hand stretched toward Marwan. Uncle Cass looked much older than my father, although I remembered my father saying they were the same age. He was as much in love with horses as my father was, and I had grown up seeing him around our stables fussing with the untamed colts every time a new shipment arrived. He would lift me up and let me caress the smooth neck of a mare and then show me how to feed her sugar cubes out of my hand.

"Sit down, please. Coffee? Or maybe lemonade for you, dear Nadia?"

Uncle Cass pointed to several wrought-iron chairs and then settled into a wooden chair between two safes.

"Lemonade will be fine," Anwar answered for all of us.

Uncle Cass pushed a tiny button behind his chair to call for the lemonade. "Tell me, Anwar, how is Kareem doing? I haven't heard from him since he closed the stables. I felt very sorry when I heard of his bad luck. Your father loved the horse trade, but I guess such a risky business does not survive on love alone. Does he have another job now?"

"Yes, a job that may not meet his ambitions, but one that puts food on the table. We have had two new brothers since he went broke. I had to leave school and get a job."

Cass pulled trays of rings from drawers and shelves and lined them on the table in front of Marwan and me.

"And are you still working now? I bet you are doing very well. You are a bright and intelligent young man, Anwar. I always thought you would have a bright future."

"For now I am running an import-export business. I share an office downtown with my cousin Kamal, Aunt Hind's son. I think you remember him." I laughed to myself at Anwar's bluff. He hadn't yet got any business off the ground.

"And you are a Rajy, too, Mr. Marwan. What do you do?"

"I work for a national bank in Haifa."

A surprised look swept over the smiling face across the table. "Haifa? How come?"

"Marwan is from a different branch of the Rajy family, one you don't know yet, Uncle Cass. His ancestors settled down in Palestine as our branch of that tribe moved north to Lebanon and Syria. Uncle Ahmad, Marwan's father, has a large business in Haifa and owns most of the shares in the bank where his son now works."

The jeweler turned to me now. "Here, let me measure the size of your fingers." Then he pulled out a silver loop with a dozen thin rings of different sizes.

When we finished, one tray remained on the table. On its dark blue velvet lay three rings, two golden ones for Marwan and me and one delicate sterling circled with countless dots of sparkling blue diamonds. "Sure, Mr. Rajy, I can engrave your names right away. But you have to bring them back for the dates to be added after the wedding takes place."

"Hey, Nadia!" A hissing sound came from the door of my room as I lay in bed Sunday morning. "Can I come in?"

"Mabel! How did you get here?" I jumped up and rushed to Mabel, whom I had not seen for a whole week.

"The door was open and no one was around. . . . Can we talk?" Her eyes swept over the room as she closed the door behind her. She was dressed for church in a white pleated silk dress.

"I think we'll be safe here for a while. Nora's at the orphanage where she works and Sharifa has taken all the kids on a picnic."

"I can't believe what your family has been telling me every time I come to see you, Nadia. It sounds crazy!"

"Everything has happened so quickly. I feel like a turtle that has been turned over on its back and then kicked and thrown in every direction. Only at night when I am finally alone can I think about what I'm going to do. How much do you know about this mess?"

"The day after the rainstorm, when I came to bring your books, your mother told me the Rajys were visiting in order to arrange your kitâb ceremony. She didn't want me to bother you. "

"Oh," I groaned. "You were the one person I needed that day! I'm sure she knew that, too."

"When I passed by your house on the way to school Saturday morning and didn't find you waiting, I began to think something was wrong. I knocked on your door and your father came to the top of the stairs. 'School is finished for Nadia,' he yelled down to me. 'You go and tell her teachers that!' I didn't tell anybody anything. They think you're sick."

A mournful silence fell over us.

"What are you going to do now? Couldn't you manage to come to school just on examination day?"

"Mabel, the thought of all of you taking the exams without me is killing me. A tiny part of me still hopes that I can pull it off. But my parents have decided against it. They've taken away my uniform, books, notebooks, everything that has to do with school."

Her warm hand reached out to mine with great compassion. "You still have me. The exam is three weeks from today. I can keep you posted on any information you may need. Now tell me what's been happening with you. I ran into Anwar on the way to school this morning, and he was bragging about your diamond ring. Did it really cost two thousand pounds?"

"I don't think it's anything to brag about. He and my father ought to be ashamed, if anything, for the way they treated our relatives."

"Don't tell me you're getting attached to those men. You are naive, Nadia. You haven't seen things as I have. Men are the same no matter how they may charm you. I've watched those men who come and go to see my mother and my two older sisters while my father is off at the horse races all day." Her voice was bitter. "I'm sure Marwan and his father knew what they were doing when they invested in a healthy young bride for their deformed sickly son."

"Marwan had nothing to do with it, Mabel. His father was the one who made the deal and dragged him into it."

"What do you mean 'dragged'? He's not a helpless sixteen-year-old girl like you who has to depend on her family to provide for her. He's ten years your senior and has his own job. He could say no if he wanted to."

"True," I said pensively, remembering that Nora had said the same thing. "I wonder why he didn't object, particularly since my father swindled him out of God knows how much money."

"Why do you say swindle? Isn't it legal for Muslim parents to demand any amount they see fit for their daughter—for what they call their daughter's dowry?"

"I can't imagine other parents making such disgraceful deals. I think its is customary for the daughter not to marry until she is eighteen so she can sign her own marriage certificate and use the dowry the way she pleases and that neither the father nor the brother has any right to it. But now my father wants me to be married while I'm still a minor so he can sign for me and get the payment promised by Uncle Ahmad as the final installment. You know they started to make payments a long time ago for the preparation of my trousseau. My father insisted on ordering the jewelry himself, and then he ordered cheaper gems than what he charged them, keeping the difference to himself. He kept dragging things out with one excuse after another. Now that he knows he can't get away with that any longer, he wants to wind up the deal as fast as possible."

"So you feel you must throw yourself to the wolves just because your family is abusing the Rajys? What about your dreams of becoming an independent career woman? You wanted to be a lawyer, remember? What about our vow that we would never let ourselves be approached by a man who would not accept us as his equal?" Her green eyes were troubled.

"What can I do? I'm unwanted here. Can't you see, Mabel? It's not only my father who makes me want to leave. A silent enmity that I can't control has grown between my mother and me ever since I told her what really caused Maria to leave our household eleven years ago."

"You never told me anything about this."

"I was only five at the time. It didn't seem that important at first. But as the years went by and I would secretly tell my mother about the horrible abuse our maids suffered at the hands of my father and my brother Anwar, the barrier between us grew. She knows I blame her for my father's behavior, and we both know that she will always deny his guilt and refuse to believe my accusations. My engagement to Marwan is a deliverance to her, a way to get me out of her way once and for all. She seems small and gentle, but she can be a strong, stubborn woman when her relationship with her husband is endangered."

"And she probably thinks she is doing you a great service at the same time, by tossing you into the lap of such a wealthy family." Mabel picked at the rug distractedly. "It sounds like breaking your engagement would just be trading one miserable situation for another. We are under our parents' mercy no matter how you look at it."

"The only reason I would stay with my parents would be if they let me continue school. But that won't happen. They can keep me at home until I rot if they choose to. If I go live with the Rajys, I will at least be in a family that loves and wants me, and might even help me with my education. I need that fresh air, Mabel. The hypocrisy around here is suffocating me. As for Marwan, I have made it clear to him and his parents that I do not love him. Our relationship will be based on kinship and respect, no more."

"You seem to have made up your mind to be a married woman!" A teasing gleam returned to Mabel's eyes.

"Why do you have to stress that word 'married'? Uncle Ahmad wants to make me his daughter. I simply have to marry for that to happen."

"Oh, come on, Nadia! You can't be that naive. Marrying someone means only one thing: being his! That means he can do anything he wants with you. That Uncle Ahmad of yours sounds like quite a joker!"

"He is a wonderful, serious man, Mabel. I trust him."

"All right. You keep on dreaming as you always do. But don't fool yourself that this husband will be different from any other."

She sounded as if she knew what she was talking about. But I did not think that Marwan would force himself on me.

"I have to go, Nadia. Anwar said your days of freedom are over this coming Friday, right? Will I be invited to that ceremony?"

"No, even I am not invited. And I don't sign in the official marriage records either. I'm not of age, remember?"

"Poor Marwan. Who will sign next to him?"

"Mr. Kareem Rajy and another male family member as guardians," I answered with a smile although I was crying inside.

In a case like mine, when a bride is not of age to sign her wedding contract, nor any official contract for that matter, people would resort to the proxy law where two of her guardians represent her.

When that date arrived my mother and her female guests gathered in our family room, waiting for my father and the chosen member of our clan to come in and have me sign the proxy. As far as those women were concerned that signature was the highlight of the whole ceremony. Linking the Rajy's two branches from Lebanon and Palestine was a great occasion and they were elated.

I stood there paralyzed by the spell of the moment, holding tightly to Nora's cold hand when my father and his chosen witness came in. The women welcomed the men with ovation and prayer songs, while my father had me put my signature at the end of a small paragraph of words that danced under my bent face. Sweetened coffee was offered and the men rushed back to the reception room where the men's party began.

Only Nora was aware of my nightmare. She looked very sad when she put her arm around my shoulders and pulled me to the back of the crowd. "I want to apologize for all the pain I've caused you, Nadia. No, please, let me finish. I've always felt that as your older sister I had to watch out for you. Every time you rebelled against something, I felt I had to get tough with you to protect you from what might happen. But now I will never be in that position again, I realize that I was a coward, afraid of what would happen if I took your side. I feel I failed you whenever you really needed my support. In two hours you will belong to someone else. I want to tell you now how much I admire your courage and your spirit, and I hope you will never change." We embraced each other and stood there motionless. "You are going to need all the courage you have to manage the new life ahead of you," she whispered.

The rooms began to hum as guests filled the reception area. Lights were on throughout the house and a cool breeze came through the open windows. Fear moved into me. Crowds of men would gather in our home to witness a serious religious occasion, people who knew nothing of the feelings the marriage couple might be hiding.

"Mama, Mama, the judge is here! Can I go in there and watch the ceremony now?" Mae burst into our bedroom that had become like a harem, a place forbidden to men. "Oh, Nadia, I wish you could come out and see Sheikh Mobarak! He looks very young to have such a big name. He is taller than everybody and wears clothes like Grandpa Mehdi in the picture."

Suddenly the noise that had filled the house died away.

"Go tell Sharifa not to make any noise and not to send any more coffee into the lounges until after the ceremony," my mother said to Mae. "You and your brothers stay out of the way, too. You can watch from the sun porch until the party is over." Her face looked as cool as marble, as if what was going on at that very moment a few steps from where we sat had nothing to do with her.

An authoritative voice reverberated through the air. "In the name of God, the almighty and only God, let it be known that on Friday, May 25 of the year 1934, a nuptial contract is being signed between Kareem ben Ali Rajy on behalf of his minor daughter Nadia Rajy and Marwan ben Ahmad Rajy. The sum of twelve hundred golden Ottomans will be paid by the groom. Half of this amount has been received by the father of the bride and the remainder will be due to the wife upon the termination of this contract: *Ajalain.*"

I turned and pulled at Nora's sleeve. "What does this mean, *Ajalain?* What's going to happen to me?"

"It means divorce or the death of your husband. Don't worry, neither of these two fates is going to happen to you, I hope."

October of that year was a month to remember, indeed.

My heavy silk wedding dress hung like a hoisted flag from the doorway between the dar and the sunporch, the long train floating down to a table where Aunt Hind arranged the cloud of tulle in a circle, then placed my floral headdress and tulle veil in the center. Since none of our close friends or relatives would be able to see me at the wedding, Aunt Huda had advised that we put the dress on display and let callers stop by to see it. "It looks like a mutilated ghost," I teased.

"You worry me, Nadia." Aunt Hind turned to me with a look of concern. "I know how much you appreciate fine clothes and gifts. Why are you acting so nonchalant? Are you frightened?" She took me by the hand and led me to the bamboo couch on the porch.

"I want you to know that I admire your strength and your patience. From the day the Rajys paid their first visit, I have been concerned about what is happening under this roof—and concerned for you, Nadia. Don't look so surprised. I never wanted to interfere with your parents or take sides, but I felt I could be here for you if you needed someone to talk to."

The emotions in her voice stunned me. I had always known her as a simple woman who kept her distance from everyone except her three children.

"I have been aware, Nadia, of the harm Kareem has done to you. I didn't know what I could do to help you, until two years ago, right after the Rajys asked for your hand. I have kept this from you because

Nadia between Her Sister and Sister-in-Law before the Wedding

I didn't want to make things even more difficult for you, especially after your mother refused to cooperate with the plan I proposed on your behalf. I knew the situation in which you were caught, and I suggested that instead of pushing you into a marriage you did not want, you could be engaged to Kamal, who admires you very much. Kamal knew how important school was to you, and he was willing to wait as long as you might need to be ready for marriage."

"I can't believe there was yet another plan to dispose of me!"

"I don't think marrying Kamal would be disposing of you, Nadia! I thought you always liked having him around. Didn't you ever wonder why Kamal was so attentive to you? I could see what a great pair you two would make. You were the only girl with whom I had seen him so talkative and at ease." The bitterness in her voice made me watch my words.

"Please don't misunderstand me, Aunt. I do like Kamal very much. He has been a better brother to me than my real ones. But most of all, he's my friend. Do you want me to marry my best friend?"

"What is the use of even talking about this now, Nadia? You are about to marry a man whose name has been written on your forehead since the beginning of time." She pulled me close. I knew she was as dear a friend as Kamal.

The wall clock chimed softly, eleven times, in the still house. I was still packing my last suitcase, the one I would keep with me during the trip. Carefully bundled inside was all the jewelry the Rajys had showered on me over the years and the gleaming set of diamonds, my wedding gift. The round chiseled stones were as large as coffee beans in the center, tapering to tiny beads at the end of the chain. In between the jewelry boxes I slipped my diary and writing pad.

I pushed the small suitcase under my bed, careful not to wake up Nora and the other two siblings who shared my room. Suddenly a lump rose up in my throat as I realized how much I was going to miss the sound of their breath and the sweet fragrance of their bodies whenever they would lie down overcome by sleep. I stepped into the dark hallway to get a glass of water before going to bed. Behind me, light footsteps sounded. I jumped. "Mama, you scared me!"

"I couldn't sleep. I want to talk to you, Nadia." Her voice was a whisper in the shadows of the hallway.

"Is something wrong? Shall I bring you a glass of water?"

"No, thank you. I'll be waiting in the liwan." Like a vision, she turned away, her long cotton nightgown floating behind her.

As I reached for a glass at the kitchen sink I saw, lying in a dish, one of my father's pigeons. Its neck was cut and a trickle of blood ran over its white feathers into the bowl. A bloody spoon lay on the counter next to it. I ran back to the liwan where Mother sat under the dark windows. She had placed her bed in such a way that she could look down into the rose garden.

"Sit down." She patted the covers next to her and straightened a cushion under her elbow. I took a deep breath, relieved that we could finally open our hearts to each other. "I am not good, Nadia, at talking about personal matters." Her eyes turned away from mine for a moment, but then she went on. "This is your last night under this roof and I have some things I want to tell you. I wish you happiness, lots of happiness in your new life with the Rajys. But your place in their family will be different than here, and it will be best for you if you learn to adapt to their expectations. We have tolerated your stubborn temperament and may have gone as far as spoiling you—especially your father, as you took advantage of his affection. But as a wife you will be expected to be prudent. . . . You cannot always insist on your needs and desires. You must learn to give way to the will of others, and to your husband."

"But Mama, how could you . . . "

"Please don't interrupt. You must learn patience and tolerance. I know that I haven't been able to provide you with the kind of home you would have liked, but I have tried to be a model for you in other ways. A woman must temper her will if she is to keep her nose above water." She gave me a steely look. "Life is harder than you may think."

My eyes were fixed on hers. "Yes, Mama, you have been an excellent model of subservience and compliance, letting your husband impose his will on this entire household. His children, Aunt Salma, Maria, Alia. . . . No matter what he did, you turned your eyes away, even moving out of your bedroom so as not to witness more of his crimes! Did it ever occur to you that keeping silent made you just as guilty as he was? Why didn't you stop him right from the beginning? You saw him gambling with your children's future, forcing some out of school and sending them to work to feed him. . . . You have deprived us of sacred rights every child is given by God, by nature, by civilized societies."

"You don't understand, Nadia!" There was an expression of pain in her face such as I had never seen before. "I could never expose myself to his retaliations. I would die if he hit me or cursed me. He is too strong for me. I cannot change him or stand in his way. You will see how it is soon enough. You will see!"

"Isn't it ironic that you should be instructing your daughter in this way! You, the maverick in the family, marrying for love, insisting on your right to choose the life you wanted!"

"I have paid dearly for that. My mother tried to stop me from marrying Kareem, closing her doors against him while my father was still alive and again after he died. When I insisted, she refused to see Kareem or attend the rushed marriage ceremony. Yes, I paid the price for going against my mother who had more experience than I did. I am responsible for that and have to accept the results of my marriage and make the best of it.

"Now let me change the subject. There is one other thing that I want to make clear to you before we leave on our trip tomorrow. I know that upon your insistence the Rajys have agreed to include Nora and Fadi in our traveling party. But not until yesterday did I realize that you intend to have them live with you there. Nadia, Ahmad Rajy has asked for your hand and that naturally makes you a member of his family. He said nothing about adopting two more of us!"

"But Mama, Uncle Ahmad is very happy to have all of us. You were there when we spoke about it. Did you notice any hesitation on his part?"

"That man is too refined to object, and too anxious to please you. He seems unable to say no to anything you want. He has been jumping from one city to the next buying furniture, carpets, and other luxuries to meet your every whim. 'I hate those huge beds where two people sleep side by side, Uncle Ahmad, I want my own single bed, please. Can I have my own piano? I need to practice, you know. What kind of radios can you find in your hometown? At Orosdi's they carry a wide range of them,' " she mimicked.

I had never heard her use such jeering humor. "What's wrong with that? The Rajys make me so comfortable that I feel free to tell them anything I want."

"I wonder why your fond feelings for them don't include Marwan. Don't you realize that if it weren't for Marwan you would never have met them?"

"He's different from the rest of them. . . . He's hard to understand." I couldn't tell her that the thought of being alone with him scared me.

"So your plan is to hold on to Nora and Fadi in order to hide from Marwan?

Let me remind you, Nadia, that by agreeing to marry Marwan, you have given away your rights. He will make the rules, and you have to follow those rules. Believe me, daughter, there is nothing you can do to keep him from demanding his marriage rights. Please, don't make things more difficult for yourself."

Suddenly I felt extremely tired. I got up from the bed. All of me felt empty, lonely. I was diminished to a little shell, and an icy wind was blowing through me. As I crossed the room I felt her hand on my arm. "Here, take this." She opened her fingers and extended her smooth palm to me. A tiny glass bottle, filled with a substance red as blood, lay in her hand. "Put this among your personal things."

I looked at her in incomprehension. "Is it medicine?"

"No. You are supposed to have this with you on your wedding night. It will stain the sheets as well as your own blood!" Her glare was dull, muddied up, without a trace of emotion.

The night was long and full of odd dreams. I woke up before dawn on what would be the last day I lived under my parents' roof. Friday, November 1, 1935, was to be my wedding day. At six o'clock on that morning I would begin the long nuptial journey that would take me across the border of my country, south to a new land.

I heard the ticking of the wall clock that hung on the wall of the dar. Through the open doors of my room I could see shadows moving in the dar and in the hallway. My father roamed out there, stopped on the threshold of my room, then retreated into the dark. Nora tossed restlessly under her quilt, and Mae and baby Fadi breathed heavily on the next bed. Mama had moved my baby brother to Mae's bed to wean him from his attachment to me before I left.

I closed my eyes and tried to push away the painful memories of my childhood, tried to hold on to the ray of hope that Friday's journey would bring. One wound in particular, though, would not yield-the grief over being robbed of my childhood and of my hopes for the future of my own dreams. The memory of my last determined effort in that direction, fruitless though I knew it to be, would not go away.

On a Sunday nearly eighteen months earlier, on the eve of the long-awaited exams that would mark the culmination of my nine years of school, Mabel had left my house carrying a paper bag containing a flowery cotton dress, a pair of shoes, socks, and my purse. "I'll meet you in the backyard at five o'clock tomorrow morning, before your father goes down to feed the pigeons, Nadia," she had whispered.

"What if someone sees me going out the kitchen door so early, Mabel? It will still be dark at five."

"There's no other way. Don't chicken out now. You can change inside the stone recess under the bottom landing of the stairs. By the time they discover your absence, we'll be halfway through the exams."

I hardly slept that night. Then, just before dawn, I slipped out. I was shivering all over by the time I reached up to the rusted iron bolt of the gate and struggled to pull it open. The dark alley leading to Mabel's house was deserted. Suddenly, a rooster's plaintive crowing filled the air, sending me back to the alcove under the stairs. That sounded like my father's favorite rooster!

I waited for what seemed like hours. Finally, her voice was next to my ear. "Sorry to be late. Here, take your clothes. I will keep a watch eye." Her confident tone lifted my spirit.

"Please, God," I prayed as I pulled my socks and shoes from the paper bag and slipped them on. I was pulling my dress over my head when I heard my father's heavy steps coming down the stairs above me.

Mabel squeezed under the stairs next to me. "Hush, he's coming!"

We froze until the shuffling died away beyond the rose garden, down by the chicken pens.

"What are we going to do now?" I moaned. The dawn had already turned to a clear June morning.

"He can't see us from down there. We can make a dash for the gate. Hurry, it's almost six o'clock!" I could tell she was no longer sure our plan was going to work.

It would have worked well, though, had not the huge gate burst open just as we got there and, Sultan, the milkman strolled in followed by his mule strapped with two tin milk jugs.

"Sorry I am late, Kareem, my friend." His thundering voice seemed as if it would wake up the whole city.

We shrank against the closest wall.

"Coming, Sultan," my father's husky voice sounded through the yard.

"Go, Mabel, please!" I pushed her out the gate but she never let go of my hand and we barely made it to school in time for the exams. By the time the official results appeared in the newspaper, with my name among those who had passed, I was hundreds of miles away, playing at being a bride.

The day the black limousine rolled away from my family's home and I left many old memories behind, I felt as if I had been reborn. As the forty-day wedding celebration continued, I was dazzled by the constant stream of visitors and parties and by the Rajys' large, warm family.

Their ten-room limestone house stood on an acre of terraced ground cresting the ridge of a hill that separated the old and new sections of Haifa. Below spread the thin crescent of the harbor and seaport, and behind it the newer buildings reached to the top of Mount Carmel. Several huge eucalyptus trees shaded the lot and towered above the one-story building which, with its front and back doors flung open, was the center of the family's constant activity. None of the windows or the French doors leading to the verandas had shades or draperies.

Each evening Marwan and I joined the family for dinner, as Aunt Najla had insisted that I not be burdened with any cooking more elaborate than fixing breakfast for Marwan in the morning. Marwan did not hide his blunt ways around his family. "I didn't wait all this time to have my own apartment and then still have to endure these hectic family dinners!"

Our apartment was the top floor of a four-story complex. While the family compound high on the ridge opened onto the mountains behind, our rooms looked toward the sea. Serving as our entryway, family room, and music lounge, the long central hall was heavily furnished with piano, radio, rocking chairs, brass planters, two bulky sofas, and several glass china cabinets that we could not fit into the salon and dining room. During the day I was alone. I would turn the radio on, play the piano, sing, dance, and feel like a princess in my own palace.

At first Marwan had been patient with my moods, perhaps believing that I was distracted by the long and demanding wedding festivities. He had hated every moment of the required rituals, furious at the constant intrusion of hundreds of callers led by Aunt Najla through our apartment. She would push back the doors of our closets so they could examine the evening dresses, skirts, jackets, blouses, and negligees of silk and Venetian lace. She opened drawers so they could run their fingers over everything.

But as the weeks passed, Marwan became increasingly embittered by my distance, spending less time with the family and more with his glass of wine. The cordial friendship we had built before we married could not be sustained under the strain of his nightly advances and my rejections of him.

Nadia on the Way to Haifa, Palestine, Away from Home for the First Time, 1935

Nadia in Her Wedding Dress, 1935

Nadia's Wedding Photo, 1935

"Nadia, please, I feel as if I am going to go crazy. Why do you keep on doing this to me?" Hands thrust deep into the pockets of his robe, a strange look in his eyes, Marwan stepped to within inches of me in the narrow bathroom as I was finishing my shower.

I grabbed my bath towel and wrapped it around me, backing away. "Don't come closer, Marwan. Can't you see I'm washing? Go away, please!"

"You are my wife, damn it! Have you forgotten that? You have been evading me for two months! Do you hate me that much?"

"I don't hate you. I just don't want you or anyone else to touch me, ever. Don't forget, we didn't marry because we wanted to. We did what our parents wanted us to do. So why do you keep chasing me around? Does your father know what you are trying to do to me?"

"Did my father suggest we marry and never touch each other? Do you really expect to share my room night after night and pretend that I'm nothing more than a log?"

"If living with you means that you think you can force me to do something against my will, I shall move in with your parents tomorrow."

He spun around and left. When I finished getting ready for bed, the house was quiet. I wrapped my woolen robe around me and tiptoed out to the privacy of the salon with a spare blanket over my shoulders. It wasn't the first night I had spent there; nor, I feared, would it be the last.

Marwan sat silently at the dining room table as I shuttled back and forth from the kitchen with his breakfast the next morning. Although not due at work until eight A.M., he insisted on having breakfast at six-thirty. By seven he would be behind the cashier's bars at the bank, just a five-minute walk from the house.

"Sit down, please, Nadia. I've made a decision that I hope will make things easier for us." He did not look at me. "I promise not to come close to you if you return to sleep in your bed and assure me you will not tell anyone about our situation. Not anyone!" I had the feeling he was fearful of what would happen if his father knew how forceful his approaches to me had been.

"I would die before I would tell a soul about such disgraceful things. Why do you think I haven't been wearing any of the short-sleeved sweaters your father gave me for the holidays?" I was rubbing the bruises on my arms, as the rising anger gripped my throat.

He pushed his chair from the table and looked at his wristwatch. "I'd better be going. See you at two."

As I was straightening the small silk cushions on the couch in the salon where I had spent the night, I noticed the door to Marwan's office cabinet was wide open. I had never seen the mysterious interior of that cabinet. It was always locked. I looked around the quiet room as if expecting to see him hiding somewhere. Why had he left it open?

On a tour of our new home when I first arrived, Marwan had pointed to the tall cabinet tucked away in the corner but did not volunteer to show me what was behind those smooth, locked doors. When I asked what he used it for, his answer was abrupt and final: "My personal documents. Nothing that would interest you, Nadia." I was even more puzzled when I noticed the precautions he took every time he used it. The tiny metal key was always kept in his vest pocket and whenever he went into the salon to work, he locked the door behind him.

Overwhelmed by curiosity, I approached the mahogany fixture. I saw a folder made of cardboard and an orange-colored fabric. The maroon leather strip on it read: "OUR HONEYMOON." I could not recall ever hearing Marwan talk about a honeymoon. I lifted the smooth cover carefully, trying not to disturb the papers inside. Two thick white envelopes lay on top of a pile of colorful travel catalogs and pictures of cruise ships with lists of departure and arrival times. One of them held a small brown book with "PASSPORT" embossed across the top in golden English letters. In the center, also in gold, were two lions with a jeweled crown between their forelegs. And beneath the emblem, "Mrs. Nadia Marwan Rajy." Excitement surging inside me, I opened the crisp pages. A woman in a black hat smiled back. It was me! The picture had been taken a few weeks earlier at a fancy studio in a shopping area called Hadar'a Carmel. Below the picture a fine Arabic script read, "Nadia Marwan Rajy, born Rajy, February 21, 1918." Why had Marwan's name replaced my father's? Why all the secrecy? Mysterious as it all was, I felt a strange wave of well-being. I had a passport, a new name, a new nationality—I was a Palestinian citizen!

The second envelope was thicker and wrapped with a blue rubberband. Out of it tumbled dozens of receipts and medical prescriptions and two small tins with French labels. I opened the tins carefully. Inside were rows of brown and yellow pills.

The sudden loud chime of the doorbell made me jump. I shoved the papers and tins back into their envelopes and put them back in their place hurriedly, trying to arrange everything as it had been.

"I thought you would like to have some macaroons while they're still hot." Aunt Najla stood holding a porcelain plate covered with waxed paper, wisps of steam rising in front of her. "Please go ahead with whatever you were doing." She followed me to the kitchen where I set the warm plate on the breakfast table and lit the gasoline stove for tea.

"I was going to help Suad with the preparations for New Year's Eve as soon as I finished tidying up," I apologized. Reaching to the cupboard for teacups, I suddenly remembered the bruises on my exposed arms, and my body stiffened.

"Is something wrong, Nadia? You look pale; it may be because honeymooners have the tendency to get wild sometimes. Why don't you tell me about what is going on, dear child. You know how much we care about you. In fact, Ahmad suggested that I ask my son to take it easy with you!"

"I can't! Marwan made me promise not to tell anybody."

"Come now, it can't be that bad!" She sounded bemused. "Is your period late? You don't want to hide such wonderful news from us."

"What?"

"The fatigue you've been feeling is normal for a new bride when she becomes pregnant."

I was dumbfounded. So that was it! They thought I was pregnant!

She reached for a glass and filled it to the top with water. "Here, have some . . ." She was staring at my arms; then her eyes searched my face in confusion.

"I was going to come to you. . . . Marwan wants to take me by force and I warned him that if he didn't stop hurting me I would . . . "

"Oh my God! What a shame!" She looked dazed. "Is he out of his mind? What will we tell Ahmad? He'll kill Marwan if he finds out!"

"Don't worry, Aunt Najla. Nobody needs to tell Uncle Ahmad about this. I can still go back home to Beirut if I have to."

"Don't ever say that, Nadia. You belong with us more than our own son does now." She fixed her eyes on mine. "I want you to be very frank with me, Nadia. This is very important. Did Marwan ever hurt you in any other way?"

I shook my head, feeling the blood rush to my face.

"Not even once? He never caused any pain or bleeding of any sort?" I shook my head again, but the bottle of pigeon blood flashed through my mind. I had left it on the dresser in my parents' house.

"I am very sorry about this, Nadia. I'm going to ask Marwan to go see Dr. Khaldoun. Put on some warm clothes and come to the house with me."

"But Aunt Najla, I have given Marwan my word not to tell anybody about this. I don't want him to think I have betrayed that promise!"

"Don't worry, child. He may scare you with his temper, but not me. I'll find a way to make him tell me the truth. I just hope he is not sick. . . ."

My mind was racing now. The medicine I had discovered. All the secrets locked away.

5

December 31, 1935

A diamond brooch sparkled on the strap of my black evening dress. In the tall mirror of the wardrobe room my head appeared small and rather childlike with its new Charleston hair cut.

"This is a big event—your very first New Year's Eve in this city. And you will probably be the newest bride at the banquet." Suad snapped my two diamond bracelets around my wrists and stepped back to look at me.

Marwan, who looked immaculate in his tuxedo, was ready half an hour ahead of me. "It's still too early," he said looking at his wrist watch. He went into the salon and locked the door. I knew he needed a drink, but did not have any alcohol when his family was around.

"Suad and I will stop by to wish your parents happy New Year, Marwan. We'll wait for you there," I called through the door. "Let's go, Suad."

"Is it all right if you leave without him?" She picked up her coat and head scarf hesitantly. "Won't he be mad?"

"He's probably mad already. He gets mad for reasons I can't comprehend."

"It may be a while before you learn to see beyond Marwan's tough surface to the big heart that's really inside. I hope you'll be patient with him. He went through a great deal of hardship when he was growing up. He was weak and sickly, and had a series of terrible diseases. At five, after having typhus for three months, he was left almost crippled. He didn't walk properly until he was six."

"Is that why his legs didn't grow longer?"

Suad nodded without a word.

"Do you know whether he still suffers from any illness?"

"Oh, no, he's healthy as can be. He takes good care of himself." She stopped suddenly. "What is it? Is there something wrong?"

"I don't know. Maybe you should ask him. Now, enough of this serious talk. Tonight is for enjoyment. Tomorrow is another day in another year."

A long black car pulled up to the Rajys' main gate shortly before seven. The night sky hung like a dark bowl above us as Marwan and I stepped out of his parents' house to meet our escort. The chilly breeze carried the wet scent of winter clouds, and small groups of people strolled the wide, paved road lit by a string of bright electric lamps. Bourje Street was the main road connecting the old section of Haifa down by the harbor with the new part of the city as it wound upward, past our home, to its end, half a mile farther, at the heart of the new shopping center.

"Good evening, Ali Bey," Marwan greeted the man who sat behind the wheel. "I hope we haven't kept you waiting." Marwan helped me into the backseat and then walked around the sedan and slipped in next to Mr. Ibrahim.

So this large man was Marwan's boss, about whom I had heard much but had never seen. He and his wife lived two blocks down the street from us. She was a fat, lively woman in her fifties, and a friend of Aunt Najla's who had called more than once during the wedding festivities. Even with only women around she would not take off her head cover, and she barely lifted her veil. I could not imagine her attending a dinner party in mixed company, so I was not surprised to see her husband coming alone to pick us up. Ali Ibrahim stopped the car in front of the wide marble stairs of City Hall where the bankers' New Year's Eve banquet was to be held, took a quick look at me as Marwan helped me out of the car, and drove around to the parking lot.

Over a hundred round tables filled the center of the spacious high-domed room. Translucent glass vases of red and yellow roses, and gleaming china and silver graced the white cloths. Marwan found the table reserved for his party, introduced me to a few of his colleagues, seated me, and disappeared. I was one of only a few women present in that imposing lounge. Apart from a handful of native young couples like us who were as fashionably dressed as the foreign guests, those accompanied by women were mostly Westerners.

"Look, Marwan, what are those clergymen doing here?" I asked as he slipped into the chair next to me a little later. A group of religious men were crossing the room. The Greek Orthodox priests, with their tall, stiff headdresses, long, knotted hair, and large, jeweled crosses on top of layers of robes, were an imposing sight. The Catholic priests wore small black caps and simple crosses. Their robes were just as plain. Not too impressive, I thought. The Muslim sheikhs looked like silver doves in their immaculate white turbans and long gray robes over snow white cotton caftans. They headed for a long table set apart in front of the lounge where the master of ceremonies greeted them and conducted them to their seats. Marwan's boss lavished much attention on them.

"In our city the religious leaders are at the top of the guest list for any public function. They are as important in running the government as the politicians."

"Don't they mind being at a party where drinks are served and music played?"

"No alcohol will be served tonight, as Muslims have been invited. You have to know the formula for these events, Nadia, since you are going to live here. For parties with strong drinks, dancing, and romancing, you don't invite either Christians or Muslims. For parties with drinks, dancing, but no romancing, you can invite the Christians but not the Muslims. For parties with soft drinks, no dancing, and no romancing, you can invite all of them!"

The men around the table burst into laughter at this, and I joined in, carried away by their gaiety.

"Good evening, everyone." The husky voice came from behind me. I turned to see Ali Ibrahim waiting for Marwan to pull out his chair. All the men had jumped to their feet to welcome him, but I waited to see whether he would finally acknowledge me.

"This is Ali Bey Ibrahim, Nadia," Marwan announced as if it were our first encounter. I nodded.

"So, your father is in public service in Beirut, Mrs. Rajy. Marwan has mentioned that he is the under-secretary of the Public Works Department." The man spoke with an accent similar to some of the Turks who had remained in Lebanon after the war.

Bewildered by the mention of my father with such an exaggeration of his status, I looked at Marwan. Was the man joking?

"That's right, Adnan," Marwan said. "Uncle Kareem is well known out there. He's one of the few Rajys who don't have their own trade business. Her brother Anwar has his own bureau of export and import." Oh, really! Anwar's small vending business for corn flour and powdered formula was an export and import bureau? My brother's habits of exaggeration were rubbing off on Marwan!

"I imagine schools in Lebanon have more facilities for females than our schools here," Adnan continued from across the table. "Your husband seems proud that you have finished your secondary education and are planning to attend the University in Haifa." Another exaggeration! These men appeared to know a great deal about me, while I barely knew their names. What had Marwan been telling them?

A waiter arrived with mineral water, fresh orange juice, and lemonade in large glass pitchers. Another placed in the center of the table a huge platter of sizzling barbecued lamb on a hill of spiced pilaf and fried nuts. Bowls of yogurt, olives, and salad appeared. The room was swarming with waiters whose dark skin glowed against their immaculate white caftans, red belts and tarbooshes.

"All the waiters look alike," I whispered in Marwan's ear. "Do they come from the same country?"

Marwan nodded. "They're Sudanese. You don't see many of them in Lebanon, but here they are well established."

"In fact, most of the Africans here are from Nubia, in the far southern part of the Sudan," Ali Bey Ibrahim interjected without looking at me. "You can find the Nubies wherever the British are. Although the two races are very different, they work well together. The British trust them. Anyway, Madame may not be interested in all this."

"On the contrary, Ali Bey. I find politics very entertaining. It's part of every serious discussion, even of historical and theological debates. So much intrigue to politics. And, please, call me Nadia; I am not accustomed to such formalities." I was enjoying myself tremendously.

"How much do you know about these intrigues, Mrs. Nadia?" he asked with a hint of amusement, as if he were not taking me seriously.

"As much as my age has allowed me to learn from storytellers, from my three languages and from the history books I put my hands on. But I would like very much to know more about what is really going on today in the Middle East in general and Palestine in particular." The other men quieted as they sat watching us.

"Marwan, what have you been teaching your bride? I wouldn't have expected a newly married young lady to show such enthusiasm for politics!"

"Don't look at me, dear friend. Nadia has a mind of her own."

"Your husband has a mind of his own, too, when it comes to politics, Mrs. Rajy. Did you know that?" Mahmoud, on Marwan's left, leaned toward me.

"I'm aware of the flexible approach he advocates for handling the conflict between Arabs and Jews. I know, too, that he seems to blame both camps for what the leaders got involved with in previous years." Marwan knew that my sympathies had grown for the Arab revolutionaries in the short time I had been in Haifa.

"Beware of what you are going to say, Mahmoud!" Marwan interrupted. "I'm afraid Nadia is taking this matter much too seriously."

"You had better take it seriously, all of you!" Rashid snapped. Thick curly dark hair framed his thin face. His black coat hung loosely on his narrow shoulders as if he had borrowed it for the occasion.

"All right, my friend, let's not spoil this special evening," Ali Ibrahim cut in. "We owe you an apology, Mrs. Nadia. This is hardly the time for such talk. The Palestinian conflict is dividing the people of this country so severely that we might ruin our dinner if we continue this discussion. Marwan, does your perceptive bride know about the changes at our bank?" He seemed anxious to change the subject.

"My father and I have mentioned it. I think this plan needs more research before we talk about it." Now it seemed that Marwan wanted to change the subject.

"This could be a matter of great importance for your future, now that you are married and in need of a promotion." I could not help noticing the tone of superiority in his boss's voice. Marwan stiffened but did not rush to answer.

"I understand that the issue is about changing the bank's name and function, not its structure," I volunteered.

"A name change?" Ali Ibrahim turned to face Marwan. "Is that how you see it, son?" He looked at me. "This is a split at the root level, Mrs. Nadia, if it takes place in Jerusalem between those who would support the commercial exchange between this country and the rest of the world and people like myself who would rather use the money inside Palestine to support our agricultural resources instead." His impassioned explanation forced his small audience to keep their mouths shut. "I cannot spend my time and energy working to fill the pockets of our shareholders when our children need schools, the sick and the elderly need hospitals, and our landowners cannot profit enough to keep that land in their possession. Could you, Marwan?"

"It's not that simple, Ali Bey," Marwan said, trying to control his voice. "I sure can if my commitment in either of these two banks is to the investors who trusted me with their money. My sympathy goes to the Palestinian people who have put all of their faith in leaders who have failed them so consistently."

"I'm sorry, Marwan, that after all our discussions you are still unable to see the importance of financial institutions investing in their people. I am glad, however, that your father is more objective than you are. He will agree with me, you'll see." Ali Ibrahim no longer seemed to care if a serious discussion spoiled our evening. I was impressed by how sincere and eloquent he sounded. On the other hand, I had a hunch that Marwan was right in sticking to his professional views against the passionate patriotism of his boss.

"Nadia?" Marwan's voice came softly through the quiet of our bedroom. "Wake up. The coffee is ready." His eyes sparkled at me through his thick eyelashes. I could smell the aftershave on his long, thin face.

"Marwan! Good morning. Sorry I overslept."

"That's all right. It will be my turn on Fridays to fix you breakfast. Put your robe on and come see what a beautiful day this new year has brought." We stepped out to the large veranda where a silver coffee tray sat atop the bamboo table.

"I am not completely helpless around the house." He sounded very proud of himself. But my mind at that moment was on what motive could prompt such a charming gesture. In the two months we had been married I had never seen him so cheerful in the morning.

I pulled out a chair for him and another one for me. "This is an unusually bright day for this time of year. Is it always like this in Haifa? In Beirut the chill doesn't lift until February."

"Yes, Haifa is much warmer. Palestine doesn't have snow-capped mountains like those that tower over Beirut.

"Sometimes I get the feeling you would rather live in Beirut than here. Why didn't you ever set up a home there as your Uncles Hussein and Muhammad have done?"

"Believe me, Nadia, I tried several times to convince my father to delay my marriage until he and I could reach an agreement about that. In fact, I suggested that he could open a branch there and save us the pain of living in this pitiful country. But it is very hard to make him see that the sooner we all leave, the better off we will all be."

"Couldn't you have decided to move to Beirut even if your father prefers to live here? Aren't you independent from him yet? To my knowledge a man your age is supposed to be on his own."

"Perhaps you don't know how overprotected I have been, Nadia. I cannot imagine stepping out into the world by myself, without money or a job or a place to live. But now, for the first time in my life, I realize that I have something very special to come home to." His eyes avoided mine, but this was the first time he had expressed his feelings to me with such ease and comfort.

"Tell me, Marwan, what sort of social life did you have before you married me?"

"I'm a member of a few social clubs we have in Haifa. The most interesting is the very active nonsectarian Greek Orthodox Club, established about twenty years ago by the Orthodox Church to provide a place for its young people to attend lectures and socialize, since those run by the British or the Jews were not open to Arabs. They host political debates, social activities, lectures on art and music, and open their doors to Muslims, Jews, and Christians alike. I don't attend many of their events, but most of my friends are members."

"Did you exchange any visits with those friends?"

"It was almost impossible to have them over at my parents', since that place is such a madhouse. But now that you are here and we have our own place, we can invite whomever we please, and accept invitations as well. You must promise me one thing, though. If we are to entertain our friends here, we must be on our own. I mean I want you to spend less time with my family and more with me in our apartment. I am tired of eating their food, hearing their chaos, and letting their schedules dominate our lives."

"My God, Marwan! You don't seem to understand how valuable the love and support of your family is to me. Why do you hate them so much?"

"I just want to be free from them. You spend more time with them than with me."

"Stop talking like a spoiled child. I consider your family to be my own and I hope you won't interfere in my relationship with them . . . or with my own family, for that matter."

"Nadia, please. If you miss your parents and the rest of your family, I will send you to visit them any time you want. At least they're far enough away not to come between us. You can spend a couple of weeks with them, how about that?"

Oh my God, I thought, not back there. But I said nothing, knowing that sooner or later such a visit was unavoidable.

I had spent most of my day preparing kibbe, one of Marwan's favorite dishes, hoping it would cheer him some. Since Monday, when his father had left Haifa to go to Jerusalem to meet with the pasha, who was president of the board of the original bank, Marwan had been inconsolable, as if his world depended on the decision his father would make on that trip.

He burst through the door. He was almost in tears.

"What's wrong Marwan? Are you sick?" I asked when I saw his gray face.

"The thing I was afraid of has happened. It's over."

"What do you mean?"

"I knew that schemer Ibrahim would get what he wanted eventually, but I didn't think it would happen so soon. The Rajys' shares that my father has invested in the original bank are exchanged with an equal number of shares in a new bank that is established by Ibrahim and a bunch of his political affiliates. There is a big difference in the value of these shares. While the original bank is backed by businesses and commercial corporations, the new one is backed by politicians only." I had never seen Marwan so distraught.

"I can see you have no trust in that man, but you mustn't let it upset you so, Marwan."

"I warned Mother this would happen. My father doesn't take seriously any advice I try to offer. He's gambling with a large part of his fortune by believing in the promises of a friend who is involved with those damned politicians. And I guarantee you Ibrahim has no intention whatsoever of promoting me to the managerial post he told Father he's saving for me. He's saving that for his own son, Saleem." At this he seemed to choke. "I have sweated over that bank for years, working long hours, and taking charge of matters that are his responsibility as manager. I have even taken the risk of carrying both keys of the bank's safe because Ibrahim is busy with his political commitments and is seldom behind his desk when I need him. Now, I have to move to the new bank and start from scratch again. It is his son who will be the manager now."

His bitter outburst subsided over the next several days into a morose silence that I could not penetrate.

"Marwan, getting angry and sick will not change what is done. Besides, perhaps this is all for the best. This could be your chance to leave that business and do whatever you please. Why should you be stuck in a job that makes your life miserable?"

"You don't understand, Nadia. I can't turn my back on my father. There is nothing else I could do except work in my father's store. No, my life is over."

He sounded so resigned, I felt my anger rising. "What life, Marwan? For God's sake, you're not yet thirty! With your experience you could have any job you wanted in another bank. There are many new banks in this area to choose from. I know you've put a lot into that bank and it's dear to your heart, but . . . "

"That's right. It was mine. No one else seems to be aware of that. I didn't even realize how much that four-room bank meant to me. I feel as if a part of my body has died with it."

Marwan was napping one afternoon some days later when the doorbell rang and Aunt Najla came in carrying a large envelope similar to those Marwan brought home from work. She kissed my head and followed me into the salon. "This is for you from Ahmad," she said softly, handing me the envelope. She seemed uneasy.

"For me? Are you sure it's not for Marwan?" But below the black print of the bank's name and address at the top, in large Arabic calligraphy, my name was written.

"Go ahead, my dear. Open it. It was supposed to have come on your birthday, but the paperwork took longer than Ahmad expected."

I pulled a bundle of light blue papers out of the envelope. They looked like enlarged money notes framed with a golden garland. My name appeared at the center above several unreadable signatures.

"These are shares of the new bank, Aunt Najla! So many! Does this mean I'm part owner of this new bank?" Excitement raced through me as I realized these glossy certificates that were making my heart dance were the source of Marwan's pain.

"Yes, you are, my dear daughter. All of our children have been given an equal number of shares." Her smile almost vanished now. "Please, Nadia, try to help me smooth the feelings between Marwan and his father over this bank conflict."

"I don't know, Aunt Najla. They're so very different. They seem to disagree about almost everything. Yet Marwan has such a blind loyalty to his father!"

"These are hard times for my Marwan. I feel utterly helpless in the face of his pain. I'm afraid that son of ours has been trailed by an evil eye for the last few years. He seems to be a magnet for misery."

"Come on, there is no such thing as an evil eye!" I had to suppress a laugh.

"I know you are a modern, educated young lady who does not believe in the super powers that live beneath this world, but I do. Let me ask you this—how do you explain the fact that Marwan, who I'm sure worships you, has been unable to gain your trust and perform his marital duties?"

"To tell you the truth, I don't expect anything from him."

"You are very kind to say so. But don't tell me you are not suffering because of his misfortune."

I felt the blood rush to my face. How could I tell her I had no desire for her son to perform his marital duties? I couldn't understand how any woman would want such a painful thing. "Why do you make such a fuss about something so unimportant?"

"Unimportant? You amaze me, Nadia. You are aware of so much in some ways, yet you know so little about the relations between husband and wife. Men do not marry fine brides like you just to set them aside and bury themselves in a hole of misery and sickness. Marwan has a sacred duty toward you. If he is sick, he needs to seek medical help. We can't let this go on any longer. Maybe you are not aware that your marriage is considered annulled if it is not consummated within a certain time, but my son knows that he may lose you. Hundreds of people are watching us. Believe me, Nadia, they would like nothing better than to nibble on gossip like this. People expect us to abide by our traditions. I have been afraid to set a date for your visit to your family because of this problem."

"What visit?"

"It is traditional, once the bride is with child, that the groom's family accompany her back to her parents' to show their appreciation for the kinship. That visit is overdue, and I don't know what to tell Ahmad and the rest of our relatives who are concerned about it also." Her sad eyes looked into mine for an answer, as if I, too, should be in a hurry to correct these wrongs.

"I'm terribly sorry this matter is taking such a toll on you. Don't worry, we can go on the trip to my parents' any time you would like. I promise not to give them any reason to suspect that there is something wrong. But really, I don't think it's anyone's business how Marwan and I handle our personal relationship."

"Your family has a right to know, my dear. It is because they love you that they want to be sure you are all right."

I nodded my head. She would never understand that some parents could be less loving and concerned than she and her husband were.

"Let me ask a favor of you. Try to talk Marwan into cooperating with our family physician, Dr. Khaldoun, who has advised him to see a specialist."

I looked up in surprise.

"No, it's not what you think. Marwan consulted Imad only because of his poor appetite and insomnia. I was the one who told the doctor what was really going on. He was shocked to know how serious Marwan's condition was and recommended a young German specialist who opened a clinic in Haifa recently. Marwan might have difficulty facing a friend like Imad with that kind of problem. God have mercy on us! I really don't understand how this other doctor is supposed to help him."

"How do you think I can help? Marwan doesn't trust me with any of his feelings. All he does is toss and turn in his bed, moaning as if he's in pain. He scares me, Aunt Najla!"

"Oh, honey! I'm so sorry things have turned out so bad for you two. Believe me, I know who is behind this sort of witchcraft—an old Turkish woman who lived in this neighborhood for decades and is known to be cursed with an envious eye. Please, Nadia, talk to him about the doctor, will you?"

"I have a better idea. Why don't you ask Dr. Khaldoun to come unannounced one day with his specialist, pretending it is a social call. If Marwan meets him first, he might feel more comfortable."

Aunt Najla stopped in the doorway and stared at me with surprise. "How clever of you! That's a splendid idea, Nadia. I will send a note to him right away."

The moment I shut the door behind her, I ran back to the salon. The envelope was on the side table where I had left it. I counted them. Forty handsomely printed shares, the name of the new bank in bold black letters across the top. What would Marwan do if he knew Uncle Ahmad had given them to me? "Do you have to tell him?" a naughty voice whispered in my mind.

I was straightening the couch when my fingers touched a rough object between the cushions. It was a piece of greasy brown fabric wrapped around and around with black thread. It looked like a dried fig wrapped up in rags. A safety pin pierced the bundle from one side to the other, as if through someone's heart. Oh my dear! I was amazed that such a practical woman as Aunt Najla could still believe in witches and charms. I turned the amulet over, wondering if I should unwrap it. I remembered unwrapping some that Aunt Huda used to leave all around, to find nothing more than a lock of hair, or a slip of paper with senseless scribbling on it.

I slipped Aunt Najla's charm into my pocket. Just in case!!

"My daughter-in-law is not going to a hospital, Dr. Khaldoun." What was Uncle Ahmad doing in my bedroom? Why was he talking about a hospital? An unbearable heat surrounded my whole body and my eyelids were stuck together as if glued. I felt a soothing, cool palm press on my brows. My head was throbbing.

"Nadia, darling!" Aunt Najla's breath brushed my ear. "Do you hear me?" I heard her sob.

"But Ahmad Effendi, your daughter-in-law needs a tonsillectomy immediately. What do you expect me to do?"

"I want you to perform the operation here. You can bring in whatever medical team you choose." Uncle Ahmad's voice grew louder.

"Please, Doctor, don't interrupt me. You know how I feel about hospitals where my family is concerned."

"Have the operation in here, Father?" Marwan's voice broke in. "That is not done anymore. Nadia will be better off at the hospital."

"I don't trust the way they treat a lady there, son, don't you understand?"

"For God's sake, Father, women don't care nowadays if a man sees them lying down in bed. You know only female nurses are allowed to care for them."

"Still, I don't want our Nadia to go through such an experience. She is just a child, and she needs her family around her, not a bunch of strangers from God knows where!"

The doctor came to the side of my bed and pressed his strong fingers into my wrist. "Her fever is very high. I suggest someone come with me to my clinic where I have samples of a new drug that should help."

"Marwan will go with you. When can the operation be performed?"

"Not until her fever goes down and the infection is under control. I will keep an eye on her, Ahmad Effendi, don't worry, and I will consult with a physician friend of mine who has recently arrived from Europe. He will know more about the newest drugs available to help fight this infection."

As the men's voices faded away down the hallway, I thought about all the times I had to lie in bed when my tonsils were inflamed, with only Maria's soft voice to comfort me. I was awakened by Suad when she came in to change my nightgown and sheets. Her eyes were wet with tears as she helped me out of bed to a chair. "Nadia, how could a simple sore throat turn into something this nasty? My father says you are to have an operation. Is that true?" she asked as she tucked in the clean sheets all around me.

I tried to smile to cheer her up.

"Thank God, Nadia, you are awake." Marwan came into the room with a young lady behind him, a tall and heavily built Egyptian woman with friendly dark eyes. Her white dress covered her to the ankles and a thin blue scarf wrapped her head, hiding her brows, ears, and neck. "This is Khadeeja. She is a nurse, and will give you the shots Dr. Khaldoun has prescribed. Three times a day for three days." Marwan placed a package in the nurse's hand and she stepped to my side.

"Hello, Mrs. Rajy. I'm sorry to have to meet you for the first time under these circumstances. I have heard so much about you." Her warm voice was as deep as a man's. She unbuttoned the embroidered cuff of my nightgown and pulled the sleeve up high. As she talked with Suad I felt a light prick on my upper arm. "There you are! Thank you for your cooperation, Mrs. Rajy. You are as sweet and beautiful as everyone in the neighborhood says." Her broad smile lifted my spirits. "Now if you will excuse me, I will be back later for your next shot."

After three days my fever was down, and Dr. Khaldoun announced that the operation could take place Monday at noon. Uncle Ahmad would be the only family member allowed to watch. When he arrived he handed me a lemon twig in full blossom and looked at me closely. "I hope you are not frightened."

"There's nothing to be afraid of. The operation is quite simple. I saw my brother Sami go through it when I was ten or eleven."

"Where?"

"At home. It was done while he was standing on his feet, too. Most of my sisters and brothers were born with bad tonsils. My mother, also."

After Dr. Khaldoun and nurse Khadeeja arrived, we waited in the salon for the surgeon. Dr. Khaldoun turned to me. "We can still send for a hospital bed if you wish to change your mind about standing up." He spoke in a slow monotone as if I were a child who did not fully understand what I was about to go through.

"I will be fine, doctor. You won't be disappointed in me. I would rather be fully conscious and watch Dr. Tabari as he works."

Labeled glass jars and first-aid bottles quivered next to the syringe tray as Khadeeja drove our stainless steel tea cart from the kitchen to the salon. She had draped it with white cloths, transforming it into a sterile service table. Dr. Khaldoun scrutinized each item and then pulled a small envelope from his vest pocket. "This is a sedative, Mrs. Rajy. I want you to place it under your tongue now. This is one of the new medicines that my friend, Dr. Zhurbach, brought from Europe last summer. It is just a muscle relaxant."

I looked at him curiously. "Is he a general practitioner like you?"

"No, he is a psychiatrist, if you know what that means. I met Ralph in medical school in Berlin. He has just recently come to Palestine." His voice faltered for a moment. "He is a Jew. You know, the kind of Jew who is fair and understanding. The kind that I, as an Arab, like to be with." There was an unemotional gaze to his eyes, and he kept on staring at me all the time he talked.

My hunch was right, I thought. This was probably the doctor to whom Marwan was to be referred.

Dr. Tabari arrived right on time. He seemed younger and more relaxed than the two men in gray suits next to him. In his flannel pants and white short-sleeved shirt, he looked as if he were going to watch a tennis match after the operation.

"Hello, Mrs. Rajy. I'm glad you look so well today. Dr. Khaldoun assured me you were in good shape for the operation, but I hope you don't mind if I take a look at your throat before we start."

The smile that came through his bushy mustache was radiant and reassuring. I nodded assent. After he snapped his bulky case open and put on his white gauze mask, a lighted forehead mirror, gloves, and a white coat, only a small part of him was left to be seen.

"Well?" Uncle Ahmad snapped, unable to control his mounting emotions.

"Don't worry, Ahmad Effendi. The infection is gone. But one of her tonsils could cause some trouble. It looks like someone has punctured it, probably when it was still badly infected. That old-fashioned procedure may bring relief, but it always causes trouble when an operation is required. The scar tissue where the tonsil was poked becomes hard as a pebble, and is difficult to remove."

"Perhaps you should not try to remove it then, Doctor. You must spare Nadia any extra pain and distress. She has suffered enough this last week."

"I'm sure I can manage it. You must not worry."

The more I listened to them, the more my heart began to pound. I wished they would stop talking and get the operation over with. My eyes turned to Dr. Khaldoun, but he was looking at his colleague with tightly pressed lips. A dark air of uncertainty hung over our heads.

Uncle Ahmad stood on one side of me and Dr. Khaldoun on the other, holding my arms straight against the wide wooden frame of the door. "Open your mouth as wide as possible, please, Mrs. Rajy. I want you to bear with me for just a few seconds. You will not feel anything once the morphine takes effect." I squeezed my eyes shut and gathered all my strength to keep from jumping as the long needle full of anesthetic punctured my throat again and again. As soon as a numb coolness spread through my tonsils, I heard the clicking scissors cutting into my flesh. I tried to take a deep breath to keep from fainting, but the blood seemed to have drained from my whole body.

"Are you through, Doctor?"

"That was the easy one. We still have to deal with the other."

"I'm afraid you'll have to stop. She's fainting. . . . "

Mist, and then I sank into darkness, steamy darkness.

Several long miserable nights of fever following that hectic tonsil operation had worn me out and I so much wanted one long night of sleep. But
shortly after midnight I was awakened by the heavy shuffling of boots and
sounds of furniture being moved in the apartment below ours.

The Aaron family who lived there could often be heard shouting and
quarreling late at night, but these shrieks and cries were louder than
usual. I sat up, trying to figure out what to do. Marwan's frame heaved
rhythmically under his unruffled covers. The sounds came clearer and
there seemed to be more than just a family quarrel.

The Aarons were a strange family. They had rented both apartments
on the floor below us from the Rajys for more than a decade, yet no
one seemed to know very much about them. The rabbi, his wife, and
their teenage son, Naten, lived in one apartment and the rabbi claimed
he used the second apartment, which faced the Hadar'a Carmel and
had an entrance on the side of the street, to deliver his religious ser-
mons. He always wore the same black clerical robe, and greeted people by nodding his head with vigor, the shoulder-length curled
whiskers bouncing up and down; he would never reach out to shake
hands.

His wife was even weirder than he was. She was rumored to be
mentally ill, and no one in the neighborhood had ever come face to
face with her; she apparently never left the house. No one even knew
her name. She wore nothing but long black dresses.

The other odd thing about this family was their preference for darkness. Every evening around eight o'clock they would switch off their
electric lamps, replacing them with one candle. As Marwan and I
walked back to our apartment some nights after dinner, we would see
through the panels of their glass door the flickering candle light being
carried around like a phantom inside that dark house.

I wrapped a blanket around me, tiptoed out to the landing and
leaned over the cold marble balustrade overlooking the Aarons' landing. A dank pungent stench filled the night air; the doors to both

apartments were wide open, and a crowd of people were rushing about. I saw a large covered truck parked under a street light right across from our main gate. Three or four large men in khaki uniforms wielding heavy sticks were chasing a group of screaming people, forcing them from the apartment down to the waiting vehicle. As the crowd passed under the street light I could see the contorted faces of men, women, and children half covered by large, dark hats. Their clothes were foreign looking, and their large boots clamped on the cement as the uniformed men hustled them into the back of the truck. Within a couple of minutes the truck doors slammed shut and the truck rolled noiselessly down the street, headlights off.

Back in the warmth of my bed, I wondered . . . did the Rajys know what was going on? Or was this the first time something like this had happened? Marwan had never mentioned anything this strange. Did he know about this?

Marwan was gone when I woke up the next morning. Suad was in the kitchen, stirring my milk and cacao pudding. She had been in charge of the cooking, washing, and ironing since I became ill.

"Good morning, Nadia," she called when she heard my footsteps behind her.

"Sorry I overslept. Did you hear the noise last night?" I asked.

"You mean the commotion at the Aarons'? Yes, I heard it," she said indifferently.

"How can you sound so casual?" I looked at her in disbelief. "A crime was committed last night!"

"What 'crime'? That's part of the men's job. We should probably ask Father to tell them to try to be quieter now that you are living above them. Marwan didn't mention anything when I served him his breakfast."

"He slept through the whole thing. But if you had seen those poor people being kicked and shoved into the back of that truck, you wouldn't sound so unconcerned."

Suad brought the warm plate of brown pudding to the breakfast table and pulled my chair out. "Sit down, Nadia, please. It might seem strange to you, coming from a country that has no political conflict, but here we have become used to this kind of violence between the Jewish groups and the British authority ever since the latter put a quota on the flow of Jewish immigrants into Palestine."

"But this is not the same, Suad," I interrupted. "A man is hiding under the Rajys' roof, pretending to be a rabbi, when in fact he seems to be a kidnapper! Does your family want to help someone like that?"

"Oh, dear Nadia! I wish I could answer all your questions. My father and Marwan might be able to tell you more about this delicate matter. To tell you the truth, I don't interfere with the way my father handles his affairs." I had seldom heard her speak in such a serious tone. "You must learn to be tougher and not let such incidents affect you. You won't survive in Palestine if you get upset every time you come face to face with the ugly truth about our lives here. Now cheer up and finish your breakfast. By the way, Dr. Khaldoun sent a note to my mother saying that he will come this evening to visit you and see how you are recovering. He is going to bring his European friend, Dr. Zhurbach, with him. Will you and Marwan be at home?"

I caught my breath. So the psychiatrist would be coming to see Marwan this evening! "Yes, that will be fine. Marwan doesn't want me to go out in the evening for a while yet."

A nagging apprehension filled me after Suad left. What if the doctors, after speaking with Marwan, realized that I was the one they needed to talk to? What if they tried to convince me I must perform *my* marital duty? The old familiar feeling of being trapped began to take hold of me again.

It was almost six, one of those special March evenings when the Mediterranean winds carry the warm breath of the coming spring. The sun seemed unwilling to part from the blazing horizon. I had the feeling I was watching two desperate lovers who were burning themselves out in a slow deliberate ritual. But even my poetic sentiments did nothing to appease the anguish I felt as I realized that in another hour Drs. Khaldoun and Zhurbach would arrive, supposedly for a casual visit.

Poor Marwan, I thought! He had no idea that it was his mother who had arranged this friendly visit by the family doctor, who would present his colleague just as a friend, in the hope that Marwan would later voluntarily confide more to a stranger than he did to Dr. Khaldoun.

Even now, as I saw Marwan fall into the trap, I still wanted to believe that he would refrain from forcing himself on me. He had been quite aloof for the last few weeks and had kept his distance as he had promised. But now those men were sneaking in on us. Oh, I hoped

Marwan was as much against that sex stuff as I was! Even so, would those highly qualified doctors convince him to go ahead and do it?

And what about me? Would they have a special assignment for me too?

∾℃

"I want you to be happy and beautiful tonight, Nadia. Don't look so edgy and nervous. Imad is a very interesting and fine man, and this is a chance for you to know him in a nonprofessional situation." Marwan seemed to be in a happy mood. He was probably flattered, thinking that those two important people were really after his company.

"Is he married?" The question popped out as if somebody else wanted to know.

"He was. To a German lady. She left him a year ago and took their five-year-old daughter with her. Imad doesn't talk about that sad episode easily. Arab men do not discuss their wives. It is taboo among them, and Imad comes from an especially conservative background."

Imad grew up in the Rajys' neighborhood and became active politically from an early age. He was popular as a family practitioner and could be a big charmer, but all of a sudden he could turn into an arrogant and stubborn man. My husband held him in high esteem for his gratuitous services in the city, but he was at odds with him politically.

Marwan rushed to answer the door. When the greetings ended I took a deep breath and stepped out. Marwan was talking with Imad as a stocky red-haired man was leafing through the music notes piled on top of my piano. Everything I had expected to see in a young German collapsed as the freckled face turned to me while I shook hands with Imad, who towered over the three of us.

"Nadia, this is Dr. Ralph Zhurbach, the friend Imad has spoken so much about."

"Welcome, Dr. Zhurbach, we are delighted to have you with us." My voice squeaked like that of a trapped mouse.

"It is my honor, Madame. You are held in great esteem by my friend Imad." He lowered his round curly head and touched the back of my hand with a light kiss. "Excuse me, Madame, if I use my English; Arabic is an intimidating language for us newcomers. I was told that you speak both French and English. And now, permit me to congratulate you on your distinguished fine taste in this elegant house that seems touched by the magic of music and beauty."

His eloquence lifted my spirit as I observed his square frame in its too-tight clothing, topped with a crown of hair that shimmered like burnished copper.

I liked him instantly.

"Please, come in and make yourselves comfortable." I flung the door to the salon wide open and switched the light on. The gloomy mood that had engulfed me all afternoon vanished, giving way to an inexplicable sense of excitement. I left the men to settle down and I switched on the radio before I left for the kitchen. The soft notes of a Beethoven sonata soothed my troubled heart.

But it did not seem to have the same effect on the men, who were involved in a heated argument, more like adversaries than friends.

I placed the serving cart next to Marwan and sat down. He poured a cup of tea for me and then served wine to Imad; Ralph chose a beer, and seemed to watch every move around him, especially Marwan's. Imad and Marwan began exchanging stories about their families and their childhood years. "So you were not born in Haifa, Marwan?" Ralph inquired.

"No, I was born in Acre, which was the formal location of the Turkish officers and representatives for the whole Mediterranean front until the Allies took over. Haifa was just a small town on the bay at that time; it was only about ten years ago that it started taking the shape of a city."

"As I recall, the Rajys didn't move to Haifa until after World War I," Imad volunteered. "But apparently they were already known around here because one of their grandfathers had donated a large piece of land to the city"

"Yes, I couldn't believe it when my father told me a few years ago that the Bourje Mosque on top of that little hill around the corner was built on our own land. Imagine how valuable that land has become now. What an absurd thing to do!"

"My God, man, you don't sound like a Rajy at all tonight!" Imad seemed quite at ease.

"Nor would I like to be one if all they did was to spend their lives in search of a religious mythology. Would you want your ancestors to be such zealots, Imad?"

"Let's keep our discussion in perspective, please. Those people were well appreciated in their own time. To the Rajys!" Imad raised his half-full glass and the rest of us cheered in response. "I've met some relatives who still consider the Rajys Moroccans, even though the family first arrived here more than two hundred years ago."

"Oh! How interesting," Ralph commented. "It's fascinating the way human beings keep on roaming around and changing identities."

"To tell you the truth, Ralph, I will never be able to understand how religion motivates some groups of people to uproot themselves from their countries and travel for thousands of miles to spread their faith. Look at our family, they belonged to the Shadhiliyah movement, a Sufi order, and moved eastward with Mecca and the holy land in mind. They finally came to Palestine to sink new roots. It is not as if we don't have enough people belonging to different religions and denominations, including your forefathers, who believe this miserable land is holy and therefore they would be closer to God."

"Come on, Marwan, be fair," Imad reproached. "Don't blame your ancestors for the bad luck of this country. In spite of all the friction among the different Muslim denominations, this area remained a peaceful haven for centuries before this malignant Western plot hit it this century."

"Where do the Rajys come from originally?" Ralph asked Marwan, apparently oblivious to the hint in his friend's statement.

"Well, I've heard several conflicting stories about the precise origin of this large tribe that seems to have dwelled for centuries along the southern shores of the Mediterranean. They left their traces in most of the important ports of North Africa, from Tunisia all the way to Izmir in western Turkey, trading mostly in finely aged cheeses, pickled products, raisins, nuts, and spices. The tribe came to number tens of thousands," said Marwan.

"What kind of ties exist between such a widely scattered number of relatives?" Ralph's bright eyes shifted between Marwan and me.

"Not many, I'm afraid. Except for business communications among the family patriarchs in neighboring locations, we know of only one intermarriage, which took place at the turn of the century. Nadia's and mine is the second."

"Excuse me, Marwan, if I seem nosy, but how closely are you two related?" Dr. Imad's professional instinct seemed to override his innate discretion.

"Not too closely, by any means," I said.

"All I recall is that my grandfather, whose name was Marwan too, used to reminisce about a place called Mahdia, always in a confusing story about his great-grandfather, Sheikh Ibrahim ben-Marwan, who apparently did not survive the odyssey of the migration to the Holy Land from Mahdia. He was buried somewhere deep in the Sinai. Two years later his survivors, six sons, their wives and children, made it to Acre." Marwan was silent for a few seconds. "Holy Land, indeed!" His sense of irony finally got the best of him.

"My father used to talk with great admiration about your grandfather, who was the imam of that old mosque up the hill, spending every Friday teaching and praying. You must be proud of that man, and so happy to have known him."

"I don't know, Imad, that depends. I can't see any value in the kind of religious zeal that he and his ancestors were hooked on and had to face torture and persecution for. You're probably well aware that Islam has spread over foreign lands in many forms. None of these seem to have reached very far beneath the surface of Islam's basic doctrine. Instead, most of them emphasized the day-to-day rituals while the rest went as far as wrongly advocating harsh interpretations that have nothing to do with the spirit of Islam. Actually, I believe the followers of the original leaders were more like mercenaries who made of religion a very profitable business."

"My, my, Marwan! Aren't we being too radical now?" Imad interrupted with irony. "I don't see how a guy who was raised in a foreign Catholic school could be a fair critic in that domain. I am curious, though, to know how you came to this point of view against these denominations. It could be easy to propose but hard to prove."

"Because when you let your mind be exposed to other religions and doctrines, you become more aware and appreciative of your own values. I was able to learn more about the intellectual substance of the Koran concerning, among other things, freedom of all faiths, human rights, justice, and evolution. I am not interested in the recommended list of dull readings about men's superiority over women or daily dieting, hygiene, and sex rituals." I had the feeling Marwan was scoring well.

"That's not fair, Marwan. You don't expect simple people to live by such philosophical abstracts. You have to be fair."

"You are right, Doctor, you just said what Marwan was trying to express all along," I said. "To those simple chieftains who were probably self-taught sheikhs, their religious readings provided practical wisdom. It is possible they could have left their original home for economic reasons ... simply to find more fertile land." I felt the blood rush up to my brows as the three of them looked intently at me.

I had to speak. "Do you think, Dr. Zhurbach, that the Jewish invasion of this country is based on this theory? I mean, that the reasons are economic?"

"You could be right, Mrs. Nadia. In spite of its religious umbrella, this move is in my view mostly economic. You see? The Jews have the capacity to survive and prosper almost anywhere in the world because of their long experience in dealing in political powers. Yet, it's high time they win their own state. It is not a joke to be a second-class citizen eternally."

"I wonder, though, how they have come to the conclusion that Palestine is their best choice. We all know that this has been debated for decades. I remember reading that many other choices have been suggested." That was Marwan. What he had just said came as a surprise to me.

"I don't know either, Marwan. To me, this decision together with the rigid way it was projected is a disaster for all concerned. But to put things in perspective, I believe the leaders had to take any option that could win the support of the Allies—Great Britain and the United States—and of the Jewish powers—Zionists, the clergy, the orthodox, and the Jewish secret resistance. No one asked ordinary people like you and me," said Dr. Zharbach.

Something in the analyses I had heard until now did not fit. Why would the Allies support such a policy and use force to apply it? For centuries the Jews had been subjected to incredible prejudice at the hands of those same powers. What could be the reason behind that shift?

"I don't see how such a plan could work. From the standpoint of the Jews, it sounds too good to be true," I said. Seeing the shocked look in Imad's dark eyes, I hastened to explain. "Excuse me, Dr. Khaldoun, let me finish. It is obvious those big empires are not doing this because of their love for the Jewish people. They want something in return from them, right?"

"What is the difference, Mrs. Rajy?" Imad said. "To us Arabs it could be devastating if not fatal to wait until the Jews come to that discovery. I hope you will permit me to be frank with you; I do not believe your theory is valid."

"But I do, Imad," Ralph said. "What is more, a large number of my people agree with me. We certainly need to have a state of our own, but not one that is based on misleading factors, prejudice, and wars. In Europe we are split against the decision to establish our state in this country. Hundreds of Jewish families are tricked and shipped here by force. I wonder whether any of you are aware of the horrible traps those Jews end up in when, after selling all their belongings to buy their way out of Europe to America, they find themselves in the hands of some mysterious people or on the shores of this unwelcoming land instead." Emotions were high, Ralph's words were powerful.

Oh, yes, I was aware, indeed! It hasn't yet been twenty-four hours since I watched our neighbor the Rabbi and his son help abductors shove those miserable people into the back of that truck which fled into the dark night.

Marwan ignored Ralph's statement and addressed Imad. "Do you think that if we take to violence, we are going to solve the problem?"

"Can you suggest a kind of defense that replaces violence, Marwan? Our nationalists have no other option. They have to fight back."

"With what? What kind of arms do they have against the superpowers' fleets, air force, and new weapons that support their enemy?"

"You will never understand, Marwan! That's because you happen to be one Palestinian who could turn your back on this country any time he pleases. You have the means to go anywhere in the world and live happily ever after. But ninety percent of the people who have lived off this fertile land for centuries do not have that luxury. You have a case here where a bitter enemy is threatening to take their land, the only source of every drop of blood in their veins. What do you expect them to do?"

"Sorry, my friend, I should be the last one to be asked for advice on that matter. I can tell you one thing, though; I wouldn't want to be around when the scourge of war ravages this land."

A solemn silence fell over us as Imad and Marwan started smoking again while Ralph slumped deep into his soft chair, his eyes shut and his freckled face as expressionless as that of a sphinx.

6

April 1936

"Thanks for coming to meet me in this nasty weather, Suad." She and our young housemaid, Warrood, were waiting for me as they did every Monday and Thursday when I left my math class at the Technicom Institute a few blocks uphill from our home. We leaned against each other as we walked under two umbrellas and headed toward the narrow pathway of the campus. Except for the students, the streets were almost empty. Not one car passed us, and police officers stood on each corner in pairs or in groups of three.

"I've never seen these streets so quiet. Is it because of the storm, or is something wrong, Suad?"

"As usual, one minute we are on top of the world and the next minute we are down under," Suad joked. Then she became more serious. "I'm not sure. The bombing yesterday in Jaffa was pretty drastic, I'm afraid. Um Saad told us when she came back from the bakery that the British had blown up a large part of Jaffa's old dwellings and the surrounding suburban area, killing more than a hundred workers."

"Oh, I've heard about that area; it was on the news all through the weekend. But I do not understand why the authorities took such rough measures against that particular neighborhood. Unless it's because Tel Aviv happens to be too close and such slums could be a nuisance to the settlers there!" Suad appeared not to hear the last part of my comment.

"I recall hearing that many of the people who have settled there recently were refugees from rural areas in Palestine. They had been evicted from their farms by absentee landlords who sold their lands for a high price. The British and the Arab land owners have had a number of clashes with these peasants, and it's clear they are armed. That's probably the reason the authorities are clamping down on them so hard. They'll put someone in jail for ten years just for carrying a knife."

Um Saad, Warrood's mother, was the Rajys' housemaid. The daughter of a poor peasant family, she had been sent to work for the Rajys when she was ten. She later married one of her relatives who worked as a porter at Uncle Ahmad's storehouse. The couple had settled into a two-room basement apartment under the Rajy home, where they raised four daughters and three sons.

"My brothers were sent home from school shortly after they arrived this morning, Miss Nadia," Warrood's voice cut in. "They were told not to come back because this time the strike was going to spread all over."

"This is not the first time a strike has taken place in our country, nor will it be the last," Suad said. "Nothing is going to happen, Warrood. Don't sound so serious." Suad patted the girl on the head and turned to me. "Did you enjoy your math class today? I saw your teacher leaving the room while we were waiting. He looks so young!"

"Don't let his looks fool you. He's a tough teacher. And I'm the only girl in class. As you can understand, I hate to make mistakes in front of all those watchful eyes. He's fair, though, and the competition in class is very stimulating."

"I'm so glad you have the freedom to study before you start a family, Nadia. My parents can't wait to have grandchildren!"

I felt the blood rush to my ears, but managed a calm smile. "I'm not sure Marwan wants to have children. Not so soon, anyway. He is very concerned about what's going to happen in Palestine."

She gazed at me in bewilderment. "Oh, dear Nadia. You really know very little about these matters. Having children has nothing to do with what Marwan thinks or wants. Only God knows who will have children and who won't. When he wants you to have children, he is not going to ask either of you."

We moved to the kitchen to have a cup of tea. Suad held my cold hands between her palms and gazed down into my eyes. "I don't want you to worry, Nadia. We have been living under unpredictable circumstances ever since I can remember. Yet, as you can see, nothing has happened to us."

I lowered my eyes, trying to find the right words to tell her the real reason for my fear. "The strike is not the reason for my dilemma, Suad. Your brother's reaction is what worries me. I hate to think what he might do if people turn to violence as he has been predicting. He seems to be possessed by a haunting fear that something awful is going to happen to him in this country."

"Is that all? Don't pay any attention to him, Nadia. Marwan has been crying wolf for years. Believe me, honey, in case of emergency he will be the last to actually leave Palestine."

Oh, Suad! How little you know about that brother of yours! I refrained from telling her about the changes in his schedule and behavior that had taken place since the two doctors had visited our house. In addition to the twice-a-week therapy sessions, under the pretense of extra work duties, he had started drinking stronger liquor steadily.

"Well, there is something strange in his character. One minute he's sweet and sure of himself, the next he's harsh and aloof. Especially with company."

"That's because he loves you so much, he doesn't want to share you with anyone." She was not joking.

"What do you mean 'share'? Do you think he owns me?"

"You know what I mean. Men have had the right to control us ever since time began. Probably for good reason, too. Can you imagine being on your own without their support?"

"I think we are born stronger than men," I countered. "Who told you that we cannot be on our own and do remarkable things? I feel capable of challenging men in any area. I want to finish school and get a job."

Suad laughed as if she had heard a joke.

"I'm serious, Suad. Your father knows that, too. That's what I like about him. He understands me better than my own family."

"Oh, I know he wouldn't deny you any favor. But he would never let you go out to work on your own. He makes enough money to provide for all the family, especially for you. He knows Marwan can't give you all the things you deserve and he's not happy about that."

"Your father is no different from any father who wants his children to have wings of their own. Maybe if Marwan were less spoiled and had more strength of character there would be less friction between them, and Uncle Ahmad might listen more closely to his advice on matters about the bank."

I crossed the hall and turned on the radio to see whether there would be news of the strike. After a few minutes the music was interrupted by the sound of Big Ben. Before the echo faded, a deep Arabic voice filled the lounge.

"Since the regrettable incident Wednesday evening in the peaceful suburbs of Jaffa, the authorities have stepped in to put an end to the bloody insurrection started by a group of outlaws who appear to have been supported by intruders from the outside. The incident has been reported to the Arab Higher Committee, which has issued a statement calling for an end to the violence."

The sound of the doorbell broke through the speaker's voice on the radio. The door of my apartment was pushed ajar and Warroud's thick-curled head came to sight. "Sorry to interrupt, Miss Suad," the young girl's eyes were filled with concern, "the whole family is waiting for you two to join them for dinner."

"At this early hour?" Suad inquired. It was barely three o'clock.

"Master Ahmad and your husband too, Miss Nadia." Warroud continued while still keeping most of her body outside the apartment.

Taken aback by the news that her father had closed his shop and come home that early, Suad stood up, "Come Nadia, let's go."

The whole family sat around the dinner table. Uncle Ahmad stood at the head of the table and served chicken and potatoes onto the plates that were passed down to him. Everyone was chattering in loud, agitated voices. I was relieved to see Marwan talking with his younger brothers about the new political development "I have some good news for you, Nadia." He whispered into my ear when we were halfway through dinner.

Excitement mounted inside me as I followed him back to the apartment. My arms were loaded with the gray files he had brought home with him. He went straight to his file cabinet, unlocked it, and then turned to me. "These are important documents Ali Ibrahim wants me to keep here until we come back."

"What do you mean 'come back'? Are we going somewhere?" I asked, happy he sounded unusually excited. His back was turned toward me as I was kneeling in front of his file cabinet and making room for the documents.

"We're going to Egypt on our honeymoon."

"What honeymoon? I did not know you were planning on a honeymoon!"

There was calm in his eyes, the calm of a dark pool of water. He finally locked the file cabinet and turned around to face me. "The Board of Managers in Jerusalem finally granted me my long over-due vacation. They probably figured out the bank will be closed because of the strike. You don't want to stay here and live in a state of siege?"

"So I am the last one to know about my honeymoon! You and your board decide when and how I will be shipped away for that special event, is that it?" My frustration had the best of me. "How long have you been keeping this from me, Marwan? One month? Two months? I may have been stupid enough to think you are more considerate than most men around here. Are decisions your specialty? Women can do nothing but bow their heads and follow orders." I whirled around furiously and took to the hall. "I am going nowhere with you!"

The whole apartment shook when I slammed the bedroom door. To this day I remember how much better I felt, how all it takes sometimes is slamming a door.

The days dragged on heavy and fearful. It had been ten days since the Arab Higher Committee declared a General Strike with the aim of halting Jewish immigration, it first settled into the big cities, then through the country. The uprising raged like wildfire burning into every corner of life: schools, banks, shops, clubs, restaurants were all immobilized. Eventually, the city's activity ground to a halt and, in the absence of responsible leadership, the people were left to struggle for survival on their own. The same thing was happening all over the country, according to the news.

In the few months I had lived in Haifa, I had learned much about the destructive effect of the strikes the Palestinian nationalists had used as an economic weapon against the British. I knew I had to learn more about politics in general and especially about Palestinian politics, now that I had come to live there as a citizen. It was difficult, however, to develop a clear point of view about what was happening; I heard so many contradictory reports and opinions from the people around me. All I could do was to listen and watch carefully, combining new information with common sense and my instinctive reactions to events.

As the strike gained momentum I found myself applauding the rebels—silently, as this position was far from that of my in-laws and even farther from Marwan's. He was willing, however, to bring me all the books and materials on Palestinian politics recommended by his boss, a consummate politician. This national awareness, so new to me, gratified me and provided me with a sense of purpose and importance and a yearning for knowledge and action.

During the strike we lacked nothing. The family's ample storage room had an abundant supply of food. Fresh meat and produce were obtained by whatever means possible from Abou Maarouf and his son. Abou Maarouf worked most of his life at the Rajy stores. He and his son were the only ones who stayed around after the strike began. I spent most of the daytime with my in-laws. Their home was full of activity. Marwan kept up his working routine at our apartment, joining me from time to time. We heard news, read papers and magazines. We also played cards and, occasionally, a game of backgammon. Invariably, we ended up arguing about the upheaval that gathered force all over the country and became more violent by the day. I looked forward to such political arguments, especially when two close friends of my brother-in-law Farid, Darweesh and Ameen, were visiting. These teenage friends seemed to have strong ties with the nationalists and became a valuable source of news for me concerning the impact of the strike on the poor, both in the countryside and in the cities. The press never mentioned them.

Halfway through one meal, Darweesh's agitated voice interrupted Uncle Ahmad's argument that the country's resources were being wasted since nothing was reaching the cities where the money to support the peasants was. "No, Uncle Ahmad, there are good reasons why very little of our peasants' produce is reaching the cities. You see, not even an ounce of our produce should get to the enemy's market. It is sorely needed by the volunteer fighters and their families."

"And you think that is wise, young man? What happens when the next crop is due in a few months? Who is going to give them money for their crops?" Uncle Ahmad sounded like a father giving advice to those young rebels.

"You don't have to ask, Father," Marwan interjected. "They will rob us. They will start with you businessmen and finish with us bankers."

"Well, I don't mind giving away everything I have to a successful national movement, Darweesh." Uncle Ahmad continued and avoided Marwan's angry gaze. Are you confident that the revolt will succeed?"

"Yes, I am, sir. But we could all be confident if, as you said, if all our power, dedication, and money went into this revolt." He looked at all of us, not just at Uncle Ahmad.

"Oh, we could indeed, son. That is, if our sole enemy were the outsider. As I see it, the threat doesn't come from the British, the French, or the Germans alone. It comes from inside this country and from all the countries surrounding it. Do you agree?" Uncle Ahmad answered alluding to factions within the country and the governments of other Arab countries.

"I don't, sir!" Ameen's pale green eyes were alert and defiant. "You are talking about the regimes of these countries, Uncle Ahmad, not the people. We have heroes from the whole region who are fighting among our nationalists. Did you know that?"

"What people and what heroes?" Marwan shrieked before his father could answer. "The couple of hundred drifters who crossed our borders infiltrating the nationalists' camps for God knows what reason? Or, are you talking about those Arabs who have been trained, armed, and supported by the Russians and Germans?"

"Calm down, Marwan," Uncle Ahmad ordered. "These young men have just as much right to believe in whatever they wish as the rest of us here do. Neither of us, I reckon, has the means to prove the other wrong."

"It doesn't do the young generation any good to build high hopes on untrue factors, father. They are the future of our Arab world and their lives are at stake here." Marwan had stopped eating, his face taut and angry. "Where is the united front that can protect them from becoming victims of their own adventure? Look at the struggling Palestinians who, thanks to the feudal system that's still protected by our leaders, are the majority and do not even own the land they toil. The whole work force of this country: peasants, ordinary workers, women, children, just about everyone, is poorly paid. They will all be bled to death before this irrational upheaval ends."

"But this majority is beyond hope anyway, my friend," Darweesh responded, "they have nothing to lose. And we, the young generation, as you call us, are willing to fight, regardless of whether we are weak or strong. No matter what the older generation does, this country will not be given up."

An outbreak of heavy shooting split the air for a full hour during our dinner that evening. Later I could hear the agony in the voices of the people who had gathered at the foot of the slope near our home. They were waiting to hear the news through the windows of the privileged few who owned radios and felt obligated to increase the volume at prime news time. At eight, BBC News repeated a list of emergency regulations, citing a new set of emergency laws against civil disobedience and armed insurrection: six years imprisonment for possessing a revolver; twelve years imprisonment for possessing a bomb; five years in jail plus hard labor for possessing twelve bullets. In defiance, shouts of "Allah O Akbar," and "victory to the Arabs," filled the air.

Then the husky voice of an Arab commentator who had lately become quite popular, broadcasting his political news from a new station called "The Arab Voice," rose in the air, strong and distinct.

"Good evening, friends. This is a special report which we were advised to bring to you without delay. A few hours ago hundreds of armed men joined the bands of nationalists in our mountains. This move by rebels from neighboring countries, Lebanon, Syria, and the Trans-Jordan, came as no surprise. It is the fruit of a long and slow battle that arose from the oppression of the Arab peasants and workers under Ottoman bureaucracy. There is no doubt that this act of solidarity is an important step in showing the British and their collaborators how serious this revolt is. Let me remind you, my friends, of a significant event that took place in Tel Aviv less than two weeks ago. On April 23, Weizmann, the leader of the Zionist movement, gave a speech to a Jewish audience in which he described the Arab-Zionist struggle as *a struggle between destructive and constructive forces,* thereby exposing the true face of Zionist forces. These forces are an instrument of colonialism on the eve of the armed clash. This report proves how committed the British are to handing over the colonialist heritage of Palestine to the Zionist movement by throwing all their weight into supporting that movement and securing its growth. Here we have an empire that has forced itself on many peoples, and especially on the Arab world. It is the wish of this station to declare its full support of all that have thus suffered, all the way to the day of victory. . . . "

This astonishing and exciting announcement was greeted by a triumphant end and prayerful clamor, "Allah O Akbar!"

"Sorry, Marwan; I didn't expect you to be doing this here. How stupid of me to think tea is what you need," I said as I purposefully took a cup of tea to him. As usual, he had secluded himself again.

"Please, Nadia, don't assume this attitude. I can explain."

"Explain what? Your secret drinking? The medicines you have hidden in this damned file cabinet? Your notorious visits to the clinic run by Imad's friend? You can't hide all these secrets living with me and surrounded by your big family."

"I have had it up to here with this nosy family! Everything you're accusing me of is a result of their interference."

"That's not true; your family worships you, though you certainly don't deserve it. I am not responsible for any of your troubles, and you know it. Do you really think that alcohol would bring us closer together?"

"Can't you understand how I feel when you lie so close to me in bed, and yet I can't touch you? All your attention goes to the family, to your hobbies, and now to politics." He picked up his glass and handed it to me. "Have a little sip, Nadia, please!"

The first thing that occurred to me was to turn away and run, but he was closer to the door. "No thank you. Look Marwan, how I fill my time has nothing to do with how we act toward each other. If I am destined to live in this country, I'd better learn about its problems. It's important to know what really is going to happen now that the strike has been so effective. It might even change the dynamics of the conflict."

"Wishful thinking! I can tell you what will really happen! This country is marching to its ruin no matter what. Some day, and that won't be far from now, you'll find out how right I am." He moved with unsteady steps closer to me. "Come on, Nadia, let's go to our bedroom and forget about politics."

"You go, Marwan." I stepped aside, my heart racing with fear. "Something happened in downtown Haifa earlier. The BBC has said nothing about it yet. I want to hear what the new station might say. Do you realize how lucky we are to be able to hear another voice besides that of the BBC? How can we be objective if we hear only half of the story?"

"So, now the BBC isn't good enough for you anymore! Now you trust this obscure station believing that it's pro-Arab. You may not know that it's run by the Germans who are interested only in getting back at Britain. The Arabs here are just a tool—no more, no less. I don't trust either the British or the Germans. Those superpowers need pawns for their game, honey, and the Arabs are it. And they're both after the destruction of those ill-fated nationalists. I'm sorry you have adopted such a futile position. You're still too young to appreciate my way of thinking. I hate to see you involve yourself in the problems of this damned country so much that you refuse to discuss other options like leaving, going on a honeymoon, or at least visiting your family. Can't you see I'm worried about you. Let us go to Beirut for only a little while, it's almost six months since you've seen your family. Don't you miss them?"

"Oh, I do!" I moaned, not sure whether he was sobering up or losing his mind.

"Well, then!" He came over to me. "Do you want me to arrange your trip? My father knows a trustworthy driver who can see that you arrive safely at your father's house. How about it?" He followed closely as I moved away from him; the stench of alcohol on his breath and on his skin turned my stomach. His reddened eyes were moving from side to side and the tone of his voice was getting harsh.

"I can't leave all of you here and go, but we can all go and spend the coming Adha there," I said.

"I might be able to go with you if that would make you feel better."

"Well, I think we had better wait, and stay with the rest of the family."

"Let's go to bed now, Nadia, please!" He swayed as he grabbed at my wrist, trying to pull me down the hall.

"Let me go, Marwan. You seem to have drunk too much this evening."

A strange giggle escaped his lips. "I wonder what my parents would do if they knew that their favorite doctor and his recommended colleague prescribed the whiskey as a cure for me."

This statement stunned me. Could Imad and Ralph be the reason for Marwan's excessive drinking? Marwan didn't give me time to think. He suddenly threw his arms around me, crushing my body against his chest.

"Let go of me, Marwan, you're hurting me. Please let me go!" I felt as though I had to flee, but I was too weak to do it.

"No, I'm not going to. You are driving me crazy! Dr. Ralph says if I keep living with you like this, I may end up in a sanitarium. Is that what you want?" His fingernails cut through flesh as he dug down the neckline of my nightgown. I pushed him away from me and ran back to the lounge and locked myself in. I was gripped by awful pain. I could not see at all.

It was a sad May morning. The fog rolled in from the bay, bringing with it the sharp salt smell of the sea and the promise of a warm summery day.

The limousine arrived, and the whole family gathered to say good-bye to Suad and me. Yes! Suad was my only escort on my *Raddit al-Ajr* visit to Beirut—the bride's first visit to her parents, which is traditionally a gracious exchange of visits between the two families of the newlyweds and as lavish as their wedding. But this farewell party was as doleful as a funeral. That traditional visit meant a great deal to people of the Rajy's status. And that opportunity should have been as popular, costly and festive as the wedding party Nadia got from her inlaws. The son had brought shame on his family by failing his duties as a husband. His bride is going on her special trip back to her parents with bruises over her body and a broken heart instead of a baby in her arms or inside her belly.

Aunt Najla clung to me in a long anxious hug; this was the first time I'd ever seen her give way to her emotions. "I'm very sad that you have to leave under these grim circumstances, Nadia! God knows how guilty I feel to let you go burdened by all the pain we have caused you."

Uncle Ahmad kissed the top of my head. "Forgive me, my child, for letting you down. This trip should be taking place with the dignity you deserve. Let us pray this dark cloud will soon disperse. Then with God's will I shall make it up to you." He turned to Suad. "Remember, my daughter, you will be representing all of us. Don't forget the envelope I gave you; be sure to hand it to your Uncle Kareem as soon as you arrive. And take good care of Nadia. Give her all the things she needs. I don't want her to ask favors of anybody there. You understand?"

So, another envelope of money was on its way to the father of the bride!

My heart went out to that generous man. His instinctive sense of obligation stretched far beyond his household. Many times I had seen him go out of his way to help needy cousins and relatives. My father had abused him enough and I didn't want Uncle Hassam to have to buy me this kind of trip.

When our suitcases were all loaded, Marwan pulled a large packet out of his coat pocket. "Here! Both passports, Ali Ibrahim's address and telephone number, and a recommendation letter to the rebel authorities from him. It is not likely that anybody would stop you, but just in case. After the crazy thing the British did last night, arresting sixty of the leaders who supported the revolt, God knows how desperate those fighters could get. How long are you going to stay there?"

Suad took the packet and threw her arms around him for a brief hug. "Oh, probably two or three weeks. Don't worry, everything will be fine. Write to us. We will want to know how things are going at home."

"Well Nadia, the trip is, after all, taking place." He walked with me to the gate. He walked with his head lowered. Anger seethed in him.

The elderly driver guided the car out of the city through unfamiliar back roads where the long strike had left its ugly mark of decay piled up in the corners. Soon we were on the highway heading north.

"Good morning, ladies," the driver said without turning his head. "I am Hadj Uthman. It is my wish that you enjoy this journey and not have any worries about your safety. I do this trip almost daily. If you want me to stop for anything, please let me know."

"Thank you, Hadj." Suad turned to me. "How do you feel now, Nadia? Would you like to have some tea? I have it right here." It was clear she was concerned more about my emotional condition than the discomfort of my usual car sickness.

"Oh, Suad! I'm sorry my problems follow you everywhere. I don't know what I'd do without you!"

"You know you don't have to apologize to me. You are not alone, and these problems are not simply yours only. At home we all feel guilty because Marwan is making things so difficult for you. My mother is extremely worried about the whole thing. It amazes us how a girl who is barely seventeen could bear this burden without complaint."

I had the feeling she was aware of more than Marwan's bad temper and hostile relations with most of the family. Could he have opened up to her? "You seem troubled, Suad. Have you talked to Marwan lately?"

She shook her head. "I didn't have to. Mother told me about the bruises she saw on your arms. I could never imagine that something that cruel would happen to a girl when she got married, especially at the hands of someone as peaceful and refined as my brother Marwan!"

"I don't know if Aunt Najla wanted you to know the whole truth about Marwan's behavior toward me, but I think you should. In a way she shares the responsibility of what Marwan has been driven to do."

"My mother? How?"

"She is always pushing him on me, urging him to do his duty as a husband. She once went as far as to tell him that the bride could be taken away if this problem dragged on too long. 'People are curious as to why you are not pregnant yet,' she said. She even arranged for him to see a doctor without telling him about it. I don't know whether I am to be blamed for refusing to let him touch me. I feel that it is my right not to be touched. You know I wasn't aware of such obligations when this marriage was decided by our parents. I want you to know how I feel about this complicated situation, Suad. You are the only one I can turn to. Now that your mother is openly taking Marwan's side, which is understandable, I can't turn to her as I could before."

"I'm here for you, Nadia. You know that. But do you really doubt my mother's intentions? She loves you so very much."

"I know that, believe me. You see, people like your mother who have been raised to give in to every one of their husband's whims are not likely to understand how I feel. They could never accept that I have the right to prevent my husband from violating my body. To people who have been brought up to think like this, a good wife is only a submissive wife; that's all."

The car stopped suddenly at a gas station on the corner of a huge citrus grove. We were so engrossed in our discussion that we had not been aware of entering the big old gate of Acre. Half an hour later we reached Nakoorah, the frontier chosen by the Allies to separate Palestine from Lebanon. We stopped a few yards from a barrier blocking the road. Directly beyond it an armored tank stood at the center of the road facing in our direction. The blue enamel stop sign fixed on the side of a high stone pillar to the left was written in both Arabic and English. The place was deserted now; our car was the only one in line.

"We have to wait here," Hadj Uthman said, sitting calmly behind his wheel. "Be sure to have your passports ready; the officer in charge will come soon."

A knock on the window soon confirmed that statement. "Passports, please." Dark, tall, and lean with a hint of arrogance in his bearing, the uniformed man took a swift look at the inside of the car.

The long thin fingers leafed with deliberate slowness through our passports and lingered on my exit permit. The man paid special attention to our faces and photos. "Where is the husband of this minor? And what is the purpose of this trip, if I may ask? Shopping, I suppose. Your family must be very rich to send you across the border for that. What kind of currency are you carrying?"

"We are going to visit close relatives, Nadia's parents," Suad stuttered nervously, unable to continue.

"Well?" he snapped in coarse Arabic that was heavily flavored with English, "how much money do you have on you?"

"Um. I don't know. Enough for a couple of weeks' visit, I guess." Her hands shook as she groped for her purse in an attempt to find the two envelopes her father had given her.

But he suddenly changed his mind and pounded his fist on the side of the car, yelling at Hadj to open the trunk for inspection. Finally he lifted the barrier and let us out. It took us a few moments to recover our wits and breathe freely. "My God, what a scare!" I managed a pale smile. "It was much easier when we crossed this border last November on the wedding trip. Is it because of the strike?"

"Oh, no! This officer was really different, and I think it's not the same with only women in the car. But this time we are women alone. I have never crossed this border without my father or some of my brothers."

"If you excuse me, Miss," Hadj interrupted. "That man is not of the immigration corps that was in charge before this revolt. He is one of the quasi-agents in an undercover Jewish force trained to do police work. To replace the large number of Arabs who were on strike, the British put Jewish men in uniform. They are using them to gain control of the situation."

In another few minutes the crossing process had to be repeated at the Lebanese checkpoint. Carts loaded with fresh vegetables, fruit, and all sort of food appeared as soon as our car reached a wooden kiosk with a big stop sign. Instead of a barrier, two uniformed men with their guns planted at their sides stood on guard on either side of the kiosk. Not far to the right was a long gray structure with small screened windows and one wide-open door. There was no flag, but the whole roof of the structure and the sides of the kiosk were painted with two long red streaks separated by a white one: the colors of the Lebanese banner. A white enamel sign nailed to the trunk of a huge oak tree read: "Welcome to Lebanon" in big Arabic letters above smaller French ones.

Hadj Uthman took care of the entry procedure and we were on our way again in about half an hour. Marwan, the strike, and all the marital problems had been left behind. My mind now drifted ahead to other problems that might be waiting for me at my parents'. Very suddenly, I felt a sting of guilt for dreading a visit to the dear old house that contained everything I treasured in my whole life. My memories, secrets, aspirations, and childhood dreams were all embossed on the majestic walls of that beautiful house. The brothers and sisters I had missed so much were still there. So were the parents who, despite our differences, could not be replaced by any surrogates, not even by Uncle Ahmad and his loving wife. After all, I owed them everything I had inherited from my ancestors. I owed my innate love for art and music, as well as my tenderness for pets and plants, to my father. My courage and initiative clearly came from my mother. I recalled those rare moments when my father's good side overpowered the bad one and the house glowed with warmth and a keen sense of belonging. Precious moments indeed, both to me and to the rest of my family. We were all at the mercy of a sick man whose unpredictable moods swung from one extreme to the other. If only one could know when and why a man with my father's remarkable potential could be the victim of such an illness.

Come to think of it, symptoms of such a disorder weren't that rare in the world, nor was such a condition considered a mental impairment if the deranged person was male. Manliness, cruelty, and a generous share of high intelligence have frequently done many male heroes no discredit.

In a closed society like ours, however, such domineering providers have been both loved and hated by many women. I had seen this in the admiring eyes of Grandma Rajy, who was obsessed with her talented son, Kareem.

As our car rolled through the familiar streets and buildings of my beloved city, I tried again to sort out the confusing image of Grandma Rajy. The short time I had known her left me with a memory of her as a very domineering woman. She openly favored our brothers over us "girls, who are good for nothing." She just couldn't stand my mother, who to her was a snobbish, demanding doll who took advantage of

Kareem's good nature and wanted to ruin his future. "This son of mine should have been born in a great city like Cairo or Istanbul where people revel in all sorts of activities, where he could expand and excel, rather than in this dull city," she would lament. "It took me two years to convince his father and older brother that Kareem deserves the financial sacrifice needed for his higher education in Istanbul. I just knew he would make all of us proud of his achievement once he finished his studies and came back!" Grandma Rajy's words echoed in my mind as our car began to find its way through the crowds swarming in the boulevard leading to the residential area of Beirut. Thank God she did not live long enough to see her beloved Kareem fall on his face, blinded by the lure of fast money, never allowing the study of money management, architecture, and three European languages to bring him fame and fortune. He had studied all this in Istanbul. The first thing he did when he returned to Beirut was to grab the easiest job available and to spend his free time watching his neighbor's daughter. He had been in love with her for a long time. He showed off every morning in his elegant uniform as a brass-and-stars bodyguard to the city's Turkish commandant, waiting by the same old eucalyptus tree at the Mehdi mansion, unaware yet that the prominent old scholar had passed away and his family was still in the three-month mourning observance. This modest job would soon push him into the society of the rich and the famous, where he buried himself for the best years of his productive life. When that wicked society had its fill of him, his reputation was beyond redemption. But he was the only father I had, and the god of the household where my siblings were living. Our house was the house where my Grandpa Mehdi's spirit lingered. My heart raced wildly when Hadj Uthman turned his vehicle onto Mehdi Street where our trip would end.

The newly asphalted street buzzed with the lively sound of children and parents returning home on that warm and bright afternoon in May. Beirut seemed to have a magic touch. Healthy or sick, wealthy or poor, it didn't matter—a feeling of well-being would encompass anyone who found himself in the city. In contrast to the grim and tense atmosphere that dominated Haifa even before the strike, Beirut inspired merriment and an urge to sing in the streets. I became aware of what I had been missing—our vibrant mountain air, the tall pines, and the soothing fragrance of the first drops of rain on the soil of our rose garden. I missed Aunt Salma, Maria, Alia, and all our old summer houses in the mountains and the fruit groves around them. My city, my home, all the moments of my childhood, were anchored deep in my soul.

"Happy arrival, ladies," Hadj Uthman called. "Is anybody expecting you or shall I ring for you?"

We looked at each other. No, nobody knew we were coming! My knees were numb with yearning as I watched the old man's knotted fingers pressing the round black button on the huge wood gate. Suddenly the gate snapped open and my three young brothers, who had seen the limousine from the western veranda, bolted out, roaring in delight.

"Nadia is here! Nadia is back!" Mae shrieked as she ran down the last flight of stairs following Akram, Ameen, and Fadi. As they wrapped their arms around my shoulders and buried their faces in my neck, I realized how much I had missed them. At that moment my apprehension about returning home for the first time since my marriage disappeared. God only knew what sort of pain I would be subjected to, being home and under the same roof with my father.

The two weeks went very fast. Suad and I had a lot of fun visiting the rest of the Rajy clan and attending the parties they threw for us. And, we had a lot of shopping to do.

I tried to stay away from being alone with my father who watched me carefully whenever the conversation centered around Marwan and me. He was dying to read the letters I received from Haifa, hoping for confirmation that our marriage was not a happy one.

The four letters I had received from Haifa in the two weeks I spent in Beirut were all from Marwan. Much to my astonishment, he wrote beautiful letters. Neat Arabic handwriting, right to the point and, in a way, humorous. I wouldn't have made this discovery were it not for this trip precipitated by his physical attack on me when he was drunk. He called me endearing names I never heard from him in person, such as "dearest bride," "prettiest lady," and "most beautiful Nadia." He used lofty idioms I didn't imagine him capable of writing in Arabic, simply because all the books he enjoyed reading were in French. He wrote: "Since you left, the apartment has become depressingly oppressive and full of ghosts. . . . The fragrance of your hair is the only air I breathe! Your voice floats everywhere around me, soothing like the sound of music. . . . I can't read, your face covers the pages. . . . Please, dearest, come back! I promise never to harm you again."

The last letter I received from him left me with a sense of relief, and a welcome message: Hadj would come to take me and Suad home Saturday morning. "Today!" I thought, and a lump in my heart grew large with expectation. I was returning to Haifa with a new appreciation of my new home. I had had enough to compare the two homes and decide I no longer belonged with my parents. Although in Haifa I lived in a small apartment with a confused man surrounded by warring factions, I knew I belonged there, the Rajys were my family.

Suad and I were the first to wake up that morning and take advantage of the sleeping house to wash and finish packing. The poor woman was still struggling with the blow she received from my brother Anwar. After years spent hoping she would become Anwar's wife, Suad had caught him in the arms of his girlfriend.

"You can't be serious, Nadia. Why should all those newspapers be packed between our clothes instead of stuffing them under the car seat as we always do? We barely have space for the pile of presents as it is."

"I just can't." I explained. "These are foreign magazines and opposition newspapers that are forbidden in Palestine. They have the whole story about that meeting between some of the Arab leaders and the British Colonial Secretary to discuss the revolt in Palestine. Your brother Farid and his gang would love to read them so I intend to smuggle them." I made a face at her in an attempt to cheer her up. "Don't worry, Suad. There is no reason for the border inspector to go into our suitcases. Do we look like smugglers? Two pretty and elegant ladies in a limousine. Relax, if Hadj arrives today at ten as he promised, we can leave long before noon and be home before dark."

While Suad was saying goodbye to my parents, Nora came in with the coffee. "Oh, Nadia, why are you going back so soon? That country is involved in a nasty war. God knows how it is going to end, and here you are taking it all with a smile." "You know I have to go. I didn't choose that country or the man I live with. All I wanted was to get away from this house. And these two weeks have proved that I do belong there, I have a family who needs me and a man who may die if I stay away from him."

Shock darkened her brown eyes but she was silent for a long moment before she asked, "How about your feelings for him?"

"All I know is that he is as close as my brothers Anwar or Sam. I don't know where this feeling will take us."

"I do understand your attachment to all of them, but how about us? I'm beginning to worry that because of the old frictions you had with your parents you might become a stranger to your own brothers and sisters. And what about Mama, I saw you kept your distance from her! Are you going to continue to blame her for the rest of your life? She didn't do you any harm."

"Well, she has always covered up for him, refusing to acknowledge his wrongdoing and failing to provide the protection she owes her own children. She was never there for us when we needed her, and she still isn't. You have to face the truth of what is going on here. I do miss this crazy house and I am not going to let anyone come between my family and me, but the neglect that I see Mae and the three boys facing really worries me." My parents seemed hardly able to keep the roof over their heads. They did not have the means to provide an education for their children. Mae, almost thirteen, was treated like a housemaid, going to school one day and spending the rest of the week doing errands Sharifa herself wouldn't want to do. She had a great sense of humor, but didn't know a thing about books.

"Well, what do you expect me to do?" Nora moaned through her tears. "You have seen how I spend days working at the boarding school to avoid this trauma, worrying about the unsteady income of this household and the safety and care of those children. And then I worry through the night about your living under siege, the precariousness of your health, and the distance between us, in case there is an emergency. Worry, Nadia, that's all I can do for you."

"I want you to stop worrying about me, Nora. Strange as it may seem, I feel stronger every time I face some difficulty. It is as though I could face the whole world, all alone. Stop worrying."

The suitcases were lined up in the hallway and we were waiting for Hadj to arrive. The doorbell rang and my father went to answer it. Suddenly Marwan's sharp voice came through the hall over the other voices at the door. Suad saw him first and she was hugging him when I followed, not believing my eyes.

"What a beautiful surprise, Marwan! Your letter didn't mention anything about coming with Hadj!" Intimidated by the watchful eyes around us, I shook his hand timidly.

"Sorry, Nadia, but I made this decision only last night. I hope you are ready!" He stepped over and kissed my cheek lightly.

I nodded. His lips sent a thrill all the way down to my toes. I watched him as he tried to answer questions coming to him from every direction, while his eyes met mine for a quick exchange of glances.

"No, there is a cease-fire today but I really can't stay. . . . We have to return before they resume the fighting. . . . Food is not a problem. . . . No, I don't expect the schools to open now that the academic year is almost over. . . . My parents might come later if this truce holds. . . . No, we don't have time to have lunch. . . . We will eat on the way. . . . "

Halfway to our destination, Hadj slowed down and took a right turn into a corner gas station. A young teenager with worn-out black pants and striped white shirt rushed to his service. Happy to be on our feet after the three hours' drive, we started walking down the side road leading westward. The road sign on our right read: Welcome to Tyre.

The sun blazed high on a cloudless sky. Cutting through the middle of a long stretch of bare land, the deserted sandy road shimmered like a mirage reaching out to the horizon through the hazy dunes of Tyre's peninsula. Nothing there looked like a city to me. All I could see were some wooden shacks scattered along the shore on both sides and a pile of multicolored small buildings far away at the end of the peninsula.

"Is that all that remains of the city called Tyre?" I pointed out to the glaring dunes.

"That's it," Marwan said. "You're disappointed, aren't you? The same thing happened to me some twenty years ago when I saw it for the first time. But what you see is not actually the ancient city of Tyre; this is a recent settlement, not more than a few hundred years old."

"What happened to the magic and fame that filled hundreds of history books about Tyre thousands of years ago?"

"The original city is buried way down under your feet. Its discovery was reported a long time ago, but only after the turn of this century did some international archaeologists show an interest in verifying it. I recently read an article saying that the Association of European Archaeologists is planning to start digging at the site of the original Tyre. Amazing, huh?"

We left the road and stepped down to the white pebbled beach. "See those empty shores?" Marwan said. "This is where, four thousand years ago, your ancestors, the Phoenicians, built one famous fleet after another to invade the world with the wealth of their trade."

A tranquil silence fell on us as we strolled, forgetful of time. The waves ebbed and flowed gently, translucent over the sparkling pebbles. "As kids we used to come here often," Suad reminisced. "There were no cars yet. For trips outside the urban areas people used bulky open-air wooden-wheeled carriages. It was hectic but fun."

"Fun, indeed!" Marwan mocked. "Oh, how I hated those clumsy rides. Dust covered us from top to bottom and got into my eyes, my ears, my mouth. . . . And why did our parents love to drag the entire clan along every time they wanted to go out on a picnic? One carriage was never enough to hold us; the convoy would contain two or sometimes three of those noisy carriages. Piled on top of each other on stiff narrow banks with bundles of food, extra clothes, and blankets suffocating us . . . we looked like nomads on the move." Marwan's tone carried a pinch of sarcasm.

"That's the way your parents are, Marwan. They just love to be with their children, is that so bad?" I teased.

"I could do without that kind of love, dear Nadia, believe me. To tell you the truth, that dominating love is behind all the misery I have ever had."

"That's not fair, Marwan!" His sister said. "What will Nadia think, hearing you expressing your feelings this way?"

"Don't worry, I know your parents' intentions are beyond criticism, but I don't mind hearing more about Marwan's point of view. Do you feel you were ever forced into a situation your parents had imposed on you? I mean an important one?"

"Our whole lives were planned the moment we were born, Nadia. The apartments where we have to live; the schools, languages, and futures we have and the wives we have to marry, all these decisions are not for us to make." Suddenly, Marwan stopped and looked me in the eye. "Do you know that when your Uncle Ahmad first spoke of you it was as a future daughter-in-law, not as a wife for me? I was not consulted. I was twenty-two then and marriage was the farthest thing from my mind." He stopped abruptly, and he gently slapped his lips with his hand.

"That's all right; it's important that I know the truth now. I'm glad you brought it up, Marwan. That puts us both in the same boat." In a way I felt overwhelmingly relieved.

"All I wanted to say is that, in spite of the fact that I had nothing to do with the decision making of this marriage, you have become everything in my life now. You do know that, don't you?"

I nodded, praying to God to place the wonderful blend of love and harmony I felt, in Marwan's heart as well. We resumed walking silently, thoughtfully, at peace. Hadj Uthman brought us back to reality, as he rolled the car down and next to us. "Do you want me to drive you to the harbor to have lunch now?"

"Yes, Hadj, please do! We are famished," I said.

7

September 1936

I lost count of the long, very long, days that brought nothing but grief following my return from Beirut. All I wanted to remember were the few moments of companionship and harmony that Marwan and I had joyfully spent together while away from the menaces of the destiny we were forced to share in his homeland. Those moments led me to wonder whether he might have been a better mate had he grown up in a different environment.

As though the revolt and vengeful reaction to it that terrorized the country weren't enough, an acute epidemic of typhoid fever swept through the city. It erupted first in the originally unpopulated seaside not far from Haifa where thousands of middle-class families had fled their besieged dwellings for the safety of the enchanting shores of the Mediterranean. The killer epidemic struck the Rajy family at the end of August, claiming within a period of three weeks two victims in the prime of their youth. The first one was a fifteen-year-old cousin of Marwan's; the second one was Marwan's seventeen-year-old brother, Jihad, who collapsed within one week of his doomed cousin. A good six feet tall already, Jihad was a close friend who doubled with me in softball games, brought me flowers and chocolates, looked after my little cat that Warrood took with her and kept at my in-laws' because Marwan wouldn't let it into our apartment.

"I told you, Mother, that Jihad would end up bringing this disaster right into our home by spending so much time clinging to the bed of that poor dying boy. But you wouldn't listen to me," Marwan screamed at his mother the day Dr. Imad announced his diagnosis for Jihad's high fever. "Now he has infected us all with that killer fever."

His mother tried to soothe him. "Stop worrying, Marwan! Nothing is going to happen to Jihad, believe me. You are too pessimistic, dear." Her hand tapped his cheek affectionately.

"Don't touch me!" he screamed, pulling away from her. "Your hands are probably full of germs. I've had my share of your damned touch, Mother, remember? I was barely a year old when you just left me to the mercy of that high fever that poisoned my entire life."

"But, son, sickness and death are not in our hands. If we get sick, it is our fate. That is all God's will!"

"All right, you keep up your optimism in that almighty God of yours whom you blame for all your mistakes. Let's just wait and see what he does to your beloved son now. I hope Jihad will, at least, be spared the chronic ailment I still have to bear. That is, if he makes it."

"God have mercy on us, Marwan. I can blame only myself for sending you to that atheist school where they brainwashed you against the sacred truths of our faith."

"Oh, yah! Well, I hope you will live long enough, Mother, to see how wrong you are, running away from your responsibilities as a human being and leaving everything in the hands of some god you cannot define."

It broke my heart to see Jihad whither away in the arms of that mournful mother, who watched helplessly with the rest of the family as the days wearily succeeded one another. Dr. Imad, the only physician who remained in the neighborhood, defying the spreading danger with his team of nurses and aides, shuttled day and night between his nearby clinic and the house. But nothing helped. The boy's delicate system succumbed to the cruel disease after a few hours of convulsive struggle.

I worried myself sick as I watched the effect of this tragedy on Marwan. As a frightened turtle draws head, legs, and tail into its shell, so he crawled into the safety of our apartment the day he was told the bad news. He stubbornly refused to join us throughout the family ordeal, and he did not touch any food or drink made at his parents' home after that. His irrational attitude put me in an awkward position. My heart was with the bereaved parents, who needed nothing more than to be close to their loved ones; they were deeply hurt by Marwan's behavior and responded gratefully to my constant attention.

Yet Marwan's crisis weighed on me as well. He seemed inconsolably obsessed by his fear of the disease. "Nobody will ever understand the way I feel about being sick!" he once shouted at me when I argued in favor of his parents' need for his support and compassion. "I'm no good at supporting anybody, Nadia, can't you see that? My life has been a constant ordeal. My parents were both there, all right, but their presence did nothing to change the fact that I was crippled, and remained crippled. I was confined to my crib while my younger brothers and sisters crawled, toddled, and walked away from me." "Look at her," he pointed his finger at his mother. "She filled this house with all those devils. What for? I hate children; they are nothing but trouble."

"But you have survived to walk, talk, and prevail over most of your problems. Poor Jihad did not."

"I survived all right. But for what? To be a dwarf in a world of giants? For God's sake, Nadia, try to understand how I feel!"

I did care tremendously. I had come to realize how poor his resistance to colds was, and how stomach disorders and other simple ailments got the best of him. Toothaches and headaches plagued him if we so much as changed our daily routine. And the jealousy! How embarrassing it was to see him overcome with envy and frustration in the presence of his vigorous teenage brothers who were extremely friendly with me; he would pick a fight for the smallest reason.

On a hot morning at eight o'clock, the cortege of four black limousines headed our sad journey. It was led by the ambulance carrying the body. A large framed picture of Jihad adorned its front windshield.

Gradually, as the small convoy moved northward to the Rajy cemetery in Acre, scattered groups of agitated armed men joined in, and before we were halfway there, our procession became the center of a huge patriotic demonstration. The road swarmed with horses stamping on the pavement only inches away from our vehicles. Heads wrapped tightly with kaffiyehs, guns pointed to the sky, these unwelcome guests chanted national songs and rebel slogans.

"Oh, my God, Suad!" Aunt Najla fretted as she pulled up the side of her veil and peeked through the window. "Those people think this is a martyr's funeral. Why are they circling us like that?"

"Death to the traitors!" Their harsh voices cried in unison. "Glory to the martyr. . . . In Heaven may you rest, brother . . . We are here to avenge your sacred blood . . . " Deafening rounds of gunfire followed each thunderous shout.

"I don't understand, Aunt Najla!" I whispered. "If nobody asked them to join in, why are they doing this?"

The weeping mother shook her head helplessly.

"A lot of strange things are happening nowadays, Nadia," Suad volunteered. "Abou Maarouf told my father last week that in the South, secret agents helped authorities find the families of martyred rebels. The police took the men from these families to jail and demolished their houses. In retaliation, the rebels assassinated the informants. Abou Maarouf said the rebels now try to make all funerals, martyrs' or otherwise, look the same to make it more difficult for the authorities to identify the families of the rebels."

"But it's not fair!" Aunt Najla moaned. "My son had nothing to do with that bloody revolution." Ordinarily quite reserved in the way she judged political issues, the poor mother's grief boiled over into anger.

The young Rajy was indeed a martyr claimed by a decadence caused by fear and confusion, one that seemed to have taken over all the sensibilities we had accumulated throughout our history. People reacted strangely to hazards like the one we were busy surviving; they could become hysterically self-destructive. For instance, the typhoid, which ordinarily was an easy-to-conquer disease, was now turning fatal. One had only to look at the decay setting in all over the city, with sewage excavation by the harbor left open and piles of uncollected garbage filling both sides of the streets, to realize why that bacterial epidemic was raging beyond control. People worried that deadlier plagues that could overtake the city if the panic persisted. I remembered how clean the downtown was when I first saw it less than a year earlier. Marwan may have been right when he attacked the politicians who didn't take any precautions before using the strike as a political weapon. "They don't want to see that the invasion of scavenging rats and mosquitoes could be as lethal as colonialism and partition," he'd say time and again.

Relatives and friends waiting for us at the Acre cemetery were not surprised to see that the armed mobs of horsemen and street followers not only attended, but led Jihad's funeral. "What's going to happen now, Suad?" I whispered in her ear as the cars stopped in a line at the entrance of an unfenced sandy piece of ground dotted with gravestones.

"God knows!" she whispered back, her swollen eyes blinking nervously. "Until this moment, our family has never had any contact with rebels, revolutionaries, or anyone who goes against the law. Nor would any of us wish to be in conflict with the authorities. I'm very worried, Nadia. After today my father and the rest of my brothers may be in great danger of retaliation. The authorities might not believe that this crazy thing was out of our control."

"Couldn't Uncle Ahmad just ask these people to go away and to leave us in peace? The poor man is under enough stress as it is."

"Oh, I don't think he could do that. It would be disgraceful to denounce the nationalists openly at a time when danger of failure is closing in on them. And after all, he's still a proud Arab."

We sat in our car waiting for the burial ceremony to begin. The vigorous strangers seemed to be in control, efficiently arranging an impressive ceremony with separate stages for religious lecturers, political rabble-rousers, and female mourners. There was even a donation stand. Shoulders stooped, arms locked behind his back, Uncle Ahmad walked slowly down the narrow path of the cemetery looking lost. His five other sons, formally dressed in suits, ties, and tarbooshes, followed ahead of the rest of the relatives. Surrounded by the unknown intruders, the small family procession looked meager and pitiful.

In midst of all the sorrow and confusion, the curfew imposed by martial law in Haifa was forgotten. By the time the ceremony was over, we found ourselves forced to spend the night in Acre with the Sallooms, Aunt Najla's two brothers and their families who had taken over her family's property after she and her sister had married and the parents had died.

Although the painful memory of that night in September 1936 was deeply engraved in my memory, time would prove it to be the beginning of a blissful awakening that shaped the faith inside me. I slept very little, but I got more valuable rest in being awake. I was more in control of my thoughts. It was a strange feeling to look with wide open eyes into the darkness and discover how to get solace through meditation or through the power of quoting from memory anything I wished! Only in this way was I able to talk to Grandpa Mehdi's soul again, and to ask for his guidance at a time when my faith faltered.

By mid-November the tragic Palestinian revolution came abruptly to its end, an end scripted by Britain and financed and produced by all Arab seats of power. Formally, it was the Higher Arab Committee that imposed it on Palestine.

As weary and disappointed as we and those around us were,

Marwan and I plunged head-first into the social life we had missed for so long. Ever since that memorable day we spent on the shores of Tyre's peninsula, Marwan had become less guarded in talking to me about things that bothered him at his work or at home. He even shared with me personal decisions on business problems and he introduced me to a circle of old friends and financiers. Some were foreign representatives who lived in Haifa with their wives and children.

The newfound pleasures of our social life brought us closer and helped open my eyes to the truly vulnerable man Marwan was. Behind the harsh image there was a scared and helpless man. He wholeheartedly abdicated all social responsibilities and day-to-day decisions to me. He did this with a sense of great relief and I found myself thriving in the combined role of protective friend and loving sister. I welcomed the change, but still, there were thorny issues: his need for intimacy, his excessive drinking, and his silence on money matters. It never occurred to him that if I wanted to buy anything, I had to come up with cash just like everybody else. As far as Marwan was concerned, it was his father who should cover all our expenses, since he ordered the marriage and chose the bride. Marwan would have never taken such responsibility on his own.

Dr. Ralph picked us up about seven in the evening three days before Christmas. He and Dr. Imad were invited to be our guests at a restaurant a few miles away from the city. It was a lovely starry night, quite mild for that time of year. Marwan helped me into the backseat of the green cabriolet, and then hopped up to the front seat. "Congratulations, Ralph! Is this a new car?"

Ralph nodded his red head, pressing his lips on his new pipe. His formal dark suit made him look older. Next to me on the stiff back seat Imad sat silently after we said hello. His long muscular legs were folded clumsily behind the driver's seat. I felt ill at ease sitting so close to him.

The Refuge, on a cliff at the top of Carmel Mountain, was a perfect restaurant, both for its location and its genial atmosphere. "What a fantastic place!" Imad cheered quietly, strolling ahead with Marwan. Ralph and I followed along the winding path leading to the discreetly lit cabin. Like huge white mushrooms, embedded spotlights led our steps to the entrance.

"This restaurant is owned by a Hungarian couple who take good care of their customers. The whole hill, in fact, is well guarded. It belongs to the Franciscan convent nearby," I assured Ralph.

Our table, as usual, was right by the wide French doors next to a squarish covered veranda. A few yards to the left stood two pianos, back to back, where Evan and his wife Tatyanna played in concert, usually soft classical music.

Marwan was attending to our drinks just as a soft-spoken waiter took our orders. He poured small portions of whiskey from an exquisite triangular bottle with dimpled sides and golden stamps around its narrow neck.

"No, thanks, Marwan," I whispered, covering the top of my glass with the tips of my fingers as my turn came.

"But why, Nadia? Just a little, please!"

"You know I don't drink this, Marwan!" My face suddenly felt hot. Imad and Ralph kept their eyes on their drinks.

"Be practical, honey, try it. Just a drop, please!" Marwan insisted. "Do advise her, Imad. Will you?"

My heart raced. The last thing I wanted was to become intoxicated while those two men watched. It was useless to deny that Marwan's abuse of alcohol was entirely Imad's fault.

"What's the big deal, my friend?" Imad uttered innocently. Evading my watchful eyes, he patted Marwan's hand soothingly. "Let the lady take her time." His smile was full of scorn.

∼ℭ

The session of classical music came to an end just as we finished our dinner. The whole lounge responded with clapping and cheering as Tatyanna bowed gracefully and disappeared behind the service curtain.

"A toast to you, Marwan, and to your fascinating bride, for this charming and delicious dinner," Ralph said. "I have enjoyed it tremendously."

"Oh, Ralph, the evening isn't over yet." Flushed and glowing with joy, Marwan cut in. "The best is yet to come."

The room grew quiet as Evan began playing romantic slow dances and tangos. I felt the sweetness of the desire for dance in my knees. "Why don't you two dance? Ralph suggested. "Don't let our presence stop you."

"I don't know how to dance, that is, not until Nadia teaches me." He looked adoring at me, then turned to his friends. "I would be grateful if you would dance with Nadia. Take turns, please, I'm sure she wouldn't mind."

Ralph held my waist with a steady arm as our feet glided swiftly to a tango. "You dance very well, Mrs. Nadia. Did you study this in school in Lebanon?"

"Oh, no! Not in schools." Mixed dancing in girls' schools? "I learned it at home. My brother Anwar is an outstanding master of tangos and waltzes."

"I would love to go and see Lebanon one of these days. It's quite a Westernized society, am I right?"

"I really don't know how to describe it, but it's nicer than here. You can feel it in the air. Our society is as colorful as Palestine's. Different races, and even different kinds of climate make for beautiful variety. The same things one does here, one enjoys more in Lebanon!"

"You don't sound quite happy living here. Is that because of the political conditions, or because of some other reason?"

"Oh, no, politics has nothing to do with it. On the contrary, I find it more interesting to see people reacting sharply to whatever is oppressing them. I don't like the wide rifts and disagreements among the people themselves over the dilemmas of their country, even in the same family sometimes."

"How did you happen to meet Marwan? You are not close relatives, as I remember hearing you say once. Was it a marriage arranged by the two families?"

I noticed a serious edge to his question. Could this encounter be part of a medical examination?

"I'm sure you are aware of the circumstances of our marriage, Dr. Ralph. You are quite close to both Marwan and Dr. Imad. Haven't you discussed this before?"

"I'm sorry, I should have known better than to beat around the bush with you. It's wonderful to talk to someone so direct and so logical. I must tell you frankly that your husband's case is quite a serious one. It was impossible to imagine that such a young, inexperienced woman could handle it without help. In fact, I expected to have great difficulty talking to you in terms of a specialist's advice. Please forgive my ignorance." The music stopped and we pulled back, applauding but still looking at each other intently.

"Are you tired?" Ralph asked as the music began again.

I shook my head. His arm reached back to my waist. "I don't expect you to know that I love Marwan very much." I was as stunned by my statement as the bewildered doctor was. "What I mean is that I love him for what he really is. He is as close to me as my own brothers. This is not the kind of love men usually expect from their wives. Do you understand now what I mean, Dr. Ralph?"

"Yes, yes, I do. But how can you be sure that is all your husband expects from you?

"I know that. But Marwan is not the type of husband you, his mother, Dr. Imad, and probably a lot of other people would like to make of him by imposing that so-called man's duty on him."

"I am really impressed, Mrs. Nadia, with the exceptional way you are dealing with this problem. I shall tell you how Marwan feels about you and try to defend myself."

I didn't say a word. I just turned my head to where Marwan and Imad waited. They seemed to be immersed in their talk, barely aware of what was going on around them.

"Marwan worships you, Madame. He has always been aware that he doesn't fit your image of a husband, and this has further complicated things. Please don't kid yourself. He is not different from other men. I happen to know that he is physically very interested in you."

"Well, if that is true, then you, as his advisor, must tell him to stop bothering me since you now know that physical contact between us is out of question. You have made a big mistake prescribing alcohol to solve his physical problem without knowing anything about my feelings. Did he ever tell you about the effect of that prescription on his behavior? Did you know that he turns into an animal when he drinks?"

"I couldn't prescribe any medicine or sedative in his case. He didn't show any sign of sickness and has no disease. It was obvious the problem was an emotional one. My suggestion that he drink a little alcohol was intended to help him become a relaxed companion instead of a frustrated and deprived animal."

"Again, I want you to know that I care little about his physical needs. He knew all along that I didn't love him in that sense. His parents knew that too. Now, it's your duty to help him either forget about physical intimacy with me or find another solution. I am amazed at the fuss you men make about this matter. Sex, in my view, is the ugliest act human beings have ever invented."

"So I was right after all. You *are* a difficult case, Mrs. Nadia. A charming challenge to a psychiatrist."

I was awakened late one blustery night in January by Marwan's coughing and calling my name. "I'm freezing, Nadia, my whole body aches."

"Oh, Marwan, you're burning with fever," I mumbled as my hand touched his forehead. "Could it be the flu?"

"I don't know. Please send someone for Dr. Imad right now!"

"I will, but not at this time of night. Meanwhile, some tisane and aspirin could help. And a couple of hot-water bottles might keep you warm until one of your brothers can find the doctor."

The windstorm grew more fierce, lashing the sturdy wooden shutters of our apartment. Dr. Imad didn't arrive until after lunch the next day. "I'm sorry, Marwan," he apologized as he checked his pulse, "half the city seems to be ill with colds. I hope you take care to stay warm, Mrs. Nadia," he teased with a conspiratorial smile. "We don't want our bride to catch a cold now, do we?" With his windblown hair and mischievous eyes, he reminded me of my brother Anwar at his most provocative. It never bothered me that Imad liked to call me "our bride"; it was an allusion to my chosen abstention. Although he had stopped talking directly to me about Marwan's physical condition, he had gradually become somewhat contemptuous of me since Ralph had taken over Marwan's case. I was sure, however, that Imad was still following the case through his colleague, who had prescribed a series of "therapeutic" sessions for Marwan. In order to involve me in the treatment, Ralph recommended that these sessions be held at our apartment, to set Marwan more at ease.

Imad stepped out of Marwan's room as I placed the tea tray on the lounge table. "I gave him a sedative to soothe his cough. He has a nasty flu and may need a couple of weeks to reach full recovery." I went on pouring the tea, trying to ease the tension his authoritative demeanor provoked in me every time I found myself alone with him. "I've been trying to find the right time to talk to you privately, Mrs. Nadia." I prepared myself for another lecture about my attitude toward Marwan.

"Watching your conflict with your husband for the last few months,

I have become convinced that, contrary to what you have told Dr. Ralph about how much you care for Marwan, in reality you are very cruel to him. It's not yet clear to me what reasons you wish to give for this unwarranted behavior, but I can see that you are deliberately ignoring Marwan's right to happiness. To put it more bluntly, you seem to be taking advantage of his love and naiveté, an attitude that puts you and me at odds."

My heart was racing, but I managed to check my temper. "Why do I get the feeling that you are more interested in what Marwan does with me than in Marwan himself? I am not sure we need any medical help, Doctor, we are enjoying our life as it is. In fact Marwan and I had no problem until you and Aunt Najla began interfering."

"Don't fool yourself, lady. When in pain, Marwan complains to me, not to you. Like all men, Marwan never admits his masculine worries to a woman, not even to one as willful as you are. Do you think you could change the biological nature of a human being all by yourself? For over a year now you have shared a room with your husband, permitting him neither to touch you nor to make love to you. As a physician, I have to warn you that you are committing a crime by inflicting such strange rules on him."

"I didn't create any rules, Dr. Khaldoun. I have caused Marwan no harm, and I have not taken advantage of him. He knew all along what kind of relationship our marriage would involve. It is your rules, not mine, that are tearing him apart. You want to mold him into your image of what a man should be. To me, that is the crime."

"I don't understand your logic. You appear to be bright and enlightened in so many aspects of life, yet you continue to demonstrate complete ignorance of the real physical needs of your husband. Where do you suggest this husband should go when his hormones overflow?"

"He can go anywhere he pleases. I don't care. You are such an expert physician, one so worried about your patient's excess of hormones, so why don't you advise him on the options he has instead of forcing him into raping his own wife?" Imad's arrogance brought out the worst in me; I could have argued for hours without giving in, but I was worried that our loud and heated discussion would disturb Marwan.

"Well, well, Mrs. Rajy! So you suggest that Marwan go to the streets. Is this your idea of ethics for marriage? And what about you, how are you meeting your own needs?"

Boiling anger rose in me. "You had better leave, mister. This talk is becoming too vulgar, and I have no intention of letting it continue. You may simply get out. I'll go check on Marwan now."

I began walking swiftly down the hall, but with one leap he was on top of me. His arms, tough as steel, formed a deadly vise of steel around my waist. He lifted me up, and brought his face close to mine. "I know your type. You're one of those women who can only be taken by force."

Twisting frantically in his grip, I buried my face into my robe. He bit my ears, breathed down the nape of my neck, and pulled my hair. "Why don't you scream, like other women?" he hissed between assaults. "Your resistance is driving me crazy." He put me down and pushed me back at arm's length. "I can't see your beautiful face, Nadia. Look at me. Oh, my God, baby, you are really shy! I know you want me too; please, let me see how you look when you're aroused." His grip lessened as he talked; he was too crazed to know the difference between hatred and desire.

I freed myself from his hold and jumped back, impulsively swinging my arm up to his face. The sound of the flat of my hand slapping his face reverberated on the silent walls. My body swayed. Had I really slapped that angry face? The sharp sting in the palm of my hand told me I had. "I will kill you if you ever try to touch me again!" My voice sounded surprisingly steady, but I didn't dare move, afraid that my taut body would collapse if he continued to glare at me. When he finally turned his back and started to walk away, I closed my eyes, praying that my trembling knees support me until he was gone from the house. When the outside door clicked shut, I took a deep breath and collapsed on the sofa.

"Damn you, Imad!" I sobbed into the sleeve of my robe. I was still in shock, trying to understand how such a respectable and well-mannered man could suddenly turn into a crazed animal, attacking the wife of his sick patient and most trusting friend.

The apartment was heavy with silence. I was grateful that Marwan had slept through the incident. I didn't know whether I could ever tell him what kind of man Imad was. My stomach lurched as I caught the stench of Imad's tobacco on my hair and skin. I wanted to wash off every trace of his presence as fast as possible. I let the hot water pour over me in steaming jets, then sat motionless in the shower stall, gradually relaxing, trying to sort out in my mind what I should do. The

Rajys were fond of Imad and trusted him implicitly. To accuse him before them would be to risk disbelief and, even worse, the goodwill I fostered and cherished. "Damn this one pig!" I cursed again, banging the enamel faucet shut and pulling myself up from the wooden shower stool. Should I just keep silent? Should I remain a speechless victim of his threats, a mute object of his advances? I wrapped a towel around myself and stared at my bewildered eyes in the mirror. There she was! The scared little girl trapped on the edge of a cliff, her parents and brothers threatening to push her off if she told about what was done to her.

"Damn you all!" I wailed into the folds of my towel.

"Please come in, Ralph, thanks for coming. Marwan is fine; in fact he woke up this morning ready to go to work. No, I convinced him to stay home a little longer. The week is almost over and he still has two more shots to go. The bank can wait." I led the way to the dining room where Marwan was reading the morning papers after breakfast. I wondered whether Imad had sent Ralph over to check on me. "Look who's here, Marwan."

"Ralph, my friend, what a pleasure to see you."

I poured tea for Ralph and excused myself, saying that I was planning to make kibbe, one of Marwan's favorite dishes. I couldn't trust myself to be there if they began talking about Imad. Marwan was perplexed by his friend's unexplained absence since the day he had tried to assault me. Imad's nurse, Hala, had been coming to give Marwan his injections. She blamed the doctor's busy schedule, but Marwan wasn't convinced and kept on asking questions. Imad's absence was a relief to me. It gave me more time to think about that horrible encounter. I wanted to prepare for some sort of special and yet decent relationship with him. Obviously he would be around, since he was as dear to the Rajy family as one of their children. And no doubt he would apologize. Would accepting his apologies be a cowardly submission to male brutality? Would it compromise the safety of my new haven?

Marwan called from the salon where he and Ralph were visiting. "Nadia come, please. Ralph is leaving."

I washed my hands and rushed to say goodbye to Ralph. The two men were standing in the middle of the lounge talking and joking.

"Ralph is engaged to be married, Nadia, did you know that?" Marwan sounded elated.

"Oh, yes." I confessed. "I did not know your fianceé had arrived from Germany. Did you decide about the date yet?"

"No, not yet," Ralph said smiling. "She likes to take her time."

"We have something very special for dinner, Ralph." Marwan said. "Nadia made one of her favored dishes, *kibbe arnabiye,* it is a meat pie marinated in sesame cream. Why don't you and your fianceé join us for dinner? Nadia and I would love to meet her. Are you free tonight?"

"We might not be able to come until after nine. Are you sure you're up to it, Marwan?"

"Of course! I feel fully recovered. Besides, your engagement calls for a celebration, and I want you two to have a chance to hear Nadia play the piano."

"My playing and singing are far from exceptional, I'm afraid," I said. "But I do try to improve. Music has always been a source of sustenance for me."

Ralph was a very capable psychiatrist and might have detected the pain I felt discussing my early attachment to music and the profound effect it had on me. But I doubted that he could ever imagine the healing role it played during my tormented childhood.

Suffering from malaria and ulcerous tonsils from early childhood, I later developed an acute case of somnambulism that stayed with me until puberty. A week would seldom pass during those early years without my having to miss school because of illness. Playing the piano became everything to me besides books and pencils. And this innocent pleasure bothered no one until the piano playing became part of the sleepwalking. That weird behavior led to a lot of family conflict and to my being tied to my bed at night to keep me from "running wild and playing the piano while the whole world is sleeping," as my mother described it.

At nine sharp the door bell rang. Heike was tall and very attractive in a tan leather suit with a pearl-white blouse and alligator belt and purse.

"This is for you, Mrs. Rajy." The sweet-voiced young woman presented me with a porcelain pot of African violets, my favorite. "This is Ralph's choice, he said you would love to add this pale color to your purple collection."

"And this is for you, Marwan." Ralph handed Marwan a silver foil-wrapped package that looked like a bottle.

"Thanks, Ralph. Is this the gin you told me about?" I didn't miss the spark in Marwan's eyes when I thanked Ralph.

"Yes, it is. Consider it a belated New Year's gift."

Ralph volunteered to fix the drinks, and by the time I rejoined the party with a carafe of tomato juice and an ice bucket, three of the four glasses were already half-filled with a clear, sparkling liquid. I requested tomato juice for the fourth.

Our evening began on an amicable note. Even my name became a topic of discussion. "Nadia is a beautiful name," said Heike. "In Germany it is considered Russian; it wasn't until I came to the Middle East that I realized its origin is Arabic. I'm really fascinated with the Orient and its many cultures. But the people of this land seem to take its beauty and the rich treasure of their cultures for granted. There is an eagerness to adopt modern and rather experimental cultures. It's beyond me to understand why."

"Isn't this due to the innate human urge for new experiences, my dear?" Ralph suggested tentatively. "We all have the tendency at one time or other to lose interest in things we own, and to envy everything others have." Their glasses almost empty, both Ralph and Marwan seemed beyond serious discussion, unlike Heike, who had barely touched her drink.

"Living on this rotten old soil, I neither see beauty nor feel exhilaration at being one of the Arabs of the Holy Land," exclaimed Marwan. "Holy, indeed! But here is my solution to this problem for you, dear lady. It is simple: All we have to do, you and I, is to exchange IDs right now. How about that?" Flushed with excitement and full of humor, he burst out laughing. "And now, ladies and gentlemen, it is time for some music." He reached his hand out to me. "Come, Nadia, let us show this fascinating lady some of the real beauty of our life."

It was after ten when I finally escaped from many heartwarming encores and convinced my audience that it was time to eat. Ralph looked at the elegantly spread table in awe. "The man in me feels so much guilt when I realize how much time you spent just to please us, Nadia. From here on, the rest of us are going to serve you!" He asked me to sit on my chair and waited for me to comply.

Marwan picked up the wine decanter and moved toward Heike. "May I introduce you to one of the best vineyards in the country. This is a 1927 rosé made by the Capuchins at a Franciscan monastery in Lebanon." Marwan held the decanter as though it were a child. "May we have the pleasure of toasting your coming of age again, Nadia?" Marwan was pleading. He picked up my glass as Ralph smiled, full of approval and encouragement.

"My goodness, Nadia, have you just turned eighteen?" Heike's dark eyes sparkled with surprise.

"That was nearly a year ago, but Marwan never tires of bringing it up whenever the occasion permits. He's not likely to recover from the shock of having an aged wife."

"How about it, honey?"

"I would be honored, Marwan. The tomato juice is right there, do you mind?" I could feel my forced smile. Marwan hesitated for a moment. Silence fell in the room.

"May I suggest something, Marwan?" Ralph interjected. "It just occurred to me, Nadia, that tomato juice is great for cocktails. Why don't I fix you one for this occasion? Just a few drops of gin with your juice will do the job. Allow me, Marwan." Ralph picked up my half-full glass of tomato juice and turned to the bar shelf behind me.

"I would rather not, Ralph, please!" I apologized. "I have never tried any alcohol before, to say nothing of this gin of yours that I'm suddenly hearing so much about."

As the dinner progressed, I realized that Ralph's suggestion had given pleasure to all but me. My stomach started playing funny games as soon as I took the first gulp. A few moments later I felt feverish and I shivered every time food came near my mouth. Could Marwan's flu have invaded my body? I didn't dare show any signs of discomfort, afraid that my guests, who were enjoying themselves tremendously, would feel obligated to end their stay.

"You seem to like this cocktail, baby. Let me fix you another." Marwan seemed eager to please, but I was too weak to say anything. My head felt heavy as a rock. Poor Marwan, I thought. It must have been terrible for him to struggle with this nasty flu for a whole week.

"You haven't touched your food, Nadia. Is something wrong?" Heike's voice came from far away. I focused all my might on opening my mouth to explain how sick I felt, but all that emerged was some sort of long, jittery laugher. Plates whirled and floated around the room, provoking more of this convulsive laughter. My hands groped at the sides of my chair as my eyelids closed, helplessly heavy. I could hear the sound of my own giggles, but I could not stop them. They had a power of their own. The chatter and hum of conversation drifted away from me. My throat felt very dry.

When I came to my senses, my mind was still at the dinner party. I felt sure that Marwan had kept our guests well entertained while they waited for me to recover. But the stiff pillow under my head and the prickly woolen blanket against my sweaty skin shattered that illusion as I realized that I was lying half-naked in bed. Groggily I tried to sort things out. This wasn't my bed. What was I doing in Marwan's bed? How did I end up there? The small room seemed empty. Where was Marwan?

My head buzzed with menacing questions. The worst scenario flashed before me: What if the symptoms I felt at dinner were not the flu? Could it be possible that I got drunk? Would Marwan and Ralph dare add too much of that powerful liquor to my juice without my sensing it? Just thinking what might have happened sent shivers all through my body. The pain between my sticky thighs confirmed that thought. Tears of frustration and anger rolled down my eyes. "Oh, Marwan! What have you done?"

"No, Aunt Najla, I am not moving back into the apartment with him. I hate everything up there, especially that haunted bedroom."

"Oh, come now, Nadia! You can't still be angry with Marwan. And I didn't know you hated your room so much. Tell me, dear, what is it you don't like?"

I knew it sounded strange to Aunt Najla, but I really hated that room. The more I thought of its passive white walls, dark imposing furniture, and impersonal drapes, the more I hated it. The room itself bore witness to that terrible night. It seemed to conspire against me with the rest of the world. The expensive perfumes on the dresser, the garlanded bedsheets with years of hand embroidery, none of these could erase the stench of what had happened. But I couldn't explain this to Aunt Najla. She was hardened by the rituals of her life and had become, like everything in that room, part of a formula she refused to question.

"Everything. Why can't I have my own room? That one is too small for us anyway."

"And where would that room be? The apartment is already crowded with your furniture. Ahmad and I were thinking that you might need an extra room or two as your family grows larger, but for now I want to ask a favor of you. It's nearly a month since you moved here with us and refused to see Marwan. Please, Nadia, let him come and talk to you now that you have regained your health! You know Marwan worships you. Don't you think it's only fair to let him apologize?" She reached over and hugged me tightly.

The implications of the phrase "You and Marwan talk to each other." left me dumbfounded. I avoided her eyes. I wasn't sure of my feelings for Marwan at that point. A lot had happened in the aftermath of that night. There were alarming changes in my body. No one else knew. Something was happening in me, something was taking over my life.

"Mother, please, take it easy on Nadia," Suad begged irritably as she came into the room carrying an armload of packages. "What's the rush? Are we going soft on our Marwan again? Let's take this one step at a time. Tomorrow is Nadia's birthday party. Let us go full-time on it! You can take over from there if you want."

My own guardian angel, as well as her brother Marwan's savior, Suad had insisted that I share her room ever since that night of madness when Marwan had run to her for help. She did me an even greater favor by refusing to let him come near me. I suffered something like a nervous breakdown that developed into a severe case of nausea that lasted the length of three whole weeks. That long period of separation from Marwan gave me time to think and to try to forgive.

The one trauma Suad couldn't protect me from was the presence of the family physician, Dr. Imad. He was the first person Suad had called on the following day of that incident. My eyes were shut, my jaws were grinding, as I listened to that hateful voice giving Suad instructions. Imad didn't come near my bed or address me directly until a three-day seizure of stomach cramps hit me and dehydrated me, it left me almost dead.

"Try to relax, Mrs. Rajy. You are being too hard on yourself." Imad sounded very proper, very professional. But the moment we were left alone he rushed to my side and grabbed my hand. "Please forgive me, Nadia, it was very foolish of me to lose control that way. I beg you, let's be friends." I turned my face away and said nothing. "You don't believe me, but the time will come when I will earn your trust again." Waiting for a response that didn't come, he pulled back and whispered to himself, "You are not hearing what I have to say. I can't blame you, especially after what happened to you lately."

Leaving Suad and her mother to their noisy planning for the next day's birthday party, I rested my head against the window pane that looked out on the graying horizon, letting my thoughts wander beyond the bustling harbor of the prosperous city. It was a crisp evening. The sky was bright and filled with stars. Still, not all was perfect. The fumes from the giant refineries by the bay bridge formed an ominous umbrella over part of the city. My mind drifted away into the glorious unknown future that awaited me, a future that seemed as great as the miracle unfolding within me.

The whole world changed for me when the fifth week ended and my period did not come. Indeed, a few weeks ago I was still that sickly confused woman who hated nothing as much as her dumb body, a sinful piece of flesh that attracted every wicked fly. But that was a long time ago, meanwhile, my body had seemingly repented and transformed the ordeal inflicted on it by Marwan into a great miracle: Could it be possible that a baby had begun to grow in it. Yes, the girl who since infancy had played mother to rag dolls, stray kittens, and younger siblings might soon become a real mother. Would I be a good mother? Would Marwan give me a fit child?

Throughout the time I spent at my in-laws, Suad kept the family away from me. Occasionally the young siblings came in with Aunt Najla to bring me flowers they had picked on their way home from school. Uncle Ahmad would come loaded with gifts of exotic fruits, silk blouses, and exquisite jewelry. Yet I had the feeling that he was more aware of my pain than he could admit and I felt compelled, by some unwritten code, to guard against disclosure of the real cause of my sickness that made me leave my apartment.

What should I do about Marwan now? How would he react if I was really pregnant? Would I ever be able to live with him again knowing how much he hated children?

"Is there something the matter, Nadia? You look very pale today, Nadia." Suad joined me in the bedroom bringing a cup of tea. "Would you like to sit for a while before we go to meet the family?" This was my birthday and I was expected to join the family out in the lounge to celebrate it.

"I'm fine, it's just that I'm curious about Marwan. I haven't seen him since that night." The fact that I carried his child inside me eased my grudge against him.

"Well, rest assured that he is dying to see you, so please relax." Suad admitted.

"It seems sometimes that he still doesn't confide in me. He is so tight-lipped toward me, you'd think I was the enemy. I wish he would allow himself to enjoy the good things life has given us."

She was silent for a moment as if gathering her thoughts. "Maybe he's feeling the constraints of marriage ... and it carries a lot of obligations, doesn't it? Take children, for instance. I have wondered what would happen if you want children and he doesn't? He's always been wary of being around them. He can't stand the constant activity, the needs that never end, the noise."

Unaware of the crucial point she had made, Suad waited to see my reaction to her dilemma. I felt a monstrous lump in my throat and I had to swallow before I could answer. "We haven't spoken about this yet. Did he ever discuss it with you? I know he trusts you the most in this house."

"Oh, he often raved at Mother for having done us a great disservice by bringing us all into the world. 'I want nothing to do with this human crime, Mother,' he yelled at her once when she preached to him about the magic of having one's own children." Suad laughed lightheartedly. She had no idea that Marwan's baby was no more than an arm's length from her.

"Hello, Nadia!" Marwan's unexpected greeting made us both jump. "I came to accompany you to the dining room. Everyone is waiting for you." Marwan crossed the room, and stood there, facing us. There was a big smile on his face and in his eyes. Suad mumbled a greeting and quickly vanished.

My ears buzzed as if wasps had been caught in them. I had no idea how I looked, but my face must have looked frightful. Marwan suddenly dropped his pretense, his confident tone disappeared, and he rushed to support my swaying body. All the force of my confused emotions erupted into a flood of tears. "Oh, darling Nadia! Please, my love, forgive me!"

I kept the news about my pregnancy secret for awhile after I moved back home with Marwan. The loss of weight I suffered covered up for all the changes happening to my body. Marwan had to be warned by his mother that his would be the last time he would be forgiven for what he did to me.

It was Suad who, after the third month of my pregnancy, caught me in my nightgown with my stomach bulging.

"No, you tell Marwan and the rest of the family, Suad," I said. "I know the family will be elated, but what about Marwan?"

"Oh, Nadia. He will be happy too," Suad defended. "Deep down he is a very soft-hearted man."

Suad loved her brother Marwan too much to know about that deep down part of him. The effect of being a father took its toll on him. The larger my stomach grew the sadder he became. For some reason I was able to understand his attitude. This man never did anything by choice. It was always his parents who forced him into the future. Not even his job was his choice. It was his father's large share in that national bank that placed him there. Then his marriage to me was arranged by his parents. And now, the pressure on him to consummate the marriage made him a father by default.

"Dear Nadia," Nora's letter began. "With great relief I received your long-awaited letter, which brought the wonderful surprise about the upcoming birth of the baby. How anxious I have been since news of your long, complicated illness reached Beirut in late January. Rumors hinted that you were involved in some kind of accident that left you with a mysterious illness. Uncle Ahmad sounded quite confident when I talked with him on the phone in mid-February. He said there was nothing to worry about and denied the rumors, saying that your illness was nothing more than a passing stomach flu. "Oh, Nadia, knowing how happy you must be about carrying a baby, I become impatient with my own dull life here and the way it consumes me. I long to be free of the duties at home that are keeping my wings from flying and being with you. But alas! With Mae, Ameen, and Fadi growing up so fast, I am not allowed that liberty. Everyone in this house seems to have the right to assert his or her ever-growing demands except for me. I had hoped to spend spring vacation with you in Haifa so I could help you out with some knitting for the baby, but my mother thought it unwise that I leave when those three siblings are on vacation, since they're too much for her to handle.

"Well, a lot of changes have taken place here since we saw each other last spring, Nadia. Not very reassuring things, I'm afraid. In addition to family obligations keeping me from social activities, our father's temper and the harsh way he treats the children are making life more and more miserable for me. Most painful is his flagrant hostility toward our brother Anwar, whose success in business in Beirut is turning him into an aggressive and independent man. My father's unpredictable moods are a constant emotional hazard to my mother's gentle spirit, especially when it comes to her favorite son.

"He became obsessed with the idea that Marwan was the cause of your illness. He argues for hours with my mother about their foolish mistake of giving in to the Rajys and letting you go. He picks a fight with Anwar if he happens to mention Marwan's name or anything happening in Palestine. More than once I've seen him sneak into my room to go to the old closet. He sorts through your summer clothes and buries his nose in their folds, clinging to them in a weird pathetic way. Some of them vanished, never to be found again. And when the family cheered to learn of your baby, he snapped, 'stop this nonsense! We want no more babies in this house, do you understand? Aren't you more than enough as it is?' The kids argued the joys of being called aunts and uncles, but he cut them short, warning that he was not about to have any child call him grandpa. Now I realize how hard it must have been for you, fighting him all alone. Even if I live a hundred years, I will never understand him.

"Forgive me, Sis, for crying on your shoulder at a time when you need clear horizons, not darksome clouds, but I have no one else to confide in. Let me brighten up now and tell you a small secret of my own. A friend of mine has introduced me to a brother of hers who is in search of a wife. He is one of those dedicated scholars who forgot all about marriage until now, when he is in his early forties. You might not think I should marry a man who is nearly double my age, but you must know that my options are nearly nil by now, especially if I keep on living in other people's shadows. I need you here more than ever, for you to meet him before the negative overtones from our parents and Anwar drive him away for good. Can you come to visit around the end of this month? Summer vacation could be a turning point for Mahmoud and me. If we become engaged, we shall have a couple of months to get to know more about each other. Please, Nadia, try to come. Write back as soon as you can and tell me how that tiny little thing inside you is doing. I love you, Nora."

Dated July 1, Nora's letter was delayed for two weeks due to a new, but hardly unexpected, round of violence that broke out in Palestine that summer of 1937 following the British Royal Commission's report on the partition of the country. Involving long years of work on Britain's decision about the Arab-Jewish conflict, the report—as the nationalists expected—had recommended partition of Palestine and the establishment of a Jewish homeland comprising Galilee, the Jezreel Valley, and the coast from Acre to Tel Aviv, a territory that would include Haifa. The Commission further suggested the partitioned Arab state merge with Transjordan. This gave the nationalist rebels their first tangible evidence of a conspiracy between Britain and all the Arab kings, sheikhs, and princes, against the Palestinians and in support of the Zionists.

Marwan took this as a confirmation of his view that the Palestinian case was hopeless. His old idea that well-to-do people like his family were better off escaping with their money to Beirut before such a plot crushed them resurfaced. One evening when Suad and Farid, one of the younger brothers, were having dinner with us we were debating the suggested demarcation of the partition and the disastrous effect it would have on all the countries surrounding Palestine. This prompted Marwan to go on one of his tirades.

"Isn't it ironic that, of all the generations that have lived on this miserable land, we have to be God's twentieth-century sacrificial victim to be immolated on Ibrahim's rock?"

"What Ibrahim are you talking about?" I knew this was his grandfather's name, but he seemed to be referring to some other Ibrahim.

"About that prophet, of course, who had made a habit of threatening to slaughter his son every time he wanted a favor from God!" I still didn't know what slaughtering he was talking about, and I said so. "I don't know, honey," Marwan said wearily. "We grew up in parochial foreign schools; surely you got as much as I did of those mythical stories. Maybe Farid can help, how about it, Farid? You attended local schools, what do they say about that issue?" Sarcasm was getting the better of him and Farid seemed reluctant to pursue such a slippery argument. Religion was a revered subject at the Rajys'. Marwan was the only voice of doubt and cynicism.

"You shouldn't mock such things, Marwan," Suad said nervously. She was probably the only Rajy who would stand up to her brother's challenges. Farid looked worried.

"Why not?" Marwan almost screamed. "Isn't that damned rock the cause of all our misery? How much blood do you think has been shed on this accursed soil in the name of that Ibrahim and his stupid act? And what about that God who rushed down with a lamb just in the nick of time? Where are those lambs now? Couldn't he come down with a lamb right now and stop these new warlords from slaughtering us?"

Godly lambs or not, the fighting continued over the crucial partition report. More and more it resembled a fast-growing civil war. Battles such as the authorities used to call disorder or disturbance were now reported with big words like civil disobedience, insurrection, rebellion. Nationalists who were identified before as anarchists, armed agents, or fundamentalists became conspirators, assassins, terrorists. Heavy government artillery was carried on huge trucks and fierce-looking vehicles outside the urban areas, especially in the north. The change in Haifa's task force was seen not so much in the type of arms as in the sort of men carrying them. Gradually, uniformed athletic bodies, tall thin frames— blond hair, blond mustaches, blue glassy eyes—became a common sight.

On the surface, Marwan seemed less agitated by the new political development than by the previous ones, but deep down he was in a state of despairing resignation. I, on the other hand, became more involved, I would glue myself to the radio for the regular newscasts and I would read everything I could get my hands on. Our social life, already slowed by my pregnancy, had almost come to a standstill since the beginning of the month.

✑

Nora's letter lay on my lap as I rocked slowly in my chair. The crystal clock on the piano declared noon to have arrived. Time for the news! I turned on the radio as the vigorous voice of pro-nationalist anchorman Bahri revealed that the revolutionary leader Mufti Hadj Ameen al-Hussaini, who since the beginning of this eruption of violence had taken refuge at the Haram al-Sharif, the Aqsa Mosque, had fled to Damascus during the night for an emergency meeting with the Arab Jihad commanders.

"Now what?" I wondered aloud, and got a sharp kick from the baby inside me as he shifted to one side. The pain brought a smile to my face. The tingling thrill of touching this child still in the making then made me think about Marwan, who was fighting the idea of fatherhood tooth and nail. "It is utterly crazy to bring a baby into this chaotic world, Nadia. Why did you let this happen to us, can't you do something about it?" I had a hunch he was afraid of that unborn baby, as though a child could be one more hazard in a land torn with violence. The concept of being fearful of a child seemed weird. If anything, we had to fear for that innocent baby instead.

The region's English broadcast came just after one o'clock: "Commissioner Andrews—the district commissioner of Galilee, who was publicly accused of demarcating Galilee in favor of the Zionists for the partition proposal—was shot dead by four armed commandos outside the Anglican Church in Nazareth." I bolted to my feet and rushed to the terrace, scanning the noon haze engulfing the city. I had expected to see Haifa on fire as a result of that news, but the city hummed drowsily in the blazing sun. I turned back to the cool of the hall and busied myself collecting the scattered pages of Nora's letter.

I lay on the long comfortable sofa, trying to make up my mind about Nora's call for help. "This is the first time Nora has allowed herself to open her heart to you," I thought. "The first time she had ever revealed her disappointment with her parents and the first time she has asked for such an important favor," a voice reasoned. "The baby isn't due for another three months." But I worried. What if things got worse in Palestine and I couldn't come back? The mere thought of giving birth under my father's eyes if I got stuck over there made me shudder. "You have to go, Nora needs you!" the voice persisted.

"Nadia, wake up! What's wrong?" Marwan's alarmed voice broke the silence around me. "Are you in pain? Why are you crying?" My hand was still holding the pages of Nora's letter. They were wet with my tears.

My voice shook with hesitation: "I have to go home!"

Marwan's eyes hardened. "What home is that?"

"Oh, Marwan, I'm sorry, I'm still drowsy. What I mean is that I need to go to Beirut for a few days. Nora needs to talk to me about a problem she's having." My words sounded incoherent even to my own ears. "Well, sister stuff, you know." I felt like a fool. How could I put it to make Marwan understand the situation? Nora's choice didn't seem to fit into any of the usual categories of acceptable suitors. And from the little Nora had said about him, the man might not even be worth the sacrifice of my rushing to Beirut. I took a deep breath. "You see, Marwan, I owe Nora the effort. She has always been there for me, helping whenever she could, listening to my dreams but never talking about her own."

"Well, I can see that you're set on making that trip," Marwan interrupted cheerfully. A smile flickered in his eyes as he continued, "I have an idea, what if I come with you? We could spend the coming week there and come back on Sunday. Would that be acceptable?"

"Acceptable? That would be wonderful! Oh, Marwan, Nora will be thrilled. She needs all the advice she can get in the next few weeks. Can you leave this Tuesday, the twentieth?" Babbling with joy over Marwan's unexpected decision to finally take a long-overdue vacation, I jumped up and into his arms. I clung to him for a few moments before I realized how unyielding his thin body was. I looked at his face and saw his bright smile fade away, replaced with apprehension as he pulled away from my expanding tummy. My arms fell from his neck and I stumbled backward.

Marwan was terrified by the feelings he had coming so close to his own unborn baby.

8

1937

I remember the chilling shock I felt when our loyal driver, Hadj Uthman, reached my family's summer house late in the afternoon with the news of Uncle Ahmad's massive heart attack. We were celebrating Nora's engagement to Mahmoud.

Marwan retired into his cocoon during our entire journey back home. I had learned to leave him alone at such times. It was after midnight when we reached home. Marwan went straight up to the apartment while I hurried down the wide staircase leading to Uncle Ahmad's big house, now silent and completely dark except for one light from the couple's bedroom. A large lump lodged in my throat and tears stung my eyes. Please, God, I prayed, don't let him die! With both hands pressed against my lips, I stood outside their closed bedroom door trying to muffle my loud sobs.

The back door was ajar and I had tiptoed to his room. There he was on his big brass bed. His bulging chest heaved audibly, as if such a natural process as breathing had suddenly become an impossible ordeal. I went to his side and touched his brow. His skin was warm and alive. Head down into the folds of her scarf, Aunt Najla slept heavily in her chair by his bed. I found a chair and for a long hour, hoped he or Aunt Najla would wake up and talk to me. When I got up to leave, the anguish was gone. I felt that God's grace filled the air and my prayers were answered.

Nevertheless, two weeks later there had been no substantial improvement despite the care of the three best-known physicians in the area. Twice a week the medical team came to consult on the case, and Dr. Imad and Ralph reported their day-to-day treatment to them. But it was always with long, grim faces that the doctors left the house.

To my horror, arrangements for the possibility of Uncle Ahmad's death were being discussed by Aunt Najla's brothers and other close family members from Beirut and Acre, casting the usually lively house into a state of mute despair. Until the late hours of the night, one could hear a lot about power of attorney, death certificates, burial ceremonies, guest lists, even the menu for the funeral gathering. But I knew in my heart that he was not going to die. I spent most of my time at his bedside, and I associated his endurance with that of the buoyant captive inside me. I kept on assuring myself that Uncle Ahmad would survive, if for nothing else, to take care of his grandchild.

The heart specialist on the medical team suggested that we try a new medicine as a last resort. Ralph had called upon the Red Cross in Jerusalem for help in obtaining it quickly, and two days later an exultant Marwan burst in carrying the little white box. Dr. Imad and Ralph decided to start giving Uncle Ahmad the precious injections at once. Ralph translated the prescription from German to Arabic: "It is critical that this medicine be administered precisely every six hours, day and night."

I offered to do it if they would teach me. "These are intramuscular shots, quite easy, anyone can give them," Ralph assured me. The challenge of performing such an important task filled me with a newfound energy. To Marwan's dismay and Aunt Najla's astonishment, I followed the procedure step by step without any problem. Everything went fine until the critical moment of driving the needle into human flesh. For a moment I thought I would faint. "Don't be afraid!" Imad shouted. "Plunge the needle down in one steady stroke." His mocking arrogance provoked me. I saw my hand guide the needle right into the designated muscle. "Again," he commanded. "Don't hesitate and don't let your emotions get in your way."

The sound of excited voices and hurried footsteps that had surrounded me for nearly two days and one whole night had finally moved into the rest of the apartment. I lay immersed in the sweet pains and marvels of birth. There it was, at arm's reach, a little miracle bundled securely beneath the colorful quilt of its lace-ruffled crib.

The labor had begun early on Wednesday as I was having my shower. With a busy day ahead, I tried not to pay attention to the cramps I felt in my abdomen. Aunt Najla had told me such pains were normal for a woman in her ninth month of pregnancy. Uncle Ahmad's medical team was meeting around noon to decide whether to change his strict diet to a more palatable one, since his condition had been steadily improving. Dr. Imad was to monitor the effect of such a change and I was to make sure the new guidelines would be followed.

The hall clock chimed eleven as I left my room. Bright sunshine filtered through the tall windows. There was a promise of a beautiful dry day after a long week of heavy fall rain that had flooded the city roads. The doorbell rang and I went to answer it. But halfway down the hall another wave of pain tore through my lower abdomen. My knees gave out and I grabbed the corner of some piece of furniture for support, wailing inarticulately. The bell rang again. "Miss Nadia, are you there?" Warrood's voice came through the thick wooden panel. She began tapping frantically on the door, and then I heard her wooden clogs fade away down the staircase.

$$\sim\!\mathcal{C}$$

"Mother, now that the doctor is sure Nadia is in labor, shouldn't we call Marwan and tell him about what's going on?" Ali whispered as I lay resting on the sofa. Aunt Najla explained to her son that husbands had nothing to do with their wives' labor, and sent him off to inform the midwife, who was waiting at the big house, that labor had begun.

The where and how of our baby's delivery had been exhaustively discussed by the grown-ups of the family. Marwan insisted that no one less than a fully qualified obstetrician could attend to his wife; male or female made no difference to him. Although nobody cared to get my opinion on a matter that usually concerned the grown-ups only, I supported Marwan openly, trying to put enough pressure on Uncle Ahmad to get him to overcome his prejudice against hospitals. But to no avail. They insisted that no Rajy woman had ever been subjected to such humiliation. Their beloved Nadia was to be no exception to this tradition.

$$\sim\!\mathcal{C}$$

Aunt Najla beamed at a tall, immaculately dressed young woman who entered my bedroom. "I'm glad Ali found you at home, Zahia. I was told your mother is out of town."

"Yes, Lady Rajy, she is. I hope you don't mind my coming instead." She stretched out a long arm and shook my hand; then she stroked it tenderly. "It is a pleasure to meet you, Mrs. Nadia. I'm glad to see you in such good health and hope your delivery will be easy." Her long fingers played with the corner of my bed cover as she asked tentatively: "Do you mind if I have a look?" "What kind of a look?" I asked with great distress. The room went suddenly silent as the half dozen women who had gathered in the room watched in anticipation. Annoyed by the offhand way Zahia proposed to expose my body to all those inquisitive eyes, I hung on to my cover, preventing her from pulling it away.

"You'd better let me rest now. I'm not sure I want you to see me." The intensity of my feeling was quite obvious and I watched with relief as Aunt Najla led the scandalized onlookers out of the room without a word. Zahia sat waiting. "A physician doesn't make a show out of his patient's body. What is it that you expect to see under my covers?" I asked.

"I am terribly sorry if I upset you, but having these women sticking around isn't my fault. It's up to your mother-in-law to decide whether they stay or not. Neither a midwife nor a physician usually dares interfere with such socially sensitive issues."

"Well, I want none of you with me. Please go and ask Suad to come and stay with me."

"I will gladly do so if you let me check on you just to see how much time you have left." But I shook my head and told her I felt quite all right. Who knows? Maybe the baby had changed its mind after all. But my wishful thought had barely taken shape when an unbearable sharp pain took my breath away. My screams brought Aunt Najla back to my side. My fingers still clutched stubbornly at my cover. I saw the wink Zahia gave her before leaving.

"Dear Nadia, I know how embarrassing it is to let a stranger infringe on your privacy. But what alternative do we have at a crucial time like this? Please, honey, don't cry!" Her palm felt so soft when she wiped the tears off my cheeks.

"But what if she isn't really qualified, as Marwan keeps on saying? With that heavy makeup, perfume, and long polished fingernails, she doesn't seem very professional. If Uncle Ahmad doesn't want me to deliver in a hospital, why can't you call a doctor here instead?"

"Don't worry! Zahia was trained by her mother, the midwife who aided in delivering most of the babies of this city, and she's very reliable in spite of her appearance."

"But what about the albumen in my blood that Dr. Imad warned us about this morning? Do you think Zahia can handle it in case something goes wrong?"

"That's nothing, honey. We all get swollen limbs a few months before the baby is due. Using fancy medical names for ordinary symptoms makes doctors sound more serious. I'm sure Zahia is capable of handling any uncomplicated situation."

"Maybe as far as the mother is concerned, but what about the effect of this blood disorder on the baby? Suppose the baby has a problem. Does she know what to do then?"

"Would you rather have Imad attending to you? It's easy to call him any time." Aunt Najla mistook my moan of resignation for the arrival of the labor pangs and she rushed out to call Zahia.

I woke up to feel Marwan's hand touching my brows, "Nadia, wake up. You were moaning, honey, are you in pain?" he said frantically.

"Oh, thank God you're home. What time is it? Did you see the baby? It's a boy, Marwan, a big boy."

"I just came in, Nadia. I wanted to see how you are doing first. Mother told me about the difficulty you had delivering this boy." Ignoring my excitement about the baby, he sat down next to my bed and grasped my hand. "You're very hot, darling, are you sure you're all right?"

"I don't know, maybe I'm running a fever. But that doesn't matter now. Go on, pick him up, please, bring him to me here. I would like to have a better look at him now that he has had some rest."

"I don't know how to lift such tiny creatures. I'd rather you let it rest. We have plenty of time to see it later. To me all babies at this stage look alike." He avoided looking at the crib, but seemed unable to take his eyes away from me. "It's you I'm worried about, and how long it's going to take you to recover from the injuries this pregnancy has caused you. I hate seeing you so worn out. You look so different now."

It was quite clear that Marwan couldn't care less about how his baby looked. Rather he felt sorry for me, as if going through the trauma of bringing a baby to life was a tragic mistake I had brought on myself. I closed my eyes and tried to remain calm.

The five days following the birth were spent in pain and misery, beginning with the fever Marwan had noticed. Then a throbbing abdominal pain started torturing my body shortly after midnight. Suad and Aunt

Najla took turns watching over me. They placed towels soaked in diluted vinegar on my forehead and they kept on feeding me a trickle of some sweetened liquid. But the thrill over the baby's presence, and the momentous effect it was having on everyday life, made my physical pains seem unimportant. In addition to being fed, cleaned, dressed, and stiffly wrapped in swaddling clothes every day, the poor infant would now have to endure the painful ceremony of circumcision, a cruel operation that had to be performed on male infants within the first week of their birth. Indeed the Rajys, who couldn't wait to make of this traditional ritual a double thanksgiving offering, observing the birth of the baby boy and his grandpa's recovery, put together a grand feast on that day. It began quite early when a dozen lambs were slaughtered and later barbecued to feed the several hundred guests invited for that special occasion. The circumcision was to take place at eleven. Because Uncle Ahmad could not climb the stairs to our apartment, it would be performed at the Rajy residence.

"Oh, Nadia, I shouldn't be introducing your baby to his grandpa as you lie sick in bed; Ahmad is waiting anxiously to see you as well," Aunt Najla said.

"Please look after my baby, Aunt Najla, and bring him back to me as soon as possible." I didn't tell her that being sick on this particular occasion was a blessing to me. I would rather have died than watched those people cheering and dancing as my baby's genitals were mutilated. Twice I had seen this deplorable crime committed upon my two youngest brothers. "In the Name of Almighty God," the brutal *mutahher* would shriek as his blade flashed over the child. Filled with an absurd pride, the audience burst into wild cheers, drowning out the loud sobs of the victim.

Followed by a mournful father and a nervous grandma, the baby came back cuddled in his aunt's arms, his piteous shrieks drowned out by the voices of his companions, who seemed involved in a heated argument. Suad carefully put the fitful child down beside me. "Here I am, Mama, back with a new name," she mimicked with a pale smile.

"Name? What name?" I asked nervously.

"Muhammad. That's one of several auspicious names given to every Muslim boy on his day of circumcision. It's second to the name you wish to bestow on your son."

"Why don't you reconsider naming him Ahmad—Muhammad

Ahmad Rajy! Doesn't that sound great?" Obviously Aunt Najla was pursuing an ongoing argument with Marwan.

From my bed I pretended to have no interest in the debate. Yet I prayed that Marwan would remain firm against the family's tradition of always naming the first born male after his grandfather. Unconsciously my hand slipped under the pillow where my long list of chosen names for the baby lay waiting. Ahmad wasn't on that list.

Aunt Najla managed an almost imperceptible smile as she pulled herself out of her chair to leave. "Please try to talk to him, honey, I'm sure you know better than I do how to reason with him." I reasoned with Marwan, all right. The list of names I showed him brought a spark of joy to his eyes, and he left it to me and Suad to find a brand new name for the baby. And that we did.

"I want him to pick his own name, Suad. You'll see." I pulled the long list of names from under my pillow. We chose five short names, very poetic ones. Then I wrote them on separate small pieces of paper, and I creased them into little balls. I held them in my palm as she went to the crib and brought the baby to my side. Driven by his urgent hunger, he swung out his little fists in all directions. His tiny fingers struck at my outstretched palm the way little minnows strike pieces of bread used for bait. I opened the ball of paper he first touched.

Usama M. Rajy! His name filled my heart with inexplicable joy.

Later, after the last group of visitors left on that long day of ceremonial activities, Aunt Najla sat next to my bed praying earnestly, her left hand pressed against my forehead while her right one counted the small ivory beads of her rosary. The fever that had gnawed at my body for five days had shot up unusually high and the pain intensified unbearably. Suad urged that Dr. Imad be called. "You know this is not a matter for a doctor to check on, Suad," her mother said. "I told you something of this sort was going to happen when the Mansour sisters were here this afternoon, didn't I?"

"Nadia's fever began long before the Mansours came to visit. I have the feeling there is something more serious here than an evil eye, Mother."

"Haven't you ever seen a woman passing through these periods of afterbirth illness? It's only five days since Nadia delivered her first child. Give her some time, my daughter, and remember, doctors do what they can, but our destiny is in God's hands, not in the hands of doctors."

"Why are you still here, Mother, is something the matter?" Marwan, already changed into his robe over his pajamas, peeked in the door.

"Nadia is in pain. Her fever has risen to over 104," Suad told him. "I think we have to let Imad come to see her. What do you say?"

"By all means, Suad. But why didn't you tell me earlier? I would've gone to him myself." His eyes turned to his mother accusingly. "Is that why you have filled our apartment with this incense of yours all afternoon?"

"Don't wake up the baby, Marwan," she urged. "Come, let's go to the hall." She continued in an even gentler tone, but words were drowned by his shouts and by the pounding of his fist on the table. "No, not tomorrow! Right now. Send one of your damn sons to him, right now. Go!"

Marwan, Imad, and Ralph showed up quite late, accompanied by a tall bearded man who spoke English with a strange accent. "Nadia, this is Dr. Evan Brennen, obstetric surgeon for the maternity wing at the German Hospital. He is here to see you."

"Hello, Madame." Dr. Brennen's large satin palm covered the back of my hand as if to steady it. My nervous fingers held on to the cool fabric of my cover in case he decided to "have a look." Against the bright light of the bedroom lamp his huge frame loomed over me like a ghost. "I'm here to help you get well, Mrs. Rajy, please relax." In contrast to his intimidating size, his basso voice was cheerful and reassuring. After a short examination, he reported to his colleagues who waited down the hall with Marwan. As they returned to my room, he was explaining to Marwan: "Sorry to have to tell you, Mr. Rajy, that your wife's illness could've been totally avoided if attended to in time. Her midwife, who must have seen the long tear caused by the delivery, committed an unforgivable error in not reporting it to your family doctor immediately so that it could have been stitched properly."

"So, what are we going to do now, Doctor?" Marwan sounded enraged at the whole world at that moment.

"Under the circumstances, I suggest we proceed immediately." Instead of addressing me—the patient—he addressed the men around him as if the only concern he had was asserting his expertise over his younger colleagues. Without a word to me, not even a good night, the four men strolled away, making plans for Dr. Imad to help the surgeon move a couple of nurses and the equipment necessary to perform the operation in my room. Marwan was to remove some of the furniture to make space for a surgical bed and the necessary tables and medical supplies.

Listless and bitterly lonely, I watched my little baby be carried away by Suad. I longed to touch that beloved son and hold him close to my heart while he struggled to recover from the trauma of circumcision. I wanted to be the one to fulfill all his needs, instead of having my in-laws and their hirelings fussing around him. I wanted to wash his ivory skin and to slip the soft embroidered shirts over his small round shoulders. I wondered how it would feel to have my baby's fingers tugging at my throbbing breasts. Instead I had to watch his wet nurse force a bulging brown nipple between his tiny lips.

My dreams were interrupted by the entrance of Dr. Brennen and two elderly nurses who were rolling in a surgical table outfitted with gleaming instruments and other supplies. I didn't know any details about the operation, but as the three of them set the stage for it I made a supreme effort to shut my mind against what was going to take place. As my eyes fell on the long syringe filled with anesthetic for my abdomen, I drifted back to the time of my baby brother Fadi's birth. Because of my mother's weakened condition he, like Mae, Akram, and Amin before him, had to survive on the milk of their wet nurses. I vowed to bounce back to life to be a fit mother to this child, a child that lived and breathed, not a rag doll.

I took a deep breath of relief as the strong arms of both nurses finally tucked my numb body under the soft quilt of my bed. The clock on the wall struck midnight when Dr. Brennen and his team rolled their equipment out of the room and shut the door behind them.

"What is it with you tonight, Marwan? Why are you making such a big fuss over your boss's visit? Is there any more to it than a social call?" Marwan's spirits had picked up after the baby was taken to the Rajys for the evening and I had joined him in the bedroom to change for the occasion.

"Of course, there is a lot more, Nadia. A man as calculating as Ali Ibrahim is not going to visit us at home just to congratulate us on having a baby. He didn't say it openly, but I know he wants to discuss my attitude toward him in view of the way the board in Jerusalem is handling my position at the bank."

"But don't you think I should know a little more about that side of your life before I can take part in a discussion of it? Although you have said that Ali Ibrahim values my common sense, the man really knows nothing about me. He met me only once. And to tell you the truth, I'm in awe of what I hear about his shrewd knowledge of the business world. I doubt that he's going to listen to what I say, don't you?" I couldn't tell him the many reasons that made me hate the man's power—the arrogant husband who had his wife covered in black and had left her to degenerate in boredom while he enjoyed his life to the fullest, the cunning manager who charted the destiny of my husband's career, the influential leader who skillfully tutored Uncle Ahmad and molded his financial fate. . . . Ali Ibrahim was now on his way over to shape my destiny too.

"Don't worry . . . he's like any other intelligent man, easy to be charmed by a beautiful woman like you. It's enough that you understand my dedication to a job that made me a slave to snobs like the pasha and his board members in Jerusalem throughout my whole career. Ali Ibrahim and I were a team working in our branch in Haifa from the time the original national corporation was established. We remained in the same place and capacity even after the split occurred and the Arab Land Bank was formed—he as manager and I as treasurer. That's a unique situation in our line of business. Even more unique is the fact that, as you know, I am probably the only treasurer in town who carries both keys to the bank's safe—mine and the manager's." He seemed so proud of himself that I felt sad to see how obsessed he was about his working domain, as though nothing else was as important, not even family or a child.

"Welcome, Ali Bey. Please come in." Marwan's cordial greeting reverberated through the apartment. The visitor's deep voice responded in like fashion and they stepped onto the terrace. I came down the hall to join them as they discussed the sudden heat wave that had enveloped the city for the last few days. By the time we shook hands and finished the obligatory chat about health, family, and children, we were seated around the terrace table looking formal but cheerful.

Soon Marwan moved the conversation to the reason for the meeting: fears over the questionable policy the Arab Land Bank's main office in Jerusalem was dictating to the branch in Haifa, Marwan's hometown and the center of his family's prestige. He was quick and to the point. "With all due respect, I believe you and your colleagues are too involved in politics to see where the bank is heading. Let me ask you this: Of the hundreds of overdrafts you and the other board members have signed for your constituents in the last two years, how many are solvent?"

This was a surprisingly bold question coming from Marwan, who usually deferred to his more aggressive boss. I knew he must have been quite desperate to speak that way. I held my breath, I expected the worst.

"You have always had rigid views about our bank's policies, Marwan, and that will probably never change, because you feel an obligation only to the well-oiled machinery of money making. This bank, unlike all the others in Palestine, was established to meet the needs of the rural Arab population, remember? It opened at a time when our poor landowners and the majority of the peasants had no access to any of the financial institutions in our country, because they were predominantly controlled by foreigners. Our aim has always been to support a national agricultural industry, in the face of the great challenge posed by the financiers of the Western world."

"I have no quarrel with that heroic aim, sir, and I'm not as indifferent to your political motivation as you seem to imply. But, as the treasurer of this bank, and with a duty to make ends meet, I'm frightened to see the road down which the board in Jerusalem is leading us. You know the bank's assets have been shrinking rapidly as the contributions from Arab countries decrease annually. This is why I believe that by opening new branches abroad, especially in politically stable countries, business could flourish steadily. I think Beirut is the best place to make this experiment. If the bank succeeds there, then you can go on to establish branches in other cities as well."

"Excuse me, Marwan, I think I'm missing a point here," I interrupted, hoping to slow down the intense discussion before it got out of hand. "How can an indigenous corporation established specifically to protect the peasants and help their landlords invest in Palestinian lands go out and invest in other countries? Why would the rich neighboring countries that are the financial support for your bank let you use their capital to set up competing banks?"

Both men rushed to comment, with Ali Ibrahim taking the lead. "That's what I call logic! Thank you Mrs. Rajy, for being so candid." He turned to Marwan. "Go ahead, my friend, tell this lady how you plan to enact your project now. Where would the money come from to set up a branch capable of competing with those already established in a city like Beirut?"

Marwan didn't seem discouraged by these remarks. "Alas, Nadia, that opportunity is lost now. But we could still maneuver this project through the organization, if the board in Jerusalem would support it wholeheartedly. Money can be very powerful as long as it keeps circulating. There are professionals who can help us do that if needed. As for the source of the money and whether we have the right to take it abroad . . . well, no one can tell us what to do, if we do good business and everyone stands to profit from new ways of investment and expansion."

After a short pause, the deep voice came alive again. "I see your point, Marwan. But I must warn you not to build too much hope on such a turn in policy. First and foremost, you have to remember that our Arab contributors have their own political motives for supporting this land bank enterprise. We're talking about regimes, kings and rulers here, not people like you and me. These men have advisors handling their investments all over the world. Secondly, I can't begin to imagine who among us is capable of convincing them to finance freelance investment, including another branch in Beirut, for a group of politically committed men like us. Do you think you could do that?"

His scornful tone made me feel that Marwan was going to be outmatched in this argument. Ever since I had known him, Marwan had longed to have his own little bank in Beirut. He spoke with touching confidence about the feasibility of his project, as if the money for such a costly enterprise were there for him to grab. For a limited time, his dream became mine as well, when the political situation grew more complicated and innocent people became pawns in the hands of self-proclaimed leaders, regional and otherwise. Like Marwan in his constant search for peace and tranquillity, I started to build hopes around going back to Lebanon after little Usama was born. I saw no point in raising a child in a troubled city when I could secure a normal life and safer future for him elsewhere. But I was shaken back to reality as I realized that nothing in the world could make Uncle Ahmad—our provider—uproot himself and leave his ancestral land.

When I came back with the coffee tray a while later, I was stunned to find my husband and his guest involved in a nasty dispute over Marwan's status in his job. Standing away from the table, Marwan shook his finger in his boss's angry flushed face, accusing the bank's board of unjust treatment over the years and rehearsing a list of promotions for which he had been passed over. Ali Ibrahim tried to interrupt but Marwan was beyond coherence. "I have nothing more to say, Ali Bey, except to offer my resignation."

Marwan's words flew through the air like hand grenades timed to explode before the very face of an enemy. Yet somehow I was not displeased to hear them. His complaints seemed thoroughly justified to me. "Resignation? From what?" Ali Ibrahim's voice was stunned and uncomprehending. "You can't be serious! Did I say something to lead you to this?"

"No, this has nothing to do with you. And it isn't an impulsive or arbitrary decision. I've been thinking about it ever since my father followed you to this bank. All of you have wanted me to do a good job in securing your interests, but no one cares enough to give me the security I need. You insist on keeping me tied to the same position. Excuse my bluntness, but I hate politics and I don't appreciate the way politicians function."

"In my view your resignation, which seems to be a spiteful act of mutiny done on the spur of the moment, constitutes a most unfair infringement on the feelings of other members of your family. Are you planning to tell your father about what is going on? I trust you haven't told him about the bank's actual financial problems?" A sharp edge of hostility could be heard in Ali Ibrahim's voice.

"Don't worry, my friend! If my father ever learns how troubled the bank is, I assure you it won't be from me. But I want out. The whole matter is taking too great a toll on me."

As I watched these two combatants maneuver into the closing of their bargain, my impulse was to run to Uncle Ahmad and warn him. But I realized it was Marwan's secret, and he would have to be the one to tell his father. "Our board has solid faith in your capability, as does your father. We believe you are better suited to the work we have laid out for you as our regional treasurer in Haifa and in the other northern branches. Furthermore, you're my right hand and a pioneer in the affairs of the bank. You know more about it than any of the staff, myself included. A substantial raise of salary beginning next month will prove to you how much I care about your well-being, Marwan. This will cover both the baby's bonus that is due at the end of the year and a two-step promotion."

So that was it. Nothing but a cat and mouse game. They shook hands and the deal was struck and sealed in less than two sad hours. Was my wealthy and generous adoptive father going to be the victim of another costly bargain?

My in-laws were obliged to make a sudden and unusual decision in the summer of 1938 about the intensified political situation in Palestine. The disruption of the city's economic and social life had left Uncle Ahmad with no choice but to gather up his family and seek the nearest refuge where they could stay out of the way for some time. That decision was particularly difficult for a hard-working businessman like Uncle Ahmad.

Having learned a lesson from the ultimate effect of the six-month strike that hit Palestine in 1936 and crippled most of its functions, the British Authority in Jerusalem resorted to their ancient policy by cutting communications between the urbanized zone and the rest of Palestine. They recognized the Haganah, the Jewish defense organization, as a legitimate force and agreed it could be trained, armed, and defend the Jewish community. Some members of Haganah were trained, uninformed, and authorized by the British to serve as auxiliary guards. With the British armed forces they surrounded the rural areas that were the stronghold of the Palestinians and of their supporters from neighboring Arab states. Like the wolf in "Little Red Riding Hood," the Zionists took full advantage of their position and bit by bit nibbled away at Palestinian properties, burning groves, closing shops, and killing anyone who stood in their way.

The British authorities, meanwhile, were confident that handing such a treat over to the Zionists would be gratifying to and appreciated by the European Zionists back home. By creating a new scapegoat in Palestine, Britain—which had bigger problems with Hitler's forces in Europe proper—could from that point let the Jews take the blame for some of the barbarous forms of punishment inflicted upon the insurgents and their families.

Until the spring of 1938, the authorities in Palestine had managed to keep a shaky peace around the urbanized zones, including Haifa. The iron-fist policy in the rest of the country had become even harsher. The army hit hard at the rural areas adjacent to the borders with Syria and Lebanon where the nationalist fighters were in power. In May rioting broke out in the cities, first in the schools where the students' movement was gaining power and then in the streets. Retaliating quickly, the authorities shut all Arab schools a few weeks before final exams.

Eventually a large number of rioters were arrested and jailed. The Rajys put their children under house arrest. They were forbidden to meet with any friends who were politically involved.

The daily papers that were sneaked in during the nights that spring were full of horrifying pictures of executed people, demolished properties, and homeless families. Things seemed to have gotten out of hand in early June as a strong flare of patriotism swept through Palestine from one end to the other. A substantial number of Arab employees and workers in public facilities threatened to call for another strike if the authorities persisted in their harsh methods. But the governments' forces retaliated by arresting thousands of protesters. In Haifa alone, more than two thousand were jailed without proper legal procedures. Promptly the British commissioner of northern Palestine filled some vital vacancies with Jewish immigrants. Inevitably the hostile measures resulted in fierce clashes with civilians and brought an unprecedented outcry from the neighboring Arab countries. Finally the British appointed the Palestine Partition Commission headed by Sir John Woodhead. His report concluded that the partition scheme was unworkable and suggested other boundaries that were equally unpopular. Not long after this the British decided to drop the idea of partition but the die was already cast.

During my few years in Haifa, I had come to realize that through the long years of the British mandate rule over the Palestinian state, the British seemed incapable of playing the role of an unbiased mediator between the various groups that claimed legitimacy and power over that holy land. In contrast to the modest growth that had taken place in the kingdoms and princedoms Britain had planted around the Arab world, the quality of life in Palestine was still inferior to that in the French-mandated state next door in terms of education, health, and public welfare in general. Obviously the Palestinians were kept in fear about their political fate from the day Britain gained power over them after World War I. That fear was clearly expressed in the lists of demands their representatives in Jerusalem had served to the British authorities in years preceding the outbreak of violence. While the text of those demands was plain, almost stark, their despair thunderously echoed throughout the whole Arab world. Theirs was the cry of a trusting population that suddenly found itself circumvented by belligerent powers that demolished their homes, tortured and killed their children, and confiscated their land before their very eyes.

The Palestinians were not the only group that expressed such urgent demands. The Zionist representatives in Palestine presented lists of their needs written in eloquent terms; their claims were couched in the pristine language of the Talmudic tradition. In addition to those two claimants, there were sovereign nations like Great Britain, France, the kingdom of Jordan, Egypt, and a few princedoms and sheikhdoms as well. Demands with contradictory goals, ill-defined concepts, and spiritual needs were put forth. Among them all, there was one common theme: Palestine was the cradle of divinity. Its history, prophets, and gods seemed to be involved in the controversy as well, swarming ominously over this ill-fated piece of land.

Friends informed about the Arab–Jewish conflict, such as the Zhurbachs, were a great help to me emotionally during that period. They understood my need for information about the Palestinian case and provided me with copies of some European studies and reviews concerning the future of the Middle East. Ralph helped me understand the concepts of the Middle East from the puzzling Western viewpoint, and in time I learned how to read between the lines, and how to draw my own conclusions. But for all the reading, listening, and discussing, it was still beyond my imagination to be persuaded that in order for British and French politicians to make their mighty countries mightier they had to plot, oppress, and kill over the ownership of a tiny and peaceful place like Palestine. Their reviews were crowded with complicated terms like land demarcation, country partition, inhabitant relocation, chopping up, swerving from, intersecting zones. They left no room for a few simple words like peace and justice.

Until now, Uncle Ahmad had stubbornly refused to acknowledge the seriousness of the revolt and had never shared his political views openly. Indeed, like most of the business-oriented class in the country, he belittled the power of the revolution and did not want the rebels to undermine the stability of the country's economy by throwing themselves into a doomed battle against the British, which he called the greatest power in our hemisphere. At the same time he did nothing that would jeopardize the welfare of his country. He sold no land to the Zionists, and he did not participate in any of the dark deals anonymous foreign agents were pushing on people at that terrible time. He regularly paid his dues to the rebel leaders without asking any questions and without allowing his vexation against their policies to interfere with that duty.

But in mid-August 1938 the danger hit too close to home to be ignored. In a sweeping tide of violence against some Arab business-men accused of treason for collaborating with the enemy, a neighbor and friend of Uncle Ahmad's was fatally shot near the public stairway leading up to the Rajy house. He was the head of the Salems, a reputa-ble wealthy family that owned thousands of fertile acres in Galilee. According to Abou Maarouf, our handyman whose sons were serving with the nationalists, the victim had been warned on previous occa-sions against signing a deal with the Zionists involving the sale of an important piece of Arab land that was estimated to extend over thou-sands of acres, linking the Litani river in Lebanon with the Houli Lake in northern Palestine. But apparently he had finalized that deal on his last trip to London, cheating his people out of their right to survival.

For the Rajys to see such a crime committed against a member of their class was devastating; especially since the killers were young men from our neighborhood who had recently joined one of the most radical units of the revolution.

Jazzin, a small town spread along one of the highest ridges in the southern part of Lebanon about 50 miles away, was chosen as our impromptu vacation site. Centrally located between Sidon, Tyre, and the northern Palestinian shore, the town was widely popular among the upper-class vacationers of that region.

In mid-September Uncle Ahmad and Aunt Najla suggested that Anwar come to visit us and bring Nora and her husband with him. It sounded like a marvelous idea to me. Nora and Mahmoud had been married during the week little Usama was born, and I was anxious to have a chance to talk with her alone. Mahmoud was an extremely private man who remained aloof from the rest of the family. Soon the familiar black limousine with Hadj Uthman at the wheel rolled down our driveway and discharged its exuberant cargo: Anwar, Nora, and—joyous surprise—my baby brother, Fadi! Our month's vacation was a welcome respite from the cares and tensions of life in Haifa. These were halcyon days compared to what lay in store for us. Only Suad, still nursing some hope of drawing Anwar close to the bonds of matri-mony, was unhappy, as Anwar didn't hide his summer flirtations with the irresistible local beauties of Jazzin.

Nadia, Vacation at Baalbech, Lebanon, 1939

"God have mercy on us, this country is in real trouble," Aunt Najla murmured to herself as she struggled out of the car when we finally arrived home just before dawn on our return from Jazzin.

Turning to where I sat exhausted to the bone, Uncle Ahmad looked at me sorrowfully. "I'm sorry I let you down, dear Nadia. God, how infuriated I felt, failing to protect you from such a terrorizing experience. Please forgive me!"

I nodded silently. No one said a word as the children dragged themselves out of the car and down toward the big, dark house. I tiptoed into the sitting area of our apartment with Usama asleep in my arms and lay him down on the soft cushions. His dimple quivered as my lips touched his flushed cheek. Marwan remained sound asleep in our bed-room. When I finally flung my exhausted body on my bed and buried my head under the pillows, I knew that many changes had taken place in the woman I had been three months earlier.

The terrifying incident that took us by surprise after we crossed the Palestinian border seemed unreal at the time. It happened a little after sunset, about twenty miles from home, when we came upon what looked like an army barricade. An armored tank blocked a passage in the densely forested area surrounding the oil refinery zone.

"Halt!" A deafening voice thundered from inside a wooden stand at the barricade. Hadj immediately stopped the car and a flock of hel-meted gunmen in fatigues jumped out of nowhere and took position around the car, their rifles pointed straight at us.

"Pull off to the right! Move!" the angry voice ordered in broken Arabic. Poor Hadj complied as the gunmen pushed against the car, forcing it off the road over the sloppy sandbank and into the thorny shrubs of a fence of clustered myrtle where the motor died. The fierce soldier who appeared to be in charge barked his order for inspection. He banged the roof of our car with his fist, and we stumbled out, thoroughly shaken by the unbelievable scene. The gunmen conferred among themselves for a few seconds before they began their investiga-tion; apart from the few Arabic words we heard, they spoke in an odd language that was neither English nor French; their accent sounded very Teutonic.

"Does anybody speak French or English here?" the chief managed in very poor English.

"She does." Young Latif pointed at me.

From that point on, despite Uncle Ahmad's loud complaints in the only language he knew, I was forced into service as interpreter during extended body searches of Uncle Ahmad and his sons, ac-companied by probing personal questions regarding work, business connections, school interests, even political affiliations. Completely disoriented, they were then lined up against the thick thorny bushes near the limousine.

Aunt Najla and Suad squatted by the car tending to the screaming and whining of the children. They were spared the indignity of a body search because of their black chiffon veils. As the wailing took on hysterical proportions, the head officer turned to me: "Tell the women to take those brats and get back in the car."

Shadows grew longer, and the evening withered to a grim starless sky. The mysterious commotion on the road above us got louder but was still incomprehensible. I waited and hoped this nightmarish ordeal would soon be over. Usama's shrieks weakened my resolve to follow orders, and I turned around to go to him but a commanding voice roared: "Stay where you are! We are not through with you yet. The road to your destination is closed for now. So tell your father and brothers to go back to the car. They have to wait there until we come back. You are supposed to report to the commanding officer at the post. Follow me. Move!"

Lined up on the road there was a pathetic circus of people, cars, and trucks. Men, women, and children were grouped on both sides of the dark road like herded ghosts. Whistling winds, sounds of arguments, moaning and wailing tested my nerves to a breaking point and pushed me to the verge of screaming.

My captor delivered me back to the wooden stand and spoke briefly to the commanding officer inside. As though I were a member of his team, the CO addressed me in pure British English: "This is an emergency, miss. Some of the women out there seem to have difficulty responding to our questioning and we have reason to believe that it is a language problem. We want you to help out."

I couldn't believe my ears. The fact that the commander of this holdup was a real British soldier eliminated all doubt that the operation had been ordered by the British authorities. This posed a fearfully perplexing question: From my naive perspective, the British could block any road anywhere at any time when there was a danger of civil disturbance or armed disobedience; also when the safety of innocent citizens was in jeopardy. So why were they engaged in this hostile, hush-hush holdup aimed at terrorizing innocent citizens, blocking their way to safety and exposing them to the dangers of the ever-impending armed confrontation with the guerrillas that often took place in the middle of the night?

My face was covered with sweat. I trailed behind two gunmen to where a flock of captive women, children, and elderly men huddled together on one side of the road. Farther down on the other side, lines of men were under surveillance, squatting submissively before their guards, their arms crossed over their heads.

I stood across from the captives for whom I had to play intermediary. I was flanked by two gunmen. The captives' eyes gazed back into mine, making me feel I had stepped into a trap worse than the obvious one. Did I look to them as though I was voluntarily collaborating with "the enemy"? Was I branded an alien by the way I talked and dressed?

As my Grandma Mehdi used to say: "God has no stones to throw." Suddenly all hell broke loose as the deafening thunder of explosions and firearms filled the air above us and sent sparks falling everywhere. Machine guns mounted on tanks spewed fire in every direction around us. People ran like rabbits in every direction as the gunmen pursued them and shot at them mercilessly.

I found myself groping aimlessly through the terrified survivors seeking refuge down by the forested fence. I was fully disoriented. When I finally recognized the spot where I left my in-laws and was able to locate the car, the place was deserted. The poor old limo, turned upside down as if a fiendish power had struck it, slumped wretchedly amidst the shredded bundles and trunks of our belongings.

Usama was all I could think of. The fear of losing him terrified me. I roamed around searching for any clue in the lonely darkness. What could have happened to make my baby disappear? What had they done to him? Eventually the rest of the family heard my screaming, and we all got together. We huddled together, sobbing and laughing at the same time. With Usama snuggled safely in my arms, I watched the men turn the battered car back on its wheels and fix things up inside so we could all fit in once more. At first, the engine puffed and belched like a tethered old goat that was choking on its cud. Finally, it chugged up the hill, and we all breathed with relief.

The scene of destruction we drove through for a couple of miles dispelled any notion that this had been just a nightmarish dream. Like a deserted battlefield, the area was a shambles of twisted vacant cars, shattered luggage, and a sad debris of shoes and clothing. I learned from the other occupants that we had been caught in the middle of a serious confrontation between the ruling authorities and a group of Arab fighters, the Commandos. Farid, a nonviolence advocate, argued that the nationalists should have been wiser than to shoot arbitrarily, knowing that hundreds of civilians were detained at that post. "The casualties were mostly among innocent civilians just because of our fighters' lack of experience. This, in my view, isn't an act of heroism. Is it?"

"These civilians were not casualties, they were killed deliberately by the Schintzes who captured us in the first place with this intention." Ali, a cumbersome nineteen-year-old, fanned the fire of revolution among his brothers. Although I didn't often agree with him on political matters, at the moment I had to since I had seen the deliberate killing with my own eyes.

The word "Schintzes" among Arab youngsters referred to the European immigrant Jews who were recruited by the British as additional policemen. This Jewish task force, which grew from less than a thousand in 1936 to about eight thousand in the summer of 1938, was reportedly trained and armed by British officers, who gave them a free hand in attacking Arab villages in Galilee, a stronghold of the nationalists. "That's always your friends' cover-up," Farid argued. "They blame it on the Arabs, the Schintzes, or the British. They never admit making mistakes."

The argument about the violent activities of the night continued among the boys until finally Farid attempted to sum it up for the rest of us. As he explained it, there was an attack on a covert operation to smuggle in about five hundred illegal Jewish immigrants who came into the bay aboard three boats from Cyprus. Apparently an unknown number of Jewish immigrants had already been smuggled into the country in spite of a recent treaty between Britain and the Arab leaders to restrict such immigration to numbers accepted by the Arabs in return for a promise to stop the revolution.

"Go on, Farid, tell her how the fighters knew about this shipment."

"It's still debatable whether the alert came from the revolution headquarters in Damascus or whether the native commandos found out about it on their own. But look, Ali, if they had been more thorough and learned ahead of time that the British were in on this with the Jews, they could have saved the lives of innocent Arabs who were killed tonight."

"Well, the point is that our fighters put their lives on the line to disclose the fact that the British, while they've been saying they're on our side, have been working with the Zionists against us. Admit it, the Arabs have no friends among those foreigners!"

"Shut up, both of you!" Uncle Ahmad, who hadn't spoken one word until then, suddenly burst out. "I want no more of this useless talk. Do you hear me? This is the last time we'll hear about what happened tonight. None of what we saw or heard shall ever be repeated. Ever."

9

July 1940

When we first saw the high-altitude reconnaissance planes hovering over Haifa, most of us in the neighborhood reacted with bewilderment. Our apprehension was minimal, since they were seen only in the daytime and appeared to be harmless. But in the spring of 1940 the hostile bombing attacks on our area began, at first distant, short, and at odd hours, but never at night. As spring turned into summer, they became heavier and more frequent, drawn by the immenseness of our harbor and our petroleum refinery with its liquid gold. Then there was the large and efficiently run railroad station that tied the three warring continents together: Europe, Asia, and Africa. Since these assets were among the ultimate sources of energy and maneuverability for waging war, the Italians spread their destructive capability to our shores to bleed the Allies to defeat. Joining forces with German air power, they started raiding those facilities at random times with little regard for the innocent people who had nothing to gain from that war.

It was in July of that hot, humid summer that my second baby chose to be born. After an early dinner because of the curfew and the blackout that had been imposed on Haifa for almost two weeks, Marwan and I left Usama with the Rajys for safety reasons and returned to our apartment. Propped up on thick pillows in my bed expecting the usual eight-o'clock raid to begin, I caressed my protruding tummy, hoping to calm the tiny hostage who was making a serious effort to rush out into a world beset with the grim business of war. "You can't be due yet, my love, you have to wait." But the soft gnawing pain persisted, reminding me of the first time I was in labor.

While our sexual intimacies had improved little since Usama's birth, with an occasional "marital privilege" granted, we had in time gained a strong sense of loyalty to each other that united our efforts to survive. We became like two horses harnessed together who knew nothing other than to go straight ahead. Marwan and I differed in our convictions and intellectual aptitudes, but we shared an irreverence for the rigidity of many observances our countries clung to. A resentment of our clan's social and quasi-religious habits forged another bond between us. We respected each other's limitations, thereby enriching our sense of camaraderie. Marwan gave me his unquestioning support whenever social and ethnic pressures stood in my way, and I learned to forgive his reckless temper that could sometimes blind his reason and drive him to the verge of insanity. Having a baby together, on the other hand, had mellowed my resistance to his increasing abuse. Otherwise the only option available to me as a wife was to leave him, and divorce was inconceivable. At my young age, I could go nowhere but back to my parents. Nor could I have custody over my sons after they reached their seventh year; after that they were the responsibility of their paternal kin. According to our traditional and religious laws, the parents and brothers of a single woman, divorcée, or widow were required to provide for all her needs until she married again.

The familiar shriek of the siren brought me back to awareness just as the wall clock finished its midnight count. "Oh, God! Here they come again." The whining bombers swooped down closer and the air started to vibrate, rocking perfume bottles and bouncing picture frames off the walls. At the same time the baby inside answered with a fury of kicks which sent a jolt down my spine.

As the deafening first blast of bombs shook the floor and then intensified in rippling whistles and explosions above my head, I stumbled out into the shadowy hall. Crippled with fear, I groped for the nearest chair and sank into its cushions. It would be some hours before the night ended. Through the open French windows I could see the blazing tongues of fire, like gaping snakes, twirling high above the refinery zone, shedding a hellish light over the city. The air was scorching, suffocating; it was filled with sooty particles saturated with the nauseating odor of burnt oil. In the meantime I stuck to my chair by the door, not daring to go anywhere; so far the labor pains had been short and rather far apart, as if the little being had sensed my reluctance to let go and decided to yield for a while.

Marwan remained buried under his covers throughout the whole episode. Frightened and uncommunicative, he just hid there until the raid was over, as he had done ever since they began. The bombing made him incoherent at times, and it gravely affected his health. His food intake had diminished drastically and his sleep became sporadic. I felt completely helpless seeing him, day after day, swallowing pills and tablets that he said should alleviate his discomfort.

I began to feel all alone, cut off from the world up in that penthouse apartment with a husband as invalid as I was. Staggering cautiously to the door, I opened it wide, calculating that I could walk down to my in-laws' house in only a few minutes.

The labor pangs hit me hard. I screamed just as hard. They heard and they knew instantly. They carried me through the hallways to their guest room, yelling for Marwan to go get the midwife. "No, I am not going out there now. Why do you have to bring that stupid midwife here, why don't we call an ambulance and take Nadia to the hospital?"

"Oh, son, that's impossible. After those raids, no hospital could give Nadia the attention she might need. Besides," his father added, "the hospitals are probably jammed with bombing victims."

Resting between two waves of pain on the flat thick mattress on which I lay in labor, I showered Suad with questions: "What is going to happen? What time is it?"

"Don't worry, we'll find somebody to go and see if Dr. Imad is in his clinic. It's eight o'clock now, we have plenty of time."

Time! What time? Suad and her mother didn't understand that this was the real thing. The forces of generation were hard at work. I could feel the baby's head emerging into light. I could also feel a lot of kicking inside me. A furious onslaught of pain lashed through me. Suddenly, the whole world stopped as my baby glided out onto the sheets beneath me.

"Oh, God have mercy on her! Mother, she did it all alone!" With disbelief, Suad looked up at her mother's white face. "What are we going to do now?"

The sudden silence that hung over our heads turned into panic. The three of us waited for that wondrous cry of life, but it didn't come.

Suad shrank back in fear. Her mother reached out and lifted my cover. She took one glimpse, and then she looked at me and whispered, "It's a boy, Nadia!" Clearly, she was unaware of the serious condition the silent newborn baby was in. She rushed away to the door. "Let me go and tell them."

"Suad, please look and see why he's not crying," I begged frantically.

"Oh, Nadia, he looks so blue. Wait, the umbilical cord seems to be wrapped around his neck. Oh, God! What are we going to do?"

"Unwrap the cord, please! Go ahead, don't be afraid, please!"

Time could not move fast enough. Finally, the baby's cry rose loud and clear into the day. The little man announced himself quite assertively. A long hour passed before Bahia, Dr. Imad's nurse who waited in a shelter on her way up from the clinic, arrived to clean up the mess we had fallen into on that memorable Saturday, July 20, 1940.

Children, indeed! A redeeming blessing that made my life worthwhile after all! My little kids added an important dimension to my life: a deep and ever-pressing concern. Chubby, well-formed, and fully independent, Usama was almost four and ready to start school very soon. Challenged by his innate artistic skills, he saw the world as having a boundless, glowing horizon, and hated to be babied or touched. His brother, a handsome, cuddly, and extremely demanding toddler, with my looks and a big chunk of his father's temper, was more dependent. From the day he was born, he claimed the family's undivided attention, Marwan's included. He glared defiantly into our faces and made us feel as though we were all to blame for his problems. Marwan had taken a gentler attitude toward this child and named him Jamal for his handsomeness.

With the two boys sharing our bedroom, Marwan became even more vexed about Uncle Ahmad's reluctance to remodel and expand our small apartment. Eventually the conflict between him and his parents over this issue erupted and affected both me and the boys. Usama, already troubled by his father's harshness, after Jamal's birth had to endure beatings that sometimes left him with bruises. Jamal was scared out of his wits when he saw his sometimes loving father suddenly turn into a monster who would scream into his face or shove his cot out to another room for the rest of the night.

Mute rage over Marwan's tyrannical behavior toward our sons tore through my soul as I began to see myself as helpless against my irascible husband as my mother was with my father. I often ask myself whether, compared to her generation, I really had more courage. How right was I in thinking of her life as a disgraceful compromise? The protection of the children within the sanctity of their own home occupied my mind all the time. Yet I did little or nothing. But my helplessness at that stage wasn't caused either by my abusive husband or by any other physical threat. It was the love and compassion that my in-laws bestowed on me that crippled me. They were a haven for my children as well, ready at any time to give them the affectionate attention they missed. In other words, it was the family structure and its efficient shock absorption system that did me in. My in-laws' love turned out to be a prison that was all too secure for me to leave.

The large manila envelope that came in the mail contained the Carmelite kindergarten's answer to my application to enroll Usama for the fall semester. "Should the child prove to be up to our requirements, the administration will be happy to take him in October 1941." Carmelite St. Joseph was a unique Catholic school run by the French mendicant order of friars established at Haifa's Mt. Carmel in 1160. They were known as the White Friars because of the white robes they wore over a brown habit. The spacious compound provided mixed classes up to the fifth grade and segregated ones up for the secondary level of education that ended with the French baccalaureate.

It was located in a scenic fragrant valley a few miles west of the old city of Haifa, surrounded by expensive stone houses, foreign office buildings, embassies, a hospital, parks, and boutiques. Marwan now talked wistfully about how our life would be much less hectic if we could live in that elegant area. But all we did was talk. Neither Marwan nor I seemed ready to take a jump into changing the monotonous rhythm of our lives. Coming from an old family with a powerful system of support which gave us access to luxury far beyond our means, we didn't even discuss the possibility of breaking away from it. I was married for three years before I learned, accidentally, any details about our financial situation. Strangely enough, women of a less privileged class who might share the bread-winning process with their mates tended to be more knowledgeable about their household finances. Sometimes they were in charge of them.

Rich wives and daughters, however, were provided for generously, often without having to ask. I remember that my mother had never owned or carried a purse. Just like Aunt Najla, she didn't even know how to count or spend money. Usually my father or some male friend or relative would shop for us, not only for food and household needs, but also for the family's personal items as well. In general, the women in a well-to-do, urbanized clan like ours were well fed, bejeweled, delicate, and pampered, like porcelain dolls. In most cases they were as defenseless as those dolls. Such dependence could be quite hazardous if the head of such a family happened to be as unpredictable as my father.

When I became Uncle Ahmad's responsibility, I realized that there were intricacies that were entirely new to me. There was no limit to the amount I could cost the Rajys as long as I remained loyal, not to my husband's expectations but to that system itself. I was showered with clothes, jewelry, and lavish gifts that would demonstrate the prominence of the Rajy clan. I never saw a bill, I never wrote a check, and I never discussed issues pertaining to money. Marwan was no better off, although he worked for a monthly income. His very job was considered a family asset, especially in view of his lack of qualification for his post. Like me, he was clothed in the most fashionable way. He was also encouraged to take expensive trips and put his children in the best schools because that would enhance the clan's visibility and renown.

When Marwan came home from work on the day I had presented Usama's application papers to Sister Xavier at the Carmelite school, I babbled joyfully: "Usama has been accepted, Marwan! Sister Xavier is a warm, wonderful, and charming woman, and she gave Usama a tour of the classrooms and the playground. They teach in both French and English and have a bus that will pick up the children at home and bring them back for an extra fee."

"That sounds great, Nadia. I'm happy for him." He handed me a thick white envelope with local stamps adorning its corner. "I have a little good news, too. You can read it while we have a glass of wine to celebrate!"

So on that starry evening in March 1941, while Italo-German troops lay in wait to invade eastern Europe and cross the borders to Russia, Marwan and I had a calm tête-à-tête dinner at home. It was one of those rare special occasions when we both felt on top of the world. In addition to the joy I felt about Usama's school, the letter Marwan had received from the bank's headquarters in Jerusalem read, "The Board of Directors is pleased to inform you that, as of May 1, you are Acting

Nadia's Husband Photographs Her with Their Two Sons, Haifa, 1941

Manager of your branch in Haifa and the Board's representative for the northern branches." The amount of the new salary was still less than Hadj Uthman's salary but we didn't care. The wine was mild and the night a friendly companion.

In the next two months a deadly epidemic of meningitis struck the city out of nowhere. This scourge destroyed our short-lived harmony as husband and wife. My ten-month-old baby, Jamal, and his Aunt Mona, Marwan's twelve-year-old sister, fell ill. I suspected that I was pregnant again and Dr. Imad had warned us that there was no vaccine against the often fatal disease, but for the moment I put all this entirely out of my mind. I spent the six days and six nights at Jamal's side. Only Imad's nurse was allowed to come in to watch him while I took a couple of hours to wash, change, and rest. Ice bags were kept tucked against his head and feet; his quivering limbs had to be restrained and a spoon-like tool had to be thrust over his tongue during the seizures.

Since his brain and spinal membranes were infected, the doctors advised that his body had to remain flat as long as the convulsions occurred. So I couldn't pick up my sick baby to hold him or hug him.

It was after Jamal was completely out of danger that I finally told Marwan about the pregnancy. What happened afterwards was much worse than what I expected. Instead of flaring into a violent temper tantrum, he heard me out in a stunned silence. He didn't come home after work that Saturday. Marwan's daily habits were as holy as prayers to a zealot, and he would never break them unless something was terribly wrong. Although I felt sure his absence was intentional, I made a prudent search within the family premises without alarming anyone. I tucked the boys into their beds early and sat alone in my rocking chair out on the dark terrace.

It was the first time in our married years that Marwan had vanished without a word. For some reason I wasn't worried that something had happened to him physically; guilt was the cause of my anguish. He was as much a victim of the clan as I was, even beyond marriage arrangements. He had been blunt about not wanting children from the beginning. He had to cope with a wife who knew nothing about birth control. On top of all of this, he was genuinely afraid that the world was overflowing with people. Many times I heard him argue that successive, unwarranted wars were an absolute proof of that. On this matter, not much was needed to test his limits.

The sky was beginning to lighten when I heard the key ramming into the lock. Marwan wasn't alone. "This is Nadim and his girlfriend Angelle," Marwan muttered vacuously as the young couple dragged him to the sofa, where he collapsed drowsily onto the cushions. The smell of liquor and tobacco filled the air.

"Hello, Madame Rajy." The young man's smile disappeared as I stared into his face. He seemed to be in his early twenties. He was unshaven and quite casually dressed. Yet, his manner and tone of voice conveyed an air of gentleness, and his hazel eyes defied my stares. "I am terribly sorry to barge in on you so late, but you know how stubborn Marwan can be sometimes. He just wouldn't stop drinking. By the way, he hasn't eaten any food all day and night."

My attention was diverted by the young girl who, detached from the whole situation, stood in front of the mirror down the hall, touching up her makeup and fluffing some discipline into her pitch-black, silky hair as though it was part of her daily routine to bring drunken husbands back to their wives before sunrise.

I stood speechless watching these people invade my home, and witness my humiliation. Their presence made me feel stupid, a stranger in my own house. This Nadim seemed to know too much about my husband. Did he know about the maddening complexities of our marriage as well? I felt as though he could see through me. Without a word, my eyes burning with tears, I moved to the outer door and flung it open. I waited until their footsteps died away into the silence of the stairway.

I had been in terrible pain for several minutes. I lay flat on my back, with my eyes shut tight, and my hands clutching frantically at the cold brass bar above my head. Suddenly, horrified by the possibility that I was in labor, I screamed for my "little" sister Mae, now a tall nineteen-year-old who had been made to stay home with Jamal and me while the rest of our Beirut family attended a New Year's party at Aunt Hind's, hosted by cousin Kamal.

Mae's sleepy eyes widened in disbelief. "What is wrong? Oh, my God, Nadia, what are you doing?"

"I'm probably dying or something, that's what I'm doing!"

"Is it the baby? Do you want me to call a doctor?" She didn't seem to realize that it was too late for her to go out in the street unaccompanied, nor was she aware that the roaring sounds that rattled through the window shutters came from a rainstorm. There was thunder and hail, too.

"I think I need to go to a hospital. I'm afraid there's something wrong inside me, Mae!"

"I'll go call Dr. Nader across the street. He isn't an obstetrician, but he can tell us what to do." She grabbed frightened little Jamal from my side, tucked him under the thick quilt of the narrow old bed which had once been mine, popped his pacifier into his mouth, and was gone.

Looking back, I realized what a mistake it had been to yield to my in-laws' pressure to take this trip in the hope of securing a "luxurious and secure delivery," as Marwan had encouragingly described it.

It was the first time I had seen my in-laws so worried about the fighting that had erupted during the fall between the Palestinians and the ever-increasing Jewish settlers. Marwan's apprehension was due to the fact that until that stage the Arabs and the Jews had been targeting the British rule with their violence, not each other. Such an escalation was tougher in a city like Haifa because the lives of Jews and Arabs were still entwined in most aspects of daily life. In other cities there was a clear-cut division. "Who knows," Uncle Ahmad would lament, "the battles are very close to the borders. In case something happens here, we may all find a temporary refuge in Lebanon. Why wait, Nadia? I think you'd better go while it's still possible."

So I left my home, the loving Rajy family, and my close friends. I also had to leave my little Usama behind as well, to avoid conflict with my father, who bore a strange malice toward my sweet child that he didn't even try to hide. It was something I couldn't even mention to my in-laws, because they wouldn't believe it could come from a Rajy grandparent. Finally I yielded, if for no other reason than to get Jamal's right leg checked by a bone specialist in Beirut. It had been almost eight months since the meningitis had finally abated, but his right leg was still thinner and weaker than the left one.

"This way, doctor." Mae's brisk voice brought me back to the present. "How do you feel now, Nadia? The doctor is here."

Behind her stood a tall middle-aged man with bright blue eyes. "I'm Dr. Nader. Sorry not to have had time to change into proper clothes. Miss Mae sounded extremely distressed by your condition. She said something about a hospital!"

"I think I'm better now, Doctor, thank you for coming. I'm still sure this baby has a problem, and that it is labor pains I'm feeling. Wouldn't it be better if I went to a hospital? Just in case."

"That decision has to wait until I can see your condition and that of the baby. If everything goes well, staying at home could be better. You have no idea how it's snowing out there, Mrs. Rajy."

"Yes, Nadia, it is just a gorgeous night for a new year and a new baby!" Mae's eyes danced with excitement. "You have never seen anything as beautiful, not in Beirut."

Silence fell again as the doctor proceeded with his examination.

"You're right, Mrs. Rajy, the baby's head is stuck, but don't worry, everything is going to be all right."

"Well," Mae said, "let's move her to my father's bedroom then. It has more space and the bed is quite large."

Finally, as the fateful year of 1941 drew to its inevitable end, and after hours of hard, complicated labor that threatened the life of the unborn child, the indefatigable doctor succeeded in straightening the baby's head in the right direction. The trying experience was a great challenge to my sister Mae, who, confronted for the first time with such a critical ordeal, threw herself wholeheartedly into the job. The city, snowed in, celebrated the first hours of the new year. For me the whole world burst into triumphant joy when Dr. Nader placed my youngest baby in my arms. "A boy!" Mae shrieked. "Oh, don't look so disappointed, Nadia, I know you wanted a girl. Here, look at him. Next time, be sure to have a girl. For now, you have to do with a boy!"

Next time? Never again!

1943

"Nadia, come here, please." Marwan called from the living room. "You will enjoy reading today's editorial. It is written by our friend Khalil Haddad." It was Sunday, and Marwan had just finished breakfast and retired to his corner in the living room where he loved to spend a couple hours taking it easy. "Sit down and listen, Nadia, then tell me how you feel about what he said. I tell you, this guy is unbelievable."

> Congratulations, the winds of World War II begin to favor the Allies [started the Sunday editorial of an Arabic daily paper]. To congratulate those winners on their victory over some satanic czar that once in a while threatens this planet is indeed a great pleasure. . . . Regrettably, in our case the Allies are not the friends the Arab world thought them to be before the turn of the century. Now that their greedy hands are free, they will soon rush back here and continue their crimes against our people. Drunk with victory, they will play God over this defenseless land, derailing the wheel of its destiny. On the Palestinian horizon, I see a ruinous storm coming from the West, an affliction that Europe had long been burdened with is on its way to us—a malignant tumor that Europe has extirpated from its land to plow it into ours. Arab readers are seeing lately a string of complicated terms applied to their land,

terms like annexation, demarcation, or distribution. On the surface they sound quite sophisticated and of no concern to these readers. Yet, what our innocent readers do not know is that the terms in question are nothing but dead menaces to them all: their land, families, and everything they own are pawns in a nasty power game the world is playing. Our people have to know how bleak the future ushered in by these high-flown words is. Indeed, for years to come, a rather intricate destiny awaits millions of my fellow citizens. An evil destiny waylays us all, one that is woven into reality by the very powers that pose as our protectors.

I recalled how impressed I had been when I met the courageous editor at a fund-raising dinner in our city's community center in 1938. Khalil Haddad was the key speaker in a spacious hall packed with noted professionals and their families who waited to hear one of their country's early heroes. More impressive were the remarkable past and distinguished credentials of that legend: a Palestinian of Lebanese origin, poet, lawyer, and editor of the cultural magazine *Karmel* published in Haifa until the late thirties, Khalil Haddad was the first to warn against the Balfour Declaration and its implications. As early as the 1920s this progressive intellect from a prominent Christian family, already a rebel at that time, had led demonstrations against the British mandate, chanting patriotic songs that he had composed and for which he was prosecuted. His son Nadim, the same fellow who brought my husband home drunk in 1941, had introduced his famous father to that appreciative audience, summing up Khalil's services to the Palestinian cause in an epic poem of his own.

It took me a while to admit that the wild companion who had charmed my husband out of his gloomy cocoon and was on his way to winning my babies' hearts with that alluring charm was the same young man I had applauded when he introduced his illustrious father. Whether by virtue of naiveté or through fear of his charismatic personality, I managed to stay out of his reach as his visits to Marwan became more frequent. I watched their involvement with girls as dull as Angelle and was unable to understand why it angered me to see Nadim with such cheap company but not my own husband. For men to take pride in their extramarital affairs was not very unusual in our world. Still, the ease with which I had handled Marwan's flirtations and love affairs puzzled me, and mystified the relatives and friends who knew about it. I myself wasn't sure whether I did so out of a feeling of guilt for not fulfilling my conjugal duties, or because I really didn't care what happened to Marwan.

Although my husband and I had reached a silent agreement on this issue, we did fail to agree on many other issues that affected other aspects of our life. The country's economy and its political condition were growing more precarious and, like most young couples of our generation who had children to plan for, Marwan and I could not agree on any plans. Most importantly, we failed to decide on a country of residence for ourselves and our children. This was an issue that put us at odds because he lacked financial power and depended totally on his father. As far as Marwan was concerned, the source of his ills came from being born in Palestine and to a father as domineering as his. But to me Uncle Ahmad was a savior and the only source of security for my children no matter where we lived. Both Marwan and I were trapped by the web of our dependency, and as the seventh anniversary of our marriage approached following Ghassan's birth, conflicts and tension between us increased to a distressing level.

Most demoralizing was the effect of Marwan's involvement with Angelle and the rest of that fun-loving group that had almost destroyed him physically and emotionally. It left me with a deep sense of helplessness and resulted in the slowing of our social life. At a time when I needed my friends the most, I had to maintain a distance to keep from drawing them into our bitter conflicts. I survived by focusing on the single blessing that had resulted from my marriage to Marwan: my children. To have such great children and to win the full right to raise them the way I wanted was a humbling reward under the circumstances of our life.

My twenty-fifth birthday party was a last-minute affair held in our apartment. Aunt Najla thought having it there would please Marwan more since some of his intimate friends had been invited, including Ralph Zhurbach and Marwan's constant companions, Nadim and Angelle. It was a hectic day for Marwan. Too many phone calls and family members shuttling between my kitchen and the Rajys' where the cooking took place. The overall chaos was rudely disrupting Marwan's Sunday, a day he adamantly insisted must be free of social functions.

As the apartment filled with guests, Marwan grew wearily impatient with the happy crowd. The abundant attention bestowed on me from all directions seemed to have irritated him more because Angelle had declined our invitation to the party. I had noticed that their relationship seemed to be cooling off. His troubled eyes followed me from place to place and he sullenly brushed off my attempts to cheer him up. Angrily I turned away, determined not to let him ruin the party for me.

When all of our guests had left and Marwan and the boys were asleep, I rested my elbows on the cold side of the washstand, awed by the swell of emotions in me. The joyous moments of the evening careened through my mind. I lowered my head, turned the faucet on full force, and let the cold water run generously over my burning face. The mental images dissolved into Nadim's longing gaze following me wherever I went and combined with the echo of his sonorous voice when, given the floor, he began his reading of "a birthday gift to you, Madame." The theme of his glowing sonnet left the rays of his thoughts all over the apartment.

Slowly I dried my face and searched the depths of the eyes gazing back at me from the mirror. Could it be possible? Am I falling for that mischievous charmer too? Could he cast his spell upon me? Could I prove as vulnerable to his charm as Marwan and his companions?

Regrettably, the rest of 1943 fell short of being memorable. World War II continued to rage, with catastrophic results for some partici-pants and triumphs for others. The Zionist leaders were quick to take advantage of the confusion and they accelerated immigration to Pales-tine from the countries where Hitler was in power. Their plans to establish a segregated Jewish state in Palestine were now obvious, and the names of some Zionist underground gangs in France, Poland, and Austria began to surface in cities like Jerusalem and Tel Aviv. The Arab regimes, together with the prewar Palestinian leadership, dis-persed in all directions, leaving the younger generation in the land to clean up the mess. Terrorists, under the pretense of protecting British interests in the area, especially the oil pipelines, claimed the lives of a number of prominent foreign and Arab leaders.

In Haifa, where the line between the Arabs and non-Arabs was not as defined as in the country's other large cities, contact between the two camps lingered on, but a wave of uncertainty began to vibrate among the Arabs who were not involved in politics. Those Arabs who were comfortable or wealthy and lived in the cities had difficulty believing an apartheid-style state was about to violate their ancient community. The Rajys were, alas, of that category, refusing to take any protective measure—economic, financial, or other—to prepare or arm themselves against the hazards of the coming civil war.

Marwan's position was different. He had taken a pessimistic attitude toward the future and resigned himself to that spreading doom. He ignored my advice to protect himself from the risks of his position at work. His safety on the job, in a city with so many armed people around, had become an increasing subject of argument between us. His promotion to acting manager doubled his working hours, and I wanted him to be well protected at all times—especially after he was required to carry the vault's two-key set in his pocket every time his boss took off on a trip, which happened more frequently as the country's political conditions deteriorated.

"I hope your worries can be put to rest now that I have my own bodyguard," Marwan boasted to me late one October afternoon that year. "Tyseer's appointment will be confirmed as of tomorrow. The man is great for the job, Nadia. Now I'm doubly insured—I carry a licensed gun and I'm followed by a bodyguard. What more do you want?"

"Well, I'm glad you decided to take this matter seriously. The country is full of armed men. At least this will give us some peace of mind." That peace of mind came to a halt the day I laid eyes on Tyseer! Instant revulsion sent a tremor through my body when I opened the door for Marwan late one evening and a huge man blocked the opening. Two bulging, repugnant eyes stared into my face. I pulled back, feeling suddenly sick with a strange sense of foreboding.

"Come in, Tyseer, put the files over there." Marwan pointed to the side table where books and magazines were kept handy. The man's big boots dug heavily into the soft fur of the carpet; the acrid odor of sweat and cheap tobacco filled the air as his massive frame lumbered in and out.

"Yuck, what a stench!" I groaned after he left. The stranger's nauseating odor turned my stomach, as though a wild beast had invaded my little hall. "Is that your bodyguard?"

"Yes, that's Tyseer. Don't look so offended. The man is a hard worker, and he's poor, so he can't afford the Soirée de Paris cologne you're used to." I didn't try to explain that it wasn't the appearance or the smell, but the intuitive foreboding that triggered my revulsion.

With the fiscal year coming to its end, Marwan was up to his ears in overtime work, both at the bank and at home. He had neither time nor patience for my feelings and intuitions, and he dismissed as unwarranted any admonitions I offered regarding the trustworthiness of his bodyguard. If Tyseer's duties had been limited to serving at the bank, I wouldn't have come in contact with him, and Marwan and I would have been spared the constant arguments about the matter. But that scary man gradually became the stranger I had to meet every day. In addition to walking Marwan through the dark alleys of the city at late hours, knocking at my door at odd times to retrieve a forgotten file, or picking up an overdue lunch, Tyseer was assigned to escort our children to school whenever the road between our home and the school was barricaded and the bus couldn't make it.

The conflict over this issue led to Marwan's demand that I back off because he intended to keep Tyseer in the position. I demanded that he keep him away from me and my children and I prayed to God to spare him the bitter regret of the choice he made.

Alas! Regret was too mild a word to describe what happened to Marwan later.

The nightmare of that episode began on Adha's Eve, which once every thirty-two Gregorian years coincides with Christmas week. The whole city was getting ready for the sacred occasions and the children and I spent the day roaming around with my in-laws, visiting boutiques and shopping centers. The joy of the Rajys' gathering, the ceremonial hustle and bustle, and the festival preparations left me unaware of Marwan's absence when we returned. Not until late in the evening did I realize I hadn't seen him since he left for work that morning. Neither had any of his brothers or his father.

I searched the neat apartment for any clue that Marwan might have left behind, but a vague silence dominated the whole place. I wondered whether he had called at any time during my absence. The December night air seemed to be filled with chilly ticking sounds that made my blood run cold. "Oh, God! Not now, please!" I prayed, suddenly overwhelmed by a paralyzing fear. I snatched the phone and I dialed Marwan's direct number at his office, hoping against all odds that he would still be there. The quick busy signal made my heart leap with hope. With whom could Marwan be talking at that late hour when all offices and shops in the city had long since closed? I rushed down to my in-laws, and I told them about their son's mysterious disappearance.

A heavy silence fell over the family. There were anxious looks and murmurs. Aunt Najla said, "Calm down, honey, Marwan wouldn't stay in his office just to talk on the phone. We'll find out in a moment." We walked down the hall to where Farid and his joyous bunch of friends played cards.

"I'll go with Farid to the bank and see what's going on," Darweesh, the only guest who had driven his car to the house, offered eagerly. "We'll be back in no time, Mrs. Nadia, don't worry."

It was almost midnight when the telephone finally rang. "Now listen to me, Nadia, and please try to be calm," Farid's earnest voice instructed me. "I'm at the police station. Wait, wait! No, Marwan is not with us, we believe he is still in his office. We are not sure who else is with him. The night guard is sure he hasn't seen him leave the building. We don't know if someone besides his bodyguard is there. The police are looking at all helpful clues they need to check before alerting others who are in the bank. Yes, the police know Marwan has a gun in his office, but no one seems to have heard any noise, or any shots coming from that floor." I hung on to the phone with both hands as Farid talked with someone there at the station. Suad and Uncle Ahmad were glued to my side trying to make sense of the few words they were able to pick up as Farid delivered his alarming message.

"Nadia, are you still there?" Farid asked breathlessly. "The police believe there is only one man in there with Marwan. They are sure now it's a holdup. Please don't panic, Nadia. You need to keep your strength to take care of the kids. No, the lines are cut. I have to go now. Yes, yes, I'll call you in case of any change."

Forgotten and overshadowed by the nightmare that befell our family, the sacred Eve and its following day of Adha dragged on in a mournful air of confusion and uncertainty, shared by the friends and relatives as it unfolded.

It took the police squad twenty-four hours to free Marwan unharmed and to force Tyseer into their custody. Saved too were the cash and the rest of the bank's valuables. Marwan was too devastated after his release to tell us in detail what had taken place during the long holdup. Apparently he did not know what had happened until the police took over. Tyseer had him bound to his chair throughout the night and he took from him the keys to the safe. Tyseer apparently was unable to escape during the night because the building was surrounded by the police and the city was under a night curfew. When he tried to escape through a bathroom window on the first floor with a handbag stuffed with banknotes and jewelry, he found the police waiting for him. The four bullets that were fired at him and forced him to surrender didn't seem to have done too much damage to his massive chest.

The terrifying incident at the bank took its toll on us. On top of that, the breakup of Marwan's two-year affair with Angelle soon afterward sent him into a bad depression. This despair placed a burden on me which I needed to share with someone. In a way, that came about one day when Ralph, who was treating Marwan for depression, prescribed another week of rest for him. Marwan insisted that important matters were waiting for him at the office. This set off an exchange of accusations between the two of us, with poor Ralph watching in bewilderment as we took turns drawing him into the fray, trying to convince him of the validity of our respective positions.

Marwan paraded before his friend my continuing complaints about the ever increasing demands made upon him at work, lamenting: "Nadia blames all of my ills on Ali Ibrahim, whom she has mistrusted from the beginning. She sees him as a manipulative politician who uses the Rajys and everybody else for his own goals. And you know what she wants me to do now? Resign! And why? A woman's intuition! That's her test for people, and none of my colleagues seem able to pass it!"

My heart simply brimmed with indignation, and I found myself yelling, "Stop it, Marwan, right now! You seem to forget that you were the first one to complain about that selfish man. Remember how many times you threatened to resign because your promotions never came through on time? It doesn't take spiritual meditation and intuition to discover how malicious that boss of yours can be, especially when dealing with people as trusting as you and your father." I turned to Ralph and apologized for losing my temper, trying to shut out of my mind the echo of Ali Ibrahim's voice making slimy passes at me whenever an opportunity occurred. Marwan was speechless, amazed by my fit of anger.

"This man is after money, wherever it comes from, and the Rajys have it. That's all. He uses many tricks to lure Marwan to his side, even when it means deciding against the interests of his own father." I was more stunned by my bluntness than Marwan himself. The memory of their discussion that night on our terrace when Marwan capitulated and agreed not to mention to his father the conditions of their ailing bank still filled me with remorse. The burden of what I heard at that meeting would come back to haunt me a decade later for not having followed my intuition and warned Uncle Ahmad on the spot about the risk involved for him and all the Rajys who had invested heavily in that bank.

"Sorry, Marwan, I may be blaming you for a past you had no control over. The important thing now is for you not to give up. You are young and surrounded by people who would do everything to help you bounce back and try again. We both have a lot to look forward to, charting a much brighter future for our boys." But my husband was loudly contradicting my accusations and suggestions. I turned back to Ralph. "Say something, Ralph, please!"

But Marwan got a word in first. "You see how impossible my wife is?" he moaned, looking terribly haggard as he pushed his quilt to the side and tumbled out of bed. Ralph stepped in and tried to talk him into sitting down. "Let's relax and come to terms with this issue, my friend. It sounds as if Nadia has been going through a hard time coping with the way you carry on with your job."

But Marwan was in no mood to hear more from me. He thought my lecturing him about the future was outrageous. "There is no sense in what she is proposing, Ralph. She wants a nearly forty-year-old husband like me to turn his back on the only career he has ever had, detach himself from the only background he has ever known, and drag his worn-out body to where her dreams are." I started to remind him that those were also *his* dreams all along, but Ralph winked at me to stop. Marwan was no longer listening. I felt weariness and sadness inside me. The truth was before my eyes. Marwan wanted to drop out of the race.

It took Marwan most of the following year to regain his health and some sense of normalcy. Nadim Haddad, his only close friend besides Ralph Zhurbach at that point, stood by him through the grim days of spring and summer when, disagreeably uncommunicative, he trusted no one else. Nadim's attention enchanted the boys as well. He knew how to please them. He also loved their energy and often bundled the two older ones into his little cabriolet and zoomed off to his parents' house on the Mediterranean shore, where they would hunt for seashells and eat homemade cookies. Indeed this man had by now become my remorseful admirer. I recalled how he had invaded the privacy of my home and aroused my combative instincts on that night several years earlier. He had dragged my drunken husband home from a night of carousing, but he would now go to any lengths to gain my approval. The small flame of attraction his poetry had lighted at the party for my twenty-fifth birthday had not dimmed. To my increased exasperation, it continued to grow.

I had watched the adventurous young Nadim change. The wild and tough playboy turned into to a romantic, soft-spoken poet and gentleman who began to show up in elegant attire, using all the courteous manners his aristocratic mother had instilled in him.

Unaware at first of the force of that emotional awakening, I let myself flirt with him, but in thought only. But that power had its own ways. His presence broke the rhythm of my daily life. His absence stole my sleep at night as well. Although we had not at that point acknowledged our feelings in words, our relationship had changed imperceptibly from courteous attention to a risky alliance. Nadim was often present not just as a family friend. From the security of my quarters, I would indulge in the thrill of hearing his voice and feeling his presence. Like no male friend I had known before, he was on my mind day and night and that attachment had become a great concern for me. He didn't seem to be aware of the perils of a relationship with a married Muslim woman. After all, it was rarely heard of in our rather conservative Muslim community that a trusted family friend of another faith would infringe on the sanctity of that family! I did not trust my feelings. I simply did not trust us together. Overwhelmed by the passion surging within me, I would seek safety behind the doors of my privacy, seldom staying with Marwan when Nadim was around.

"Nadia, would you come here for a moment, please?" Marwan called from the terrace where he had settled down for the rest of the evening. "Have you read this invitation?"

"Yes, I have. Sister Xavier handed it to me today when I took Usama to school to pick up the prize his teacher gave him for arithmetic. Why do you ask?"

"Because this is more formal than the parties they usually hold at the school. Those religious people never get tired of creating new ways to squeeze money out of us parents." He leafed through the blue booklet. Marwan never hesitated to express his dislike for the manipulative style with which religious institutions collected money.

"But this has nothing to do with money. It's an invitation for you and me to attend a very special mass celebrating the six hundredth anniversary of the founding of the Carmelite order." I tried to make my voice sound as soft as possible.

"Do you really want to go to that boring mass?"

"Yes, and I think you should go, too. We have trusted them to educate our three children, and they deserve our respect in return; sharing some of their sacred observances when they invite us is, in my view, one way to show our gratitude." I knew I had to go easy if I wanted Marwan to go to that ceremony. So far I had managed on my own for most daytime occasions, but never at night. For me, going out in the evenings unaccompanied was like being seen nude in public.

After a short silence Marwan drowned what was left of his cigarette in his half-empty coffee cup, got up from his chair, and said, "Let me call Nadim and see if he would be willing to accompany you." He didn't look my way nor did he stop to ask me! He couldn't know that I didn't trust myself to be alone with a man who, as my intuition told me, could shine brighter than the sun for me. What if Nadim refused? What if he accepted? Marwan returned from his phone conversation, sounding relieved. "Nadim will play the role of chaperon with pleasure," he said. "He was concerned whether you would mind going with him alone and suggested he could bring his sister Leila along if you like." I told him the invitation was for two.

On the next day Nadim arrived early, a little after five. It was a hot June Sunday afternoon and our apartment felt like a furnace. The kids were still out on the terrace enjoying their daily dip-and-run game, pretending that a large brass wash basin filled with water was the Mediterranean. I finished dressing in a short sleeveless dress, a silk dress with delicate layers of chiffon pleats at the hem, which Usama and Jamal had helped me choose.

Finally I took a deep breath and left my room to meet a date who was chosen by my own husband. Probably neither of them realized that this was the first time I had ever gone anywhere alone with a man who was not related to me. Marwan's impulsive move to rid himself of a simple social duty had, according to the matrimonial ethics of our society, subliminally cost him his conjugal right. Was that move really as trusting as it appeared? Could he have sensed the emotional restraint I had been practicing and wanted to try me? Was he too tired of a bond his father had pledged on his behalf and just wanted out? Those disturbing thoughts were churning in my mind, but I still think Marwan was too good a man to become an accomplice to such a plot.

As I sank timidly into the low leather seat of the dark blue Triumph, a part of me wanted so much to respond to the mutinous emotions in my veins and reach out to that beautiful body next to me. Another, more prudent part of me was scared to death of such urges. So I sat as stiff as a statue. I could hear my loud and fast heartbeat. Two hearts, not one, were beating inside me at the same time.

The mysterious solemnity of the dome's frescoes depicting saints, angels, and beautiful plump cherubs helped me return to sanity, and the glory of Bach's arias rippling from a beautiful organ on a high balcony brought my heart rate back to normal. Surrounded by the familiar faces of young parents I had come to know through our kids, I forgot about my companion, and felt quite at home and full of good spirits. After the mass was over and we were ushered into the reception lounge, I saw Nadim coming across the room with a crystal goblet in each hand. "I brought you some French champagne, Mrs. Rajy." The effervescent liquid swayed gently as I pressed my fingers around the goblet's delicate stem. I took a small sip, and gave the goblet back to him. "Thank you, Nadim." For the first time I heard myself call him by his first name. "I'm sorry, you know I don't drink." He put the drinks down and we walked through the open French doors. I moved away from him, and pretended to be enthralled by the breathtaking view as he softly began to recite the romantic poem he had composed for my birthday four years earlier. "I have something to tell you, Nadia. Please listen. It has been buried inside me ever since I saw you for the first time. I love you more than you can ever imagine!" I could hear him breathe, but I stood there by the impregnable old wall, waiting for a miracle to save me from falling in love.

Denial struck first. For a whole week after that Sunday evening, I kept telling myself it couldn't be true. I dreaded answering the phone, unable to listen to Nadim's voice for more than a few seconds if he was the caller. The whispers of his poetry frightened me. But prudence and morality were no match for a body suddenly set on fire. Gradually lack of sleep and poor appetite took their toll on my health and I began to wonder whether I was capable of pulling myself out of this mess at all. Marwan was surprised that Nadim had suddenly gotten too busy to call, unaware that I was the one who refused his friend's plea to visit.

"I have to go away," I told my mirror one morning in July. A few days later I told my in-laws the kids and I needed a vacation.

"I'm glad you made this decision, dear. Najla and I were worried that the heat is affecting your health," Uncle Ahmad said. "July is far too hot to be spent here when you can enjoy it at your parents' summer house." Aunt Najla wished that Marwan would go, too, but we all knew he hated the inconvenience of visiting my parents during the summer. My parents did not own a summer house, and the houses they rented were usually too small to accommodate all of us comfortably.

It was a very sad day when we left Haifa on that vacation. The news hadn't been good since the beginning of 1946 and it became worse as the summer began. Political assassinations and terrorist operations had intensified tremendously in Palestine after the end of World War II, especially in the cities. The conflict was spreading, not only among the Palestinian factions themselves but between the Jewish opposition and the British mandate authority as well. Britain, in disagreement with the

Jewish-American lobbyists who wanted the whole cake and not just a slice of it, considered partition of Palestine the only available solution to the mess they had created in Palestine and in the oil-rich Arab states. Meanwhile the regimes that had already consented to the partition deal, against the wishes of both Palestinians and Israelis, were busy fighting among themselves over the wages due them for that bargain.

The family good-byes on the morning of our departure lacked much of the excitement and warmth of similar occasions in years past. We were to carry memorized greetings, money, and food parcels to two of the Rajy sons. One of them was still at the boarding school in Sidon while the other one attended college in Beirut. "Ahmad and I did not want them to come back here this summer, Nadia!" Aunt Najla said. "If something should happen, I'd want them all to stay with you in Beirut." She feared her premonition that some predicament was going to separate her from those boys. They were the three ambitious younger sons who had left home for a better education in foreign institutions across the borders. Radhi had been accepted at Purdue University after graduating from the American University in Cairo. He would soon be on his way to the United States to begin his graduate studies in political science, a field unknown to his parents and most intriguing to the new generation. For Aunt Najla, the faraway continent might as well be the end of the earth, and she might never see that child again. I never regretted urging that those boys be allowed to get an education rather than to go directly into the family business, as Farid and Ali had done at an early age. They were stuck forever.

Our trip to Beirut was long and tiring. The car was crowded with over-stuffed suitcases, food, and bundles of clothing that had to be unpacked and repacked every time we were stopped at a barricade within the Palestinian territory or at border checkpoints. The children were exhausted. Ghassan, then four years old, was carsick and on the verge of collapsing. It was late when we arrived, but my brothers Fadi and Amin were waiting to help us with the luggage. The small portable radios I had brought as gifts for them were received with great excitement.

By midnight the large house had regained its majestic serenity.

Ghassan slept peacefully on the old narrow bed that used to be mine, while Usama and Jamal had settled down with their accommodating uncles. My parents were at their summer place in Broumana and for this time I had the whole house to myself.

Lying down on Nora's old bed, I surrendered to the splendid tranquillity of that huge house where the night breeze never failed to steal through. It was in this room that I had learned, when in fear or pain, how to daydream and lull myself to sleep. I used to just close my eyes and let my childish imagination calm me down. On that particular night I found myself in great need of that innocent imagination. I invited the memory of Grandpa Mehdi, whose life-sized portrait had long since disappeared because of the lasting feud between my father and his in-laws. Now I needed to rest my burdened head on his shoulder and tell him about Nadim, the dilemma I could tell no one else about. As I had done when I was a child, I wanted him to listen to my tale of anguish and direct me to a safe path. I knew he would respond!

It was strange that no one in my family had ever been able to understand my attachment to a grandfather who was known to none of us grandchildren. He was always real to me in a way I couldn't explain, and his influence on my life took many forms. I came to believe that the lasting respect he commanded and the immense library lining the walls of his mansion were not his greatest achievements. Years later I would realize that the enlightening ethno-theological essays he wrote minimizing the rifts between the various religious sects in our community were his real legacy. Regrettably, his books were not allowed to be published during the sixties and seventies because reconciliation among religious communities was not in vogue.

Although fatigued to my bones, I refused to let sleep take away my last few hours of privacy. The new day would soon sweep me into the midst of family and friends, with little time to myself. Worse yet, on the weekend we were all expected to leave this peaceful house and join my parents in Broumana.

A cool dawn breeze lifted my spirits. Ghassan stirred restively and uttered some inarticulate sounds. It was a new day, and I was next to my child. The delicate scent of his moistened skin filled me with gratitude for being the mother of this adorable child. Indeed, in the midst of all the fear and uncertainty of my maturing emotions, I found nothing as reassuring as the endearing love of my children. I knew that no matter what happened to me as a woman, the solid bond that linked me with my children would always be my source of comfort.

"Face it, Nadia, that isn't going to work this time," my inner voice scolded. "Your emotions are in control now. They are going to win the battle for your body. Worshiping your children is quite beside the point."

The trip was not the answer to anything. Staying with my fun-loving family that summer did not help me reach any decision. The struggle inside me left no room for frivolity. It claimed every bit of the living space of my soul.

10

Fall 1947

November 1947 marked the United Nations' decision to partition Palestine, still under the British mandate, to form an Arab state and a Jewish state. It was not until the winter of 1948 that the ordinary people in Palestine came to the realization that the Arab liberals and heroes who had persistently warned against impending disaster were right to fear a plot by the Allies against the Arabs. Our ancestors had had to face invasions before. European Christians had fought holy wars against them. Indeed, the destiny of Palestine has always been determined by outsiders. This latest round of crusades would feature the Israelis as the winners in the Holy Land.

Earlier, in the winter and spring of 1947, the conflict between Arabs and Jews reached new critical levels. One could see with one's own eyes how much confusion was going on as promises that looked beneficial to both Arabs and Jews were made, and then broken on a daily basis. The Allies and their associates dropped their masks and rushed to carry out the plans they had all along supported against the Arabs. In August two plans for the partition of Palestine were reported to the General Assembly. Despite the shortcomings from their point of view, the Jewish Agency supported the majority plan but the Arabs accepted neither. Before any decision was made in the United Nations, the British declared they would end the mandate by May 1948, giving notice that they would withdraw regardless of the outcome. The British Empire had pulled its horns in. In November the majority plan was accepted by the General Assembly and an ambiguous blueprint for the partition of Palestine into two states was accepted.

The dozen or so years I lived in Palestine taught me a lot about our behavior as human beings when under the pressure of a disaster as irreparable as ours. One had to be there to describe the numbing shock and confusion that immobilized the Palestinian people who suddenly found themselves totally under Zionist control. The majority of them were in a deep state of denial, not willing to admit that their passionately trusted Allies could betray them. Uncle Ahmad was a living example of that majority. He had always honored the heroes of World War I who had united the Arabs, and, in his view, helped them win many victories against the Ottoman forces. Why would such heroes betray them now and inveigle the Palestinians into what was beginning to look like a fatal trap?

The irony was that the lack of leadership among our own people caused the real damage. Most of the casualties were among the civilians who didn't know what to do or where to go. The chaos existed everywhere: inside their defense lines, on the streets, as well as in people's homes. The Rajys were a prime example. The increased bombing week after week seemed to have eroded the very structure of our family long before claiming one of us as a victim, and shattered its sense of unity and belonging.

I watched that tightly knit family fall apart before my very eyes. Uncle Ahmad, the mighty oak who had never failed to provide all of us with everything from money to emotional comfort, was the first to lose faith in his ability to control the situation. He decided to leave Haifa. This left us with the responsibility of making our own decisions about where to go and how to manage. It was a scary feeling to find myself and my little family suddenly all alone in such hard times.

The Rajys were gone before the summer of 1947 came to its end. Parents, children—even their maid—vanished as though they had nothing to hold on to, no roots to protect. Like the rest of the Arab neighbors, they vacated their home leaving behind everything they owned as though they were going on an excursion. The possibility that they might never return was not reckoned with.

My in-laws did not go very far, of course. Acre was only ten miles away where some of the Rajy clan had roots. "It's safer in Acre, you know. We are having a good time here," Aunt Najla said the first time I heard from them. Farid and Ali had both married maternal cousins from Acre and had also escaped to that safe place right after the shelling began. Marwan, the only Rajy who had always voiced his wish to leave the country years before the revolution began, was now the only member of the family determined to stay home. Although devastated by his parents' choice to flee, and chagrined over the cowardly British surrender to the Zionists, he decided to stay his ground. Our home was just a short walk from his office at the bank.

His mother's pleas to join the rest of the family proved entirely ineffectual. I too resisted her suggestion that we move to Acre and that Marwan commute to his work like Farid and Ali, whenever the road was open and it was possible to return before dark.

Worrisome to me also was the hint of aloofness I detected in Aunt Najla's voice. She talked as though she had lost interest in her affluent and privileged life in Haifa. Suddenly, she was prepared to give up her past. More depressing yet was Uncle Ahmad's reaction to the fighting. Too overwhelmed to protect his business from collapsing, he cut himself off completely from the trading arena and left the store to his old worker, Abou Maarouf, to look after. According to Marwan, his father had neglected his financial affairs to the point that the harm done might be irreparable. "You'd better talk to him, Nadia, he might accept advice from you. I know it's my mother who's keeping him away, but there's no need for him to be so scared and hide behind her skirt."

My attempts to reason with my father in-law by phone got me nowhere. He and his other sons were convinced that, if they made new trading contacts in Acre, their business would be well protected. The man who had worked all his life to promote Haifa's commercial viability assured me that "our place in Haifa will always be reserved for us, especially since we established that branch away from the harbor with Rathos, our friend in the Jewish market." They had given Rathos power of attorney over all the Rajy business proceeds "until things stabilize," as Uncle Ahmad put it. As he explained to me the new business opportunities at Acre, his tone showed no trace of concern for the 140-year-old family business or for the properties he had inherited by default. The Rajys were a legend in Haifa, renowned for their wealth and prestige. Yet Uncle Ahmad was now sloughing all this off with no visible sign of regret.

Our hill was very quiet when I heard the squeaking of our street gate. At first I thought it was in a dream. The hurried footsteps echoed up the staircase of our apartment building. It was still dark. I jumped out of bed and waited for the doorbell to ring. Ours was the last floor in the building and we were the only ones who had a key to the door leading to the rooftop that served as a veranda. There was a shuffling of feet on the roof. A few moments later someone walked down the stairs very decisively. Marwan didn't move, but I couldn't help rushing out to the terrace of our apartment where I could see the gate. Four men in what appeared to be fatigues were crossing the gate to a truck waiting for them. They looked like members of the enemy gangs, like the foreign guerrilla's pictures we saw in the daily newspapers. When the dimly lit truck turned around, I got a glimpse of the spidery signs on its sides. Then I knew.

For the first time, I felt estranged in my own home, angry that some Jewish troublemakers showed no respect for the neighborly trust the Rajys had always shown the Jewish community in our city. Why should they sneak in during the night instead of coming openly to talk to us during the day? I wondered whether Rabbi Aaron might be able to explain this untimely raid in the morning. He had apparently grown weary long ago of working with the neo-kibbutzim and extremist Jews who flooded Palestine after World War II, and he often voiced his concern about the Zionists' volatile approach to the Palestinian issue.

Marwan and I went up to the rooftop in the morning while the children were still asleep. We found the door to the roof torn from its hinges. Rabbi Aaron was already there, gazing at some chalk lines and marks drawn on the cement floor. "Good morning, Rabbi. So you heard those invaders too. Do you know who they were?" Marwan greeted him.

"Oh, no! I didn't even dare let them know I'm still here. But these marks make it seem obvious that they are bringing their filthy war right here. They are taking over. Our roof is going to be their new barricade and soon we will have some heavy artillery over our heads. You can't stay here any more, especially with your wife and kids. I'm going to move my family away. If you can do that too, we can both stay and look after our homes."

"You mean they would bring some big gun up on this roof? How could they do that?" Marwan tightened his woolen robe around his chest, waiting in disbelief for an answer that never came.

I did not believe it. How could anyone bring the war and its artillery into a civilian home? The whole matter seemed absurd. "It just isn't done," I protested.

"Oh, you are so innocent, my dear," the rabbi said. "Those people don't care if your roof tumbles down or not. Anyway, who is here to stop them? Since most of the neighbors moved away, this neighborhood has become a no-man's-land. It belongs to those who will be the first to claim it."

Marwan went to the bank early that morning, leaving to me the task of finding a place to move to that was close to the children's school. Knowing how resourceful Nadim's sister Leila was, I called her at her office. She turned her concern for our plight into action and, while I was still packing, called back to say she had found a great apartment, right by the children's school; two bedrooms, one bath, newly built. "You'll enjoy the neighborhood," she added. Within a couple of hours our loyal Abou Maarouf had secured the address and sent his son to clean the apartment. Then he showed up at my door with his truck at our gate, ready to move us. He managed to fit our large bedroom set into the smaller of the two bedrooms, so that the boys could have the larger one. The rest of the apartment was no more than a small kitchen and an extended covered terrace with a French door that opened to a small vine-clad porch. The place was like a doll house.

Clearly, these were new times. The pain I had felt since the Rajys deserted their house had to be ignored now. I had lived for twenty-nine years, and never had to worry about a home. Now I had to start growing accustomed to the idea of being taken away from home, roots and all. Included in all these agitations of the mind and the heart were three bewildered children and a weirdly detached husband.

Indeed, Marwan showed no emotion over the move. He even seemed to deny that we were in danger at all. The financial mess we found ourselves in left him indifferent. He acted as though someone else would take care of our problem. Not even the possibility of losing our whole city to the enemy provoked him to a discussion. He cared a great deal about his personal papers and his many bottles of liquor. He had these transported to the new place. Like his father, he left home with no apparent regret, but remained totally attached to his work.

The boys proved to be quite resilient. On the day we arrived at that nice residential area on the outskirts of Haifa, they immediately began exploring the small park in the center of the modern complex and were soon playing with some other children. Two days later they happily discovered that some of their classmates lived in the same neighborhood. Their greatest concern was for their nanny, Warrood, our faithful maid, who had long since gone with her parents to their village in the area that was already in Zionist hands. The possibility of going back to school thrilled them. Each time we discussed the idea, we celebrated it with a picnic.

Our first guests to the new apartment were Laura and Michael Hindi, the owners of our duplex, who lived in the apartment above us. A warm and friendly couple in their forties, they arrived late one evening with a freshly baked cake and a bottle of French red wine as a welcoming gift. They both worked at Haifa's General Hospital, he as a pediatrician and she as a staff nurse in the emergency wing. They were the best thing that could have happened to me and my distraught family. At a time when we were cut off from the comforting warmth of our family and friends, their affection and support were as welcome to our souls as a gentle rain to the thirsty desert. They helped us regain a sense of balance in our daily life. Our landlord was a man who could listen to Marwan sympathetically and offer him reassurance. They became good friends in no time.

It was such a relief to see my husband and children so happily adjusted to their new surroundings. Being on our own, without Uncle Ahmad's attention and support, helped me grow up and opened my eyes to what life was all about. Survival was now the new imperative. I wasn't sure that we could manage on Marwan's salary alone. We had no idea how much money my in-laws had been spending on us. No one kept track of such things. Our sudden move placed us on the opposite side of the combat zone, and away from the Rajy properties. Abou Maarouf was unable to continue his faithful service to us. To my great surprise, Marwan, who had never been in charge of me or my children, suddenly began to pay attention to our daily needs. He would write our shopping list for the day, order our bread or milk as though he had always done this. I wasn't sure whether this delightful change was the result of the absence of the older members of our family or was a spontaneous response to the comfortable community we had become a part of. It consisted of married couples, all of them members of the professional class. There were none of those uncouth Rajy relatives that used to swamp our house with no previous notice.

Anxiety started to build up as the warfare accelerated and stories were told about furious street battles between Arabs and Jews in some cities and villages. The loss in lives, property, and businesses was said to be tremendous as alarming news began to proclaim the fall of some important Palestinian towns. Haifa was among the cities still holding on when on December 3, 1947 the British government announced that it would consider its mandate on Palestine at an end as of May 15, 1948.

We were having our dinner when the sound of explosives thundered through our home, sending us all running to the inner room for protection. It sounded very close. We put the kids to bed and retired to our room. Overwhelmed with fear, the boys rushed into our room crying, and I squeezed them between us on our joined double beds. It was a long and endless night, the kind our nightmares bring back to us.

Next morning we followed our usual routine: the children left for school, Marwan took his time shaving and freshening up, I prepared his breakfast and waited for the morning papers to arrive. Those newspapers provided me with a wide range of fresh information that represented many viewpoints. The local ones included profitable instructions about how and when people could safely go in or out of the old city for their necessary errands. At the same time they helped me plan a few quick trips to visit with my in-laws in Acre, and to go back to our apartment where I managed to pick up some winter clothes and blankets.

Reading the papers gave Marwan a certain sense of continuity—he looked for articles about business and money matters to assure himself that the economy was still holding out. He didn't seem to mind reading all the falsified reports that glutted the papers. Both camps had constituents waiting to be fed, and the newspapers stood to profit the most from the daily mixture of lies and half truths.

But this morning I could hear him argue with Alloush, the newsboy, about which road to Haifa was open and which one was closed this morning. "No, I told you, Uncle Marwan, not even the Alemania road could be safe today. Several people were found dead there this morning." I watched them walk down to the alley where the car pool group had gathered. Marwan was apparently determined not to let the young carrier win an argument. Through the thin twill yarn of his cashmere vest I could see the outline of his pistol holster under his left armpit. I wondered whether Marwan, who had never parted with that lethal weapon since the holdup at the bank, knew how to handle it in case of need. I turned away from the window as the argument droned on.

When Marwan hadn't come back into the house by 8:30, I peeked through the window again. The crowd had grown larger, split into little groups over the newspapers they were sharing. Marwan was moving from one group to another, talking to people and sustaining animated conversation with them. It was actually a relief to see him so vigorous and so engaged in the midst of those people. I recalled vividly how hard it had been for him at first to cope with such a large number of businessmen and professionals all at once. But their easy acceptance of him and the support he received from long-time friends who lived nearby brought him out of his shell.

I left a note on Marwan's breakfast tray and went to take a shower. When I came out later, the apartment was grimly quiet. Marwan was nowhere to be found, his food untouched, tea and coffee still brewing. The area where the crowd had been was deserted. I could still hear the same incongruous sounds of explosives and gunshots that had kept us awake all night. "Something is wrong," I thought. I rushed out of the apartment and down to the vacant alley, where John Karam, a city commuter with Marwan, saw me and came out of his duplex. "Is something the matter, Madame?"

"I'm looking for Marwan, where did he go?"

"Go? What do you mean? No one could have gone anywhere. The roads to the city are all closed. Did you check with the Hindis? I heard Mr. Rajy say he needed to make a phone call."

"The Hindis left for work early. They drop our children off at school on their way."

"Oh, well, in that case, he might be at somebody else's house where there is a telephone. I'll check for you. Please go home now, it's cold out here. And don't worry, Mrs. Rajy, your husband can go nowhere without a car."

Half an hour after I had inquired of him about Marwan, John Karam appeared at our door to tell me that my husband had indeed gone to the city on his own. He had heard from neighbors that Marwan apparently phoned the bank and talked to a person called Ibrahim Bey. They heard to him saying, "Don't worry, I'll go and open the bank. I'm leaving right away. "Can you believe that, Mrs. Rajy?"

"I can believe it all right, Mr. Karam. But I don't understand the rush. Why didn't Marwan come back here, eat his breakfast, and then go?" I managed a smile as I thanked him for the trouble we had caused him and promised to have Marwan offer an apology in person when he returned from work. I tried to pretend that everything was going to be all right and remembered that it was Thursday and the children had to be picked up at twelve because of the school's mid-week break. While anxiety within me mounted with each new round of gunfire, I caught myself blaming the whole world for what was going on: Marwan, for being such a senseless workaholic; his boss, for taking such vile advantage of him; Leila, for finding us an apartment without a phone; the Hindis, for not being home to let him use their phone. . . .

"Mrs. Rajy, there's a telephone call for you," Natalie, the Karams' 14-year-old daughter called from under my kitchen window. "It is very urgent my father said. Could you come right away, please?"

I knew it! My shivering body felt it! But for an instant, as I heard the sharp Rajy voice and what I thought was Marwan's familiar accent, I relaxed somewhat. But it was his brother Ali on the phone. He was wailing frantically, babbling incomprehensibly, he wouldn't listen when I tried to interrupt.

"Hear me, Nadia, please! We don't have time to argue now, we have to be back with the body before the sun is down. Do you understand? The ambulance will pick you up at 2 o'clock."

From that moment on, things went too fast for my mind to grasp; it was as though I were split into two—one part of me hovered over the ground like a suspended balloon. The other part would be sinking into the jaws of death, deep inside the earth.

Alas, Marwan had gone . . . and left us all behind.

He had left for work on foot, as I learned later. He didn't go very far. His body was found by a passing ambulance at 9:30 that Thursday morning, January 15, a few yards away from the city limits. He was shot from a long range in the back of the head. Someone took aim at him from a distance, and he was left to die on the street our newsboy had warned him only a couple of hours earlier not to take. After his body was identified by none other than our close friend Laura Hindi, the hospital authorities, following traditional practice, had notified the Rajys in Acre. I was the last one to know. Not until they had sent someone to Haifa to make the funeral arrangements did I receive the terrible piece of news that turned my world upside down.

The journey to the cemetery began when the ambulance carrying Marwan's body picked me up. Against my objection and that of the neighbors who saw us off, Ali insisted that it was more appropriate that I ride in the back of the ambulance. The mere idea of finding myself close to a dead body behind the closed doors of that ambulance petrified me. Cowering into the dark corner of the grave-like van, I couldn't believe Marwan was inside the silent coffin at arm's length from me. Besides, Ali admitted that he didn't actually see the body, as it was already in the ambulance when he had arrived. He could be mistaken, couldn't he? The idea of a wrong identification struck me with a sudden hope. What if Marwan had spent the whole day safely, behind his desk, and what if he would come home at that moment to find no one there?

The familiar sounds of explosives and the heavy but random rattle of machine gun goaded the vehicle into high speed. Finally, it skidded to a halt, hurling my body against the cold door. Silence was followed by the loud and reproachful voice of Farid. "Thank God you're here. What took you so long?"

Ali started to mumble some angry words but Abu Riad, a close cousin of Marwan's, cut him short. "Where is she? Don't tell me you forgot to pick up Nadia!"

"Oh, for God's sake, man! She's inside the van where she's supposed to be. At least she has been protected from the dangers I had to face."

"What? Nadia is with the body? Are you crazy?" Instantly the van door opened and the wide-open arms of Farid reached out to me. Someone received me in my grief and led me to one of the waiting cars.

I spent the rest of the journey in the back seat of Hadj Uthman's sedan. A heated political argument between Farid, Ali, and three of their cousins was a gift I could not appreciate at the time. Brooding silence moved into me. Ours was the first of a dozen cars carrying Rajy friends and relatives who came from Acre earlier but had been stopped by Palestinian guards just a few miles outside Haifa. The guards had advised against crossing that heavily attacked end of the city. The main topic of conversation was the stunning news about the weakening Arab defense all throughout the country. A number of Arab footholds had been lost to the enemy across the Jordanian borders. According to an afternoon news bulletin quoted by one of the cousins, the day's casualties numbered 150 civilians in downtown Haifa, in addition to hundreds of unattended injured people who had fled inland.

I listened wearily to the dispute overshadowing the real reason for the gathering of my escorts. These men had forgotten all about their dead cousin in the van. Eulogists, sheikhs, and religious leaders were waiting to do him honor, but his next of kin seemed oblivious to everything truly important, including the children! The memory of my sons' anguished faces, weeping desolately behind the kitchen windows, their tiny hands waving good-bye as Leila, their temporary guardian, tried to comfort them, obscured everything else around me. There were many emotions inside me, but this was not the time to speak to them.

The separation from my sons lasted for three long sacramental days of tribal pageantry. I watched patiently as the Rajys and their clan of several hundred mourners prayed, wailed, danced, and feasted. They would move back and forth from their little rented house to the weed-grown cemetery. I was worn out. I, too, was dead. Yet I knew I had to support my in-laws at such an overwhelming time. This bereft family seemed determined to play the traditional role required from a patriarch of their clan at such a critical time. Dressed in black from head to toe, its members wanted to prove that their social standing was invincible. As the young, foreign-looking widow, I knew I had a crucial role to play in the tribal tragedy as well. Nothing more was demanded of me than to be there, so my young age would feed their grief and bring more tears. And why not? These benevolent people had shown me nothing but love, trust, and respect. Now they needed a heroine for their show and, by God, I owed them that! After all, with their acquisition of an expensive daughter-in-law, the addition of three healthy grandsons to the family, and the heroic martyrdom of their forty-year old son, the Rajys could not have scripted a more dramatic finale!

On the third ceremonial day after Marwan's death, when a commemorative service was to be held, the arrival of the three grandchildren rekindled the sorrow and augmented the confusion that reigned over the place. The situation emphasized my need to ask a favor of the heartbroken old grandfather, and it wouldn't be an easy one for either of us. My eyes were filled with tears when I approached Uncle Ahmad. He seemed to have aged, to have pitifully shriveled up, in the last few days.

"Come, sit here next to me." His fat, elegant hand patted the seat adjacent to him encouragingly. "God knows how much I miss you, my dear Nadia. And I have failed you in the most disgraceful manner a father could fail his daughter. Tell me, what can I do to have your forgiveness?"

"Oh, Uncle Ahmad, let's go home. Please, let's take the children and go home. I can't stand it here anymore. It will be easier on the children to be in their own home instead of this miserable place, don't you agree?"

His voice echoed in a strange, low tone: "You know we can't go there now. Not until things settle down. One victim is more than I can afford."

I tried to calm the anger rising in me, hoping our long harmonious bond would survive the difficulty we were going to face. "You can stay in Acre if you want, but I have to take my children back to their home." His fatigued eyes widened in disbelief, but he didn't interrupt. "Please Uncle, give me the chance to find something to hang onto after the disastrous vacuum I find myself in. If not for my sake, for that of the boys!"

"Nadia! Do you know what you are asking me? You want me to send you and those little kids to the war zone while I hide like a frightened rat over here? How on earth could I do that?"

"Well, my view of the disgraceful situation you are in must differ from yours. It breaks my heart to see the hero I know you to be losing faith in himself merely because of a setback in the war. Your faith doesn't allow you to be afraid of death. God wants you to free your soul from fear and maintain the dignity he has always enabled you to cherish. Please, let's all go back home and try to cope with what we still have. A lot of our Haifa's Arab inhabitants are still living there. What do you say?" All of a sudden, I looked at him more carefully. His head was lowered. His shoulders were bent, wrapped around with a woolen scarf. Tears trickled down his unshaven cheeks. "I'm sorry to have upset you, Uncle Ahmad. I'll go and attend to the boys."

"Wait, Nadia." He grabbed my hand as I turned around to leave. "You may not have my blessing to go back home right away, which I believe is unwise. However, I want you to know that you are free to make any decision concerning where you want to go and what you want to do with your children, as long as you are safe and well provided for. Does this make sense to you?"

It did indeed. The tone of his voice conveyed neither scorn nor disdain in reminding me that I was a woman who needed to be provided for. At the same time, he was granting me an unheard of freedom of choice. In reality, a young empty-handed widow who belonged to a closed society such as mine could have one of only two providers: her in-laws or her parents. A third choice would brand her as an outcast. But since both of my legal custodians were broke—the Rajys financially, and my parents ethically—why shouldn't I be my own provider? Practice began the very next day.

A cease-fire was announced on the radio and in the press confirming that in view of the effort made by "all concerned," the fighters would maintain order over their actual positions until an agreement between the two camps could be reached. That announcement came from the British authority, in theory still the custodian of the Palestinian state, who played the role of commanding some authority. The "all concerned" were none other than the leaders of both camps who had already shook hands over the partition issue behind closed doors. The skirmishes that both armies were engaged in across their lines of fire were only a scenario. The role of the Arab leaders was to defend the beloved sister state of Palestine and the honor of the Arab people. The Zionists meanwhile were crying wolf from behind a thin mask of pretense. The whole world was called upon to save them from the malice and the savagery of the Arab world.

This period of negotiations offered me a chance for a quick trip to Haifa. Farid and Ali were ordered by their father to accompany me to my apartment. Farid was genuinely encouraging, although amazed that I would embark on such a venture by myself. Except for him and Ali, who had dropped by a couple of times since the fighting began, none of the Rajys had dared to set foot in the city let alone go to a wooded hill that until a few days earlier was a part of the war zone. Ali objected when his father asked him to give me the keys to the four Rajy family homes. I knew he was nervous about bestowing so much trust and responsibility on a woman. To his mind, I needed a male escort for the performance of such duties.

"Why don't you make me a list of things to bring to you, Aunt Najla?" I suggested, trying to control the anger inside me. "Who knows when another opportunity will occur? I need to collect some clothes and books for my children and myself and, to tell you the truth, I am not sure we are doing the right thing, leaving everything we own unattended over there."

"Why don't you butt out of this property matter, Nadia?" Ali snapped heatedly. "These are our homes and we know how to protect them. In my view, you are no longer in charge of anything, not even of your apartment."

Farid left the room as quickly as he could, while both parents yelled at Ali to shut up. "How dare you talk to Nadia like that! You'd better understand that as long as I'm alive, Nadia comes first and her word is equal to mine." Uncle Ahmad was boiling mad. Apologizing for her son's flare-up, Aunt Najla grabbed Ali's arm and led him away.

Farid let me out of the car at the foot of the wide stone steps connecting the lower part of the city with our hill. He promised to call me from the store. "You do know how to reach the Iranys in case something happens while you're there?" Ali kept to himself and never addressed me.

"Yes, Farid, I do. I have their son's number at the City Hall where he works. And you know that building is just around the corner. Now remember to call and tell me when we will be going back to Acre."

The chill wind that came with the new dawn whistled plaintively through the swaying trees and swept down the hillside. It lashed my face and made me shiver. Wavering on the uneven stone steps, I tried hard to concentrate on the goal of this essential mission. Behind those sturdy stone walls were all my treasures, all my memories, and everything I owned. I tried not to listen to the roaring silence that issued forth from the surrounding houses which for years had belonged to lively and fun-loving neighbors with their flocks of vigorous children. Their tiny feet used to pound those uneven steps. Now the walls were deaf and dumb. Yet I had a feeling that hostile eyes watched me from behind those closed doors.

I unlocked the door and found myself inside my home. Although no one was there, the hall seemed crowded with phantoms of unfriendly intruders. Everything was in a shambles. Closets were wide open, drawers rummaged through, clothes heaped amidst scattered files and toys. While I was trying to comprehend the extent of the damage, the telephone rang. A heavily accented male voice inquired whether I was all right. Who could this be? It turned out to be Bahaa Irany, the family friend Farid wanted me to contact if needed. Although from different backgrounds, Marwan and Bahaa shared similar political views, such as putting the blame on the Arabs for not forming a united front to further their own interests.

Marwan had given Bahaa the keys to our apartment when we moved out to the rented place five month before. As a non-Arab, the young Baha'i had the freedom to come and go. So he promised to look after our apartment until we returned.

He expressed his sincere condolences about Marwan's death. "I'm terribly sorry about the apartment, too; the place was untouched until this week when the fighting stopped and the soldiers left your building unguarded. Most likely, the looters came from the neighborhood, and were looking for cash or jewelry. I'm coming right away, Mrs. Rajy. And don't worry, those thieves are too cowardly to come back in the middle of the day."

A few minutes after I put the phone down, I heard his truck rumbling along the vacant street. "Good morning, Mrs. Rajy. I must again offer my deepest sympathy to you for the loss of your husband. Please forgive me for not attending his funeral. Commuting was almost impossible during the last week."

"You are a friend, Mr. Irany. It is enough to know that you shared our sorrow and regrets." I invited him to come in to walk around the ravaged place with me. He suggested that even if we couldn't move back into the apartment, it was unwise to let it look vacant in case we needed to ask for protection from the authorities. After all, the current negotiations might fail. He offered his help and that of his sisters, and left with me the momentous decision of what to do.

"You are all alone now, and no one should make this decision but you. Think about it, and call me when you feel you are ready to move back."

All I could do was fight my tears and try to clear my throat to thank him for his kindness.

After he left, I decided to see which of Marwan's personal things were still there, things that should be kept for the children to see and touch as they grew up. Some day they might feel the need to know more about a father who had kept himself so distant from them. I rushed to the salon where his private file cabinet was. Both panels of that exquisite wooden cabinet were torn from their hinges. Its gold-labeled drawers were thrown all over the place, and their contents were scattered in all directions. I searched for his stamp collection, in my view the most valuable thing he had. It was a priceless collection inherited from Uthman, his idolized uncle. This childless uncle was a very prominent businessman who died after a short life full of adventurous travels and daring quests. The huge album that bore his monogram had been flung about and trampled on, but the violators were apparently too ignorant to know the value of those stamps. I persisted in my search, and I rescued our marriage certificate, some of the bonds of the bank that were torn up beyond recognition, a pile of certificates, and our Palestinian passport. That priceless document was the only solid proof of the children's link to their Palestinian nationality and family heritage.

The phone rang again. I sprang up to answer it.

I stood there, dumbfounded, as though it were the first time this velvet voice had ever whispered in my ear. Tears blinded me as a vision of Nadim's handsome face filled my mind. "Darling, please say something! I know you are there. I can hear your heartbeat through this cold-blooded instrument." A short moment of silence, and his voice pleaded again, "Can I come and see you Nadia? Now?"

"Oh, no, please!" I sobbed. "Stay where you are, just let me hear you talk." Indeed, he should never come to this house again. Marwan was his reason for coming here right from the beginning and now Marwan was gone. This house was taboo for him. Its associations were strictly conjugal, and from it Nadim had to be banned forever. We had not had a chance to be together since he and Leila had driven the children to me in Acre.

"Then let me come and pick you up, darling. We can go anyplace you want. I have to see you, just for a few moments. Please!"

"You can't," I moaned. "Don't you know how impossible it is to circulate in this dead city? Besides, what about the danger you'll be exposed to, driving to this miserable neighborhood? And the Rajys could call for me at any time if the shooting flares up." But I knew he wasn't listening; he was on his way no matter what I said.

The burning question remained and haunted me for weeks: what was I going to do? Take the boys and run away, leaving Palestine and its people forever? Do what my children longed for, return home to their toys, books, and music? Go back to school, friends, teachers, and books? Or stay where we were, like the rest of the Rajys, waiting for something to happen and things to clear up?

Until things clear up. This expression had become the Arab motto of the time, the crippling footnote to every statement, for decades to follow as well! My first choice was to run as far away from Palestine as I could, but under the circumstances this meant as far as Beirut. We would land on my parents' threshold. My second choice was to move back to Haifa, where everything I loved was waiting for me: my house, the rented apartment, the children's school, and my friends, not to mention Nadim.

The rough edge of any of those decisions was that they required the consent of my in-laws, who at that point were the closest of kin and sole source of income for me and my children. But they had lost faith in their country, and categorically refused to return home with me. They declined even to give it a try or to negotiate the liquidation of their stores and bank accounts. Besides, I felt that their pessimism would eventually rub off on my children.

The last option was mine by default: like the rest of the family, wait a little longer. I knew I couldn't consent to this somber inertia forever, because it would jeopardize my children's lives. Actually they had little in common with the docile children of our clan. They were vigorously independent and creative enough to help me make important decisions. They were even quite different from each other, although they handled their activities with a kind of mutual respect rarely found in siblings their age.

Usama, the bright, fun-loving boy who knew best how to get in trouble with the grownups around him, was the leader. His big heart and forgiving nature made it difficult for anyone to stay angry with him very long for the occasional headaches he caused the rest of the family. He asked interminable questions about our future plans, especially about the possibility of going back to his school. "Don't worry," I promised, "things are not going to stay like this much longer. And remember that no matter what happens to us, the three of you will always go to school, whether to St. Joseph's in Haifa, or to some other school on this planet. Education will be the only luxury I shall always manage to provide you."

Jamal had a mind all his own. He knew best how to stay out of trouble. If it hadn't been for the hot temper he had inherited, he would have been the leader of his group. He was a very beautiful child, and this subjected him to a good deal of unwanted attention. The soft blond hair, fair skin, and dark almond eyes invited the pampering that was usually lavished on girls. It did not help that the family was over-supplied with wiry and rowdy boys. He was more family-oriented than Usama, and did not mind changing his school.

Ghassan, the youngest, had always been sweet, and easy to raise. He never whined, even when he was teething or suffering with high fever. His good nature was noticed even by Marwan, who had seldom touched either of the other two children except to punish them with a slap or a lashing. Yet, he took a compassionate interest in this bright-eyed, calm child. He was too young to worry about school.

The differences in their natures were reflected in the way they re-acted to the disaster that threw their lives into confusion. Ghassan, just turned six, showed very little change in behavior. To a stranger he would seem too detached, as though what was taking place did not concern him. I knew, however, that behind this unruffled exterior hid an insecure little boy with a loss he could not fathom at the time. His questions were brief and never controversial just like his answers, always to the point.

Jamal's reaction was a shock to me. I had always judged him to be the toughest of the children. It overwhelmed me to see him shattered, not so much by the fear of war or by the loss of everything we owned, as by the loss of his father at the hands of an unknown killer. The sensitive little soul who wasn't yet eight refused to believe that inno-cent people like his father could get killed in a war. He couldn't stop asking questions about the details: What time did it happen? What was I doing? Why was his father at that particular site when the bullet hit him? How come no one was there to rescue him? This went on and on, but none of my answers seemed to appease him. He spoke like a soldier who had fallen into enemy hands, doubting anything we told him. His main interest seemed to be in who did it and how much did I know about it. The tone of his voice would range from reproachful to suspicious. It broke my heart to see how angry he still was that I had intentionally left him behind when I went away to his father's burial. At the end of one of our discussions, Jamal fixed his dark eyes on me and yelled: "You left us back there because you did not want us to know who killed my father!"

Usama, on the other hand, came out of this ordeal stronger. He appeared unshaken, maybe a little overconfident, when they arrived in Acre three days after Marwan was buried. The calamity that struck our family forced a touch of maturity on him. From the moment the boys joined me in Acre, I felt a strong sense of togetherness binding them together. Usama was now the man in the family.

February 21, which happened to be my thirtieth birthday, seemed like the longest day of my life. When I took my seat next to Farid and Ali on the shuttle van to Haifa during the early hours of that morning, anger was the only emotion I felt. My grim companions were in no better mood; Ali and I had had an argument before we left the house because he did not want me to go to Haifa that day. None of his reasons could intimidate me. I was determined to see that obnoxious man who had answered my husband's line at the bank, calling himself manager, and who promised to see me there today. A pension fund based on Marwan's more than twenty years of banking service was my goal. This would be my only legitimate source of income if I decided to stay in Haifa without my in-laws. I had no way of knowing what faction was actually in control of the bank at that time. My telephone calls became an ordeal as I kept getting evasive answers from the people who answered the phone. Their messages were dull and phony as if memorized.

I had a good deal of worries on my mind concerning my status with the Rajys under the changed conditions. Harmonious as our relationship had been before, the lot of a thirty-year-old widow in a community like ours was a precarious one and would now be determined by the code of tradition. The family was not as stable as when Marwan was alive and Uncle Ahmad in power. There were newly empowered members of the clan to reckon with.

Some of them, like first cousins and sisters and brothers of both Uncle Ahmad and Aunt Najla, would have loved to confiscate the privileges the Rajys had favored me with ever since I had come to live with them. The first target would probably be the children, two of whom had already passed the age of my custody rights. Ghassan would soon follow. Therefore, it was in our best interests that I move cautiously through this period of transition and guard against disastrous complications. In the worst case, my father, who was my legal guardian in widowhood, could decide what to do with me—enslave me inside his house or that of any of his married sons, or arrange for another husband to take me out of sight. Whatever the fate of the mother, the children had to go with the paternal family.

In a male-structured society such as ours, a penniless mother of three young sons had no chance whatsoever to be *given* the freedom of choice. But hanging on to the mutual trust my in-laws and I had acquired throughout our years together, I dared hope that we would continue to receive special treatment. I had failed to realize that privileges rooted in wealth would be swept away by a series of calamities that fell upon that wealth as churning winds fall upon a standing crop about to be harvested.

After Marwan's death, the Rajys' contact with Haifa dwindled even more. I watched with apprehension as the entire family of fourteen lived from day to day, sulking or lamenting but not planning—as if waiting, like Moses' people, for the manna of heaven. Farid and Ali, finding themselves increasingly in charge of their father's business by default, began to crack under the critical pressures of the country's crippled market. Even though I had little respect for the way they were handling the family's sizable estate, it is only fair to admit that working through the collapsing official institutions of that period must have been a formidable challenge. Haifa was one of a few cities on the eastern shores of the Mediterranean that had flourished magically with the petroleum boom in the Middle East, mostly because of the Baghdad-Haifa pipeline and the huge refineries that were built there. The revived city established its unique and intricate commercial and monetary trading system, which had to serve the country's multinational corporations and investors. The Arabs and Jews of Haifa, roughly equal numerically since World War II, had to rise above their differences to survive in the city's tangled market—which, under the circumstances, left the Arabs at a great disadvantage as the civil war tipped the scales to the side of their competitors. And for that sizable task the Rajys had no more than Farid and Ali!

Some changes had taken place along the familiar misty road to Haifa since my last trip. The bannered barricades, garbage heaps, and battered trucks were gone; the surface looked as clean as a tombstone. On both sides fresh green grass waved to me as our van swept along. A sense of loss and emptiness twisted my heart as the car swerved into the sleeping streets of the city, also clean. The air was crisp and sparkling. Gone were the street vendors, the pungent stench of gunpowder, and Haifa herself. Unconcerned by what had happened to me or to their city, Farid and Ali talked continuously, wearing that grim professional look men used in public. Intrigued, I tried to follow the conversation, only to realize that a great deal of hostility existed between these two brothers. Four-letter words were hissed; curses and blames were exchanged. There was something wrong at the store, very wrong!

On that same day, I discovered that our home had been burglarized for the second time. My piano was gone, the violin, all the Persian carpets I had previously wrapped up and piled for shipment in case something happened. The destructive hands had torn open a secret drawer inside Marwan's closet where he used to keep some personal papers, old pictures, and school reports. The oblong wooden box where he kept his gold jewelry lay in two pieces across the room. Gone were his gold cufflinks, collar buttons, and tie clip, as well as an engraved wrist chain his father had given him on our wedding day. I picked up some framed pictures of Marwan in his teens, his torn-up elementary diploma from the Jesuit school in Beirut, and some valuable personal items he had acquired while at boarding school.

On that day I made my last call at Marwan's bank, to receive the heartbreaking news that "under the momentous situation," the bank had closed.

On that day I received my last call from Nadim, heard his exasperated voice pleading with me to return to that little apartment I still had across town. "Bring the boys and come back here, Nadia, please! Let's marry right away and brace ourselves for what is awaiting us!"

On that day I slammed the outer door of my home behind me for the last time, with the weird sense of being watched. It was as though some infernal ghosts followed me down the vacant stairs, mocking and daring me.

On that day, though I didn't know it at the time, I saw Haifa for the last time.

I put the boys to sleep, but sleep kept on fleeing my eyes. The days had gathered speed after my husband's death. On the following day the family would observe a memorial ceremony to mark the fortieth day after Marwan's death. It was after this sacred date that the mourners would collect themselves and go back to their normal life. I needed so badly to open my heart to Uncle Ahmad and Aunt Najla and, for the last time, try to convince them to return home.

But it was Ali who cut me short and stood between us. Ten years younger than Marwan, Ali was similar to him only in temperament. A handsome and physically healthy man, he had quit school at an early age to work at a manual job in his father's store. He was much less educated then Marwan. Although he was given as much love and attention as his siblings, Ali grew up to be a very angry and envious member of that good-hearted family. He pointed to Marwan's situation as proof of his parents' favoritism. The two brothers viewed each other with smoldering hostility, and I was dragged into that awkward situation against my will. At twenty Ali married his mother's niece Karima from Acre, a timid bride of fourteen. They were given an apartment in our building. All their needs, much like ours, were taken care of by the family. From the very beginning I tried to be as nice to him as he would allow me and I hoped that he would come to feel at ease with me and be less envious of our family. But stuck with a sickly, barren wife, a boring job, and domineering father, Ali had become increasingly bitter for not having the children he yearned for.

At last, his chance had come to assert his power over me and my children. The future of the four of us was now in the grip of the family, and he jumped at the occasion. Ignoring my presence on that grim evening and avoiding his mother's persistent questions, Ali continued his conversation with his father regarding the memorial observance for Marwan. The family discussion concerned the financing of their promise to commemorate the date by adding a wing in Marwan's memory to the new mosque down by the cemetery where the Rajy ancestors were buried. Aunt Najla wanted to know how long it would take for their donation check to clear and for the building of the memorial wing to start. "Soon, Mother, very soon," Ali mumbled over his shoulder.

"Not true," I wanted to scream. The man was lying. But I kept my voice under control, stating that the check will not be cleared, nor could it be cashed for the time being. I heard Ali gasping, but I continued. "The bank is closed, Uncle Ahmad. Didn't anyone tell you that? The last time I called, there was a Jewish officer who answered." I waited a few moments and then went on, "Tell your father, Ali. He has the right to know where his business stands now and about all that has been happening there in his absence. He has to know that all his accounts now are in the hands of your Jewish partner while all the family is hiding here in this misery."

Ali finally caught his breath and was on his feet ready to fight. "It's none of your damn business what we do with our accounts nor where we choose to live!"

"It sure is. I will not sit and watch you toying with our future. It's all your fault we are stuck here while our property is robbed and our money confiscated."

Uncle Ahmad reacted quietly to Ali's heated response. "Calm down, son. Nadia means well. Listen to me, Nadia dear. You know how much I respect your advice. But returning home is too dangerous and I can't impose it on all of us."

"Isn't any one of you ever going to wake up and see what will happen to all of us if you remain in this daze? Do you expect your bank accounts, stores, and equities to come running to you here? Or is it that your Jewish partner has guaranteed that Haifa is the limit for the Jewish state? What would you do if Acre is attacked tomorrow? How are you going to protect yourselves from having that enemy destroy everything you own and everything you are?" I knew this debate had to stop. It was very late, and I was exhausted. I stood up and walked toward the door.

"Take my advice, Nadia, and stop worrying about the furniture or the stores," Ali said. "You know we still have friends among our Jewish partners who will do everything to protect our interests. Just let the men of this family handle it." Neither parent interrupted. Their heads were lowered submissively. The expression on their faces conveyed a certain chilling finality.

"Well, congratulations, Ali. But I'm not falling for this style of security. If I can't live in Haifa and protect whatever is left of my own property, I shall go there tomorrow, pack everything up, and go to Beirut. The children have had enough of this misery. At least in Beirut there will always be a chance for them to survive decently." I reached the door, shaking with anger.

Ali blocked my way. "That is impossible, I'm afraid. The apartment and furniture you keep talking about were my brother's and now they belong to my nephews. You are free to go back to Beirut if you want, but the furniture stays here for the children to use *when things clear up.*"

Marwan died again on that February night. His first memorial observance, as well as all such sacred rituals honoring his death in years to follow, would never materialize.

The spring of 1948 proved to be another of those moments in our history when life suddenly came to a halt and death took over. Indeed, the falling of Palestine was even more hideous than death, because death could be a tranquil, natural transformation, consistent with life itself. But dissecting the holy soil, hacking at its truly Semitic roots and planting an alien mixture of peoples in our midst could bring nothing but conflict and confusion.

The future looked like a bowl of fire that whirled around us and ravaged everything in its way, people, land, cultures, everything. I wondered who was feeding that fire. If the Jews were to win Palestine, which could be a very expensive passage for that small minority who had no base for its defense, there should be another power that would invest in a Jewish state surrounded by Arabs on all sides.

Until that spring, I had come to know the Jewish people as neighbors or friends, as a legitimate branch of the Semitic tree. Like the rest of us, they had historical roots that reached into the remote past of the Middle East. As a child I recall hearing of the small community of Arab Jews native to Lebanon. I did not get to know them. They were a minority that had recently established themselves in Beirut and kept to themselves. It was known that they were originally from neighboring areas like Iraq and Syria. They spoke Arabic with a thick accent, and in public they wore conservative, locally made garments, similar in style and colors to those used by non-Muslim Damascenes. Like the other ethnic groups who found refuge on Lebanese soil, they established their own schools and built their own temples within the protected area of their ghetto. The adults of that peaceful community seemed to have built a steady business relationship with the private sector in our city and survived on their limited income from traditional handicrafts, jewelry, garments, kosher products, and pawnbroker shops. A goodly number of intermarriages took place between Jewish women and men of various faiths, especially Muslim men who religiously acknowledged the legality of such unions. Members of the Jewish community were seldom convicted of any crime, either against outsiders or among themselves.

My experience with Jews, in Palestine, was quite different. In addition to the familar Arab-Jewish natives and those who had moved to Haifa from the surrounding regions, I came to know Jewish groups of whose existence I had been unaware. There were people of different races and cultures who had immigrated quite recently. They were different in race and culture, having nothing in common with our local Semitic cousins. Although much more developed and often fascinating, the immigrants seemed too involved in their own socioeconomic issues to approach the Palestinians with foresight and imagination. This self-sufficiency was all the more frustrating because the Palestinians outnumbered them by a ratio of three to one.

For some of the Arabs, the assertiveness of those alien immigrants who had become too much at home in too short a time was insulting. This was especially apparent in matters concerning the Arab woman and her social limitations. The Westernized and quite aggressive Jewish women were perceived, at least by married Arab women, as a threat.

The Arab women's fear was not groundless. Such an army of sophisticated females was a seductive novelty to the Arab male. Simple men from the countryside and city men from low-income families were more vulnerable. At that time, there were men with a lot of cash that came from selling their lands. They were especially prone to seeking adventures in the arms of more daring women. The issue became so flagrant that it called forth public derision. Some, with tongue in cheek to be sure, treated it as part of a political plot. Sarcastic Arab preachers and ribald cartoonists warned that between the Jew and his money there existed a frequently fatal attraction. If money was exchanged for non-Jewish goods, the Jewish buyer would, one way or another, succeed in getting his money back. Should a man fail to do so, his woman had to find ways to recover the money!

With a friend like Ralph Zhurbach as my model of a European Jew, how could I imagine that such people could turn into cruel enemies and maim and kill or frighten us out of our homes? There was no way I could believe that, with a faith as humanistic as the Jews professed to follow, they would resort to the same horrible crimes inflicted on them in Europe.

Was I really so naive? Couldn't I have known that wise scholars, Arabs and Jewish, who had confronted the Zionist nationalism movement could be right in their forewarning?

I did not! Not until the day Marwan was killed.

But alas! No premonition, prophecy, or regret over defeat was going to undo what had been done. On May 14, 1948, as the Rajys and I were still debating our future in Palestine, Acre was bombed, besieged, and destroyed. The same cancerous growth that had eaten Deir Yassin, Teberias, Jaffa, and Haifa came to claim Acre. This was the last grove of trees that was giving us and hundreds of thousands other Palestinians shelter.

The Rajys finally decided to leave. "We can go and spend the summer in Lebanon *until things clear up!*" Like most Palestinians at that time, the Rajys, whenever in serious trouble, recited this magic formula. They did this so frequently that eventually they failed to distinguish between wish and reality.

11

_____

The muezzin's resonant dawn prayer came to an end. I had been awake all night. The children had collapsed into a deep slumber after spending most of the evening scuttling around their uncles, who were packing for the departure. Whispers coming from my in-laws' room told me they were also unable to sleep. It was as though the flight had started from the moment they decided to leave Acre and move north to Lebanon. When the clanking noises reached my ears, I thought a heavy monster was walking through the dry weeds of our backyard. I even felt vibrations under my feet as I stood at the open window. A huge bus rolled cautiously beneath the orange branches. It was a battered military bus!

I knew the driver and his team were to come before dawn, but I didn't expect the humble men who were handling secret transportation across the borders to be that prompt. They had been recommended to my in-laws by our landlord, Hadj Tawfiq Mansour. This cunning elderly man, who lived around the corner from us and had arranged such trips for most of our neighbors, seemed to be one of Acre's astute wheeler-dealers who would go to any length for fast profit. I didn't like him. During the last few days of bombing and shelling, I had seen him roaming around the compound and watching every movement. When our neighbors began to flee the area, he was there to tap the back of their cars as they rolled out of sight. I had a hunch that he was in the business of encouraging Arabs to leave the country.

I don't know how he learned that the Rajys had decided to leave, but he was the only one who came to our house and volunteered to help us solve the transportation problem. He quite jovially explained to Uncle Ahmad how his travel agents functioned and assured him he need not worry. Farid asked for the name of the agency. He also wondered whether their cars could accommodate our large family together with the load of luggage we had. "You don't have to worry about their names," Tawfiq Mansour snapped irritably. "All you need to know is that they have access to big army vehicles. I can assure you that they are very serious and have high contacts. And no one can know the roads like they do. They even have permits that work with every authority roaming our land." He seemed to know which of the Zionist gangs were in charge of bombing the area, how many were killed, and to what locations the Arab front had retreated. "Be ready at the dawn call for prayer so you cross the border before the sun rises. And don't worry about your belongings here. I'll take care of this place for you until you come back. Soon, I hope."

Everything went as he had promised except for a few surprises that none of us had anticipated.

The first surprise was the rattling bus itself. It did not leave Acre's shores until late in the morning, since the driver took his time in choosing the other occupants as he drove the huge windowless vehicle through Acre's narrow streets. It must have been the most embarrassing time of their lives for the Rajys, the first family to be loaded onto the shabby bus: to travel like medieval criminals through the very town in which their family, for generations, had been ranked with the most privileged aristocracy.

Finally the driver threw his huge bulk behind the wheel of his bus and put it in gear. The vehicle jolted, swerved, and gained speed over the wide-open highway. The merciless sun was scorching. If the overloaded bus could stay on that regular shoreline road for the rest of the hundred-mile trip, the sea breeze would alleviate the heat.

But no, it suddenly turned off eastward and zoomed uphill toward Galilee's glaring mountains. The driver's helper explained that they did not have a permit to cross the official border. Hence, gone was the promised short two-hour trip. It was to be replaced by one lasting thirty frightful hours.

Without the proper papers for an unlicensed bus, necessary for the Lebanese authorities, the driver diverted his cattle-like load of men, women, and children from the frequented countryside road to a distant and dusty inland one. Those were very scary hours, after the sun was gone and the Mediterranean night covered the sky. The heavy vehicle had to snort and quiver through the forested Lebanese peaks. The downhill drive along the serpentine trail through the steep Litany Valley was even worse.

Then came the next surprise. We discovered that we had been aban-
doned 25 miles from Beirut—in Sidon, where the youngest Rajy son
attended school! It was midnight when the driver's husky voice barked
into the dampened silence: "Here we are, people. This is where your
journey ends," he said, curt and contemptuous as a warden to his
inmates. In response to questions and complaints like "Where are we?"
"What is this place?" "You can't just drop us off here! We have paid
you twice the amount to get us to Beirut," the angered robber jumped
right into the midst of people huddling together, and began shoveling
their trunks and bundles down onto the muddy path. It was a deserted,
shadowy location we found ourselves in—the last place a disoriented
group of refugees would choose.

"Let's try to make the best of it, Aunt Najla, please," I begged. "The
boys need to wash and rest." I knew my in-laws had some close relatives and friends living in this historic city and tried to convince Aunt
Najla to call on them, but the poor woman was greatly disheartened.
She had already given way to despair, lamenting that she wasn't going
to troop her exhausted family around knocking on doors at such an
hour. Yet the family was utterly disheveled, hungry, and very far from
being attentive or prudent. We all huddled by the side of the road until
daybreak when a passing shuttle van stopped, squeezed the fourteen of
us in, along with the bulk of our baggage, and drove us to our final
destination.

> Oh, how I wish my parents were the sun and the moon!
> Then I could have been born an ambrosial fragrance,
> free to float above any hindrance . . .
> Better yet! If, instead, I were born a tiny cloud,
> ah then, I could float unseen above all my crowd.

I found those two notes among similar prayers I had inserted in a
book of poetry written by a French prisoner who was sentenced to
death by guillotine during the French Revolution. The small gilded
book was among Marwan's personal papers at our apartment. Many
passages were underlined in his fine writing. Some of my own intimate
thoughts found their way into what had become a sort of diary. I could
do this until the day I arrived at my parents' home in Beirut, where
meditation, prayers, and soul-searching were unlikely luxuries.

Indeed the whole situation became catastrophic after we arrived in

Beirut. The Rajys went to their close relatives and I, with my three exhausted children and a scraggly trunk of clothes, books, and toys, knocked at the only door accessible to me. My parents had long since lost their beautiful inherited mansion to creditors and were living in a rented two-bedroom flat in west Beirut. Their large household had shrunk. It now consisted of both parents, my brothers Sami, Amin, and Fadi, and Nouhad, the housemaid. In addition to the two spacious bedrooms, the flat had a large central hall, a separate sunny lounge, a large dining room, and a kitchen. It was surrounded by numerous verandas, and had access to a large fenced rooftop with ample space for my father's chickens and pet pigeons.

On the surface our stay looked as natural as any previous visit I had made. My sons had a lot of fun with their three uncles, who could be with them only on weekends because of their jobs and personal obligations. We were not the only ones who had to accept the bitter road to self-exile. There were hundreds of thousands of Palestinians out there who had made the same irrevocable move. Those who lacked the luxury of Lebanese kin swarmed into parks and open spaces, and set up their tents wherever they pleased, acting as though they were out on a picnic.

The atmosphere in my parents' home was infused with anxiety and fear. In a matter of weeks my parents began to show signs of weariness of our costly and noisy presence. Instead of inviting the rest of his well-to-do children to try to find a reasonable solution, my father resorted to his secret methods of torment, and my mother, as usual, turned a deaf ear and blind eye to our plight.

At the same time the Rajys, whose number increased to seventeen when some of their married children joined them, were having their own problems with their host families, who were equally numerous. "I'm here to ask a favor of you," said Farid one morning when he dropped by, the first Rajy to come and see me at my parents' in the nearly two months of our stay in Lebanon. "Can you come with me now? My father wants to talk to you about some important matters that concern us all." Farid seemed too subdued. He had the barest resemblance to the flamboyant young gentleman I had known in Haifa. His brown eyes had lost their spark, and his sense of humor had vanished. His usually erect posture slumped dejectedly.

The boys were thrilled with the prospect of visiting their grandparents and excited to learn that their grandfather might have some suggestions concerning them. They secretly hoped some balance might return to their precarious lives. Jamal and Ghassan chatted frivolously as we walked to the Rajys', but not Usama. He had been physically and emotionally mistreated by my father, who did not try to hide his dislike for having the three of them at his house. So he now walked in the shadow of sad memories. Moreover, Usama was too observant not to notice the growing tension between me and my parents. I could tell he was trying to come up with answers.

We hugged and kissed and cried for joy. Both Aunt Najla and Uncle Ahmad had lost some weight, but looked quite well given what they had been through. The small room they occupied at Uncle Ahmad's brother's house was furnished only with the few mattresses they had brought from Acre and with some trunks which served as dressers. There were two small tables and a few chairs. But none of us seemed concerned about such an unbecoming setting. We were there to cheer each other up, to find relief for our misery.

"Sit here, next to me, Nadia." Uncle Ahmad's voice quivered with emotion. "Oh, God, how I miss calling your name! Do you miss us as much as we miss you?"

"I think you know the answer to that question! Remember? When you adopted me and I agreed to become your daughter, I married your family, not your son. Nothing will ever change that commitment as far as I am concerned."

"Yes, of course. And that is why I asked to see you today and tell you what we have decided to do."

"Let me tell her what I have in mind first, Ahmad," his wife interrupted. But he brushed her pressing hand away from his arm and went on with what he thought was more urgent. "We have come to the conclusion that the situation here is growing more unbearable by the day and we have to move out and be on our own. Since we are completely broke, Farid and Ali must get jobs that will allow us to make this move." Uncle Ahmad spoke cautiously, calculating his words and trying to avoid my unblinking eyes. "Perhaps you can help us, if you can find out whether your brother Anwar is in need of our sons' services."

My heart sank as I realized that the Rajys could not possibly be aware of how sophisticated Anwar's business had become, and what kind of employees he would be looking for, if any. Uncle Ahmad and his associates were simple people, honest and quite down to earth. He had known my brother Anwar as a penniless guy who was in need of any support Uncle Ahmad could give. How could I tell him that my brother had become one of those greedy and tight-lipped tradesman who had connections with the industrial world. Anwar sweat blood for his achievement, and I doubted he would be willing to give Farid and Ali any chance to mess up *his* establishment. The two young Rajys were poorly equipped for the tile and ceramics industries Anwar was promoting.

So the old man who had lent both arms to Anwar when he was an undecided young pup had a cheerless surprise waiting for him if his sons were to go knocking at my brother's door. I couldn't find words to tell them that should any vacancy arise at Anwar's prosperous plant it would be for some professional like a Swiss chief accountant or a Franco-German executive manager. Anwar had established a porcelain factory in Beirut representing a famous German ceramic company. How could I translate all this into a language Uncle Ahmad would not misunderstand?

Farid noticed the expression on my face and left the room. He said that he had promised to take my children out for a treat. The small room was quiet while Ali went around with a coffee tray, presenting me with an eloquent analysis of how Anwar could benefit from his inordinate skills and from the experience he had gained through his long years of work at the Rajy store. His parents were still waiting to hear what I had to say.

"I would like to do everything to help, dear Uncle, but surely Anwar is not the only possibility for you. With his background in commercial bookkeeping, Farid will have no problem finding a job right away. Such jobs are listed in most newspapers. And if Ali is willing to forget about his previous status as a boss, I'm sure he can get a good job anywhere in this crowded city. Don't worry, a number of shop owners must be in need of young trustworthy employees like your sons. We can't wait for Anwar to help us, he's leaving for Europe soon. But let's discuss your other urgent matter—what kind of place do you want to move to? I assume you want to find a place in this neighborhood?"

"Yes," Aunt Najla volunteered enthusiastically. "Ali has been looking around in this area, and he has discovered a few possibilities. Ahmad and I are very fortunate, Nadia, to have wonderful sons like Ali and Farid, the only ones who have stuck by us. Tell Nadia about those apartments you have your eyes on, son." She didn't realize how extravagant she sounded when she praised that son of hers.

"Oh, there are lots of new apartments coming up for rent. But my father and I do not agree on how much we will have to compromise if we consider quality, size, and location versus capability. A few housing developments are under construction, close to your parents' house. I expect to work out a good deal on a couple of them." He stared defiantly into my eyes. "That's why I sent Farid after you, figuring that with a prominent brother like Anwar you can't fail to secure us the job this family needs so badly."

His tone of voice infuriated me. How dare this arrogant brat hold me and my brother responsible for the mess he had put us all in! I wanted to scream in his face and tell him to go to hell. I wanted to go back to Haifa, collect the family's hundreds of thousands of dollars, and ship out the valuable furniture he had made us leave behind. I felt sorry for the parents. Also, their decision to move was eventually going to affect my situation with my own parents. It would give my father his golden chance to take the children away from me and demand that they be given back to their father's family as tradition dictated. This plot seemed to have consumed his mind long before the Rajy empire collapsed.

"What is it, honey? You seem preoccupied." Aunt Najla grabbed my hand affectionately. "Now that our hope of going back to Palestine is so slim, and since fate has led us to this beautiful city of yours, let us put our heads together and see what we can do to bring you and your children back to us. Ahmad and I have a favor to ask of you." At that point Ali leaped to his feet and asked to be excused. He closed the door behind him.

"Shall I tell her, Ahmad, or would you rather?"

"Go ahead, Najla, this is your project, not mine."

"I wanted to talk to you about this when we were in Acre, but so many things have happened to us that I didn't have the chance. Ali wants to marry you, Nadia."

I was so dumbfounded, I couldn't speak at all. My voice as cold as the blood in my veins broke through the silence: "I thought Ali was already married."

"What does that have to do with it, honey? You know our religion is tolerant in such situations. Karima has nothing to say about it. She is barren, and the doctors say a major operation will be necessary before she can even try to get pregnant."

I bolted toward the door, but Uncle Ahmad rushed after me and grabbed my shaking body in his arms, explaining apologetically that his wife meant no offense. "Please hear me out, dear Nadia!" Aunt Najla sobbed. "I am not doing this for Ali alone. It is you and your children that I am concerned about. You are young and beautiful. How can we be sure that a new husband will be as good to you and to the children as your brother-in-law will surely be? Ali worships you, believe me! We all do. You are still the princess of our household. We love your children more than we do our own, especially now that their father is gone. Ali wishes nothing more than to have some children by you. You are both the same age, young enough to have ten more children if you choose. Please, think of it, my daughter!"

Beyond myself with rage and humiliation, I felt helpless in the face of that well-meaning, naive old woman who had no idea that a woman has other needs than sleeping with a husband and bearing children. "Forgive me if I sound harsh, Aunt Najla, but I yielded a decade ago to a similar offer, and I'll be damned if I would do it again! Not for anyone or anything!"

Utterly shocked, Aunt Najla asked God to have mercy on me, but I went on. "Have you ever tried to see me as a person and not as a productive cow? Did it ever occur to you that those children you want to protect are *my* children? And they are already capable of making their own decisions as to who will look after them. As a mother yourself, you ought to realize that Ali, who is even more volatile and violent than Marwan was, would be the last person my children need to have around." The mere thought of being in bed with that mule made me sick to my stomach.

"I have to go, please, Uncle Ahmad, let me go!"

"Not before Najla and I apologize for what we did. I knew all along that this plan wasn't going to work. Please sit down, I want to show you something." From under a pillow he pulled out a long manila envelope, grease-stained and secured with a rubber band. In it was a wad of fading documents. "I want you to keep this with you. One day we might need it."

"Oh, these are Marwan's bank shares! Where did you find them, they were not in our apartment?"

"No, they were in the safe of the store. Farid brought them together with our shares right after his brother's death. They may be useless for the moment, but one of these days, when the Almighty God forgives us for what we have done to our land, you might be able to go after that bank and retrieve what is yours. You just be patient." He still believed in his return!

When we hugged and said good-bye, Uncle Ahmad wished me well, and promised once more to be there for me if I needed anything he could do. "Remember, Nadia, your children will always come first, much as their father did when he was alive."

At that moment I knew one thing: no one in the world would get control of my children. But there were some unsettled matters between me and the rest of the family that had to be resolved before I could pursue the path I had in mind. First I would go back to school and patch up whatever remained of my educational background, and then choose a field for my college studies that would help me and my children achieve the goals we wanted. A long shot, but the only way to freedom at that stage. For this plan I had one person in mind whom I could trust—Mabel, my classmate at intermediate school and my only friend before my marriage. She had succeeded in getting a steady teaching job right after she graduated from high school and finished the Ecôle Normale in our city.

When Mabel had visited me to offer her condolences in June, I was astonished at how she had changed. I remembered her a lively and naughty teenager. She now looked so sophisticated, and so charming. She had a fine marriage and two beautiful children. She was also the principal of a large public prep school. Luckily, her school was only a few minutes' walk from my parents' residence. Together we devised a program by which the boys could attend a private school with the low subsidy provided by the United Nations Relief and Works Agency (UNRWA). For the remaining few weeks of that school year, Mabel arranged for the children to spend a few hours every day at her school just to keep them busy. They were far beyond the humble curriculum of her 60–student-per-class institution, but they loved the extra attention they received because of that superiority. It was indeed a great opportunity which raised their shaken spirits and brought some sparkle back to their eyes.

Daily life at home got worse. My mother and my brothers were at a loss as to what to do about me and my three energetic boys, who were full of mischief and charm. My father resorted to devilish tricks that challenged my patience and upset my children greatly. We were too scared to talk to anyone. He would hide candy boxes and toys the children received. He would hit and torture them for the tiniest mistake. He would lock them out when no one else was around.

By the end of August it had become evident to every Palestinian waiting in Lebanon that the chances of returning to Palestine had diminished significantly. Fortunately the Rajy sons had finally found jobs that would provide them with a humble monthly income. Their small income allowed the large family to settle in an unfinished cement duplex on the ground floor. This awful structure had no doors, no running water, and no electricity. It has always served my memory as a crude, and yet accurate, symbol of the decline of the once opulent Rajy family.

When the news of that new arrangement reached my father, it became a deadly weapon against the boys and me. Fadi unintentionally struck the first blow at the dinner table at my parents' summer house. "The Rajys have finally got their new apartment in shape. And guess who installed the electricity?" We all cheered, guessing correctly that it was Fadi, then in his final year in technical school.

Suddenly my father's sonorous voice cut in: "Thanks for the good news, fellows! I'm glad the Rajys are waking up after that senseless long stay with their relatives." The room fell silent as he pulled his chair back and rose to his feet. His eyes beamed urgently in my direction. "Now it is time for your children to go back to where they belong." He strolled leisurely toward the door. "I want that to take place tomorrow so when we return home from vacation in September we can get our life back in order."

That night Fadi tearfully described the Rajys' place: "It's like a cheap clinic with nothing but old couches and flattened out mattresses lined up against the damp walls. There are ten people there, Nadia, sometimes more. Where would the boys sleep?"

I tried to explain that they would be better off with the Rajys no matter how bad the conditions. "There is love under that roof, Fadi, which is much better for them than a comfortable bed. Don't worry. You'll see, this arrangement will end up being the best for all of us."

"And what about you? Are you going with them? Why didn't you ask our father to let them stay at least until the summer is over? I can't understand that constant feud between you and our father. It's very scary. My mother takes the whole issue so lightly instead of trying to soften his heart toward his sweet grandchildren. Does she know the reason for his vengeance against you? Sometimes I think your children are in real danger when he is around. This is a raw hatred."

"Fadi, I want you to promise me that you will pretend you see nothing and hear nothing. And I promise to tell you about my plans, step by step. Believe me, this is only a temporary arrangement, and I have already planned what I will be doing for the next year or two. By then I will be ready to get a job and bring my children back to me."

"Job! What job can a woman get that will feed and educate three sons? They need the kind of support that does not come cheap!"

"There are plenty of them waiting out there for us women if we really want them. Especially if you men would stop pretending that God created us weak and unfit for responsibilities outside the house."

My sister Nora and her sons, Omar and Nidal, were waiting at their door when we arrived on that crisp fall morning. It was a beautiful day. The warm sunshine and bright blue sky matched our exuberant mood. Nora's house was an ideal place for the boys to spend a four-day holiday with their cousins before the school year began; they really needed such a treat after what they had been going through.

Before they found their large, two-bedroom graystone house with its red tile roof, large garden, and beautiful orchard, Mahmoud and Nora had had their share of loss. They lived in a small apartment when their first son, Omar, and his three brothers were born. Zaher died suddenly of meningitis before he was even a year old. Two years later Nader was born with an inoperable heart defect. His death left Nora and Mahmoud emotionally and financially broken. My sister was over thirty and her husband in his late fifties when Nidal was born. He was a handsome and strong child, and his mother vowed never to let the child out of her sight. Eventually she left her long-time job and devoted all her time to her two remaining sons.

Although extremely different in nature, temperament, and expectations, Nora and I had always been close. It was she who kept me in contact with my family through my married years. A rare kind of trust had survived all our differences, and she was the only one at home in whom I could confide. She knew, through my letters, about my falling in love with Nadim. On one issue, however, we had never agreed as we were growing up—my confrontational attitude, as she described it, toward our parents, especially my mother. Nora saw my mother as a noble victim of my father's tyranny, while I came to think of her as a bright and calculating woman whose sense of self-righteousness was more important than the protection of her children. Drifting within the boundaries imposed on women by men, society, and parents, Nora had hung on to the same poorly paid job after she married. She taught folk songs to children of kindergarten age because she did not have to go farther than around the corner from home. That gave her ample time to serve as guardian angel in that turbulent household. She seemed to have given up on finding a husband when suddenly Mahmoud came her way. Their marriage was the product of a family arrangement based on the assumption that he was a sickly man and Nora a wonderful caretaker!

While our children were enjoying the freedom of the large yard like wild monkeys who had just escaped captivity, Nora and I sat down in her room. "All right, Nadia, I want to hear from you what happened on Sunday afternoon last week at our parents' when our father and Sami were at each other's throats. Our mother can't believe that what your son Usama accused his grandfather of is true."

"Well, while Mother and I were gone, Usama came by to see whether I was home. Apparently his grandfather, who had previously seen him squirt gasoline into the lubricating holes on my sewing machine and did not like it, decided to let him in and punish him, even though I had permitted Usama to do this. Instead of telling me to prevent such a thing, our father took advantage of being alone with that boy, picked up the little spouted can full of gasoline, grabbed Usama by the hair, forced his head back, and squirted the burning liquid into both nostrils. Sami was coming home as Usama was running out of the house shrieking. He confronted his father immediately and there was an ugly fight.

"But Nadia, it seems insane to think a grandfather could do such a thing! That boy could have died because of that attack! This is becoming more of a lethal feud than a mere family conflict."

"Do I have to remind you that I have been saying this for ages? But what can you or I do about it as long as the family won't sit down to talk? Besides, his fighting with his sons Sami today or Anwar tomorrow is nothing new."

"Well, I still think that if you would just try to reason with your father you could curb his frustration over your attachment to those children. I think his attacks on them are his way of hurting you, not them."

"That man does not respond to reason, Nora. Believe me, if he were the breadwinner in that house, I would never set foot in it. But my brothers are working hard so we can have a roof over our heads, and they want me in the house for the time being. You just wait, when I finish my courses, you will see me and the boys fly from them all."

"I just hate to see you putting yourself through such a struggle. It is a lengthy commitment of studies, and you have to care for your children at the same time. Why take the hard way when you know that many men, both young and wealthy, would give anything to marry you. And it is not Ali or any other man of the Rajy family that I have in mind."

"But Nora, you know I would probably have to give up my children if I remarried. What would you do if, God forbid, you were in my place?"

"I would leave the responsibility for my children in the hands of their legal custodians. And I would go with them wherever they went. But I would not be like you, empty-handed and still ordering everybody around as to how I want my children to be raised. Face it, dear Nadia, you are not easy to reckon with."

"First of all, I am not empty-handed. You are probably the only one who knows about my jewelry box, since you are its keeper for now. I'm staying away from it as much as possible because I may need it in case of an emergency. Second, I am tired of arguing about this whole mess. Let's just stop."

"I didn't invite you here to fight with you, honey, or to urge you into a marriage you don't want. But I am curious to know whether you have anyone else in mind. Are you waiting for that young Haddad you have written so much about? I hope you don't mind my asking—have you heard from him since you left Haifa?"

Stunned by my sister's directness, I didn't know what to say. It was the first time any member of my family had asked such a blunt question concerning my relationship with Nadim.

"Oh, me and my big mouth!" she said. "Please, Nadia, forgive me."

"No, don't apologize. You're the only one I can talk to about my feelings for Nadim. No, I haven't heard from him, and I wish I knew how his wonderful relatives are coping with those fanatical Israelis back in Haifa. Nadim's parents would never leave Haifa even though they are originally from Lebanon, from a very prominent family, in fact."

"Tell me about him, Nadia!" Nora whispered. "You might feel better if you talk. Do you feel like it?" It was as though once again we were two little girls lying on our beds, whispering through the night.

"I'm not sure I can, Nora. I'm afraid to let myself remember the passion that's dormant inside me now. Sometimes I pray never to see him again, but I miss that man so much, his face keeps on haunting me. All of me, to the depths of my soul, cries for him."

Nora pondered for a long moment. Leaving her bed, she walked to the window. "It's better you stop thinking about him," she whispered to herself.

I tried to recall the last words Nadim and I had exchanged on the phone before I left Acre. "I have a hunch this is a trip without return, Nadim."

"If that happens, I will follow you to the end of the world," he answered.

Nora spoke again, still by the window, watching the boys out in the yard. "Can you imagine what would happen if, one of these days, Nadim knocks at our parents' door and Father goes and opens it for him?"

Suddenly I was struck by that possibility.

If it did happen, what would I do?

"Really, Nadia, you do seem to enjoy making an impact on the people around you, not to mention shocking them out of their wits every now and then. How can you stand all that negative fuss?" My lifelong friend Mabel was referring to the turbulent argument she had found herself part of while visiting my parents' home earlier, before we walked to her office.

"Oh, come, Mabel! You have known those people for ages, what did you expect from them? As far as they are concerned, I'm still the powerless little daughter who needs tutoring for any step she takes."

"What was your mother saying about your being a dressmaker? Is it true?"

"That's a big issue of conflict between us. Like most of the other relatives, she thinks I'm crazy to go to school and plan to get a job when I can stay right at home and use my talent for fashion and dressmaking. In other words, they want to make another Aunt Hind of me. You remember my father's sister Hind who used to spend weeks at our house, cutting and sewing? For what? Just to please her brother Kareem, who would now and then throw a few pounds into her lap. The irony of it is that both she and I married young, became widows at an early age, and were left with three young children to raise."

"So you don't want to become another Hind. But you're sure taking a long road to get to what you do want."

"You know there's no other way. What else do you want me to do?"

"I want you to look at yourself in the mirror and take advantage of the potential you already have. Doesn't it seem crazy to you to have to go to all these special schools for math, accounting, and secretarial skills? You could get any job you want by just being yourself. You're bright enough to know that your feminine charm and not your brain should be your best assets. Believe me, we live in a big zoo. See those pompous executives who dominate our lives from behind their high-powered desks? They are as rotten as all the rest of their fellow men. They look at you through your body, not your head."

The vindictive expression on Mabel's face was shockingly revealing. This was the harshest remark against men I had ever heard from her. That issue had always been my specialty, not hers. If anything, she was the one who would preach to me against taking a negative attitude toward men, "because we could never live without them," as she would put it. Yet here she was, after the long years of success she had built up side by side with some powerful men, dropping that bomb without hesitation. "Try to understand what I'm saying, Nadia. Fame and power might look great to people who don't have them, but they breed awe, and sometimes fear, along with the success."

"I'm not running after either fame or power. I just want everyone to accept that the decision is mine and that no one else can understand what is best for me and for my children who in our community are considered common property. You may be right in accusing me of being provocative to my parents and not knowing how to win them over. In your view I should either stay with them peacefully or take my belongings and leave, right? Well, according to our religious and moral code, they can't throw me out, and it works best for my plan to stay here until I'm prepared to take the boys and move on to our new life together."

An aide had placed a pile of files on Mabel desk. "You see these files, Nadia? They are just one week's crop of sick-leaves. You can do me a great service by signing a contract right now for a teacher substitute job. What do you think?"

"What? You want to give me a teaching job here in this school?"

"Really, why not?" Mabel beamed as though the idea had just popped into her mind. "I'm in desperate need of teacher substitutes.

Every week I have at least a third of my staff absent on sick leave. Some of these teachers can stay home for weeks if they choose to. The law is quite accommodating for teachers in this country. As for your credentials, I can manage that. Especially now that you have been admitted by the Ministry of Economy to its Institute for the Study of Income Tax. What do you say?"

The prospect of having this job came with problems. Substitute teaching at the elementary level was poorly paid, and the idea of working with so many kids scared me, though I didn't have the courage to admit it. Such work could consume most of my time and energy, leaving little space for the studies that were so vital to my plan. "I know you'll be mad at me if I decline such a special offer," I began as my friend's shrewd eyes watched my face. "But please try to understand the complicated position I'm in. Besides the dilemmas I face in Beirut, I have worries about what I have left behind in Haifa. So far I just haven't been able to convince myself that the political situation in Palestine is final and I haven't given up the possibility of going back there. It's as though I'm in a capsized boat in the middle of nowhere."

"Well, that's a side of you I haven't been aware of. What kind of attachment could you have had there? In spite of the misery that country has buried you under, you still have the urge to go back?"

"Sorry, Mabel, I can't go into it now, but some day you'll be able to know what that land has come to mean to me." I avoided her eyes lest she might see that I wasn't telling her the whole truth. "For the moment, I'm afraid to commit myself to any job. Training for a career is crucial for the future, whether I stay in Beirut or go back to Haifa. A substantial job is a must if I want to raise the kids on my own. Besides, earning money now, even a little money, can jeopardize my relationship with my in-laws as well as with my parents. Both households are in need of money and might well expect to share my income, a duty I am not yet ready for. But I would like to take a rain check on your offer!"

Of course I knew on that Saturday afternoon that Mabel had a strong point in questioning the way I was handling my situation. But I knew, too, that if I was pushed into independence before I was fully prepared to manage it, my whole plan could turn into a disaster. Most members of the two families that claimed me were waiting eagerly to see me fall on my knees. I knew that. Only men had the power to map the destiny of women and children in those days. Up to that point very few women had been strong enough to challenge this tradition. I didn't mind being one of them.

Mabel was my unpaid lawyer and advisor on bureaucratic tangles; Nora became a surrogate mother for me, and Fadi took on the roll of escort and chaperon for my small family. So many things seemed to be working out against all odds. With this wonderful task force I was able to circumvent most of the technical obstacles that involved the issuance of a pile of papers and decrees for reinstatement, naturalization, school records, and other documents I needed before the school year began.

We did it, and on time! That fall my children and I set the wheels of our destiny in motion!

I recall standing at my window on that October day, with tears in my eyes, as my three handsome boys galloped down the road on the first day of school, looking taller and thinner in their new pepper-and-salt suits I had finished sewing the night before. Who could have believed that in only a few months after their father was killed, their home and country destroyed, and their very identities jeopardized, I would see each one them with naturalization papers in one hand and a scholarship certificate in the other!

As the boys disappeared from view and I started to turn away from the window, another wonder unfolded before my eyes. A sporty sapphire cabriolet rolled hesitantly up the street, drawing the attention of the early risers in our neighborhood. My heart nearly stopped when that intimately familiar car stopped right under my window!

I stood in front of my mirror and looked at my chalk-white face for a long moment before the doorbell finally rang. Afraid to move, I waited behind my door to see what would happen next. My parents were still in their bedrooms but Nouhad, our housemaid, rushed to the door. The faint echo of her "Good morning to you, miss, yes, she is here, miss, can I tell her who is calling, miss," assured me that the caller wasn't a man.

"Leila, Leila Haddad." The familiar strong voice rang through the quiet house and brought back the spring to my knees.

Overwhelmed with emotion, Leila and I hugged and sobbed unaware of my parents who had rushed out to the hall and stood there staring at us inquisitively. It wasn't often that they saw me give way to such an outpouring of emotion, especially in the arms of a total stranger who expressed herself in a mixture of Arabic, French, and English! Introducing them quickly and apologizing for the interruption, I led the way to my room. Nouhad followed soon with her tray of freshly brewed coffee and some almond cookies I had baked for the children's first day of school. "Oh, Leila, what a blessed surprise! My God, I can't believe you are really here. Did your parents come to Lebanon too?"

"Nadia honey, I'm sorry, I can't talk about them now. We have to decide what to do about Nadim. I had a hard time convincing him to wait in the car and let me prepare you for this surprise. Besides, I didn't have any idea what the situation is here with your family—how they would feel about his visiting you here."

"Leila, you're an angel! Always prudent! I think the best way would be for all of us to meet at my in-laws'. The boys will be thrilled to see you. But how did you get my address?"

"I looked in the phone book for Anwar's number first thing after we arrived from Haifa last night. He was extremely pleasant, invited us to his house for breakfast, and promised to bring us over here to see you. But Sunday was too far away for Nadim to wait. You can't imagine how excited he has been at the prospect of seeing you now that he has decided he would have a much better chance to achieve the career he wants in Beirut than in Haifa. He can't wait to let you know about his decision. My parents decided that this concept should apply to me too. So, here we are."

We arranged to meet near the train station at the curve of the street at nine A.M. I left with my books under my arm, as though going to my ten o'clock class, with no notion of what to expect when I saw Nadim. The autumn sky suddenly clouded and a soft drizzle began to gather on my glasses, but that didn't bother me. A few more steps and I would be embracing two wonderful friends.

Nadim's elegant Triumph was attracting the admiring looks of curious teenagers when I arrived. Leila wasn't there. I didn't ask, and he didn't explain. We were too overwhelmed even to say hello. In a few moments the car was zooming toward the mountains that towered over the humming city. Words did not come at all in the beginning, and we made no effort to coax them out of our silent hearts. We reached the renowned village of Dair el-Kamar (Convent of the Moon) long before noon. Stretched out along a breathtaking precipice in the heart of the Shooff mountains, Dair el-Kamar was established in the tenth century by Christians seeking refuge in Lebanon's majestic mountain peaks. Nadim's ancestors traced their origins back to the people who settled in this area in those ancient times. The church's little square was vacant when we pulled alongside an old Ford sedan, the only car there. Apart from a drowsy old pointer who seemed undisturbed by our invasion of his friendly territory, there was no one in sight.

On that emerald hill our journey came to an end, and with it the blessed silence that had given me some time to sort out my feelings about this man whose presence always threw my emotions into a tempest. "Hello, angel! Is this really my Nadia, or am I dreaming?" I thought I would faint at the sound of that beloved voice.

The weather-beaten door of the calm house of worship was suddenly flung open and a middle-age priest emerged and, leaning lightly on his wooden cane, limped down the large landing. His face brightened the moment he saw who had interrupted the quiet of his haven. "Oh, good day, my friends," the surprised priest greeted us in French. "Please, come in, you must be tired coming all the way from the city." His serene face seemed enchanted that some foreign-looking guests would make that long trip just to visit his remote sanctuary.

"Thank you, Father, I came to see Reverend Haddad, George Haddad. Is he still around?"

"I am sorry, His Excellency doesn't live here anymore; he comes on Sundays only. Can I help?"

"You are very kind, it is a personal matter. The bishop is my uncle, and I haven't seen him for a while."

"Oh, oh! How wonderful to meet you, Mr. and Mrs. Haddad." The kindly priest shook Nadim's hand with informal warmth. "Please allow me to prepare something for you to eat. Meanwhile, I can send someone to see if, by any chance, His Excellency is visiting with his mother. You know she lives down in Dibbeyye."

I was shocked over the assumption in his address, but Nadim gave my hand an imploring squeeze while his conversation continued. "Thanks, Father, you needn't go to such trouble. We were planning to visit Grandma anyway, so let us hope my uncle will be there. But for the moment, we will be grateful for a cup of tea, if you don't mind."

Leading the way to a small apartment directly behind the chapel, our eager host begged us to please feel at home and promised to return shortly, which he did, with a generous plate of food, tea, coffee, and steamed milk. In this tranquil, holy place we had all the peace we needed to turn our simple visit and cup of tea into a long, soul-searching discussion. Indeed, it's hard to imagine another place that could have given me the strength to face my obligations toward a relationship that was born in drought and raised in famine. Nadim and I talked, argued, laughed, and cried. I had not anticipated the dilemma I had come to face.

"I don't understand you anymore, Nadia," Nadim fumed after a strained silence. "Why are you now so reluctant to consider my offer? The last thing I expected was your refusal to marry me. What happened?"

"But marriage was never part of my expectations! Can't you see that no matter how strong our feelings are for each other, marriage is out of the question? There is a huge gap between your status as a carefree man with a bright future and mine as a widow with three children who need all the dedication I can provide. I don't own myself, Nadim. I can't make you happy the way you deserve. Not until these kids are ready to fly away."

"Will you stop using the children as a pretext! You know how much I love them. I'm not convinced that they can't fit into our marriage. Are they the reason, Nadia, or is there someone else in your life?"

I pretended not to hear that jealous remark. It was clear to me that if we were married, Nadim would not give me the freedom I wanted to care for my children in my own way. Nor would he understand the difference between loving a husband and loving a child. He refused to believe that the Rajy family's sense of honor would not permit them to allow their grandchildren to be raised by a stranger, let alone adopted by a Christian who married the widow of their lost son.

As a Muslim woman I could not marry Nadim unless he converted and even then, my children would only be allowed to stay with me while they were minors. Nadim could be their guardian but never their father for they were seen as belonging to their father's lineage. Conversion to Christianity would make it possible for him to adopt them but this was a decision I would not have made for my children for it would have cut them off forever from both their paternal and maternal families.

Nadim and I never discussed the issue of religion since we never agreed on the marriage conditions. He and I had the same belief in the

Almighty Creator which stemmed from the conviction that God is one for all religions. But this conviction was not shared by our relatives. Even had we been able to overcome these hurdles, I did not believe my marriage would be good for my children. While Nadim was the man closest to my heart and it would be wonderful to spend the rest of my life with him, I would not subject my children to another trauma that would further remove them from their past.

His Excellency's wall clock suddenly chimed three times. I jumped to my feet, remembering that the children were expecting me to pick them up after school.

"Oh, my God, Nadia, the day is almost gone." Nadim was composed again, almost a little formal. "I'm sorry, I shouldn't barge into your life like this."

"That's all right, Nadim. We deserve to have one whole day to ourselves after this long separation. I wish you could come with me to meet the boys, though. They'll kill me if they find out I've seen you and kept it a secret. Would you, please?"

I knew he would. He had loved my children since they were babies, easing his way into their little hearts long before he even acknowledged my presence. They considered him part of the family, getting from him the attention and appreciation their own father didn't know how to express. His arrival at the Rajys' doorstep was a touching scene, with the three excited boys jumping all over him as though he had been gone for years and had suddenly materialized in the flesh. The Rajys received him with hugs and tears, and everyone had questions about "back home." Usama kept asking about his school and the toys and books we had left in our little rented apartment near the Haddads. Ghassan, plopped on Nadim's lap, sat contentedly, as Jamal got angry again when he heard his father's killer was not sitting in jail. Uncle Ahmad expressed concern about his assets back home, about the banks and shops that housed his dreams and his wealth. Farid wanted to know what would be the effect of a cease-fire on the Palestinians should it succeed in the near future, as was being predicted.

Watching the happy charade filled me with a sense of gratification regarding the decision I had made against Nadim's plans. I wanted him to remain the romantic friend and carefree admirer who could soothe me when in pain and who would be a beloved "uncle" to my children. If he were my husband, he would claim every moment of my life and find it difficult to handle my relationship with my children. I was certain he would get jealous if I left to be with one of my sons and angry if they refused to obey him. Moreover, our society thrived on tribal ethics and was not kind to children with step-fathers. I feared that as a consequence of my act, my children would be subject to ceaseless harassment. Of course, at that point I was confident that the story of Nadim and me had not come to an end.

My parents' place was buzzing with activity on that Thursday evening in June 1949. Family members, friends, and children of all ages filled every corner of their crowded flat. The weekly Thursday gathering was the most important event in my mother's social life. The myriad Beirutans who were members of the Rajy clan simply booked Thursdays in advance for her open-house receptions.

These occasions were one of the few old traditions of the community that had survived the disastrous post–World War II era. Such receptions were held by each of the original clans to commemorate past events, celebrate new ones, and serve as a welcoming gesture to newcomers. My mother must have worked hard to preserve such a costly practice throughout the ups and downs of her married life. She had always been a generous and charming hostess.

That particular Thursday was more than an ordinary weekly gathering. It was a farewell party for my brother Sami, marking the end of over thirty years of life at home with his parents. He was a married man now and he and his wife would move out into a new apartment. Sami was the neglected middle son whose undisguised affection for his beautiful mother filled her with remorse. Her real idol was Anwar, the older son who hated Sami. As a peaceful and inarticulate child in a large family headed by two domineering tyrants, his father and his brother Anwar, Sami had learned to distance himself from everyone, growing from a shy, studious boy to a hardened cynic shut behind a thick wall of contempt with a small opening for his mother and the younger children in the family. Regrettably, his sexual activities followed the pattern of his father's, for whom he felt nothing but hatred.

Sami would have preferred to spend his life with his books, stamp collection, music sheets, and opera singing. In spite of the paradoxical elements of his personality, however, he had won recognition as an engineer and artist, had a prestigious job that filled his pockets with

money, and found himself drawn into the establishment he had zeal-
ously shunned. Marriage became a must. I feared, however, that the
marriage he was entering into was a big mistake. He needed a selfless
and compassionate mate who would help him recover his faith in
humanity and stand by him whenever he needed support for various
social obligations. But his bride was twenty years old with nothing to
offer but a high school education and a pretty, demanding body. This
mismatched alliance might turn out to be his undoing.

The party ended fairly early when Sami left with quite a few relatives and friends. The rest of us settled down for a quiet visit. But
Anwar wanted to pursue some unfinished business between the two of
us concerning the Haddads. This was obviously a matter that had provoked an undue curiosity in him. "I want to talk to you, Nadia," he
whispered as I served the tray of fruits and ice cream. "Meet me in
your room." I wasn't eager at all, but I was afraid that if I ignored his
order he might talk about what was on his mind in front of everybody.

Once inside my room, Anwar locked the door, looked straight into
my eyes, and said, "Sit down, please. It is important that, once and for
all, you hear what I have to say about your relationship with Mr.
Haddad." Ever since Leila called Anwar to ask for my address, they
had been working together on my "case." They agreed with Nadim on
the marriage issue but disagreed about his adopting the children. "You
are aware that Leila and I have been trying to find a solution to this
unfortunate predicament," Anwar began calmly. "She is very concerned about the fix into which you have driven her brother, not to
mention her surprise that you have turned him down. The man is
determined not to take no for an answer, and she has good reason to
worry about him. I can't understand what he sees in you, and I think
you're crazy to refuse such a great proposal, but I'm not here to argue.
However, the fact that you two are still socializing is utterly unaccept-
able. You either have to marry this Romeo of yours or stop playing
around with him."

"Listen to me, Anwar, you and I have never agreed about emotional
matters, and I don't expect you to change for the simple reason that
you have no respect for women or their rights. You have to understand,
however, that I am no longer that fifteen-year-old girl you can shove
around and decide her destiny just because you have the muscle to play
God. This time I decide what I want to do."

"Oh, no, you don't!" he shrieked. "As long as you are part of this family, you have to abide by our rules. Otherwise take your clothes and leave. That sucker is waiting."

"You sold me into marriage once and I'm not going to let you do it again. Nor can you control my emotions. I can live for a hundred years loving Nadim without even seeing him. Can't you see that a marriage between us at this point would only complicate matters for all of us? A mother with three sons has more things to worry about than just her own emotions."

Pacing back and forth, Anwar stopped, his eyes wide with disbelief. "What? Do you consider yourself in charge of those three boys? Who has given you that privilege? And since when does a woman determine such matters? Are any of your in-laws aware about this crazy idea of yours?"

"Of course they are. And who are you to tell me what to do with my own children? Don't you dare come close to them. They are mine alone, God's gift to me for what you and the rest of the Rajy family did to me." Shaken but utterly confident, I glared into my brother's angry face. We had a long history of such confrontations, some of which had left me with cuts and bruises.

Seeing that tossing his weight about wasn't going to serve his purpose at the moment, Anwar switched to intimidation. "Well, if that's where you stand, let it be. I must warn you, though, that no matter what your plans might be for those unfortunate kids, I shall see to it that none of us Rajys, as you call us, will ever support you. And it won't be long before we find out what kind of Rajys your children are going to be. With you wearing pants in the family, we may indeed expect spectacular developments."

Anwar kept his word. On the surface he played the part of a model brother genuinely concerned about a needy sister. But soon after that heated argument he struck his first blow. Anwar abruptly cut off the money he had been giving to our parents on my behalf. This act changed the atmosphere in our house and intensified my father's contempt for me and anyone who supported me.

The second blow was even more lethal. Suddenly, my in-laws started a campaign of murmurs and hints. The children's behavior at home was found to be very unruly. Uncle Ahmad complained that my father was ungrateful and ignored the years of help he had received from their family when he was in need of support. I didn't have to look far to find the culprit behind their change of heart. My brother's fingerprints were all over catalogs and application forms to charity institutions and orphanages in the city, which Uncle Ahmad called boarding schools.

After we returned from summer vacation, the boys went back to their grandparents' house and began preparations for the new school year. One day on his way to school, Usama stopped by to tell me that there would be a family meeting, and his grandpa wanted me to be there. "Uncle Anwar is going to be there, too."

When I arrived, Aunt Najla was in bed with a cold, and Uncle Ahmad was in the lounge with Ali and Anwar. School catalogs that I had already seen were scattered on the table around which they were gathered. There was no question in my mind as to what the meeting was going to be about.

Anwar informed me, like a public prosecutor addressing a dumb defendant, that Uncle Ahmad had some serious complaints about the behavior of the children. Ali, counsel for the plaintiff, rushed to explain to me how difficult it was with the exuberant boys jammed into a tiny hallway in their crowded home, especially during the school year. He suggested that my family might share some of the responsibility for the children on a permanent basis. "Maybe one of the boys should stay there with you."

In spite of my foreboding, I managed to sound cheerful. "That would be great! Is this possible, Anwar?" Ali exchanged a quick glance with Anwar before continuing. "We thought it might be better yet if one of the boys were sent to a boarding school. Usama is older now than Marwan was when he was sent to the Jesuits in Beirut, as you may know."

"Oh? And who would pay the expenses for such a school?"

"There are some that take students free of charge. They are subsidized by the government, as Cousin Anwar was telling us. . . . "

I cut him short. "Are you referring to an orphanage? Is that it—you have already decided to send Usama to an orphanage? Why?"

"Why not?" Ali retorted with all the contempt that had been brewing inside him. "You keep closing one door after another in our faces. No matter how much we love you, you still belittle every single proposal we make on behalf of those children."

"Don't talk to me about your stupid proposals. And let me remind you that if it weren't for your stubbornness, the children and I would be right where we belong, living in our own house back in Haifa and sleeping on our own beds. It is useless to talk about this now. God punishes people like you. You wait and see."

"Stop it, Nadia!" Anwar stepped in with all the arrogance he was capable of. "You can keep your comments to yourself. We are facing a problem here that has to be solved. Your father-in-law and I have agreed on how to solve it. If you have a better solution, let us hear it."

I did not have the power to stand against them all at that point.

The family verdict was issued. The application for the Schuller orphanage was handled by Anwar, signed, and sent to me on Sunday, October 16. Usama became genuinely excited over the thought of a new adventure, unaware of the impact such a sudden change might have on him. The catalogs pictured glorious landscapes and forested hills surrounding the fortress-like establishment, conveying no hint of doom or penury. Monday, October 24, was a chilly day. Huge clusters of dark clouds filled the sky. The shuttle van snaked cautiously along the narrow road leading to our destination. The view of Ras el-Matn's peaks was indeed breathtaking. There were icicles everywhere, reflecting brilliant colors through the clusters of pine trees. The fragrance of wet soil and peeling bark was almost intoxicating.

But when we stepped inside the bleak, shadowy lobby of the orphanage, Usama's cold fingers tightened their grip on my hand. He was taken aback by the huge deaf and mute janitor who let us in, looking as ancient as a laborer in Victor Hugo's *Les Miserables*, and breathed a sigh of relief when we finally were led to what appeared to be the superintendent's office. Father Mark did all the talking while escorting us on a little tour of the dingy classrooms, kitchen, and dormitory area. As he set up a collapsible iron cot for Usama along the row of similar beds, he explained that most of the students were out in the forest working. "There's a lot of work to be done before winter—logs to chop, produce to be harvested, foods to be preserved. Our students do most of the jobs. Otherwise, we cannot feed them."

Later Usama and I walked hand in hand back to the gate to say good-bye. "What are you going to do?" my inner voice shouted. "You can't just leave this child here all by himself! You have to take him back, right now." Another voice mocked, "But where to?" Out on the open grounds, it had begun to rain again. Soft as mist, the autumn drizzle fell noiselessly on my head and seeped slowly through my hair, merging with the tears that blurred my vision. The shuttle van rattled up to take me back home. Usama's widened eyes followed me until I disappeared, his sleeved arm waving gently. I shrank back into my corner seat and closed my eyes, thinking of nothing but how to return to claim Usama back.

The sun was almost gone when the shuttle van reached the city crossing near Nora's house. With the world seeming to close in on me, I needed her to help dissipate some of the fear and anger I felt against both my parents and the Rajys. Mahmoud, who objected to the decision to expose a city student who excelled in academic skills like Usama to the rough requirements of that vocational institution, could help me out of that pit too, I thought.

My mother opened the door, her beautiful eyes puffed with grief. "Nora is at the hospital," she wailed mournfully. "Mahmoud was admitted last night for some tests after a convulsive stomach pain seized him at dinner time. Oh, Nadia! He seemed to be very ill!"

I took care of Omar and Nidal that appalling week while we waited for the pathologist's report on Mahmoud. He had pancreatic cancer. He wasn't told how advanced it was, but I wondered how my soft-hearted sister could endure the six months her beloved husband was given to survive.

In retrospect, the similarity between Nora's life and mine until 1950 is quite striking. Although we went our separate ways after my marriage to Marwan, we eventually found ourselves at the same crossroads. She married Mahmoud two years after I married Marwan, gave birth to Omar two years after Usama was born, and Mahmoud died two years after Marwan was killed. She was thrown back on her parents' doorstep two years after I had arrived there. In October of 1950 she found herself in a struggle with her father and brother over the custody of Omar, similar to mine over Usama. Just as in my case, the decision was made without her consent, her son's papers were handled by my brother Anwar, and the ten-year-old boy was ordered out of his mother's life and into an orphanage. It was the same miserable orphanage I had taken my son Usama to a couple years earlier. But there was a big difference between those two episodes and the effect they had on our two sons. In my case, my plan was to abide by the family decision and send Usama to that orphanage and appease Uncle Ahmad momentarily. But a week later, on my first visit to that cold place, I brought my son back and got him back into school where he belonged. Seeing how much weight Usama had lost in one week, the family was easily convinced that the climate had affected his health. Unfortunately, Nora's obedience to the family meant she was separated from her son Omar forever. He remained in that orphanage until he came of age, then enlisted in the army until he graduated and married. Omar died tragically at age twenty-one of a heart attack.

But even in 1950, Nora's life and my life were going in different directions. I was leaving my parents' to follow my career, and she was going back to live with them. Such a misfortune was not rare in a community that held on to its tribal habits. It struck women and children every time a husband or any male breadwinner died. Most of the women of our clan were unprepared to take charge of themselves. They also were not trusted to be given custody of their children. I have often reflected on how women of ancient times enjoyed a high status, a sacred one. They were put on pedestals and worshipped merely for being the source of procreation and preservation of the human race. Feminine fitness and beauty were the Creator's blessing, a human symbol of grace and love that made woman the inspiration for faith, culture, and art. The decline of woman began when man became aware of his biological power. I have found it difficult to accept the rigidity that some religious figures have imposed on their disciples, fashioning God after man's mortal image and appointing man a god over woman. I would rather believe that gender is carnal while the human spirituality and its link to the universe are not. My role models were those select men and women who had overcome the fear of mortality, using the power of their minds rather than their flesh to meet the challenge of equalizing that natural balance.

12

January 1951

Ready to conquer the world, I set out looking for a job in January 1951 armed with nothing but a sublime confidence, a patched list of credentials, and a meager résumé. I had no idea what to expect. At first I was nervous, finding myself in line with stinking strangers, pushing through chaotic offices, and fumbling for positions which in some cases had little in common with my uneven educational background. Then came the interviews, a daring process in which I found myself faced with scornful employers, or glared at by prying eyes that made my heart swing wildly between hope and fear.

The search for a job was dreary. It dragged on through that winter, giving me the chance to gain some valuable knowledge about a domain I knew very little about. Among other things, I learned that becoming employed had very little to do with the quality of one's credentials, especially in competition with male applicants. Such a realization was quite disheartening for a woman with little exposure to life in the business world. I was stunned to learn how different men were from women in terms of natural logic and reactions to each other in public, or the way their minds functioned away from the bedroom. Most intriguing was the rivalry, jealousy, and insecurity they unconsciously expressed behind their desks. Some were messy, vulgar, and negligent, without the discipline a mother or wife would impose in the domestic setting. Their offices were crowded with laws, scripts, and publications displayed ostensibly as part of the decor, while unfinished work cruised in all directions. These revelations made it obvious that I had a lot of adjusting to do if I were to survive and succeed in a man's world.

As the time approached to make a choice from among the jobs available to me as an Arab woman, I was appalled to discover that a woman could not accept a job outside her country unless she had the consent of a male member of her immediate family when applying for a passport or requesting a visa. With the skills I had, my choices were limited to a handful of ordinary secretarial positions, mostly in the private sector where foreign women were my competitors. In the public sector, that domain was still in the hands of men. In addition to these problems, I knew it was going to be tough gaining the agreement from my zealous family. They had already expressed great concern that female secretaries were subjected to sexual abuse in almost every kind of office work, let alone the private sector, where the hazards of being at the mercy of one's boss could be overwhelming.

The first positive response came from an embassy that needed a secretary with multilingual skills. They notified me of an interview appointment in February 1951, to be held in the office of a well-known lawyer in downtown Beirut. I was surprised they did not have a permanent residence in Lebanon.

During the few days just before the interview I was nervous and jittery, but not for fear of failing the test. On the contrary, I was afraid the embassy would want me to sign a contract right away. This secretarial position, although ranking high in wages and potential, had some rough edges to be dealt with. Since the embassy's representation covered more than one country in the Middle East, its headquarters were in Baghdad during the winter and in Broumana during the summer. This would require me to move from one city to the other and be separated from my children for months at a time. On the bright side, the generous salary was three times what my late husband was getting when we were married.

My son Usama accompanied me to the interview on February 1, a cold dark-gray school holiday morning. Looking a lot older than his thirteen years in his dark formal suit, striped necktie, and shining shoes, my son carried his bulky umbrella in one hand and held my arm with the other, his olive skin gleaming with pride and excitement. "It won't be long, Mama, hold on," he said soothingly. He surely sensed my uneasy mood.

Sayed, the embassy's personnel officer, spoke candidly about his conviction that so far my qualifications were ideal for the job. He had the looks of a Persian but addressed himself to Usama in eloquent literary Arabic. Swiftly, he switched from generalities to familial issues, showing a genuine sympathy when he learned that we were survivors of the Palestinian situation. That made it easy for both of us to be frank with him.

"Do you think it is all right that your mother is applying for a job that will take her away from you?" he asked Usama.

"To tell you the truth, sir, I don't know how to answer this question. We have never been separated for more than a few days at a time." Usama's answer was prompt and his tone quite confident. "But we will sure try to take care of ourselves if my mother promises to do so herself. After all, she is doing it for all of us."

Sayed congratulated Usama on his prudence in supporting my efforts and said that we should hear from the embassy by the end of May since the vacancy had to be filled no later than mid-June. "This is the time when our representation in Lebanon begins," he explained. "We usually rent a floor at one of the hotels in Broumana. I hope that will be convenient for you, Mrs. Rajy."

The meeting I held with my sons over that offer did not last too long, but was quite important to all of us. I would have to be away for nine months, which involved some change in their daily life. But they were too excited about the financial independence I would gain from working to hesitate. They agreed to accept the new responsibilities each of them had to carry during that long period of time. By the time the envelope arrived from the embassy, everything was in order. I did not stay in the hotel with the rest of the embassy staff but instead found a cheerful spacious room in Broumana for the four us, and the rent was very reasonable. We did not mind sharing the kitchen facility with the landlady, nor did she object to our uninterrupted music and the extra energy we displayed in her little house.

My sister Nora and brother Fadi were the only family members who were invited to our party celebrating the new move. Usama played the host at that dinner which we held at the same hotel in Broumana where, eighteen years ago, Marwan and I had our engagement. Since Usama was still a minor, my brother Fadi, who was barely eighteen, became my guardian by default. He was the one who later would sign, with me, the papers for the passport required for that job.

On the Way to Baghdad

From the corner seat of the racing sedan, my mind was swept back in time and memory almost seventeen years to my first trip across the border to another country, a move as uncertain as this one. Driven by a wild imagination and boundless ambition in both cases, I seemed to be searching for a dream, an identity lost somewhere in the vast world. It was October and here I was on the road again, on a second journey far away from home, still searching. But this time it wasn't a dream I was following, only a specific identity. There was a great test waiting for me out there and I had decided to meet the challenge and explore my capabilities. Even if I was a little late in doing so, earning the freedom to excel brought a novel, unknown excitement to my life.

The elegant Mercedes climbed the Lebanese mountain peaks and rolled easily behind its diplomatic flag flipping in the crisp air. The embassy's van and the convoy of its employees followed. Inside, the Banums and their four daughters chatted vivaciously in air-conditioned comfort. Ambassador Banum conducted the conversation in his native tongue, to my ears a loud hum of Persian, Armenian, and Arabic. From the front seat, my boss argued heatedly with Anissa, his wife, who was next to me in the back seat. The subject matter of their talk sounded political; several prominent names on the international list were mentioned. Once in a while the couple, who spoke French with me, would attempt to draw me out of my pensive mood with a question or two, but to no avail. My throat was too tight for any conversation.

Resting my head against the cool window glass, I shut my eyes and ears to the rest of the world as the powerful car cruised swiftly over the last hills of the Lebanese western mountain chain and began to wind its way downhill. Soon the road would unfold rapidly through the Beka'a Valley and eastward to our border with Syria. The last three months working with Ambassador Banum and his staff had been one of the happiest summers of my life and probably of my children's as well.

The Almighty had indeed blessed me with a package of wonderful things when I received the thick bundle from the embassy in June. Inside that envelope was a signed contract for my first assignment as a working woman. I remembered reading the details and seeing the words dancing like happy butterflies when I reached the item defining my post: Executive Secretary, Interpreter, and Editor. Along with the papers were two checks for 20 guineas each—one the first month's wages in advance and the other a boarding bonus. While in Lebanon, I received funds to cover rent for a place near my work since I did not stay at the hotel which housed the embassy. The personnel officer made sure he explained the job's duties and rewards when we met again in Broumana. "In some cases the translation of an urgent report compels us to call you late in the night. It will be more convenient for you and your family, I think, to have your own place close by, if you don't mind."

Mind? Why should I mind such a luxury? It was a dream come true for the children and me to live together on our own—our first haven, a place where we could receive our own friends, eat and sleep at any time we wished, or fill our hearts with all the music we craved.

Of course the arrangement was only temporary, but it was long enough to give the boys a taste of what their life would be like once we were on our own. I had the feeling that, saturated by the gossip they heard in family circles about my rebellious move, they could well wonder whether I should really take them away from their clan. After all, they were as masculine as the rest of the males their age and probably as doubtful too. It was only fair, therefore, to give them the opportunity to assess my unpopular decision.

During the three months we spent in Broumana, the only relative who came to visit us apart from Fadi and Nora was my cousin Kamal, Mae's husband. His visit was on behalf of my parents and brothers who, according to him, were shocked by my behavior. Kamal had come to convince me to go back home!

"You are too delicate to take on such a harsh responsibility, dear Nadia," Kamal began. He explained with emotion how worried everyone in the family was. "Please try to understand, Nadia, what an awkward position you have put all of us in. Can you imagine how our business colleagues who think highly of the success we have reached are going to react when they learn that Anwar and I cannot support a widow and take care of her children? It is a disgrace to all of us men in this family to let a young woman as beautiful as you work for her own bread and butter. It is our honor that is at stake here. I can understand how you feel about your father, but what about me? You are my cousin and my sister in-law. Why can't you allow me the pleasure of taking care of you at this critical moment of your life? You know how much that would mean to me!"

Wrapped firmly in the family cape, he sounded so naively romantic, seeing me as the little princess who was snatched away from him years ago because he was poor and couldn't compete with a wealthy outsider. I knew he meant well, trying to bribe me back into the harem of his clan, but he was blind to the transformation I had gone through.

If my job at the embassy was harsh and humiliating, as Kamal seemed to be assuming, I had no time to find out. But I surely had come to the conclusion that working for a boss as kind and considerate as Ambassador Banum was delightfully honorable. In fact, the whole team I worked with throughout that summer was great, as was the Banum family. They had touched my heart with the warmth and good company of their flock of four boys and four girls.

I was awakened from my reverie by the sound of shrieking brakes and a staggering jolt as the vehicle came to a sudden halt. Surrounded by pitch-black space, the powerful headlights of our car beamed away through an endless darkness. Mrs. Banum was thrown against the middle row of seats where three of her daughters were dozing. I was able to hold onto the two-year-old baby asleep on my lap. From the front seat came the shocked exclamation of the father: "What happened? Vartan, is something wrong with the car?"

But the answer came from outside the car. "Turn off those lights!" barked a commanding voice.

Still trying to collect my wits, I saw four tall shadows jump out of the darkness and encircle us, their long rifles pointed right at us. The ambassador was the first to recover. "Please be quiet back there, all of you. Anissa dear, try to calm the children. I'll go out and talk to those people, whoever they are. This must be some kind of a mistake. Nothing like this has happened before."

Through the ghostly shadows I could see his frail frame surrounded by a group of soldiers trying to push him back into the car with the tips of their rifles, seemingly unaware that he could not understand their language. "Are you deaf?" hissed one voice in plain Damascene Arabic. "I told you, you have to drive back to the proper road. No civilians are allowed to take this trail."

While the ambassador shouted in French, another voice responded in the same Syrian accent, "What did you say? Baghdad? You can't reach Baghdad from here, this is too far north!" I couldn't believe what I was hearing.

God have mercy on us, we are lost! Lost in the middle of the Syrian desert and those faceless officers didn't seem inclined to help us find our way out. Why didn't that stupid driver realize his mistake before leading us into this mess? There he sat, calmly erect behind his wheel, showing no remorse, as though someone else was to blame for his lapse.

The whole situation seemed so mysterious that I had a hunch someone had deliberately planned this incident. Otherwise, why would this driver disregard the convoy's rules, break off from the rest of our convoy, and drive north when Ravi, the embassy's head chauffeur, had given clear orders at the Syrian checkpoint out of Damascus: "Stay behind me, east all the way."

Not until we found our way out of that mess and the Banums were reunited was I able to weigh the disquieting circumstances—and consequences—of that incident. In Baghdad the issue remained more under the control of the authorities than in Syria, where the incident took place. I was afraid the media in Lebanon would pick it up, which could cause my children some concern because they had as yet no means to contact me. It had been an unlikely occurrence for travelers of the Banums' rank. In addition to their diplomatic status, Ambassador H. Banum and his wife Anissa Buchador belonged to nobility by birth. He was a prominent member of an old dynasty that paralleled in rank and wealth the reigning rulers in his country. Even after we had been in Baghdad for quite a while, he and his wife seemed to be struggling with the new fear that had shattered their harmony at home. According to H. Banum Junior, fingers were being pointed at his mother's tribe who allegedly were in competition politically with her husband's constituents.

On the bright side, the incident brought the Banums and me closer than ever, easing my adjustment to life away from home. When I applied for that job in Lebanon, I agreed to reside at the embassy quarters when in Baghdad and to give English lessons to the younger Banums and help them with their homework in return for my boarding expenses. I soon became accustomed to living with strangers day and night and found myself charmed by the couple and their well-bred children. Their affection came as a remedy for the yearning I felt for my own boys.

The two-story embassy mansion was built inside an impressive compound of gardens, recreational facilities, stables, and service quarters. The ten-member family lived on the upper floor, which was spacious enough to contain their guest wing in addition to their own living quarters. The lower floor was yet larger and housed the embassy's offices, parlor, library, and reception lounges.

My room was the smallest in the upper floor, at the end of the guest wing. It became my safe, secluded refuge once I finished putting my personal touches on it—a set of white lacy curtains against its French doors and a display of my children's photos that encircled the mirror. Those were the pictures I had collected from family and friends in Beirut after we lost all our family albums in Haifa.

The work was plenty to keep me busy throughout the day, the nights were mine alone. In my sanctuary I could be found in the late hours following up on my studies, painting, reading, and writing. My writing consisted of either my own diary or letters to my children, again staying with their father's family, in answer to their generous load of news, fiction, and nonfiction matters which they put in the form of a weekly magazine. That wonderful homemade magazine was established by Usama, a drama critic since his early years. He, Jamal, and Ghassan would report every item of interest they could get their hands on. There were items like their complaints about the inadequacy of the school curriculum and their accommodations at home; the plight of the Palestinians in the refugee camps; their empty drawers for the coming winter; also, their hopes of getting some new underwear, a camera, or a radio "made the news." It was a delightful source of information that became my lifeline as the weeks grew into months.

My diary was a different matter, a sad and soul-searching pursuit. I had been writing journals all my life but they were destroyed the moment someone began to ask questions, especially during the last few years of destitution. It was not until I found myself in the privacy of my tiny room under the Banums' roof that I relaxed enough to entertain the idea of trying my luck again.

Confined within the fences of the embassy, I did indeed miss the tentative freedom to which I had been accustomed. Having such a famous and intriguing city like Baghdad at arm's reach fostered in me a desire to go out and explore it, but still, there were a lot of social activities that I shared by way of my work, and running around alone in the streets of Baghdad would not have been a prudent choice anyway. Instead, the security of my room and the tranquillity of the grounds allowed me to look into my mind, face my mistakes, and see how rainbows looked inside that mind. That peaceful practice continued undisturbed until the early afternoon of February 21, 1952, when the embassy doorman came into my office babbling, "Miss Nadia, come quick, please! Your cousin from Beirut is here to see you."

"Cousin, what cousin?" I wondered whether the man had come to the right person. No cousin of mine would have made such a lengthy trip to see me.

"I don't know which cousin. The young man didn't give his name. Nevertheless, I let him in. He is in the study waiting. Please, miss, hurry."

On my way through the parlor, my mind whirled at great speed through scary images of my children being sick or injured, and my knees turned to jelly. Slowly the familiar scent of lavender mixed with Virginia tobacco penetrated my thoughts, and as if in a waking dream I followed it to the study. Through my tears I saw Nadim's eyes gazing beseechingly into mine. "Hello, stranger!" the vibrant voice murmured. "What's wrong, sweetheart? You look pale. I didn't mean to frighten you, but I was so mad at you for leaving home without consulting with me, I had to come the moment I was able to get your address. Besides, today is your birthday, or have you forgotten?"

Totally hypnotized by Nadim's sudden appearance, I debated whether I should turn and run up to the security of my room or throw myself into his beloved arms.

I requested a few hours leave to go out for a ride with my "cousin," and so I found myself snuggling into the princely front seat of a black Jaguar speeding through the lush suburbs of Baghdad. Finally the mysterious capital where Scheherazade was born and where she told her tales would unfold its secrets for me. The whole experience seemed as unreal as the handsome escort who sat by my side on that miraculous birthday.

Nadim told me how Leila was able to get all the information about me from my children. We laughed, cried, touched, and argued fervently over our differing views regarding our relationship. He stubbornly insisted that our marriage had to be right away or else. I wanted to wait until the boys finished their education. "There is no need for you to be afraid of what your people will do, Nadia. We can go away tomorrow. Please, darling, let's go pick up the boys and leave that damn country for good."

Then like a child describing a wondrous Christmas gift, he told me about his cousin Michael, who was the major shareholder in an oil pipeline company in the Middle East. "I'm his lawyer now and there's a big chance I will join the company in the London headquarters—an ideal city for you and me. Nadia, please relieve me from the critical situation you have thrown me into. I really want to settle down and start a new life with you. The children would love to join us in London too. What do you think?"

If only I could be sure that marrying Nadim would work for all of us. My heart yearned for him, but not my mind. I knew I should not share my boys with anyone, nor would I want any man to replace their father. I was their mother and believed I owed them all the attention they needed until they left home. Selfish? Well, maybe that was my understanding of a parental commitment. Nadim had always been aware of my attitude towards his proposal. And I told him again during that stormy meeting that if we ever married, I wanted to give him the same kind of commitment, which would be to share him with no one but his own offspring! I could see no way to fulfill both roles at the same time.

Finally the packed bus rolled swiftly out of Nern Station and along the empty highway. It was already midnight, a little late for the thirty-hour trip from Baghdad to Beirut if the interstate coach was to cross the Syrian desert before the early June sun could rise again and burn the hardened sand under its massive wheels. Lights dimmed as the air-conditioned liner gained speed heading westward through the deepening night, allowing its sixty-plus passengers some rest before its first stop at the Iraqi-Syrian border. I snuggled down into the soft upholstery of my seat and allowed my thoughts to find their way back to the nine months that had passed since I crossed that same desert.

At that time I was breaking away from the clannish bond to which I had been hostage ever since my birth, and to do so had run hundreds of miles in search of an identity. Here I was again, crossing the borders back home, as a totally changed person with hard-won confidence and the strength to stand up to any challenge. The experience had far exceeded the expectations I gambled on when I took the embassy job.

I recalled the sorrowful days in February, after Nadim's visit, when Ambassador Banum was suddenly called by his superiors in his hometown. He was ordered to report immediately, in person. I was stunned by the alarming effect that urgent message had on the whole family, especially Anissa Banum, who was known among the staff as a tough lady. She took ill, retired to her room, and left the heavy job of packing the family's belongings to her confused and frightened children. It was as if they suspected some great threat would follow that urgent call.

In just a few minutes, gates were bolted, windows shut, files packed, and drawers locked. Asked to remain with the family on the upper floor, I watched with disbelief as arrangements were hastily made. Sayed was promoted to Wakil (chargé d'affaires), the domestic staff were given indefinite leave, and the few remaining employees at the consular department took over. The Iraqi authorities were contacted, and a special airplane was assigned to fly the ambassador back home. The rest of the family would remain until further orders.

The fatigued diplomat had tears in his eyes when he said good-bye that night before dawn. "You are a great friend, Mrs. Rajy. Please keep an eye on the children. My wife is going to need all the help she can get in the coming few days."

That was it. The end of a brief era of happiness. The security I had been promised was now over. Before me there was a blank page to read and no clue as to what would be written on it.

Ambassador H. Banum was shot in the head by an unidentified gunman as he stepped from the plane only a few hours after leaving Baghdad. His wife and children were secretly taken out of the embassy during the following night and the stately residence became as silent as a grave. Not until a week later did we learn the details of that incident, when the official report from the Banums' country arrived with the delegation's diplomatic courier. According to that report, the assassin, an unknown mercenary who acted all alone, was instantly taken by the airport guards and executed on the spot! But the general belief was that Anissa Buchador's tribe was responsible for the assassination.

I spent the rest of that fateful week in bed, sick with sadness, trying to assess the situation from all sides. Meanwhile, the few colleagues who were asked to stay walked on tiptoe around the vacant mansion where the voice of our late boss was still reverberating. The idea of losing my job, which would oblige me to return to Beirut before the year was over, scared me and I tried not to panic every time the embassy doorbell rang or a message was delivered. The whole staff was in an insecure state of mind, waiting for something to happen.

Finally, on a late Sunday afternoon in March, an envelope was hand-delivered to the chargé d'affairs, who quickly reacted to what he read: "Congratulations, everybody! Here's the news we were all waiting for. The new delegate replacing our late ambassador is here." He shot a quick look at me before turning toward the others. "You can go rest now, Mrs. Rajy. I'll see you in your office in the morning."

I still remember the haggard look on Sayed's face as he led the way to the main office where a graying fat man sat in Ambassador Banum's chair. Files were scattered on top of the stately desk and his hands were leafing through one that was similar to my files. "Please, come in, miss." I felt ill at ease seeing the new delegate, wrapped in his flowing gray robe and sitting erectly behind the desk, fumbling nervously through the documents in front of him to find my name.

"This is Ambassador Samad, Mrs. Rajy. His excellency is anxious to resume the work here as soon as possible." Sayed sounded too formal.

Mr. Samad hummed a short greeting as his hands fumbled with his eyeglasses, taking them off, cleaning the lenses with the corner of his shawl, and returning them to his flushed face.

His message was brief and to the point. "I'm sorry your contract has to be altered to accommodate the embassy's new regulations, Mrs. Rajy. However, you may keep the job as long as you please if you don't mind staying in Baghdad all year around. Our representation in Lebanon is going to be handled by my colleague in Istanbul from now on." The unexpected verdict was delivered in colloquial Arabic as though rehearsed beforehand. "My wife and I have no children, nor do we plan to continue the social life the Banums had been maintaining in this absurdly expensive mansion. Hence, for economical reasons, I decided to close down the upper floor altogether. You are free to live anywhere you like. Maybe my aide here can help you find a place to live and an afternoon job if the salary you will be getting as of today is not enough to cover your room and board elsewhere. This will be all for the moment."

The coachman's loud voice brought me back to life as the bus slowed to a stop. "Your attention, please. We are now at the border between Iraq and Syria. Passports are required to be presented to both authorities. Only the Lebanese among you do not need a visa; otherwise, you have one hour to stretch your limbs before we take to the road again."

The desert air was refreshingly crisp as I walked down the dim alley following the aroma of brewing coffee. It was 3:00 A.M. when the bus took off again, crossed the Syrian border, and swerved away from the paved road down the uncharted desert path of tough sun-baked sand and hardened shrubbery. That was the same path we crossed nine months ago coming to Baghdad.

Lulled by the undulating movement of the vehicle, I gave way to my thoughts, trying to make use of the remaining precious hours before arriving home. . . . Home? A bitter taste flooded my mouth as the concept of home started to take form in my mind. Up to that moment, such a reality was still a dream. The homes I had used during my thirty-four years were not mine. They were family-owned spaces loaned to family constituents who had the qualifications for such a facility: reside and abide. A simple law, not much different from that applied to domestic hens that were generously stuffed with hormones and fish oil and cooped up in small cells. In return, their eggs were securely hatched and their breasts well-rounded.

The home I had been dreaming about lately was quite small and with very light furniture. It had to have a small garden, though. I wanted to share it with no one but my children—not a father, not a brother, not even a husband—just like the charming little apartment I rented at the YMCA Alaweyya Club in Baghdad in March when I accepted Ambassador Samad's conditions for keeping my job until June. That nonprofit organization provided access to many activities on its spacious grounds that relieved its tenants from seeking such service elsewhere. The swimming pool, tennis courts, and coffee shop were just a blessing, allowing contact with a distinguished class of professional women, most of whom were from Europe.

It seemed crazy at the time to take on such a challenge, having no idea where I'd go tomorrow, especially since my income shrank in half after the departure of the Banums. I was afraid of falling short of covering the new expenses for room, board, and transportation in case an afternoon job wasn't that easy to find. But being crazy seemed to have been working for me so far.

Most importantly the Y residence was ideal in terms of fees and convenience. And my tiny suite was the closest I had ever come to feeling at home. As for an afternoon job, it was much easier than I expected in that prosperous city of oil. Luckily, the good referral I got from Sayed at the embassy and the accounting I had studied back in Lebanon were good assets for the new job I found. The work at a pharmaceutical company was not only challenging, it paid twice as much as my half-day job at the dear old embassy. By the end of April I was securely settled for the rest of my working year with a bank account that transferred my savings directly to the account they opened in my name at their branch in Beirut.

The greatest advantage, however, was in my social life. For the first time I was left to face the business world all alone in an industrial capital four times the size of Beirut. It wasn't easy to socialize as a single woman in a community where married men and women had their own separate activities. That made it awkward for me to make the choice between the identity of a Muslim Arab woman or that of a foreigner. Being Lebanese played to my advantage, and I had much more freedom than that allowed to young native women of that era.

For a woman who had been choked by masculine control all her life, it was an amazing experience to associate with men as colleagues or acquaintances and then forget all about them back in the privacy of my haven at the Y. At the same time I began to know my own self better and to learn the skills of survival in the man's world to which I was attracted. At first, I was mystified to find myself a better communicator with men colleagues than with women, especially when they happened to be bright and mischievous. With time, I became aware that my attraction was more of an obsession to know the man in his own world. I was fascinated by the instinctive differences between women and men and wanted to know how men's minds functioned. I doubted that the mask of might and assurance most men wore was real.

Those discoveries ultimately cured the fear of men I had harbored all my life, putting me at ease with myself and turning that fear into more defined opinions. When I looked at men as a group, good ones and bad ones, I tended to consider them responsible for the destruction of the human race. Their achievements through written history were minor compared to their crimes: wars, political plots, covert operations, genocide, colonization, invasion, terrorism, the arms race, rape, molestation, all these and more were acts of male power. I began to sense the spark of fear in some men's eyes as they debated certain issues: coups, assassinations, gangs, robbing, and killing, not to mention destruction of wildlife—too many crimes committed just to boost the low self-esteem of the men who did them!

The price for these discoveries was, alas, high. I saw myself changing from a sensible trusting person to an opinionated, rather hardened one. Of course I knew we humans have to sacrifice for our learning; we must burn a finger to learn how hot fire is. And I knew the price I would sooner or later pay could be emotionally painful. But it didn't occur to me that the fire would claim part of my heart rather than my finger!

My mind buzzed with the memory of that warm April afternoon at the beginning of a four-day Easter vacation which I planned to spend back at the Y Club resting and reading. I stretched out on a deck chair to go through my weekly mail when the receptionist in the Y office called my name across the pool. "You have visitors, Mrs. Rajy. Three of them. They are waiting in the reception hall." The Y was a women's residence and male visitors were not allowed in the dorms and recreation areas.

I wondered who those visitors were, since few of my friends in the city knew where I lived. I went directly to my room, showered, and changed before going down to the reception hall.

Of all people, Nadim Haddad was right there, impatiently circling the room. My heart skipped a beat when I saw his tanned neck under the thick bush of brown hair he never cared to groom. I watched him move to the fireplace, with his back turned toward me. There he stopped to talk to a couple, a foreign woman in her forties and a tall, middle-aged man dressed in an English colonial outfit. This man was holding his white cork hat across his lap, very much like the Britons in some pictures taken in Africa or India.

"Welcome to Baghdad, stranger!" I recalled tapping Nadim's shoulder and waiting to see his face. "I should have guessed it would be you who makes a habit of dropping by unexpectedly."

Turning quickly, Nadim grabbed both my hands and brought me closer. "What else can I do, Nadia! That is the only way I can see you! No matter where you choose to run, I will always find you." We stood for a few seconds in each other's arms, lost in our emotions. My legs were shaking. "Oh, sorry, my friends! Here, let me introduce you to Mrs. Nadia Rajy—the idol I told you about on our way here."

"Jeffrey Malcom, at your service, madame, and this is my friend, Ms. Daisy Sandberg," the handsome Briton mumbled, taking my outstretched hand and touching its back with his thin cold lips. "Pleased to meet you, Mrs. Rajy, after hearing so much about you from Nadim." The lady acknowledged me with sparkling eyes.

"The pleasure is mine. I hope you are not disappointed. Seeing me through Nadim's eyes can be misleading. Well, what brought you out here, if I may ask? And, Nadim, how did you find my address? I thought you were in London."

"Sorry, darling, I have gone behind your back again. You have given me no choice but keep on searching for your whereabouts every time I come east. This time I passed by Beirut on my way here and took the boys out to dinner. Didn't they mention this to you in that magazine they write for you?"

"They probably did. Usama wouldn't let such an exciting piece of news escape his tabloid section. But this week's issue will not reach Baghdad for ten days. How are they doing, is everything all right with their families and with school?"

"They looked great, and school seems to be going very well. They told me about Ambassador Banum's misfortune. I'm sorry you had to go through all that stress." Nadim stiffened while talking about my work as if it were a rival. I turned to his companions.

"Excuse us, Miss Daisy and Mr. Malcom, we are being selfish talking about personal matters. Do you two live in Baghdad or are you here on business?"

"I'm on a business trip," Mr. Malcom said. "London is my home now. Daisy is one of our team here." Jeffery and his friend Daisy kept reminiscing about the long period of time they were assigned to work in the Middle East as I led the way to the seats near the French doors. "It's an extremely interesting country," Daisy admitted, "but I'm afraid the horrible policy with which our government in England is handling this beautiful region has increased the number of our enemies wherever we go." Jeffery sounded yet more serious when he said: "I wish we had enough time to apologize for that and for what happened in Palestine. But alas, my lady, this is a very short trip, and my last to the Middle East I am afraid." Nadim must have told these two colleagues a good deal about my life in Palestine, for which I felt grateful.

"That's true, Nadia. We are here on assignment, it may not be longer than a few days. Could I book your evenings until we leave, if you have no other engagements?" Of course I detected Nadim's scornful hint, but I did not respond. "How about having dinner with us tonight as a start? We can pick you up in an hour or so."

Although relieved to see Nadim respecting the promise he had made not to pressure me when we had last seen each other in February, I knew that one way or another, he would open the old wound. It was the same old conflict concerning our marriage, and Nadim and I didn't agree. He wanted us to marry right away, and I wanted him to wait. This awkward situation grew more complicated after he went to work for his wealthy cousin in London and money became more of a priority to him than it had been for the spirited man I had known. From the letters we exchanged between February and this week in April, I could see the witty lawyer and mirthful poet I had admired turning into a total stranger before my eyes. Sad as it was, I had to face the fact that Nadim and I were no longer the romantic couple who had built their relationship on a treasure of sentimental poems, long love letters, and short phone calls. The man who appeared that spring was a tough, cunning professional who seemed capable of acting much like the other businessmen and politicians I had encountered lately.

Of course, everything in our world had changed. Like all those of our generation who had been hit by the Palestinian disaster and had suffered the consequences of being part of an Arab world doomed by its own wealth, we had been forced to change. There we were, after four years of struggling and readjusting, still separated from our loved ones, trying to pick up the pieces of our shattered lives. And yet, being of Lebanese origin and members of a privileged nationality, Nadim and I were lucky compared to hundreds of thousands of Palestinians, some of whom remained in a state of siege while others were thrown behind the barbed-wire fences of refugee camps. We were free to go anywhere on this planet; the Palestinians were stuck wherever they happened to end up. Their identity was denied to them. Their nationhood was insulted on a daily basis. They were cast out of the human race.

The change in us was not limited to those circumstances caused by political or social pressures. Nadim and I seemed unable to surmount our differences over our commitment to each other, my duties as a parent and my insistence on improving my status as a career woman. He was never able to understand my need as a person to pursue that path of independence, relating the issue instead to how much money he made. Nor was I sure if Nadim belonged to a minority in that regard. For centuries men had taken that role as part of their dominance, and women complied, not to say, demanded it.

I will never forget the night Nadim and I challenged our relationship, killing in a few moments what we had built over those long enduring years. He and his two companions, Jeffery and Daisy, had had a call from their main office in London, asking them to return as soon as possible. Jeffery and his girlfriend had arrived early; their flight was a few hours earlier than Nadim's. We were to have dinner at the Y restaurant, with me as the hostess.

Nadim arrived late and in a fretful mood, but otherwise the party went smoothly. When it was time for his two companions to leave, Nadim didn't move. I strolled with my two guests down the long terrace to the parking lot. I went through the routine of polite expressions and tried to be as graceful as I could.

Jeffery rushed to rescue me. "I apologize for what we have put you through, Mrs. Rajy. Please don't blame it all on Nadim. He has been under a lot of pressure lately. You know, the oil business is not as smooth as it appears from the outside." I was surprised by his apologizing on behalf of Nadim, who should have been apologizing to all of us for his moody behavior. And I said so. Jeffery wouldn't let me finish. "He probably doesn't want you to know what the trip to Baghdad was about, but since you are involved anyway, I feel it is my obligation to clear that up before we leave. It involves the assassination of an important personality." I thanked him even though his statement stunned me. But I did not probe further, I did not want to know any more about the political intrigue then shaking the Middle East and all our lives. Daisy managed a pale smile as Jeffrey reached for my hand to say good-bye, "We have to leave now Mrs. Rajy. Please be patient with Nadim, he loves you more than you can imagine."

Nadim and I talked very little the rest of that evening. I was at a loss whether to tackle the conflict of our relationship again or ignore it. But it was obvious from the tension that hovered in the air that Nadim had nothing else in mind. I felt tired and hurt seeing him behave so childishly on a night that seemed a unique opportunity for us to open our hearts to each other and face whatever options we still had. When the evening was over, I took a long time to say good-bye, unable to quiet the alarm of an emotional explosion I sensed coming between us.

I was already in bed when the phone rang. I picked up the receiver and placed it on the pillow next to my ear.

"Darling, are you awake?" Nadim whispered. "I want to ask a favor of you!" He sounded serious.

"Oh, yes, by all means, Nadim. What is it, is something wrong?"

"You know, Nadia, it's ironic that it is my profession to solve other people's problems. Yet, I find myself stupidly helpless when my own future is on the line and I can do nothing about it." I could hear his anger growing hotter as he talked and knew he was annoyed with me. "The last time I was in Baghdad, I realized how mixed up you were about our relationship, and I vowed never to pressure you. But now I can't let this opportunity slip out of my hands; it may well be the last, who knows? I love you, Nadia, and I can't live without you. Now, of all times, I need you right here with me. Please, bring your passport and let's go."

Dumbfounded, I didn't know what to say. Never before had I heard such a forlorn cry from Nadim, a tough unbending man who tolerated no weaknesses.

"Are you there, Nadia? For God's sake, say something!"

"Calm down, darling, please. You think you are the only one who is collapsing under this commitment? Can't you see what a dilemma it is for me? Please don't do this to me. You know as well as I do what will happen if we run away like two crazy fugitives. Please, Nadim, just try to be a bit more patient with me."

"No, I will not wait one more second," he yelled into the wires that connected us, suddenly almost incoherent. "My plane takes off at noon, ten hours from now. You be there if you really love me." He went on shouting and warning, but I wasn't listening.

The sun was high and sizzling when the bus crossed the last stretch of flatness and started to mount Lebanon's winding road westward. I could hear my heart beat faster as we approached the familiar mountains where villages I had known since childhood smiled at me. Memories of them had brought me nothing but enchantment and happiness every time I crossed a road or passed by a house where my family spent a summer or two as I grew up. But on that June day of 1952 the lump in my throat grew tighter as my destination got closer. I felt heavy with the emptiness of having left the glowing ashes of a precious romance I had nurtured lovingly for years to be blown away by the desert wind of that captivating city.

I knew at that moment that the nine months of happiness and sorrow Baghdad had taken from my life were a small sacrifice for the knowledge I had gained and the decisions I had chosen to make. No one would ever be able to take away from me memories of the past that echoed in the present. Nadim's last warnings on the phone would be engraved in my memory for years to come. "You are going to regret it, I tell you, Nadia! Next time we see each other, I'll be married and have a flock of kids behind me. You'll live to regret not being the mother of those kids. You wait and see!"

Neither of us could know then that nearly a decade later he would be married, a famous corporate lawyer, and rich with all that money could provide. When his heart failed and he passed away in 1961, he was survived by a very sick wife who had spent her best years in private clinics for emotional depression. Nadim was forty-two and childless!

13

The first thing I noticed on arriving at the Beirut bus station that warm June day in 1952 was the magnificent new cluster of high-rise office buildings on the far left side of the bustling downtown area known as the Tower Plaza. Then another pleasant surprise caught my attention and stirred my emotions. It was the familiar warm face of someone I had met in Baghdad not too long before. A full-length picture of Camille Cham'oun, dressed in black tie and dinner jacket, hung on one of the electric poles surrounding the Plaza. The campaign for elections to parliament that had begun a few months earlier appeared to be in full swing. As I stood in line for a taxicab, I saw the faces of candidates displayed everywhere, from telephone wires to store windows, and wondered whether the campaign would indeed be as bloody as our ambassador in Baghdad had predicted. Mr. Salah had been in the diplomatic service long enough to know how to judge such events. "The Maronites will have a tough time in these elections," he warned.

The ambassador and his wife, Jacqueline Towmey, were family friends. They were from Broumana, and I had spent time with them during summer vacations. They were among the few Christians who sympathized with the Muslim community's view of the sectarian regime. They had a lot of reservations about the irresponsible dictatorial rule of their fellow Christians, the Maronites, which deprived the majority of the Lebanese of their natural share in the government of the country. "We will pay dearly for this mistake," Jacqueline lamented. "Sooner or later the frustration of the majority will explode and bring about the downfall of the country."

The roads felt smooth as the car rolled swiftly over a thick mat of newly spread asphalt. Shop windows were elegantly dressed with fashionable foreign-made apparel and accessories, while food markets and delicatessen stands were piled with a colorful display of fruit, flowers, and sweets. Recalling the provincial appearance of Baghdad's wide streets and the maladroit displays of the Iraqis' valuable artifacts and bountiful crops, I was delighted to let my eyes feast on the Lebanese spontaneity and cosmopolitan taste I had so missed.

In an attempt to avoid the heavy traffic that choked Beirut at such hours, the cheerful driver swerved away from his destination toward Rass Beirut Boulevard where fewer cars and more pedestrians would be found around sunset. He seemed as much in need of such a tranquil passage as I. The wide circular road provided a breathtaking view of the long summer day as the setting sun wrapped the Mediterranean shores in a panorama of soft colors.

"You look tired, miss, have you come from far away?" The driver's eyes caught mine in his rear-view mirror, but he went on with his second question before I could answer. "You are Lebanese, right?"

Here we go, back to where people have to be identified wherever they go, I thought, seeing his eyes glide from the mirror to the road. "Yes, I am. But I have been in Baghdad on business." The old man instantly became alert and his rough hands tightened on the steering wheel.

"Oh, Iraq, Kerbala and Nejef!" his voice chanted with nostalgia. "The holiest of all holy lands! It's in that blood-soaked soil that my ancestors are buried and . . ." He shot an apprehensive look at my face in his mirror. I didn't have to ask. Only a devout Shi'ite would bestow such profound reverence on the two places he had just eulogized. He was silent for a moment, then looked in his mirror again, "Excuse the indiscretion, miss—you aren't a Christian? Are you?" His apologetic tone twisted my heart.

"Stop worrying, Hadj. What difference does it make, everybody on this planet worships the same God! Just relax." To call any Muslim elder "Hadj"—pilgrim—was a respectful gesture regardless of whether that person had made a pilgrimage to Jerusalem, Mecca, or any other holy place. My nameless Hadj then drove the few remaining miles talking nonstop about his wife and eleven children, domestic politics, and the candidates he was supporting. "This time, Cham'oun will get our votes. He is our last hope and the only politician who sits with us and listens to our grievances. If he is accused of befriending the Engeleez, so what? Aren't we all?"

Most of his conversation was lost on me as my mind darted back to the evening in early January when Camille Cham'oun and I were introduced to each other at our embassy in Baghdad. Jacqueline was a relative of Cham'oun's wife and she insisted I meet the future boss, as she always called Cham'oun. After that brief introduction, the three of us had a chance to socialize as we strolled down the hall to the dining room where the cocktail tables were set. Cham'oun was well known in Baghdad. He received substantial support from the Iraqi royal family because of his strong stand toward the British government. His appearance at the embassy on that chilly evening caused a lively commotion, especially since his arrival had been delayed long enough to cause some concern. No picture I had seen of him had prepared me for his tall, handsome looks and regal carriage.

The elegant embassy hall was filled with the romantic strains of tango music, and I was swept away to the adjacent dancing lounge and eventually into the arms of the guest of honor. He was a very appealing man, and I enjoyed being so close to him as he diverted our preliminary small talk to questions about my relationship with the Haddads and the Towmeys and about my being all alone in that mysterious city. Later, when we sat down in the lounge area with the Salahs, Cham'oun's shrewd eyes softened when I asked him about Nadim's parents who, to my knowledge, were still back in Haifa. He reminisced about playing with Rose when they were kids but said, "Khalil is a little older than I am, and I haven't seen him since he committed himself to his political movement at an early age over in Palestine. I heard lately that he was taken ill at home in Haifa and that probably his son Nadim would have arranged for him and his wife to go to London for treatment." His dark blue eyes seemed to penetrate my soul when Nadim's name was mentioned, and I hesitated to inquire further into his relationship with that family, especially Nadim's cousin Paul, who was running his oil business from London during Cham'oun's diplomatic career there. I returned to my little room at the YMCA that night profoundly humbled by the experience. Electing the president in Lebanon was still the parliament's responsibility. The common people had little or nothing to do with it. Coming as close to a future president as I did was very rare, something most people could never hope for.

The signs of prosperity became less visible as my taxicab crossed Beirut to the humble suburbs where both my in-laws and my parents lived. Tears of joy came to my eyes when I thought of the boys busy studying for their finals at that time of the year. At fifteen, twelve, and ten, they had grown to be remarkably independent. The money I sent from Baghdad should have helped them to cope with the humdrum life at their grandparents'. I knew they might have changed during those long months. I also knew that the woman who had crossed the border to find work had gained more in those nine months on her own than during the three decades of "protected" years. The family prejudice against the idea of a career woman in their midst now seemed like a cruel absurdity.

Nothing appeared to have changed on Mazra street where my in-laws and my children lived. The familiar crowds still surrounded the carts of vegetables and fruit lining both sides of the narrow street, and the young vendors competed for the business of late shoppers by providing them with the best bargains of the day.

Since the land trip did not have a precise schedule, no reception party had been planned. The thrill of surprise bubbled inside me as the cab stopped across from the designated building, the driver rushed to the trunk, unloaded my luggage, and carried it to the Rajys' door. It was almost 8 o'clock in the evening and I knew the boys would be back from school and probably studying. The door was ajar and the sound of after-dinner bustle came from the kitchen. I pushed open the door, entered the unlit lounge and tiptoed to the boys' room.

We stood in the middle of the room hugging and kissing and it was a long time before we were ready to let go of one another. I sat on the edge of their bed and remained there as the whole household came in to welcome me and then left us to be by ourselves.

I did not leave them that night but instead squeezed in between them on the two single beds they had pushed together. We talked and talked until the early hours of the dawn. Their priority at that time was to have us live on our own as a family.

A few years earlier I wouldn't have approached the public sector for an administrative job. Aside from traditional jobs for women like school teacher and health worker, that domain was reserved for the male elite who ruled the country. But 1952 was an exceptional year for us in Lebanon as well as in other Middle Eastern communities eager to take action. If I wasn't sure of the political stability of our country at that stage, I was sure of my will to proceed at once to find my way through the complexities of government administration. I did know that neither Lebanon nor the Middle East were in for an easy future, not when the world's militarization depended on the oil of our Arab neighbors.

The atmosphere in the country was jubilant in August of that year. Cham'oun's ticket was well in the lead with the two camps in the parliamentary representation too much at odds with each other to threaten the support he needed for his radical plans. This sent a joyful message to the people who were eager to have a president as competitive as Cham'oun force the conservatives out of their seats for the first time since the end of the French mandate. It was an exciting time. We were all busy analyzing editorials and listening to people express their views with passion. One thing was clear, the French were on their way out and the Anglo-Americans were marching in to the tune of a new political order.

The cool September breeze helped me keep up a brisk pace on my way to the Bureau of Public Employment where applicants could fill out forms for their choice of positions. Mine was Rank 5, Grade A, an advanced clerical appointment, involving confidential archives, bilingual shorthand, translation, and accounting. There was a great need for such skills now that Cham'oun's new cabinet, under Prime Minister Solh, had drawn up its list of priorities for the reform it had promised. Selected from well-established professionals in the private sector, the cabinet members had the obligation to enact the plan they had prepared during the campaign. In return, the parliament had suspended the constitution, freeing the cabinet to do the paperwork within six months, after which they would resign and a parliamentary cabinet would be nominated to turn the reform into reality. Under normal circumstances, an application for a civil service position at that modest level had to be based on a qualifying examination given by the specific bureau. But the suspension of the constitution cleared the way for such appointments to bypass the regular restrictions, thus allowing me and the rest of the applicants a fair chance.

A sudden gush of rain chased me up the wide steps of the Presidential Grand Palace on Monday, October 20, almost a month after I had applied for employment. At 8:30 A.M. I was to attend the swearing-in ceremony held by the chief of protocol for the dozen or so secretaries who had been hired. My wet shoes slipped on the marble floor of the long hall and I found myself thrown into the arms of a passing priest. Unruffled, the elderly clergyman touched the top of my head with his rosary cross and gave me an encouraging smile. I whispered my thanks and rushed ahead, looking for Room 2 where the ceremony was to take place in just a few seconds. Although I was confident my employment was assured, I still couldn't stop the unsettling buzz in my ears. There was too much at stake. My hopes and those of my three sons depended on that appointment. That day was also the eve of Usama's fifteenth birthday and I had promised to take the three of them out to dinner.

The dinner reservation fell through, and so did the birthday party, but not the job. Immediately after the ceremony I found myself surrounded by the brand-new secretaries and the members of the cabinet who would be our bosses. Proper introductions were made.

Minister Hamada, a pleasant, robust man in his sixties, sounded preoccupied when we exchanged a formal greeting. Leading the way to his office, he chatted about the kind of work he expected me to do, giving me no time to say anything. "I am sure you won't mind starting right away, miss. . . . " Not expecting an answer, he expressed his pleasure at finding a secretary who had experience in office work, and spoke three languages. "You are a lifesaver, coming in at a time when I have a pile of urgent correspondence, all from English sources. . . . " I started to tell him that I didn't plan on staying, but he interrupted enthusiastically, "Oh, don't worry about the nature of the work I ask you to do. It will be very helpful if you just give brief translations for colleagues who speak no English. The rest is routine stuff, and please make a dozen carbon copies of each document for our cabinet members."

A second later my new boss was rushed out of his office by a group of visitors. "Please, miss, look for the notes I left on the letters," Hamada called over his shoulder, assured that his orders would be followed faithfully.

I lost track of time sitting behind the stacks of papers piled on both sides of my desk. The day moved quickly as the typewriter, telephone, and overworked cabinet drawers conspired to test my limits. I was startled when I heard Minister Hamada say goodnight to someone in the adjacent room. "Oh, you are still here, miss!" Hamada stammered, and stepped in to go through the day's outgoing correspondence. I nodded, and whispered my name. "Honored, madame. I'm sorry things are so hectic here, but glad you've survived the day. Monday is usually the busiest day for everyone who works under this roof." His weary, square face creased as his groomed fingers pulled a chained watch out of his vest pocket. "Excuse me, Mrs. Rajy, do you have someone waiting for you? It is sort of late. . . . " He must have seen the bewilderment on my face as I confessed I was without transportation. "All right, then, let me see if my driver is back. I hope you don't mind going alone with him. It will be a while before I finish here."

Dressed up in their new white shirts and colorful ties, the boys were lined up against the terrace railing at the Rajys' street-level apartment when the Cadillac pulled up to the curb. Usama was out first, his eyes wide with amazement at the uniformed chauffeur who brought out the flowers and birthday cake and handed them to him. "Glad you are all right, Mother. What happened?" I apologized for not making the dinner reservations, and promised to make amends. We did have chocolate milk and birthday cake while I told them about my unbelievable day. I was grateful my in-laws had retired to their bedrooms so we had the kitchen to ourselves.

I didn't go home to my parents' that night but tried to get some sleep squeezed in between the three boys on the bed they shared. After they fell asleep, all sorts of thoughts about the kind of relationship my children and I really had kept nagging me. I often saw myself more as a friend than a traditional mother to them. When no one else was around, we enjoyed a comradely closeness. Yet, I was aware of a difference in their attitude toward me in the company of their male friends or relatives. The compassion in their eyes would be replaced by a vacant look that seemed to put a distance between us, and I would suddenly feel miles away from them.

Whether this was a natural transformation that happens as children grow older or a result of the unsettling conditions of our life was not clear at that point. In those soul-searching moments before dawn, I yearned to be able to read their thoughts as men, and to be not only a mother but also a special friend to them. I hoped they would rise above the stereotypes imposed by social convention. But I knew, deep in my heart, that what I yearned for was only a remote possibility. I had to face the fact that the older my sons grew, the less I would be able to predict what kind of men they would be. Our culture puts great pressure on men as well as women. Women had countless obligations and men were loaded down with duties. Life itself was a duty for them.

The thrill of the new job and the excitement of working with politicians and national leaders did not last. The long hours of clerical work became very boring as the mission of the reform cabinet was completed, its members resigned, and seats were left for parliamentary appointees to take over. In mid-December of that year, my overtime income and the bonuses generated throughout those four months suddenly dried up. I had to face the fact that my basic salary was too meager for a family of four who were on their way to building their own little home. My plans to find our own place were to start soon after the approaching holidays.

The only option I had at that point was to get an afternoon job and go back to school to take more courses to allow for a specific career that could open new opportunities for me.

Fortunately, the opportunity for such a change came faster than I expected when a new governmental department was established and the minister who would take charge of it happened to be Professor Hamada himself. This was the Ministry of Education and Fine Arts, a ministry the reform prized very highly. The new opening offered a wider range of jobs and a number of training opportunities for the few incumbents who were transferred from other sectors of the administration like myself.

This was the manna of heaven falling into my lap! The challenging functions of that new ministry were just what I wanted, and I moved to the new building while the offices were still under renovation. The move was during the Christmas holiday of 1952, and I agreed to help Minister Hamada's team set up his office where I would be in charge of establishing the administrative archives. For the two decades since Lebanon had had its independence from the French mandate, issues of an educational nature were handled by other branches of the administration.

According to the recent report circulated by the reform cabinet concerning education in Lebanon, the new ministry was charged with the mission of imposing a structure on the educational system of the country. Two of the most urgent tasks were establishing public schools at all levels and developing a national curriculum that would serve the interests of all the people in Lebanon, so that they could define their own civic ideals. Until then, 90 percent of all the schools in Lebanon were private. Most were founded during the Ottoman occupation by the various missionaries who were guided from abroad and had their own interests in our region. My role in this department was to collect educational data for the United Nations agency. My new boss would be Fuad Salem, the man charged with establishing a department especially for statistical research.

The narrow horizon of my life began to widen. All of a sudden the future held the possibility of studying educational statistics and data processing under the auspices of a project supported by the United Nations. In less than three weeks after I heard about these scholarships, I was back on the student bench, working on mathematics and gaining familiarity with computers at the American University, which hosted the program. Minister Hamada supported my decision by allowing me to take the required time to attend the classes. All this happened in February 1953, a memorable month of unexpected blessings.

I really enjoyed receptions given at the ministry. One evening, in Minister Hamada's office, I met a man who captured my attention from the moment I saw him. It was one of those mysterious instances in life when the future of two human beings could be determined by a flashing glance or an innocent smile. His eyes looked into mine for just a second before a few colleagues strolled over and came between us. He didn't know who I was, but I recognized him from the picture in the previous night's paper: Fuad Salem, the new chief of cabinet of the Ministry of Education and Fine Arts, my boss!

Startled by the sudden throbbing in my veins, I headed to where Minister Hamada and General Director Najib were surrounded by reporters and their cameramen. Hamada introduced me to G.D. Najib, praising the resilience with which I had performed my duties during the four months I had worked for him. "You will see for yourself, Najib, how energetic this young lady is. But be sure to take it easy on her for a while. She has just won one of those UN scholarships I was telling you about." When Fuad Salem and Lara Hafiz, the new head of the Curriculum Committee, joined us, Minister Hamada made the introductions: "This is my chief of cabinet, Fuad Salem, and this is Mrs. Nadia Rajy, until a few weeks ago my secretary. She is yours from now on."

It was at that stage of my life that I began to feel free from the fear of insecurity that complicated my past. At home, I was still the daughter of my own overprotective family and a member of the Rajys'

Nadia and Her Sons Celebrating a Birthday Just Before Her Trip to the United States, 1954

unwieldy clan. I was content to have a steady job. But the doors to a brighter future and a challenging career were flung wide open for me and I began to sense a new woman emerging within me.

Life became hectic, exhilarating, full of wonder at times. Things just happened. Gone, for that marvelous stretch of time, was the stagnation of earlier years. Shows, concerts, lectures, glittering receptions became an almost daily routine. Perhaps vanity got hold of me, but it could not all be vanity. Some of the people I met, mostly men, had so much going for them. Charm, wit, beautiful hobbies, rare books, rare tastes, they had it all.

In January 1954 I was transferred to a new assignment while I was still attending the special course offered by the UN. This assignment came with a promotion and was part of a project that would lead to an exhaustive statistical survey of the changes recommended by the reform of 1952. I moved to another floor in the Ministry's building and had my office equipped with the staff and material needed for the planned survey.

The opportunity to further my studies came in May 1954. This time it was a grant from the Point IV Agency, an American program for Technical Cooperation with other Governments administered by the

Office of Education, to receive advanced academic and practical training. This offer was beyond all my expectations and came when I finally felt secure enough to settle down. At the time, the boys were looking for an apartment for us to move into, but going to the United States would change these plans. I had only a few weeks to decide, since the program began in September. The Rajy clan were tired of looking after my children, and my children by then were bored by the way their grandparents took care of them. I don't know if I convinced my in-laws or my sons about the worth of my venture for they would again be living together in my absence. Perhaps I wore them out and they did not care to argue with me anymore, or maybe they understood what a great opportunity I had been given.

The visit to America turned out to be one of the greatest landmarks in my life. Such distant journeys usually are, and there was nothing casual about this trip. It was so important for me, for my career, for my freedom to be on that TWA flight to New York. I sat next to a nice couple whose American English I could not understand all the time. They were very friendly people, happy to be flying home. "Everything will work out just fine," the man told me. "Oh, you say that about everything, honey!" his wife said. "This young woman has a pretty long road ahead of her," she said, as she smiled at me with womanly understanding. I knew the road would be long and not always smooth, but I had the strength I needed.

All the details were inside my elegant black briefcase. My itinerary was outlined in three separate files and on paper of three different colors. It included the academic program, the training sessions, and the pedagogical activities. The white file contained information and registration papers for three university trimesters, two at Michigan State in East Lansing and Ann Arbor, and a third at the University of California, Berkeley. The green file described six pedagogical seminars in six cities and two special seminars on the use of computers, plus a visit to the Remington Rand plant in Rhode Island, where its giant Univac was on display. The pink was the largest file in that package. It included bulletins and illustrated catalogues of a good number of special schools I would visit between semesters. This third assignment, I discovered later, was the hardest but the most gratifying in terms of direct human contact. It was very important to me personally to discover some common ground between Americans and Lebanese.

It was still Friday afternoon in New York when my trip by air finally ended, and the land journey began. The vast airport was jammed with travelers. Powerful loudspeakers announced arrivals and departures by the minute. I was disappointed by the bare walls and roofs, which reminded me of army barracks. Nothing in this place was as romantic as I had anticipated from having read some moving stories written by immigrants to the New World.

According to my traveling instructions, a Mrs. Molly Monroe would be meeting me at the New York airport. There was no information as to how she looked. All I knew was that she would pick me up at the immigration desk to accompany me to my hotel. The fact that there were several such desks worried me, and my mind raced for a quick decision I might have to make if we missed each other. I was left with no choice but to follow my instincts, a system of defense my body had long since adopted and trusted.

The unfriendly atmosphere around that crowded lounge seemed to put both passengers and officers under some kind of tension as if they were afraid of each other. This was not reassuring to someone who wasn't certain of her next step. The crowd comprised the widest range of races and colors I had ever seen in one place. Western clothing and regally colorful national robes and people of various lands mingled to form a rich quilt. The line moved slowly and I was afraid it was going to take ages before my turn came. The clock over the large exit indicated 5:30 New York time. My bedtime was long overdue, my feet were killing me, and I felt as fretful as a weaned child.

She was taller than most of those who stood waiting behind the immigration line. I could not read the identity card dangling from her blazer lapel, but I watched her searching eyes sorting out the faces from one line to another. I waited until our eyes met. Unconsciously my arm hailed up, waving in her direction. One moment and she was gone. "Well, hello there!" the brisk voice came from behind me. I turned and there she was, the lady with the pleated skirt and formal blazer, smiling at me. I smiled back with relief. "I'm curious to know how you happened to single me out before you got to immigration where we were to meet," she said. "Oh, I don't know. Probably fear or instinct!" I joked. "But what about you? You seem to have as sure an instinct as I do! I thought only people like us in the Orient had such mysterious talents."

That night Molly and her friend Scott took me out to dinner and I began my year in America. So much was about to happen. The vastness of America and the huge distances that separated places did not seem frightening. In so many ways I had left home to find home, to lose it, and to find it again. I did not know all this on that important day. I just had a feeling that sometimes one's home is like an airplane. Home can move with you and can take you places. But what about the people you leave behind? What about the tearful eyes, and the sad smiles?

Almost one year and many miles and experiences later, I was in New York again, being escorted to the airport. Leaving the terminal, I turned once more and raised my arm high above the crowd. I was waving to a woman and a man who stood by the immigration desk and waved back. The small bouquet of pink carnations they had given me carried in them a card that read: "See you soon, Nadia. From Molly and Scott."

Beirut's International Airport, under construction when I left for the States in 1954, looked huge compared to the domestic two-runway airfield we had before. My heart raced crazily as the airplane taxied around the newly asphalted runway and came to a halt across from an elegant structure of concrete and glass. There they were, my welcoming party of family and friends, and they looked larger than the rest of the other groups who watched our plane slow down and roll to a halt.

When I stepped out of the plane I was met by my boss, Fuad, my colleague, Lara, and a relative of hers who apparently worked at the airport's customs bureau. They accompanied me to the VIP lounge, where we visited for a few minutes while Lara's relative took care of my passport and luggage. Lara was full of news about the changes that had taken place during my absence. "You wait and see the size of your dear old statistical center, Nadia, new responsibilities are waiting for you now. And, oh! we have a new general director, replacing our dear old one, too. Remember Charles Nader, the UNESCO representative down in the UN bureau in the Palace? Well, that is the man. Yes, I know he is charming. Take my advice, Nadia, stay away from that handsome man, Doctor Charles Nader is single and eligible. . . ." She wanted to go on but Fuad interrupted her, "We had better go now,

Lara, Nadia's children must be very anxious to see her." His voice faltered as he addressed me, praising my looks and attire, "This is a beautiful haircut, Nadia, and this tan. . . . Apparently you enjoyed the beach during your stop in Italy. . . . I wish we had more time to talk, but there is a big party of Rajys waiting for you in the reception lounge. I was told you would be spending this weekend at your parents' summer house in Bikfayya, so I'll see you Monday at 10 A.M. in my office. You have to come and meet with G.D. Nader, I have already told him you would be back this weekend."

September 30 wasn't only a long traveling day. It came with a dazzling evening as well. The welcoming party that began at the airport's reception lounge was followed by a fancy dinner with the family in the mountains that continued late into the night. Despite the differing motives of those who congratulated me on my successful trip abroad and safe return home, I enjoyed this belated acknowledgment of my worth. That was, indeed, a triumphant victory over the relatives who, until I left home a year ago, stood against every decision I had ever made.

Work was even more gratifying than home. As Lara had briefed me the day I arrived back from the States, the statistical center I had set up in the ministry's basement a couple of years ago now had a name and a steady budget. It became the Department of Statistics and Educational Subsidies, and our boss would not be Fuad. This latter designation might seem unimportant in situations where the public schools carried a heavier load than the private ones, but not in Lebanon. Ninety percent of the educational task was still in the hands of the private institutions, dominated from kindergarten to vocational schools and universities by churches and other establishments from abroad.

The need for these private schools, most of which were located in areas far from Muslim enclaves, began to diminish soon after the Ministry of Education and Fine Arts was established and took charge of a national education. Together with UN support and agencies like Point IV, the ministry created a new curriculum and built public schools wherever there was need. Their doors were open to children who had been neglected up to that point. From then on, elementary education became compulsory in Lebanon. Still, the best-equipped institutions were mostly parochial and located in cities and their adjacent suburbs. It was at this time that the administration enacted balanced subsidy laws to distribute funds to all free elementary schools. Finally, a special commission was appointed to put some discipline into the way money was distributed. The private sector was represented in that commission alongside the ministry's representatives. I was its secretary.

The professional benefits I earned from working in that powerful domain were tremendous. I became acquainted with most of the leaders and administrators who were involved in that educational revolution. The work was very gratifying in terms of the valuable experience I gained in the public sector. However, as my team and I compiled the statistical data for our project, I was surprised by the amount of fraud we found in the educational private sector. Some very prominent parochial and non-religious institutions applying for the Ministry's subvention falsified information about their students to obtain extra aid. When I presented the case to my superiors and submitted to them proof of this fraud, my team and I understood we were making influential enemies who could destroy the trust we needed from those above us to continue our work. Fortunately my superiors were willing to support our project to the end.

My income, however, was still short of covering my expenses when, in August 1956, I rented a small apartment, picked up the boys at my in-laws, and finally left the family shelter. I got back my afternoon job at the Conservatoire National de Musique and the wheels of the new Rajy home began to spin. The decade-long struggle of vigorous work, penny saving, and belt tightening produced my happiest days. Determination became a password between me and my teenage sons who, like me, had evening jobs in addition to their school assignments and extracurricular activities. Family and relatives watched at a distance, still not fully sure I could pull my plan through without their help.

When I finally left the clan and moved with the children out of their reach, Uncle Ahmad was the only member of that family who suffered because of my departure. Nothing could have been as belittling to his sense of fatherhood than seeing a daughter of his working to feed his grown-up grandsons. I begged him to come see how well organized our life was and how proud the boys and I were of our little achievement. He was my father by choice, and for him, I was the preferred daughter.

But, alas! Uncle Ahmad didn't have the chance to respond—a fatal heart attack was faster. He died forty days after we put together a new Rajy home for him.

"This is Fuad, Nadia. I wonder if you can stop by at my office before you go home." My ex-boss stammered on the phone as if he wasn't sure what to say next. . . . "No, it is a personal matter. I won't take much of your time, but I need to talk to you today."

This wasn't the first time Fuad and I had sought one another's advice and exchanged views about our personal problems. Why did I have the impression he was reluctant asking for me to come by? Our relationship was unreserved from the first day we met some three years ago, always sincere and friendly. It became more intimate when I was away, as though the thousands of miles that separated us brought us closer. His thoroughness and candor had compelled me to listen to him and open my heart to his profound sorrows. Fuad wrote to me all about his intimate relationships, his arranged marriage, and his extramarital affairs while in Europe. I reciprocated by writing in great detail about the marital hardships Marwan and I had endured at the hands of our families who abused us in many different ways, not always intentionally, to be sure. Utterly confident that he would understand, I took pains to criticize men for the institutionalized oppression that was passed from father to son to grandson. I explained the irreparable disaster that befell my marriage because of that trend. "He was pushed by those who loved him most," I recalled complaining to Fuad in one of my letters, "to fit their standard of masculinity and become the monster I dreaded throughout my marriage." I confessed my grueling drama with Nadim Haddad as I had done to no one before. We exchanged thoughts on our tight budgets, problems with children, and political developments in the world.

In one of the last letters I received before I left the States, Fuad opened his heart about intimate family dilemmas, the marriage his father had planned at his birth, and the cousin/wife who was as dear as an older sister to him. He hinted at some serious illness his wife was struggling with on her own. "She refused to follow the doctors' advice," Fuad had lamented in that letter. "I just don't want her life to be as short as her father's. She was as much a family victim as I when our parents put our necks to the yoke of marriage."

Although Fuad and I differed in background and religion, we had gone through the same tenacious abuse in the hands of our traditional clans. To them we were family assets, just like all the husbands, wives, and other uncles and aunts who didn't know better.

I did not know whether it was because of a similarity in our pasts, or because of a pain we both had to allay, but we were attracted to each other. As time passed, our precious friendship ripened into a profound devotion that followed its course without either of us acknowledging it. Fuad and I were seen together with a group of friends everywhere, invited to the same parties and welcomed with geniality. Having had ample time to build up his friendship with my sons during my absence, Fuad became a family friend as well and often joined us for dinner. The boys enjoyed man-to-man arguments with him tremendously.

Fuad was on the balcony of his office when I finally left my office building and crossed the little square separating us. It was an unusually cool summer day and the sun was still high above our heads when I joined him there. His blue eyes darkened when he saw me.

"Something wrong, Fuad? You sounded strange on the phone! What is it?" He looked young and vulnerable, searching for words.

"Why didn't you tell me you have been seeing Nadim Haddad? I saw you two walking down to the UN Palace today." His blond mane moved with a rising breeze as he stepped forward to confront me. His face was extremely pale.

"That's all? My God, Fuad, you look as if disaster has fallen on your head! You know Nadim's uncle has his research office down in the UNESCO wing. I was the one who introduced you two to each other last year, remember?" His unexpected flare of jealousy twisted my heart, and I felt guilty for letting Nadim flirt with me sometimes. "You know more than anyone else in this world how I feel about him. Besides, I never question your relationships with your personal friends. You have to trust me, too." There was something in me that was happy about Fuad's jealousy.

Nadim Haddad had caught up with me at the ministry that morning by accident. A famous lawyer, rich and popular with his clan, he was visiting a cousin, a well known scholar in Lebanon who worked for our ministry. Married to a young beauty who was the only descendant of a Beirutan millionaire, Nadim had grown into a successful business-man, tougher and with a harder ego than the man I had resisted some eight years ago. Regrettably, the wealthy couple had difficulty having children. During the short visits he made to my office, his voice would falter whenever we talked about my children and my late husband.

That side of him made me wonder if all along he had looked at me more as a potential mother to healthy children than as the romantic object of his poetic imagination.

The encounter with Fuad was intensely emotional and I had to restrain myself from throwing my arms around him right there and then and letting the whole world see how much I loved him. Instead, I heard myself whispering, "Please, let's go out for dinner, Fuad! Just the two of us."

It was long after midnight when I got back home from the restaurant where we spent the evening talking, dreaming, and hoping. Although neither of us proposed a toast, we heard our hearts pronouncing: Yes, I do!

There had been many challenges, obstacles, and blessings in my life, but loving Fuad was the gravest responsibility I had willingly undertaken. From the moment I met him, I felt as though I had known him before. He was the soulmate I had subconsciously been waiting for. The burden of knowing that he was a married man had never bothered me because I took it for granted that we belonged together. We didn't try to hide the joy of our relationship from anyone who knew us. As time went by, our colleagues and friends talked of us as a couple, invited us to the same parties, and expected us to respond to their notices and invitations. At the same time, we respected each other's circumstances and gave space for privacy, including the separate activities we pursued on our own. Even when Fuad continued his hit-and-run affairs with women I knew, I did not feel the urge to disturb our harmonious relationship. I was convinced it would be frivolous to compare myself to any other woman he went with when deep inside I knew ours was the ultimate love.

Fuad's presence during those years was a blessing from God. He was the undemanding friend who stood by me when doubt lingered or a crisis occurred. He, too, needed my help since his three teenage children were on their way to adulthood and their mother's illness was pronounced terminal. Being an ambitious father who had spent most of his life abroad, Fuad had a hard time applying his lofty standards of education to children who were raised by relatives who didn't care. He, too, had his share of sorrow when his wife passed away. His older son and daughter dropped out of school and his twelve-year-old daughter did not even care to try attending school.

It was a golden year in 1965, devoted to healing and fulfillment. After seventeen years of living only for my sons, I was ready to fly away. In my case, the flight was at arm's reach. Fuad and I vowed to marry and finish raising his three children. It was Fuad's goal to see them as successful as my children. This was a memorable occasion for all of us, and Ghassan, the last of my children to leave home, proposed to honor it in his own way. He accompanied us to my parents' house and directed our intimate ceremony in the presence of his bewildered grandparents, uncles, and aunts. He was magnificent. They watched with astonishment as Ghassan performed the role of the groom's best man. With refined grace, he first introduced Fuad Salem to the in-laws who hadn't met him yet, then turned and addressed his grandfather Kareem, asking for my hand on behalf of the forty-nine-year-old groom. Fuad's eyes sparkled as he fought tears of joy and observed the young man take our hands and join them forever.

Fuad and I were married in September. We rented a large apartment in the city and his three children moved in with us. When evil winds began to blow in Lebanon in the early seventies, Fuad's two daughters were already married and his son had graduated from the university and was looking for a job. Up to that point, the tanks and mortars of the Israelis made it their business to raid the Lebanese villages in the south where most of the Palestinian refugee camps were located. In 1971 they invaded our skies as well. The Palestinian Liberation Organization had succeeded in persuading the Arab states to sign an agreement that allowed its fighters to carry arms and defend themselves against any attacker. These were rights that only the Lebanese army had; the Lebanese people were not allowed to carry arms. This caused dangerous rifts in Lebanon's social structure and in its communities as well. The Christians, who had been promised Lebanon all to themselves, were dead-set against the PLO's men carrying their weapons outside the camps. The Muslims, on the other hand, were as insecure in their own country as the Palestinians had been in Palestine before their destitution. They supported the Palestinians and shared their armed struggle against Israel in the south.

Fuad, 1935

But life moved fast in Lebanon and the cracks in the system weren't obvious enough for the general public to become concerned. Fuad and I were totally oblivious of the impending dangers and busy planning for our future together. Finally on our own, free to choose the style of life we had dreamed about, we decided to move away from the city and up to one of the surrounding hills. We wanted to detach ourselves from the politics surrounding us and spend the rest of our lives taking care of each other. Our one-acre lot was part of a panoramic development on a cliff in Shemlan, just a ten-mile drive from our offices in Beirut. A year later our permanent residence was ready. We bought a new sports car and moved up to the peaceful little town which seemed to be the safest place in the world.

We were not the only people who responded to the economic boom in our country. Many sons and daughters who, for long stretches of time, had been absorbed by the industrial countries of the world came back from abroad to stay. My son Jamal and his American wife, Kay, were among the first couples to do so. They were in Beirut in 1972 when we moved up to our residence in the mountains and they were expecting their first child. Their summer house was a few miles down the hill from us. Usama, my eldest son, followed a year later. In the summer of 1973 he arrived from Copenhagen with his beautiful wife Eva and their two adorable little boys. "We can't let our children freeze in that gray country when we can raise them here, Mom," he said. "Eva is expecting another baby next winter, she wants her children to grow up in the place Scandinavians dream about."

Usama's rented house was just around the corner from our little town. Ainab was a traditional village, calm and conveniently located for city commuters. In one week he found a job and bought a small car. Eva, a bilingual nursery teacher, now had time to take her two little boys, Oliver and Sven, on walks and strolls all over the beautiful green countryside.

The first disaster hit my family in September 1973 and claimed Eva's life. A fatal rupture of her fallopian tube killed her instantly. She was twenty-seven years old. Alas! She had only a few months to live her dream of tanning and exploring our Biblical mountains. From that date on, everything around us seemed to change. Evil winds were at work again. Fuad and I listened to them howling from afar. Israel, which continued its air attacks on the refugee camps with American bombers, took to the habit of scanning our skies on the way in and out and used sonic booms to intimidate all those who supported the Palestinians.

The beginning of 1975 signaled a sharp turn in Lebanon's future. It marked as critical a shift in my life and Fuad's as well. In January, while entertaining guests for dinner, we were attacked by an armed group of burglars. Six young men with automatic weapons, gloves, light tennis shoes, and tightly wrapped heads pushed us back as we opened the outer door to let our guests out. We were ordered into a corner where one of the attackers watched over us while the others

went from room to room, rampaging and filling their bags with anything they desired. Apart from the little money the guests and we had
on us, there was nothing of value at home that could have motivated
such a costly assault. Each man carried a machine gun, and each machine gun must have cost a fortune. They arrogantly warned us against
trying to follow them: "We cut the brake lines on all the fancy cars in
the driveway and the telephone line," one of them barked, leaping out
into the hideous night.

We were left under the frightening spell of what had happened to us
during the long time we spent under their surveillance. The possibility
of them coming back paralyzed us and for a long moment no one
moved or talked. A lady friend lay unconscious on her seat. Stiff with
fear, Fuad leaned against the wall. His nose was bleeding. The outer
door was left wide open to the chilling winds. Without telephone,
electricity, or heat at a 2,400 feet elevation, the air felt very cold. I was
the first to get my senses back and I rushed to the outside door,
slammed it shut, and locked it. I lit some candles and together with the
guests who were not hurt, revived the unconscious woman and placed
Fuad on his long chair with cotton and towels over his bleeding nose. I
brought blankets and quilts out to the lounge and we huddled together
throughout the night. It was not until the sun rose and I had braved the
freezing utility room to fix the phone line that we were able to call for
help. My son Jamal, who lived not far from our place, was the first to
come to our help. He checked the cars and offered to go to Beirut and
bring back a mechanic to repair them. It was already Sunday. My
guests were worried about the family members they had left behind.
No one knew when the cars would be repaired. Beirut seemed like a
very distant place, way at the end of a desert, at the edge of night.

Fuad's bleeding didn't stop for the next three nights. It slowed down
during the daytime, but increased when darkness fell over us and the
sounds of normal life died away. He would spend the nights propped
up in bed with ice pads on his forehead. His blood pressure was still
very high and the doctor recommended that we let the disquieting
trickle of blood help relieve the pressure on his veins. He was a good
friend of Fuad's family and he knew of the Salems' history of stroke
and brain hemorrhage.

I spent the rest of the 1975 winter shuttling to work whenever the
situation permitted, watching over Fuad's condition at night and trying
to help Usama and his children through their hardship. My son had

moved closer to us after his wife's death, making it easy for me to visit him and my grandchildren on my way back from the city. It broke my heart to see how he struggled to cope with his sorrows at a time when his little boys needed all the attention they could get. The older boy had watched his mother's funeral from the moment her coffin was carried away from the house until it went down into the grave. He knew she would never come back and he reacted to this dread by repressing his feelings and nursing a rage deep within himself. Oliver spoke Danish only, a language none of us understood, and this made him more dependent on his father. Sven seemed lost. The poor child was unable to relate to those who suddenly took Eva's place, fed and dressed him but understood none of his childish babbling. Luckily Kay, Jamal's wife, and her son, who was Sven's age, became the two family members who brightened his life. She was there for him the day his mother died.

We were all shaken with grief again, two weeks after the burglary incident, when a sudden wave of violence broke in Saïda, south of the capital. A popular member of the parliament, the leader of the Nasserist party, was shot while leading a street demonstration in support of the Fishermen's Union in the South. This veteran political leader and advocate of workers' rights in parliament stood against Cham'oun's project for an industrial fishing shipyard that would dominate the Lebanese shores. So fingers were pointed at Cham'oun's followers, and violence spread to Beirut and the neighboring suburbs where the Salem clan lived. By then, Fuad and I had moved to a temporary place that could accommodate us through the working days of the week. It was a one-bedroom apartment at Fuad's property in the suburbs of Beirut.

After that unfortunate development, barricades, kidnappings, and vengeful executions became the norm. These changes drove Fuad to despair. The need to commute to our house in Shemlan now put too much stress on him. On top of that, he seemed to have lost faith in our adoptive town. Shemlan was a unique little town in a large district that had accommodated a mixture of Christians and Muslims of all sects, in addition to a number of foreign diplomats and missionaries who had become permanent residents in Lebanon. Our house was within walking distance of an international school for Arabic, established to accommodate foreign diplomats and officials. Some of its graduates had, in fact, created a little colony not too far from "our cliff." Not a few of them had been educated by the missionary who founded the well-known American University and Hospital in Beirut. That particular district, however, had been Druze territory for almost two centuries. Fuad was still considered a Cham'ounist at a time when Cham'oun himself had fallen out of grace in that district, and he felt less secure staying in Shemlan.

Fuad had a long history in local politics. He ran for a seat in parliament when he graduated from the American University in the early forties and later when he returned from diplomatic service in Europe. In a system that required that all religious communities be represented, candidates ran for parliament in groups. Fuad, a Shi'ite, shared the ticket led by Camille Cham'oun in more than one election but he was not elected. They were opposed by the Progressive Socialist party led by the Druze leader Kamal Jumblat. Although Fuad later became a personal friend of Jumblat, he remained tainted by his early association with the Christian camp.

Eventually, we were obliged to spend more time in our tiny apartment surrounded by the Salem clan. I had known all along that Fuad's close relatives weren't too thrilled to lose him to a Beirutan wife, especially when we adopted Shemlan as a residence. Up to that point I had stayed away from the Salems on Fuad's recommendation. I was accused of uprooting my husband from his clan, who considered him a leader by birth. After the burglary incident their complaints grew louder. It was during those unsettling times that I learned more about the basic codes of the tribal structure and its benefits and disadvantages. When danger pressed close to our heels, tribal connections offered refuge. Then again, tribal law dictated alliances through marriage. But Fuad and I saw no reason to abide by such ancient laws. We were blinded by our love, but we had broken the tribal code and had to pay the price for that mistake.

June brought back a little hope as PLO leaders and army officers sat together and tried to work out a solution. We took advantage of the calm and decided to celebrate our tenth anniversary up at the villa where the weather was gorgeous. But calamity descended on us on October 3. Fuad and I had just said good-bye to the last guests who celebrated our anniversary with us and were discussing remodeling our temporary apartment in the city in case the roads to Shemlan became unsafe again.

It was a wet Friday and a bit chilly that first week of October. The hill seemed quiet apart from the voices of our neighbors attending to their swimming pool in preparation for the winter. Fuad had settled in his favorite chair by the fireplace and was reading the newspaper out loud. He loved to do this when I was busy cooking or tidying up. From across the kitchen, I listened to his cheerful comments on the positive talks between the military and the PLO.

Suddenly, ear-splitting explosives and heavy artillery shook the ground under my feet. The kitchen door panels were blown to bits and I heard Fuad's agonized howl mixed with the sounds of barking dogs and children's screams.

I remembered rushing down the hall to the lounge and seeing Fuad's body lying face down on the carpet by the bay window.

I can still hear myself scream like a wounded animal.

Our neighbor, Bashir, rushed through the door and came to my help. Tears streamed down my cheeks and everything was a frightening blur. I pressed my ear to Fuad's chest and was relieved to hear his heartbeat, loud and regular.

I have no recollection of how we managed to carry Fuad to our two-door sedan and lay his sturdy frame on the back seat. Nor can I remember the road that my neighbor took, driving us safely down to the American Hospital in Rass Beirut.

The hospital entrance and alleyways swarmed with ambulances, casualties, and terrified relatives. It was obvious that the emergency team of doctors, nurses, and assistants were trying their best to cope, and we had to wait for a few minutes before an attendant could help us get Fuad's body into the emergency lounge.

I will never forget the sweating face of the emergency physician who, after examining Fuad's body for a few minutes, turned to Bashir and asked, "Is this patient a relative of yours? Do you know how he was injured? "

"No!" I protested. "My husband is not injured. He is in shock. Please, have a specialist see him, he has been unconscious for two hours now."

"I'm sorry, madame, this patient is not in shock, he is in a coma. Most probably bleeding internally. . . . You said you drove him down from Shemlan? Well, he is lucky you were able to make it under such circumstances. . . . But I regret to have to tell you, his chances of recovery are very slim. . . . " He turned to leave but I stopped him and asked for more information about the help Fuad needed. "Oh, no, the specialists are all busy. Besides they can do nothing in the next twenty-four hours. Hopeless cases are left to their good luck. . . . A room? No way. We have orders not to admit any more casualties." I wanted to kill that blunt man.

Our wonderful neighbor sensed my anguish and stepped in. "Thank you, Doctor. I will stay with Fuad while Mrs. Salem calls and notifies the family of her husband's condition." His eyes watched the emergency doctor leave and then turned to me, "Don't worry, Nadia, I teach at the university here and have some connections among the medical staff. Let me take care of the registration process so Fuad can be admitted first. I'm sure we can find a specialist whose diagnosis we can trust. Just give me an hour or so, and, please, try to calm down. Remember, Fuad needs all the attention you can give him now." He was halfway down the lounge when he turned back, "I forgot to ask you, did you lock the door of your home in Shemlan? . . . All right, give me the key and don't worry, I will take care of whatever is needed to be done while you are here. I'm not sure how long this attack will go on. The Gemayyl Phalanges and Cham'oun's Ahrar are both in on it. Their target is the Palestinian camps, but only God knows whether they'll extend their operations to other areas. Their future allies are unknown to us."

The shelling got heavier as that fateful day came to its end. It was almost six o'clock in the evening when Bashir came back with the registration papers he had vouched for with his personal account at the university. Less than twenty minutes later Fuad's motionless body was transferred to his room on the eighth floor, and the medical team of the intensive care unit took charge of his case. Before he left, Bashir made sure that a long chair was brought to the room for me to rest and that the head of that floor was notified of Fuad's need for immediate attention. "You are God's angel for us, Bashir!" I whispered as I accompanied him to the door, unsuccessful in hiding my tears. I wondered what would have happened had I been all alone up in Shemlan when Fuad collapsed. Outside our room the news about the ongoing attack was contradictory. There were some rumors that the Maronite forces from East Beirut had broken the front line in West Beirut. I dreaded the thought of what might happen to Fuad if the battle moved closer to the American compound which was guarded by a few squads of the Lebanese Army. There were a lot of decisions to be made concerning my husband's well-being, and after the Salems got my message about his collapse, more than a dozen men and women of his family came and started debating the dangers in West Beirut. Up to that point, they hadn't decided whether Rass Beirut, which was located at the other end of the city from them, was safe enough for Fuad to stay there, or whether he should be moved to a clinic in their area. They seemed to have more control out there. I was a minority among them but, with Bashir's help, I insisted on keeping my husband where he was. I would entrust Fuad's recovery to no other place than this renowned hospital.

The specialist assigned to Fuad's case made his first call late that night. Dr. Khalifé was the head of neurosurgery in that hospital. Handsome and reassuring in every way, he exuded confidence. His advice was built on the medical report of the emergency team of doctors, but his report was put in more technical terms after he spent a few minutes examining Fuad's pulse and the tubes connected to his body. It had been almost eight hours since the accident took place. Khalifé's assessment sounded grim, far more unsettling than that of his colleagues down at the emergency room. It was a short visit, one interrupted by the increasing commotion that reached our room. Terribly lonesome, I stood by the window, looking at dear old Beirut in total darkness. Its destiny, like Fuad's, teetered on the brink of irreversible catastrophe. I tried to collect my thoughts and analyze the situation I was in. According to the preliminary diagnosis, Fuad's condition was hopeless.

It took some fourteen months of deathlike coma before Fuad opened his eyes and breathed on his own. Our stay at the hospital lasted only five weeks because of the ongoing warfare, and then I had to set up my own intensive care unit at home. At first a team of doctors helped me sustain his system; later, physical and speech therapists worked with him. Our little apartment, with its generator humming at odd intervals, lights on throughout the nights, and open door, looked more like an emergency hall than a private home. The best thing about this ground-floor apartment was the large gardens that stretched out and around the back side. Fruit trees, luxuriant vines, and long lanes of exotic plants stood there, ever beautiful reminders that life can be that way, too.

The warfare in Beirut and the surrounding area escalated after October 1975 and left us vulnerable whether we went out or stayed indoors. Roads were blocked at random, vehicles derailed or trapped, and sudden shelling targeted schools, hospitals, offices, and apartment buildings. Those hazards became a tremendous hindrance to Fuad's recovery since he had to be rushed to emergency centers several times.

In early 1977 my husband came back to life. Paralyzed from head to toe on his right side, Fuad began by communicating through a subtle movement of his left eye. There was a light in that eye that guided me, told me how he felt, and what he wanted. I learned to read this bright signal of communication, and to respond to it. As a matter of fact, his eyes projected enough love to sustain me throughout his very long, slow recovery. He improved ever so slowly from total disability in 1975 to a point where he could recognize those he loved most. He'd lift his head, sit in a wheelchair, and finally stand up and balance his head above his shoulders. He would do much more when in an extraordinarily cheerful mood, especially in the presence of beautiful women.

We took our first trip abroad for his physical therapy in the summer of 1977, realizing how great were the results of treatments such as Aslan's in Romania and Carlo Vivari's in Czechoslovakia. The progress was miraculous and I was thrilled to see Fuad so confident, going on his own to crowded places like a dining room or a coffee shop and learning how to walk downstairs, backwards, while holding to the rail with his left hand. He even made some friends who spoke English, asking them to join us for a glass of wine.

In Christmas of 1979 we headed down to Egypt's Halwan, a famous health resort with hot mineral spas and herbal baths. There, Fuad was able to meet his new son-in-law and the two grandchildren born in Cairo; his younger daughter Mimi had remarried while he was sick and moved down to Egypt.

My own spiritual revival was as promising as Fuad's physical and emotional rebirth. By 1980 he had regained most of his cheerfulness and was reconciled to his disability. He did all this with singular charm. Deep, very deep inside me, I nurtured the hope of seeing Fuad and me settled down to the peaceful life we so desired. The shocking experience of almost losing him had undermined that hope, yet I kept talking about our new plans for 1981, hoping to fulfill an old dream of our visiting the United States. We had nursed that fantasy since 1955 when I came back from that country and told him how great it was.

Meanwhile, we stayed put in our renovated residence in the overpopulated suburbs where Fuad's clan lived. Originally that suburb, called the Tower, had been developed on the side of Beirut rich in archaeological treasures.

I had vivid memories of that part of the city because my family's favorite beach was there. The huge ruins of an old tower and a small mosque dedicated to Sheikh Owza'i dominated the place in those days. The mosque stands out in my memory as a serene white structure topped by a slender minaret and surrounded by a small rose garden. I hid there to be alone and to dream.

It was rather late in life that I discovered the holiness of that site and its special meaning to my family. On the first visit Fuad paid to my parents in the spring of 1965—it was our engagement party—my mother disappeared for a few minutes and came back with an old family album she always kept locked away. The picture she picked out was of Grandpa Mehdi in one of his religious councils held in Sheikh Owza'i mosque, with my mother—then thirteen years old—sitting on his lap. Among the religious scholars in his juridical council was Fuad's paternal grandfather, a well-known jurist of the Shi'ite sect. The seventy-two-year-old picture and the profound message it conveyed had a memorable effect on all of us in the party. It was the first time I had seen such vivid proof of the gentleness of the grandfather I had so dearly loved. To see a thirteen-year-old daughter with no head cover or special attire attending this interfaith meeting presided over by that revered man filled my heart with pride.

The Tower area and the southern side of Beirut had deteriorated since I was a child. Over a half million homeless and jobless people had found refuge in its fertile land and inviting shores. They were a mixture of dirt-poor people, Lebanese and Palestinians, most of whom were victims of wars and ethnic persecution.

The war of the seventies had finally eradicated the whole district that surrounded Beirut, including the Tower and the Salem neighborhoods. It was our fate to be trapped there at a critical time in our life together. We were drained financially and unable to think about moving so we stayed and watched the country collapse bit by bit. One after the other, Beirut International Airport, the seaport, electric power plants, and water supplies became targets. The warring camps were many: Israelis, Syrians, Palestinians, Iranians, Libyans, destitute southerners, Beirut's new cantons of East and West, and others. The army had split into several camps as well. Unexpected rifts between the warlords and so-called generals often changed the previous configuration of power. The list of armed belligerents grew longer and our opportunities for escape lessened. It overwhelmed me to realize that, if this war did not come to an end soon, I would never be able to salvage whatever remained of our assets, bundle up my beloved husband, and fly away to a safe place.

My turn came in March 1981. I was in the kitchen preparing dinner for some of Fuad's relatives when I collapsed with a heart attack. It was a Sunday, a day when the Syrian troops who had lately reinforced their lines around Beirut International Airport were engaged in a deadly battle with East Beirut forces. In other words, we were at the center of a war zone. Ever since Syrian troops entered Lebanon on the pretext of helping the Christians in their battle against the PLO in Tell Zaatar, their commanders had continued to shift their allegiance from one camp to another.

The family physician who was called insisted I be taken to the hospital. It was a rainy day in March and the few ambulances available in our area were all out on the roads. We waited four hours before a taxi driver agreed to take me to the American Hospital. Usama, the only one of my children who lived in the Middle East then, was out of town. My sister Nora, whose apartment was a couple of miles from the American Hospital, was the first to come to my bedside. By the time my other sons, both living in the United States, flew home to see me, I was out of danger but still very weak.

I survived that heart attack and, after four long weeks of intensive care, an angiogram, and loads of medicine, was ready to leave the hospital. The diagnosis showed some partial blockage in the coronary arteries. Seeing how anxious I was to go home, my doctor insisted I stay close to the hospital. "I need to keep an eye on your condition, madame," he warned. "There is a good possibility you may have a relapse. I advise you to have someone at home to watch over your diet and administer the prescribed treatment with precision." Nora watched with apprehension as he went on explaining how dangerous another attack could be. "The worst thing you can do now is to exert your heart. Remember, a part of that muscle is dead now."

I recall Nora begging me to spend some time at her place before I returned home. "Fuad can come and visit every day, Nadia. Please, think how much he needs to see you back on your feet and healthy enough to take care of him." My sister had lived alone in her two-bedroom apartment ever since she lost her son Omar a decade ago. Omar and his wife were expecting their first baby when, at the age of twenty-three, he collapsed. The last one of her four sons, Nidal, was happily married and lived in the same neighborhood.

Fuad, who was devastated to be suddenly without me, survived the shock by visiting me at the hospital every day. It was the first time we had been separated from each other since we had married sixteen years earlier. He had his chauffeur bring him over at precisely the same time every day, no matter how dangerous the roads to the hospital were. Our romantic rendezvous, as we called them, became the thrill of the patients and nurses on the tenth floor. People would see Fuad leaning on his driver's arm, looking as handsome as ever and beaming smiles at everyone. Later, he'd lean on my arm and refuse to use his cane in public.

My second heart attack in June 1982 was more severe, and its timing could not have been more critical. The Israeli Army, whose invasion of Lebanon came with a big show of might, had surrounded Beirut, and their tanks were a few miles south of our home when an ambulance arrived at our gate. Fuad watched helplessly as I was carried away on a stretcher. He couldn't even pull himself up from his chair. His eyes were red with tears as he waved his left arm toward me. Our farewell was mute, swift as the passing of a shadow. I felt weaker and weaker as the ambulance shrieked its way out of our lot and raced through the city's empty streets.

I recall the ambulance driving in circles through West Beirut, probably avoiding obstacles or shells. As I lay on my stretcher, I wondered what was going to happen to Fuad if I didn't make it! I felt the urge to go back to Fuad and never leave him behind. But no sound came from my throat. Where had my voice gone and why didn't I have the power to reach up to the window that separated me from the driver of that ambulance and ask him to take me back home? It made no difference to me where I died, as long as I could spend those last few moments with Fuad.

I lost contact with Fuad after we were separated in the beginning of June. My son Usama, who had finally returned to the city and caught up with me at the hospital, had unconfirmed information about the Salems, how their residence was hit, and how the whole family had fled somewhere.

By the end of June, a new coronary blockage was discovered, and my doctor felt that surgery was imperative, probably a bypass.

On the first of July I found myself on the road to Damascus with my two grandsons, Oliver and Hussam, who were also separated from their father. My son's penthouse in Rass Beirut was too dangerous for the boys to stay alone while Usama was frequently forced to stay in his office. Mona, his second wife of two years, and their baby girl Leila, were stuck back in Saida and separated from the family as well.

Luckily, we had our passports and I had enough money to pay for airfare to the States, where my son Jamal was expecting us. I had no idea how long it was going to take to get visas. The boys were traveling with a Lebanese grandmother who, strictly speaking, was not their legal guardian. Ever since the American consulate offices in Beirut had been closed, the Lebanese were found waiting in long lines at the door of the American consulate in Damascus.

At the end of the four days I spent in Damascus preparing for yet another dreaded journey in my life, I knew I would have died of fear had it not been for the attentive company of my two grandchildren.

I flew with my grandsons to St. Louis, where we stayed with Jamal and his family. There were many worries that weighed on my mind during the first few weeks I spent in St. Louis, but my health and the expected operation were not even among them. It was intensely painful to see me and my grandchildren going through the same anguish my children and I had experienced thirty-some years before. Then, my children and I had found ourselves at the door of my parents with nothing but the clothes on our backs. Indeed, leaving Beirut as we did, the boys had very few things to hold onto after they left their father behind. I felt compelled to forget about myself and give them as much attention as I could.

This was another precarious time in my life when I forced my body to perform. I found myself bouncing back to life. The cardiologist who put me under a restricted plan of rest and medicines had no idea that the progressive recovery of my heart condition should have been attributed to the work I was doing to help my grandsons adjust to their new life. Around the end of September, I decided against the surgery and my doctor hesitantly agreed, on the condition that he obtain and review the angiographic films taken earlier by my doctor in Beirut.

Fuad was alive! I received a letter from him shortly after I had declined surgery. When Doctor Nordlicht contacted the main office of the Red Cross and asked if they could get that film from the American Hospital in Beirut, my sister Mae had to sign a document on my behalf. When the film arrived, it contained an unexpected surprise, a letter from Fuad. "I thought I would never see you again, darling," he complained. His handwriting was irregular and faint. "Now that you are alive, I can wait. I couldn't believe you went to America without me!" His reproachful words filled my eyes with tears. "Usama said you needed a major operation. I hope you change your mind and just come back, please, Nadia. We have wonderful doctors here who can take care of you. At least I can visit you while in the hospital like before, remember?"

It was not until the beginning of October that we heard from Usama. He had finally found his way out of Lebanon and gone to one of the Gulf states, where he had found a job. The boys, already in school in Saint Louis, were elated to talk to their father and to know he was all right. They were very happy to hear that they would now take a plane from Saint Louis to London, and then to Cyprus, where their father would be waiting for them.

Only then was I free to sit down and plan for the few months my doctor required for observation before I could go back home. I enrolled in several classes in art and English literature, surrounded myself with art materials, papers, and dictionaries, and bought a portable second-hand typewriter. There was a new page in my memoirs, one I had started to design. The driving force behind me then was to go back home and spend the rest of my life with Fuad, painting and writing. At age sixty-four, I knew I had many stories to tell, especially to my grandchildren.

"Welcome back, Mom," Usama whispered in my ear as we hugged at the airport. It had been a year since I had seen my son. From the look we exchanged, he knew I had neither the strength nor desire to be with anyone but Fuad. "It is almost dawn," Usama tried again while maneuvering his car out of the airport's exit and keeping an eye on the military barricades that appeared to have increased since I left. "Don't you think I'd better take you to my place so you can rest and change first?"

I shook my head, trying to control my sobs. All I wanted at that moment was to see Fuad and know how serious his condition was. Nothing else mattered. When I called Usama from Paris about the delay of my flight, he prepared me for the worst. "He seems to have given up, Mom, please hurry! Check with other lines, see if there is any possibility for an earlier flight." His urgent tone drove me out of my mind. "Fuad wouldn't believe you are coming back."

Usama didn't hear me when I said I had tried all those possibilities. He was too troubled over Fuad's recent relapse to remember that Beirut's airport was crippled for several months since the Israeli attack a year earlier. Nor did I have the time to explain how difficult it was for me to book a seat on that flight at a time when very few international airlines were flying to Beirut.

The streets were dark when we crossed the Salems' sleeping compound to our house. The light in my bedroom and in Fuad's were on. Otherwise the house looked grim in the twilight. The burned trees and gaping bird cages in the middle of the garden stood as reminders of the July 1982 attack on that area. I rushed down the alley to the main entrance. The doors were left ajar—all doors used to be left unlocked in our neighborhood. I could recognize the stern voice of Fuad's younger brother arguing with someone inside our lounge, probably one of the family members who had been looking after Fuad since they returned to their homes after the Israelis left. Usama followed me to Fuad's room, put down my two suitcases, asked me to call him later, and left as swiftly as he had come in. No one saw us coming.

Fuad's back was turned to me. He was covered up to his waist with the blue quilt that had his initials on it. His left arm rested peacefully on the fading F. S. emblem. I had ordered a pair of beautiful, embroidered quilts when I took Fuad to Romania for his therapy. The room looked bare. The side table by his bed was empty with no evidence of medicine, water, or food. The pictures of our children were not on the walls anymore. His clothing dangled from gaping drawers. Where life had once teemed, desolation had moved in. I tiptoed to the other side of his bed and bent down over him. I raised his head and shoulders as high as I could. "Darling, this is me!" It took him a while to focus his startled eyes on mine. The pale skin slowly came alive and his face brightened up. "Yes, I finally made it, Fuad." His left arm fell twice before it gathered the strength to reach out and touch the tears that streamed down my face. His lips moved but with no sound. He was breathing heavily.

I pulled up a chair and sat by his bed, very close so he would be able to see me and stroke my hand. He was trying to tell me something. . . . "Oh, I missed you too, Fuad! God knows how much I love you, now more than ever before. Don't worry, my love, I will stay in this room with you as long as you want me to. Otherwise, I can move you right away to a hospital where . . . " I could see he was trying to shake his head. "All right, Mr. Salem, no hospital."

Five days had passed since I had returned from the States. I never left Fuad's bedside. Nothing in the whole world was as important to me at that moment as Fuad's last moments on this earth. I knew his body was succumbing. All I could offer was soothing words. During those precious days, Fuad seldom let go of my hand. He responded to my words with enormous patience, and memories of old times brought a smile to his face. I paid no attention to the people around us. They could come in, watch, weep, gasp, or leave, unnoticed. Fuad was declared almost brain-dead a few days before I arrived. No system of life support seemed to have been provided since his relapse. A little juice and water was all my beloved man needed from this world. The same was true for me, and I lived off the nourishment of sharing with him the precious moments he had on this earth. I knew that his body would soon succumb but that his soul would be with me forever. It was in the early hours of June 18, 1983, that I heard Fuad moan in his sleep. I pulled out of my chair. Perhaps I had fallen asleep. Perhaps I made those moaning sounds. I had never heard him make such a sound. I bent down and pressed my hand over his forehead. "What is it," I asked, "is it that pain again?" But now silence fell over him and over the room. Even noises that I had been hearing from outside were suddenly hushed. There was a creak at the door as it opened gently and almost imperceptibly. Yet there was no one there, no one I could see. I put my hand on his forehead again, but there was no reaction this time. His forehead was cold, the way the night breeze or water is cold. I looked at his face anxiously, searching for signs of reassurance. His face had the color of life: yes, even a glow of good health. It was everything around him that began to feel strange. Everything made of wood looked as though it was made of stone, maybe of marble. All the shining metal of the furniture now had the color of pewter. I am dreaming, I thought. I am sinking into stupor. I did not feel alone with Fuad; yet there could be no one else in the room intruding on this extraordinary moment. "Please, listen to me, love," I said, "listen to me." There was no response, not even the faintest sound. Many times in the eight long years of Fuad's ailment I had felt penned in by the four bare walls of that room, the walls I wanted to bring down on that day.

But Fuad was alive. He was breathing, a quiet, shallow breath. I wanted to break through the walls, to reach out into the streets of the great city, to cry out. Instead, I took his hand in mine, and all the voice in me came out, not like a yell but like a gentle complaint. He suddenly held my hand fast. All his strength is back, I thought. Never mind these awful walls and these dull colors around us. His hand was so strong and so warm. "Nadia . . . darling," he whispered softly but firmly. There was the distinct trace of a smile on his face, his beautiful, his very alert and radiant face. I wrapped my arms around him, to hold him in them forever. I put three words together for him, "I love you, Fuad," but something, some power, commanded me to be silent and to just hold him fast. "Nadia," he whispered again, but from a distant, very distant place now, "please, darling, don't leave me here when you go."

Afterword

Afaf Kanafani was just over age thirty in 1948 when she fled the war in Palestine and went to Beirut as a refugee. She had lost her husband, her home, and all her belongings. In 1984, she was a sixty-six-year-old "refugee" leaving Lebanon for the United States. This time she escaped a civil war responsible for her second husband's death and her own precarious health. Once again she had lost a home and her belongings, and was fleeing political and personal tragedy.

Afaf chose California's bay area with its view of the mountains and the sea because it is so reminiscent of Beirut. Although she has continued to travel a great deal, especially to visit family, Oakland has become her home.

Over the years, Afaf has lived five different lives in four countries. Born in Beirut, she spent her childhood in Lebanon under the French mandate. She pursued her second life in Palestine under the British mandate where she lived with her husband, surrounded by his extended family, and bore three children. When the war to establish Israel as a state destroyed everything, she became a refugee in post-colonial Lebanon. Back in Beirut, Afaf returned to school, gained the credentials necessary for a career, and established a home with her three sons. She remarried after they left for graduate school and lived her fourth life with Fuad, her soulmate and companion. In 1975, Lebanon's civil war shattered their lives: Fuad received injuries from which he never recovered and she suffered heart attacks. After Fuad's death, Afaf came to the United States and began her fifth life as an artist, writer, and peace activist.

This memoir, many years in the making, emerged from a writing class Afaf took to improve her English. Her mother tongue is Arabic but like many Lebanese of her generation, she is also fluent in French. As a child, Afaf attended an American parochial school and later used English in the course of her professional life. She enrolled in an En-

335

glish class in California to improve her writing in preparation for art classes. When she decided to write about her own life and the instructor reacted favorably, the die was cast. Afaf kept writing, finding it easier to explore painful memories in "foreign" English than in her native Arabic. Before long, she was writing a book.

Once the work had taken shape, Afaf's friend, Apostolos Athanassakis, a professor at University of California, Santa Barbara, agreed to edit it. At this point Afaf contacted me. She had heard about the Foremother Legacies series of first-person narratives and asked if I would like to see her manuscript.

As a professor of history, I was struck by the memoir's value as a twentieth-century document. Here was a gendered account of fifty years of Middle Eastern wars that connected the personal with the political. At the same time, I was impressed by Afaf's tenacity in the face of opposition, her survival skills, and her frankness about intrafamily relationships and sexuality. As a feminist historian, I was intrigued by her experiential feminism.

When I teach Middle Eastern history, I confront deeply entrenched stereotypes about veiled and submissive women. These ideas do not emerge out of thin air; they are embedded in our literature and consciousness. Orientalists and fiction writers have exoticized and eroticized the harem; and colonial governments have compared their "enlightened" treatment of women to "degraded" and "exploitive" Arab custom. What has been missing is the Arab point of view and, especially, the voices of Arab women.

It was not until the 1960s that people in the West began to hear the voices of Arab women. Elizabeth Fernea's *Guests of the Sheik* (1965), about her experiences in Iraq, presented Western readers with women who were rational, made decisions, and exercised power. The 1967 war led to increased interest in the Middle East at the same time feminist scholars were awakening to international women. By the 1970s, Western readers were learning about the lives of Arab women through Fatima Mernissi's *Beyond the Veil, Women in the Muslim World,* edited by Lois Beck and Nikki Keddy, and translations of Nawal el Sadaawi's writings. In the past twenty years, the list has grown considerably. Monographs on the Egyptian women's movement and feminism by Leila Ahmad and Margot Badran; memoirs and autobiographies by women such as Huda Shaarawi, Fadwa Tuqan, and Fatima Mernissi; and edited collections now stock the shelves. Nevertheless, journalists' accounts and sensational novels continue to shape popular opinion about Middle Eastern women.

Afaf Kanafani's memoir is a welcome addition to the corpus of serious literature on Middle Eastern women. She has not been involved in politics like Huda Shaarawi, yet this is an intensely political account. She is not a professional writer like Fadwa Tuqan, Nawal el Sadaawi, and Fatima Mernissi, yet her prose is often passionate and poetic. She is not a social scientist like Lois Beck or Nikki Keddy, but she is capable of critically analyzing her society. Above all, this is a personal account of one woman's struggle for autonomy and therein lies its value for all women and men. Afaf reminds us that essentializing any group—Arabs, Palestinians, Muslims or women—is both futile and dangerous.

Afaf and I talked with each other by phone, and corresponded through e-mail while the manuscript was being edited and considered for publication. Once the decision had been made, I flew to California to spend a few days with her. We wanted to get to know one another, select photographs for the book, and discuss publication details. I discovered that, in person, Afaf Kanafani is the woman you read. She is strong and resilient, charming and eloquent, animated and affectionate, artistic and analytical.

Afaf's fifth life is an active one. Once she had settled in California, she returned to her art. She joined the Oakland Art Association and became editor of the *Oakland Art Association Bulletin*. Her oils, watercolors, and acrylics have been included in art association shows and on display in various locations. In recent years, a watercolor style of computer-generated art has claimed Afaf's attention (she calls it her "obsession"), and she is preparing for an exhibit of this work.

Committed to peace in the Middle East, Afaf is president of Women's Interfaith Dialogue on the Middle East and a member of the American Interreligious Council for Peace in the Middle East. Her interest in promoting Arab culture and American understanding of this culture is manifested in her work as a founder of the East Bay Arab American Community Center in Berkeley, and with the National Arab American Association and the Arab Cultural Center in San Francisco.

Although she lives by herself in Oakland, Afaf is rarely alone. Two of her sons live with their families in California (her eldest son and his family are in Beirut). She has eight grandchildren, ranging in age from three to twenty-eight, who live in Denmark and throughout the United

States. All of her family visit her and add more events to a schedule already crowded with appointments, meetings, and engagements with innumerable friends from all walks of life.

When I stayed with Afaf Kanafani and had the pleasure of getting to know the woman behind the story, I realized an Afterword was essential. She ended her memoirs with her husband's death and at that point it seemed as if her life, too, was over. The Afaf who now lives in California, creating watercolor art on computer, composing piano music, attending Arab-Israeli reconciliation meetings, entertaining friends and relatives, and going for swimming lessons is not quite what the reader might expect after completing chapter 13. Hers is an indomitable spirit and that spirit has served her well.

Geraldine Forbes
Series Editor
July 1998

Glossary

Adha's Eve: Yearly feast-day commemoration of the prophet Abraham's offering to sacrifice his son to Allah and instead receiving a lamb to slaughter. Mount Arafat, in Saudi Arabia, is the revered site of the original event, and is the most revered of Islamic holy places.

Ajalain: The word *ajal* in Arabic means "time"; *ajalain* refers to the two situations, death and divorce, that require the husband to complete the payment promised to his wife in the marriage contract if the total amount has not yet been paid.

Dar: Literally, house or dwelling. In this book it is used to refer to the central hall in Mediterranean-style mansions found in Lebanon, Syria and Iraq. The dar, a large hall which is surrounded by reception rooms, bedrooms, dining room, entrance hallway, and kitchen hallway, is furnished to accommodate a large number of people and is used for family gatherings, receptions for women, or parties for children. This is the room where musical instruments are kept.

Hadj: Lebanese pronunciation of the Arabic word for those who have made the Haj, that is, the pilgrimage to Mecca.

Jubba: A long open coat with wide sleeves worn by men over lighter everyday clothes. Its color and fabric may signify rank and occupation.

Kitab ceremony: The word *kitab* in Arabic means "book" and the verb *kataba* means "write." In popular usage, *kitab* is used for the marriage contract because the marriage is only finalized with the writing and signing of the marriage contract in a large book brought to the ceremony by a judge. The information recorded includes the names of the couple, their ages, the names of the witnesses, and the amount of the groom's payment to the bride.

Liwan: The central reception room, located in front of the dar. The liwan is for family gatherings, especially morning coffee and evening tea, which might be shared with close relatives.

Manzoul: A large room off the entrance hallway. It serves many functions, for example, as a place to meet those who come for business or officials, such as tax collectors, as a guest room for family visitors, and as a room where parents review schoolwork with their children.

Salia: The largest reception room, used primarily for formal gatherings, is adjacent to the dar and across from the main entrance. It is furnished with the best quality chairs and divans, carpets, side tables and book shelves, and is decorated with fine paintings and family portraits. The salia has only two doors; one to the dar and another to the sun room that leads to the manzoul and out to the entrance hallway. This allows visitors, especially male visitors and officials, to come and go out without entering the family's quarters.

Sambousic: Small, deep-fried pies made of unsweetened dough, ground meat, onions, and pine nuts.

Shadhiliyah movement: One of the four oldest tariqas (Sufi orders) in the Muslim world. Its name comes from Moroccan-born Abu al-Hasan Ali al-Shadhili (d. 1258) who established an order in Alexandria. This "path" or "way" of worshipping is now spread over a large part of the Muslim world.

Tabbouli: A Lebanese salad made of parsley, fresh mint, onions, and tomatoes, which is mixed with lemon juice, spices, and olive oil. This mixture is added to a small amount of bulgur (crushed wheat).

Tarboosh: The fez, a man's head covering popular in the Ottoman Empire. It is still worn in some countries of the Middle East and North Africa.

Index